普通高等教育"十一五"国家级规划教材

 北京市高等教育精品教材立项项目

APPROACHING FICTION
英语小说导读

(第二版)

袁宪军 编

北京大学出版社
PEKING UNIVERSITY PRESS

图书在版编目(CIP)数据

英语小说导读(第二版)/袁宪军编.—北京:北京大学出版社,2010.9

ISBN 978-7-301-17745-7

Ⅰ.英… Ⅱ.袁… Ⅲ.①英语－高等学校－教材 Ⅳ.①H319

中国版本图书馆 CIP 数据核字(2010)第 174160 号

书　　　名:英语小说导读(第二版)
著作责任者:袁宪军　编
责 任 编 辑:孙　莹
标 准 书 号:ISBN 978-7-301-17745-7/H·2634
出 版 发 行:北京大学出版社
地　　　址:北京市海淀区成府路 205 号　100871
网　　　址:http://www.pup.cn　电子信箱:zpup@pup.pku.edu.cn
电　　　话:邮购部 62752015　发行部 62750672　编辑部 62759634
　　　　　　出版部 62754962
印　刷　者:天津和萱印刷有限公司
　　　　　890 毫米×1240 毫米　A5　14.5 印张　415 千字
　　　　　2004 年 4 月第 1 版　2010 年 9 月第 2 版
　　　　　2023 年 1 月第 5 次印刷(总第 10 次印刷)
定　　　价:39.00 元

未经许可,不得以任何方式复制或抄袭本书之部分或全部内容。
版权所有,翻版必究
举报电话:(010)62752024　电子信箱:fd@pup.pku.edu.cn

《21世纪英语专业系列教材》编写委员会

(以姓氏笔画排序)

王守仁　王克非　申　丹

刘意青　李　力　胡壮麟

桂诗春　梅德明　程朝翔

总　　序

　　北京大学出版社自 2005 年以来已出版《语言学与应用语言学知识系列读本》多种，为了配合第十一个五年计划，现又策划陆续出版《21 世纪英语专业系列教材》。这个重大举措势必受到英语专业广大教师和学生的欢迎。

　　作为英语教师，最让人揪心的莫过于听人说英语不是一个专业，只是一个工具。说这些话的领导和教师的用心是好的，为英语专业的毕业生将来找工作着想，因此要为英语专业的学生多多开设诸如新闻、法律、国际商务、经济、旅游等其他专业的课程。但事与愿违，英语专业的教师们很快发现，学生投入英语学习的时间少了，掌握英语专业课程知识甚微，即使对四个技能的掌握也并不比大学英语学生高明多少，而那个所谓的第二专业在有关专家的眼中只是学到些皮毛而已。

　　英语专业的路在何方？有没有其他路可走？这是需要我们英语专业教师思索的问题。中央领导关于创新是一个民族的灵魂和要培养创新人才等的指示精神，让我们在层层迷雾中找到了航向。显然，培养学生具有自主学习能力和能进行创造性思维是我们更为重要的战略目标，使英语专业的人才更能适应 21 世纪的需要，迎接 21 世纪的挑战。

　　如今，北京大学出版社外语部的领导和编辑同志们，也从教材出版的视角探索英语专业的教材问题，从而为贯彻英语专业教学大纲做些有益的工作，为教师们开设大纲中所规定的必修、选修课程提供各种教材。《21 世纪英语专业系列教材》是普通高等教育"十一五"国家级规划教材和国家"十一五"重点出版规划项目《面向新世纪的

《立体化网络化英语学科建设丛书》的重要组成部分。这套系列教材要体现新世纪英语教学的自主化、协作化、模块化和超文本化,结合外语教材的具体情况,既要解决语言、教学内容、教学方法和教育技术的时代化,也要坚持弘扬以爱国主义为核心的民族精神。因此,今天北京大学出版社在大力提倡专业英语教学改革的基础上,编辑出版各种英语专业技能、英语专业知识和相关专业知识课程的教材,以培养具有创新性思维的和具有实际工作能力的学生,充分体现了时代精神。

北京大学出版社的远见卓识,也反映了英语专业广大师生盼望已久的心愿。由北京大学等全国几十所院校具体组织力量,积极编写相关教材。这就是说,这套教材是由一些高等院校有水平有经验的第一线教师们制定编写大纲,反复讨论,特别是考虑到在不同层次、不同背景学校之间取得平衡,避免了先前的教材或偏难或偏易的弊病。与此同时,一批知名专家教授参与策划和教材审定工作,保证了教材质量。

当然,这套系列教材出版只是初步实现了出版社和编者们的预期目标。为了获得更大效果,希望使用本系列教材的教师和同学不吝指教,及时将意见反馈给我们,使教材更加完善。

航道已经开通,我们有决心乘风破浪,奋勇前进!

胡壮麟

北京大学蓝旗营

Preface to the Second Edition

This revised edition of *Approaching Fiction* is based on the consideration of the possibility of self study by university students and those who are interested in English fiction with sound English proficiency though not studying in university. In addition to substitute of several short stories, most stories in this edition are provided with a brief but poignant discussion written by a British or American critic so that the reader will see clearly how a critic approaches the story. Thinking about the popularity of experimental fiction in the literary world, I have added a new chapter, "New Fiction," in order that the students get a glimpse of how fiction rebels against the traditional notion in the 20th century and, nonetheless, in what way(s) it shows itself to be still rooted in social reality. I have found that documentation is commonly a problem for students in their writing of academic papers, and thus the section concerning citation and documentation has been supplemented with more examples, including citations of an online posting and other sources. Another change is that I have cancelled "Nathaniel Hawthorne's 'Young Goodman Brown': Historical Imagining and Critical Responses" from the appendixes since the Internet is getting more and more convenient and students interested in the background information and critical responses to this story may avail themselves from online sources. With the cultivation of critical thinking being still the focus in the revision, some knowledge about how a writer writes a story, that is, the process of the creation of fiction, may also be of help in students' deeper understanding of fiction. Thus Eudora Welty's "How I Write" is added to the appendixes.

    I remain in the debt of many people who have contributed in one way or another to the completion of the first and this revised edition. Qian Kunqiang（钱坤强）and Tang Cuiyun（唐翠云）have not only offered random but significant suggestions but also done some work in the revision. There have been students and readers who have microscopically scanned the book and sent me their understandings of certain stories. I would like to extend my thanks to them all.

Yuan Xianjun

July 10, 2009

PREFACE

For Chinese students majoring in English language and literature, English literature is one of the compulsory and most important courses. However, the English literature courses offered at most universities and colleges are taught merely at the level of learning general information and developing literal understanding. Admittedly, such courses help them a lot in their acquisition of the English language. But the function of English literature reaches far beyond that. In reading English literature, a student should have the power to discern how human beings translate their experience into artistic expression and representation; how writers, through their creative impulses, convey to us their insights into human destiny and human life; and how social concern is involved in a specific form of human imagination. In addition, students should elevate to the level of cultivating a curiosity for the unknown, thinking cogently and logically, expressing themselves clearly and concisely, and observing the world around them critically and objectively. But most students are still at a loss as to how they can effectively analyze a literary work by themselves in any of these respects, even though they have read plenty of excerpts from representative works in the British and American literary canon. And they tend to have little idea what role the beginning part plays in the whole story, how the plot develops and comes to resolution, in what way point of view determines a reader's understanding of the story, and how the images and symbols are related to the theme. Upon consideration of these factors, we have compiled this book with the intention of cultivating both students' literary sensibilities and their critical power when reading English short stories and novels. This book, intended for senior university students and postgraduate students, not only discusses the essential structural elements of fiction but also enlightens students as to the basic concepts and principal terms in literary criticism with regard to fiction. With a cherished ambition to compile the best book available in China in this area and to make it of true benefit to students, the compiler has carefully selected fictional works of various styles and in different categories of subject matter, and has referred to many an authoritative work of criticism, assimilating important ideas from them. The bibliography at the end of this book can serve as a source for students' reference in further research work on fiction as well as an acknowledgment of my sources. Special thanks are extended to X. J. Kennedy and Dana Gioia (*Literature*, 1995); to C. Hugh Holman and William Harmon (*A Handbook to Literature*, 1986); to Cleanth Brooks, John Thibaut Purser, and Robert Penn Warren (*An Approach to Literature*, 1964); and to the Beijing Municipal Committee of Education for many of the valuable ideas, literary concepts and comments, and financial assistance received in compiling and publishing this book.

Yuan Xianjun
October 26, 2003

TABLE OF CONTENTS

Introduction Reading a Story ·· (1)

Chapter One Plot ··· (5)
  A & P
      by John Updike ·· (9)
  The Furnished Room
      by O. Henry ··· (21)
  A Rose for Emily
      by William Faulkner ··· (34)
Chapter Two Point of View ·· (51)
  The Tell-Tale Heart
      by Edgar Allan Poe ··· (63)
  Araby
      by James Joyce ··· (72)
Chapter Three Character ·· (85)
  The Jilting of Granny Weatherall
      by Katherine Anne Porter ·· (94)
  Tickets, Please
      by D. H. Lawrence ·· (111)
Chapter Four Setting ··· (130)
  The Storm
      by Kate Chopin ·· (137)
  The Three Strangers
      by Thomas Hardy ·· (145)
Chapter Five Style ··· (174)
  A Clean, Well-Lighted Place
      by Ernest Hemingway ·· (185)

Barn Burning
    by William Faulkner ·················· (193)
Chapter Six Theme ························ (219)
    Young Goodman Brown
        by Nathaniel Hawthorne ·············· (223)
    The Killers
        by Ernest Hemingway ················ (243)
Chapter Seven Symbol ···················· (267)
    The Lottery
        by Shirley Jackson ·················· (273)
Chapter Eight Reading Long Stories and Novels ·········· (292)
    The Metamorphosis
        by Franz Kafka, Translated by
        Willa and Edwin Muir ················ (315)
Chapter Nine New Fiction ·················· (370)
    The Balloon
        by Donald Barthelme ················ (374)
Chapter Ten Writing about a Story ············· (384)

Appendix I
    Why Do We Read Fiction?
        by Robert Penn Warren ··············· (415)
Appendix II
    How I Write
        by Eudora Welty ··················· (429)
Appendix III
    Samples of MLA Style "Works Cited" in
    Research Papers ······················ (441)
Bibliography ···························· (446)

Introduction

Reading a Story

    A woman is sitting in her old, shuttered house. She knows that she is alone in the whole world; every other thing is dead.
    The doorbell rings.

    At one glance, we know for certain that what we have just read is a story. If we are asked why it is a story, we may answer immediately that it tells us something imagined rather than real. And it has something to do with an image of people we meet in our daily life. This may be our natural response to a story. If we are informed of the structure of a story, we may say that it is a story because it has a character and the character does something in a certain place at a certain time. Although in reading such a short story we do not come to know the character well, for a moment we enter her thoughts and begin to share her feelings. Then something amazing happens. The story ends with suspense, and it leaves us in a wonder or, perhaps, in deep thought: Who or what rang the bell? And we may even have a series of questions: Is this a haunted house? Why is the character a woman rather than a man? Why is the present tense used rather than the past? Why is the house old and shuttered? Who is recounting the story? What effect is produced by the word "knows"? Why does the author select the word "dead" in ending the paragraph? Why does the author arrange another paragraph with just three words? What is characteristic of the wording and of the sentence structure? What is the moral sense of the story? In asking such questions and trying to answer them, we are actually approaching the story. Like many longer and more complicated stories, this one, in its few words, stimulates our imagination.

  To examine a story we must have a framework of ideas about its structure and functions. In this book, we are going to read fifteen short stories(though much longer than this one), and one novel, and by breaking them into their parts, we shall have a keener sense of how a work of fiction is constructed. Our analysis will involve **plot**, concerning what happens; **character**, generally considered a person who takes certain actions; **point of view**, concerning the angle from which a story is related; **setting**, the place and time in which events happen; **theme**, which requires us to investigate the meaning of the characters' action; and **style**, focusing our attention upon the linguistic features of the work.

  Fiction, originating from the Latin word *fictio*, meaning "a shaping, a counterfeiting", is a general term for such an imaginative work in prose as briefly discussed above: it is a story told in prose, a story which is assumed to be made up so as to express and explore the author's feelings and ideas about life through the imagery of characters and action. In modern criticism, the category of fiction includes the short story, the novel, the novella and related genres. Whether a text is fiction or not does not depend on its length but on its structure and function. All novels, novellas and short stories share generally the same structure with similar basic elements. Therefore short stories are selected in our analysis of "fiction" for the convenience of teaching multiple texts within a single course.

Although fiction, as the original meaning of the word indicates, is essentially imagined (and may even be completely counterfeited), that does not mean that in a work of fiction there is nothing real and that a writer of fiction may not use material drawn from real life; in fact most of his/her material comes from or conforms to life. But in reading fiction we are concerned not with where the writer gets his/her material, nor even with the material itself, but with what he/she does with it—with the pattern and meaning he/she gives it, with how strongly he/she charges it with emotion, with how persuasively he/she makes it embody his/her view of life. In works such as Balzac's *The Human Comedy*, Stephen Crane's *The Red Badge of Courage*, and Tolstoy's *War and Peace*, we see a great amount of "facts". In reading such fiction we almost always have a sense of "verisimilitude to life." But the factual information is of secondary importance. Authenticity in fiction, in an Aristotelian sense, is authenticity to art of fiction rather than to reality as understood from a sociological or historical perspective. A historical novel may be based on historical events but the focus is concentrated on quite different things than would be found in a history book. Perhaps Novalis's analogy of dancing and walking—literary works and non-literary works respectively—may well tell the major difference between a work of fiction and a work of non-fiction: dancing is for its own sake, while walking is a means to a certain destination. The "facts"—what happens to whom on the literal level—are very important in our reading of fiction. In fact, having a firm command of the facts of a story, a novella or a novel is the first step to approach fiction. Unless the literal facts of a work of fiction are clearly understood, we can never construe its total meaning, not to speak of its significance. Nevertheless, we have to keep in mind that the facts in fiction are not the facts in reality.

As we have said, fiction is a means, like other forms of art, for a writer to explore his/her experience of life and to understand his/her vision of life. We should say that the impulse that leads people to read fiction is fundamentally the same as the impulse that leads to its creation. The reader enters, consciously or unconsciously, into a fuller understanding of life by reading fiction. Fiction, while providing the reader with an aesthetic experience produced by the writer through his/her mastery of language, also extends the reader's own experience of life, and at the same time feeds his/her fundamental curiosity about life and its meaning.

Chapter One

Plot

Plot, or the structure of action, carries a variety of meanings in modern criticism. But it generally refers to the scheme or pattern of events in a work of fiction. The word *plot* has been used to indicate almost any kind of action found in a story. The concept of plot even in modern times is derived from Aristotle's use of the Greek word *mythos* in his definition of tragedy: *mythos* is the imitation of an action(*Poetics*). Aristotle lists six basic elements of the structure of tragedy but regards plot as the soul of tragedy. Of the structural whole, plot constitutes the dynamic framework to which the other five elements affiliate and around which the story develops. For Aristotle, plot must assume a certain form (for instance, the reversal of a situation, such as when the main character moves from a favorable situation to an unfavorable one); it must have a certain order of development (that is, it must have a beginning, a middle, and an end and a certain trajectory); it must involve certain agents whose actions compose its development; and it usually has a certain social background. The gradual building of the mental tension of the protagonist is also part of the plot, and the inevitable change in the fate of the protagonist, or even other characters, produces a psychological effect on the reader (or, in traditional tragedy, the spectator). This effect consists of arousing and purging certain feelings (*catharsis*). In addition, plot must abide by the law of probability: the development of the plot in a story must be logically probable rather than factually possible. Of course, all these are realized by means of language.

Aristotle's theory of plot is based on his analysis of some Greek tragedies, most especially Sophocles's *Oedipus Rex*. The theory doubtless applies to classical tragedy, and elements of his concept can be found in use in many novels and stories.

However, few modern critics approach plot from this complicated Aristotelian perspective. Plot, under the pens of modern novelists and storytellers, has become much more flexible than that envisaged by Aristotle. Perhaps a simple but serviceable approach to plot is that of E. M. Foster: "We have defined a story as a narrative of events arranged in their time-sequence. A plot is also a narrative of events, the emphasis falling upon causality. 'The king died and the queen died,' is a story. 'The king died and then the queen died of grief,' is a plot. The time sequence is preserved, but the sense of causality overshadows it. Or again: 'The queen died, no one knew why, until it was discovered that it was through grief at the death of the king.' This is a plot with a mystery in it, a form capable of high development. It suspends the time-sequence, it moves as far away from the story as its limitations will allow."(*Aspects of the Novel*, 1927)

Like any shapely story, the story we read at the beginning of the introduction, though very short, involves the unfolding of a **dramatic situation**: the woman believes that she is the only person alive in the world, and it is in such a state of mind that she hears the doorbell ringing. Here we first discern a **conflict** within the woman's mind, and then we see a conflict between her knowledge and the outer world. A dramatic situation thus refers to the fact that a person is involved in some conflict. The plot of a story is abundant of such situations in which clashes of wills, desires, or powers occur—whether it be a conflict of character against character, character against society, one society against another, character against some natural force, or character against himself/ herself.

Like anything, a plot, according to Aristotle (*Poetics*), has a beginning, "that which does not itself follow anything by causal necessity, but after which something naturally is or comes to be"; a middle, "that which follows something as some other thing follows it"; and an end, "that which itself naturally follows some other thing, either by necessity, or as a rule, but has nothing following it"—though sometimes the three parts are not clearly distinguished. But the three parts must make a **unity**: a plot should "imitate one action and that a whole, the structural union of the parts being such that, if any one of them is displaced or removed, the whole will be disjoined and disturbed." The beginning part of a plot or story we usually call **exposition**: it is the opening portion that sets the scene (if any), establishes the atmosphere, introduces the major character(s), tells the reader what has happened before the story opens, and provides other background information in order that the reader may understand and care about the events to follow. In a novel, the part that we call exposition may be rather long, while in a short story the exposition may end in the first or second paragraph. After the exposition, as Kennedy and Gioia observe, the author of a story generally arranges some other events which involve the development of the plot. (*Literature*, 1995) It is not uncommon for the writer to build up the **suspense**, or a series of suspense as in a novel, to incite the reader's curiosity as to how it will all turn out. At that point the reader usually feels a pleasurable anxiety that heightens his/her attention to the development of the plot. An artistic storyteller can develop a feeling of anticipation in the reader by arranging some **foreshadowing** to indicate what is to happen. As the story goes on and as the clash becomes apparent, we shall have a **crisis**, a moment of high tension. The crisis may be momentarily resolved. Then an even greater crisis—the turning point in the action—may occur. At last events come to a **climax**, the moment of the greatest tension at which the outcome is to be decided. The **conclusion**—also called the **falling action, resolution** or **denouement** (the final unraveling of the plot in fiction, the solution of the mystery, generally involving not only a satisfactory outcome of the main situation but an explanation of all the secrets and misunderstandings connected with the plot complication)— quickly follows.

   Such a structure of events may be called the plot of the story. By the word **plot** we simply mean the artistic arrangement of those events in the story. It would be possible, though tedious, to relate all incidents, all events, all thoughts passing through the minds of one or more characters during a certain period of time. But the plot demands that the author select from the welter of incidents or events and make an arrangement that has a certain unity, points to a certain end, and has a common relation representing not more than two or three threads of interest and activity. Different arrangements of the same material are possible. It depends upon how the writer executes with his/her narrative techniques. A writer may choose to tell of the events in chronological order, the sequence of events as they happen naturally; or he/she may begin the story with the last event and then tell what led to it or start *in midias res* (Latin, "in the midst of things"), first presenting some significant moment and then filling what happened earlier. Common narrative devices employed by writers in their stories are the **flashback** (as in George Eliot's *Silas Marner*, where the protagonist's early life is recounted in the later part of the book); the **interleaving** (as in Flaubert's *Madam Bovary*, where the narrative at one point jumps backwards from the lovers on a balcony to the busy market place below); the **cliffhanger** (as commonly used by Charles Dickens in his novels, where one episode ends with a moment of uncertainty about what will happen next—suspense—and leads closely to another episode); and random jumping backwards and forwards in time to create thematic juxtaposition or connection (as in Aldous Huxley's novel *Eyeless in Gaza*).

   Like many other terms in literary discussion, "plot" is blessed with several meanings, which might even arouse ambiguity. For instance, some critics try to distinguish a plot of action (*mythos*) in Aristotle's sense from a plot of character (*ethos*) or a plot of thought (*dianoia*), all of which involve actually potentially great change. Some try to distinguish such terms as *syuzhet* and *fabula* (as Russian formalists do in their discussion of plot and story). Some attempt to extend the meaning of plot to make it a function of a number of elements in fiction. Ronald S. Crane says (*Critics and Criticism*, 1952), "The form of a given plot is a function of the particular correlation among... three variables which the completed work is calculated to establish, consistently and progressively, in our minds." The three variables are "(1) the general estimate we are induced to form... of the moral character and deserts of the hero... (2) the judgments we are led similarly to make about the nature of the events that actually befall the hero... as having either painful or pleasurable consequences for him... permanently or temporarily; and (3) the opinions we are made to entertain concerning the degree and kind of his responsibility for what happens to him." In such a definition (which sounds Aristotelian), although much has been added to the simple idea of an arrangement of incidents or events, the basic view of plot as some large controlling frame is still present.

Although a highly dramatic story may tend to assume a clearly recognizable structure of conflict, crisis, climax, and conclusion, many contemporary writers avoid the foregrounding of the plot in their stories, perhaps indicating the dullness and dryness of modern life. Nevertheless, to whatever extent the plot of a story unfolds itself, it provides the author's significant interpretation of some phase of life. Plot brings order out of life and it focuses and clarifies life.

A & P

by John Updike, 1961

In walks three girls in nothing but bathing suits. I'm in the third check-out slot, with my back to the door, so I don't see them until they're over by the bread. The one that caught my eye first was the one in the plaid green two-piece. She was a chunky kid, with a good tan and a sweet broad soft-looking can with those two crescents of white just under it, where the sun never seems to hit, at the top of the backs of her legs. I stood there with my hand on a box of HiHo crackers trying to remember if I rang it up or not. I ring it up again and the customer starts giving me hell. She's one of these cash-register-watchers, a witch about fifty with rouge on her cheekbones and no eyebrows, and I know it made her day to trip me up. She'd been watching cash registers for fifty years and probably never seen a mistake before.

  By the time I got her feathers smoothed and her goodies into a bag—she gives me a little snort in passing, if she'd been born at the right time they would have burned her over in Salem—by the time I get her on her way the girls had circled around the bread and were coming back, without a pushcart, back my way along the counters, in the aisle between the check-outs and the Special bins. They didn't even have shoes on. There was this chunky one, with the two-piece—it was bright green and the seams on the bra were still sharp and her belly was still pretty pale so I guessed she just got it (the suit)—there was this one, with one of those chubby berry-faces, the lips all bunched together under her nose, this one, and a tall one, with black hair that hadn't quite frizzed right, and one of these sunburns right across under the eyes, and a chin that was too long—you know, the kind of girl other girls think is very "striking" and "attractive" but never quite makes it, as they very well know, which is why they like her so much—and then the third one, that wasn't quite so tall. She was the queen. She kind of led them, the other two peeking around and making their shoulders round. She didn't look around, not this queen, she just walked straight on slowly, on these long white prima-donna legs. She came down a little hard on her heels, as if she didn't walk in her bare feet that much, putting down her heels and then letting the weight move along to her toes as if she was testing the floor with every step, putting a little deliberate extra action into it. You

Chapter One

never know for sure how girls' minds work (do you really think it's a mind in there or just a little buzz like a bee in a glass jar?) but you got the idea she had talked the other two into coming in here with her, and now she was showing them how to do it, walk slow and hold yourself straight.

She had on a kind of dirty-pink—beige maybe, I don't know—bathing suit with a little nubble all over it and, what got me, the straps were down. They were off her shoulders looped loose around the cool tops of her arms, and I guess as a result the suit had slipped a little on her, so all around the top of the cloth there was this shining rim. If it hadn't been there you wouldn't have known there could have been anything whiter than those shoulders. With the straps pushed off, there was nothing between the top of the suit and the top of her head except just *her*, this clean bare plane of the top of her chest down from the shoulder bones like a dented sheet of metal tilted in the light. I mean, it was more than pretty.

She had sort of oaky hair that the sun and salt had bleached, done up in a bun that was unraveling, and a kind of prim face. Walking into the A & P with your straps down, I suppose it's the only kind of face you *can* have. She held her head so high her neck, coming up out of those white shoulders, looked kind of stretched, but I didn't mind. The longer her neck was, the more of her there was.

5   She must have felt in the corner of her eye me and over my shoulder Stokesie in the second slot watching, but she didn't tip. Not this queen. She kept her eyes moving across the racks, and stopped, and turned so slow it made my stomach rub the inside of my apron, and buzzed to the other two, who kind of huddled against her for relief, and they all three of them went up the cat-and-dog-food-breakfast-cereal-macaroni-rice-raisins-seasonings-spreads-spaghetti-soft-drinks-crackers-and-cookies aisle. From the third slot I look straight up this aisle to the meat counter, and I watched them all the way. The fat one with the tan sort of fumbled with the cookies, but on second thought she put the packages back. The

sheep pushing their carts down the aisle—the girls were walking against the usual traffic (not that we have one-way signs or anything)—were pretty hilarious. You could see them, when Queenie's white shoulders dawned on them, kind of jerk, or hop, or hiccup, but their eyes snapped back to their own baskets and on they pushed. I bet you could set off dynamite in an A & P and the people would by and large keep reaching and checking oatmeal off their lists and muttering "Let me see, there was a third thing, began with A, asparagus, no, ah, yes, applesauce!" or whatever it is they do mutter. But there was no doubt, this jiggled them. A few houseslaves in pin curlers even looked around after pushing their carts past to make sure what they had seen was correct.

You know, it's one thing to have a girl in a bathing suit down on the beach, where what with the glare nobody can look at each other much anyway, and another thing in the cool of the A & P, under the fluorescent lights, against all those stacked packages, with her feet padding along naked over our checkerboard green-and-cream rubber-tile floor.

"Oh Daddy," Stokesie said beside me. "I feel so faint."

"Darling," I said. "Hold me tight." Stokesie's married, with two babies chalked up on his fuselage already, but as far as I can tell that's the only difference. He's twenty-two, and I was nineteen this April.

"Is it done?" he asks, the responsible married man finding his voice. I forgot to say he thinks he's going to be manager some sunny day, maybe in 1990 when it's called the Great Alexandrov and Petrooshki Tea Company or something.

10   What he meant was, our town is five miles from a beach, with a big summer colony out on the Point, but we're right in the middle of town, and the women generally put on a shirt or shorts or something before they get out of the car into the street. And anyway these are usually women with six children and varicose veins mapping their legs and nobody, including them, could care less. As I say, we're right in the middle of town, and if you stand

Chapter One

at our front doors you can see two banks and the Congregational church and the newspaper store and three real-estate offices and about twenty-seven old freeloaders tearing up Central Street because the sewer broke again. It's not as if we're on the Cape; we're north of Boston and there's people in this town haven't seen the ocean for twenty years. The girls had reached the meat counter and were asking McMahon something. He pointed, they pointed, and they shuffled out of sight behind a pyramid of Diet Delight peaches. All that was left for us to see was old McMahon patting his mouth and looking after them sizing up their joints. Poor kids, I began to feel sorry for them, they couldn't help it.

Now here comes the sad part of the story, at least my family says it's sad but I don't think it's sad myself. The store's pretty empty, it being Thursday afternoon, so there was nothing much to do except lean on the register and wait for the girls to show up again. The whole store was like a pinball machine and I didn't know which tunnel they'd come out of. After a while they come around out of the far aisle, around the light bulbs, records at discount of the Caribbean Six or Tony Martin Sings or some such gunk you wonder they waste the wax on, six-packs of candy bars, and plastic toys done up in cellophane that fall apart when a kid looks at them anyway. Around they come, Queenie still leading the way, and holding a little gray jar in her hand. Slots Three through Seven are unmanned and I could see her wondering between Stokes and me, but Stokesie with his usual luck draws an old party in baggy gray pants who stumbles up with four giant cans of pineapple juice (what do these bums *do* with all that pineapple juice? I've often asked myself) so the girls come to me. Queenie puts down the jar and I take it into my fingers icy cold. Kingfish Fancy Herring Snacks in Pure Sour Cream: 49¢. Now her hands are empty, not a ring or a bracelet, bare as God made them, and I wonder where the money's coming from. Still with that prim look she lifts a folded dollar bill out of the hollow at the center of her nubbled pink top. The jar went heavy in my hand. Really, I thought that was so cute.

Then everybody's luck begins to run out. Lengel comes in from haggling with a truck full of cabbages on the lot and is about to scuttle into that door marked MANAGER behind which he hides all day when the girls touch his eye. Lengel's pretty dreary, teaches Sunday school and the rest, but he doesn't miss that much. He comes over and says, "Girls, this isn't the beach."

Queenie blushes, though maybe it's just a brush of sunburn I was noticing for the first time, now that she was so close. "My mother asked me to pick up a jar of herring snacks." Her voice kind of startled me, the way voices do when you see the people first, coming out so flat and dumb yet kind of tony, too, the way it ticked over "pick up" and "snacks." All of a sudden I slid right down her voice into her living room. Her father and the other men were standing around in icecream coats and bow ties and the women were in sandals picking up herring snacks on toothpicks off a big plate and they were all holding drinks the color of water with olives and sprigs of mint in them. When my parents have somebody over they get lemonade and if it's a real racy affair Schlitz in tall glasses with "They'll Do It Every Time" cartoons stencilled on.

"That's all right," Lengel said. "But this isn't the beach." His repeating this struck me as funny, as if it had just occurred to him, and he had been thinking all these years the A&P was a great big dune and he was the head lifeguard. He didn't like my smiling—as I say he doesn't miss much—but he concentrates on giving the girls that sad Sunday-school-superintendent stare.

15 Queenie's blush is no sunburn now, and the plump one in plaid, that I liked better from the back—a really sweet can—pipes up, "We weren't doing any shopping. We just came in for the one thing."

"That makes no difference," Lengel tells her, and I could see from the way his eyes went that he hadn't noticed she was wearing a two-piece before. "We want you decently dressed when you come in here."

"We *are* decent," Queenie says suddenly, her lower lip pushing, getting sore now that she remembers her place, a place from which the crowd that runs the A & P must look pretty crummy. Fancy Herring Snacks flashed in her very blue eyes.

"Girls, I don't want to argue with you. After this come in here with your shoulders covered. It's our policy." He turns his back. That's policy for you. Policy is what the kingpins want. What the others want is juvenile delinquency.

All this while, the customers had been showing up with their carts but, you know, sheep, seeing a scene, they had all bunched up on Stokesie, who shook open a paper bag as gently as peeling a peach, not wanting to miss a word. I could feel in the silence everybody getting nervous, most of all Lengel, who asks me, "Sammy, have you rung up this purchase?"

20 I thought and said "No" but it wasn't about that I was thinking. I go through the punches, 4, 9, GROC, TOT—it's more complicated than you think, and after you do it often enough, it begins to make a little song, that you hear words to, in my case "Hello (*bing*) there, you (*gung*) hap-py *pee*-pul (*splat*)!"—the *splat* being the drawer flying out. I uncrease the bill, tenderly as you may imagine, it just having come from between the two smoothest scoops of vanilla I had ever known were there, and pass a half and a penny into her narrow pink palm, and nestle the herrings in a bag and twist its neck and hand it over, all the time thinking.

The girls, and who'd blame them, are in a hurry to get out, so I say "I quit" to Lengel quick enough for them to hear, hoping they'll stop and watch me, their unsuspected hero. They keep right on going, into the electric eye; the door flies open and they flicker across the lot to their car, Queenie and Plaid and Big Tall Goony-Goony (not that as raw material she was so bad), leaving me with Lengel and a kink in his eyebrow.

"Did you say something, Sammy?"

"I said I quit."

"I thought you did."
25 "You didn't have to embarrass them."
"It was they who were embarrassing us."
I started to say something that came out "Fiddle-de-doo." It's a saying of my grandmother's, and I know she would have been pleased.

"I don't think you know what you're saying," Lengel said.

"I know you don't." I said. "But I do." I pull the bow at the back of my apron and start shrugging it off my shoulders. A couple cusromers that had been heading for my slot begin to knock against each other, like scared pigs in a chute.

30 Lengel sighs and begins to look very patient and old and gray. He's been a friend of my parents for years. "Sammy, you don't want to do this to your Mom and Dad," he tells me. It's true, I don't. But it seems to me that once you begin a gesture it's fatal not to go through with it. I fold the apron, "Sammy" stitched in red on the pocket, and put it on the counter, and drop the bow tie on top of it. The bow tie is theirs, if you've ever wondered. "You'll feel this for the rest of your life," Lengel says, and I know that's true, too, but remembering how he made that pretty girl blush makes me so scrunchy inside I punch the No Sale tab and the machine whirs "pee-pul" and the drawer splats out. One advantage to this scene taking place in summer, I can follow this up with a clean exit, there's no fumbling around getting your coat and galoshes, I just saunter into the electric eye in my white shirt that my mother ironed the night before, and the door heaves itself open, and outside the sunshine is skating around on the asphalt.

I look around for my girls, but they're gone, of course. There wasn't anybody but some young married screaming with her children about some candy they didn't get by the door of a powder-blue Falcon station wagon. Looking back in the big windows, over the bags of peat moss and aluminum lawn furniture stacked on the pavement, I could see Lengel in my place in the slot, checking the sheep through. His face was dark gray and his back stiff, as if he'd just had an injection of iron, and my stomach kind of fell as I felt how hard the world was going to be to me hereafter.

Discussion

Reduced to a plot summary, John Updike's "A&P" is unpromising: a grocery store manager admonishes some girls for shopping in their bathing suits, and a young cashier quits his job because he has been attracted to one of them and wants to make an impression. Updike, however, has constructed a highly entertaining moral tale in "A&P," guaranteed to amuse but in the end to instruct with bittersweet wisdom that grows from the magic in the telling.

The girls are merely summer visitors who will leave at the end of the season, just as they leave at the end of the story, while Sammy, Updike's teenage narrator, must stay on. But this is only one of the distinctions between work and play, innocence and experience, public and private codes of morality, that enhance "A&P." Updike achieves this through Sammy's slangy speaking voice. His casual vocabulary and eye for highly selective details give the story both its humor and its truth. Moreover, Sammy's easy transitions from present tense to past tense and back again allow for an off-the-cuff monologue to keep its seeming innocence intact until the conclusion, while at the same time being faithful to his point of view. As its narrator, Sammy knows the story's end before he begins to tell it. Inevitably that must influence his narration to reflect what he knows; he never loses his cheeky voice, but subtly it has been colored throughout by what has already happened.

Written over 30 years ago and included in Updike's *Pigeon Feathers and Other Stories* (1962), "A&P" reflects a more decorous time through the social mores it details, but readers — especially those of Sammy's age — are likely to find it astonishingly contemporary. Even long after the so-called sexual revolution, Sammy is easily recognizable and, withal, sympathetic to anyone who ever fell in love at first sight and learned to see more clearly afterward. Updike's timeless fable insures that through its careful language, as any number of seemingly inconsequential details demonstrate. When Sammy first sees the girls, he is standing with his hand on a box of crackers and cannot remember whether or not he had rung them up. They might have been Ritz or Saltines or even unidentified, but they are "HiHo crackers": accidentally or by design an invitation, a greeting. Similarly, as Sammy watches the girls parade up one aisle and down the next, Updike arranges appropriate backdrops: the girls stroll by the meat counter, which provides the butcher an excuse to be "patting his mouth and looking after them sizing up their joints" before they disappear from sight momentarily "behind a pyramid of Diet Delight peaches." Updike might have placed them at some other counter or built that pyramid of some other canned goods, but the story is richer because he did not.

Sammy sees "these three girls" in the first paragraph of the story; in its last paragraph they have become "my girls." In between, as he follows them on their journey in search of a jar of herring snacks, fiction's artifice seems unerringly natural. Sammy reflects exactly what the grocery store manager will eventually pronounce: "You know, it's one thing to have a girl in a bathing suit down on the beach, where what with the glare nobody can look at each other much anyway," but in the A&P, the lights are fluorescent, and bare feet look naked on a rubber-tile floor. Sammy first registers the chubby girl with "a sweet broad soft-looking can," wearing a two-piece green suit, then the tallest one, who is "the kind of girl other girls think is very 'striking' and 'attractive' but never quite makes it, as they very well know, which is why they like her so much." But they are merely attendants to "the queen," later "Queenie," who, Sammy says, "made my stomach rub against the inside of my apron." Her suit is "a kind of dirty-pink — beige maybe" and of a nubbly material, with its shoulder straps

Chapter One

down. Although Sammy does not consciously realize it — surely he would say so if he did — she must look quite nude from the distance. Later the effect is even more staggering for Sammy when the girl comes to his register and "lifts a folded dollar bill out the hollow at the center of her nubbled pink top," or as Sammy describes it, stashed "between the two smoothest scoops of vanilla I had ever known were there."

Although Sammy focuses almost exclusively on the girls, Updike weaves into his narrative a succession of casual observations that open the intentions of the story to embrace an entire range of social variations. When Sammy first hears Queenie's voice, "so flat and dumb yet kind of tony, too," he has a momentary fantasy about a party her family will give, the men in bow ties and the women in sandals, all drinking martinis, while his own family would serve lemonade or, "if it's a real racy affair Schlitz." His distance from the girls exacerbates his distance from the older generation in other instances as well, for in a broader sense he cares not only about the girls but about the rest of a younger generation's punishments. In a throwaway line, he complains that "about twenty-seven old freeloaders [are] tearing up Central Street because the sewer broke again," while the story verifies through seemingly impertinent details that he takes some implicit pride in his day's labor at the grocery store. Even so, he resents the "plastic toys done up in cellophane that fall apart when a kid looks at them anyway," and mothers "screaming with her children about some candy they didn't get." Adults are the enemy: Lengel, the "pretty dreary" manager who "teaches Sunday school and the rest"; "a witch of about fifty with rouge on her cheekbones and no eyebrows," who bawls out Sammy when he gets sidetracked by the girls and rings up her HiHos twice; the "sheep, pushing their carts" and the "houseslaves in pincurlers." Customers and manager alike have power over the younger generation in various ways, even though Sammy's smart mouth is no more innocent than the actions of the girls who are clearly aware of the effect they are making. "We *are* decent," the leader of the three retaliates when

Lengel tells her that their bathing suits are against A&P policy. "That's policy for you," Sammy says to himself. "Policy is what kingpins want. What the others want is juvenile delinquency." Sammy's bravado in quitting is vainglorious but only partly romantically so: the girls have disappeared by the time he gets to the parking lot, and when he registers that, he adds, "of course."

On first reading or last, the words on the pages of "A&P" do not change, but Sammy changes. He comes to learn "how hard the world was going to be... hereafter." So, perhaps, does the reader who looks closely at Updike's canny tale.

(Bruce Kellner)

Questions

1. **Descriptive details** create a picture of an event, a character, or a place and often reveal clues to main ideas in the story. Notice how fully the author arranges details to set the story in an ordinary supermarket. What details stand out for you as particularly true to life? What does this close attention to detail contribute to the significance of the story?
2. What part of the story seems like the exposition? Where in "A & P" does the dramatic conflict become apparent? What moment in the story brings the crisis? What is the climax of the story?
3. How fully does the author draw the character of Sammy? **Character traits** are the qualities of a character's personality. They are revealed through a character's actions and words and through description (See a brief discussion about character in Chapter Three). What traits does Sammy show? Is he any less a hero for wanting the girls to notice his heroism? Of what value to the story is the carefully detailed portrait of Queenie, the leader of the three girls?
4. As the plot develops, do you detect any change in Sammy's

feelings towards the girls? Does anything lead you to expect Sammy to make some gesture of sympathy for the three girls? What incident earlier in the story (before Sammy quits) seems a foreshadowing? Why, exactly, does Sammy quit the job?
5. What do you understand from the conclusion of the story? What does Sammy mean when he acknowledges "how hard the world was going to be... hereafter"?
6. What comment does Updike make on the supermarket society?

The Furnished Room
by O. Henry, 1945

    Restless, shifting, fugacious as time itself is a certain vast bulk of the population of the red brick district of the lower West Side. Homeless, they have a hundred homes. They flit from furnished room to furnished room, transients forever—transients in abode, transients in heart and mind. They sing "Home, Sweet Home" in ragtime; they carry their *lares et penates*[1] in a bandbox; their vine is entwined about a picture hat; a rubber plant is their fig tree.

    Hence the houses of this district, having had a thousand dwellers, should have a thousand tales to tell, mostly dull ones, no doubt; but it would be strange if there could not be found a ghost or two in the wake of all these vagrant guests.

    One evening after dark a young man prowled among these crumbling red mansions, ringing their bells. At the twelfth he rested his lean hand baggage upon the step and wiped the dust from his hatband and forehead. The bell sounded faint and far away in some remote, hollow depths.

    To the door of this, the twelfth house whose bell he had rung,

---

[1] *lares et penates*: household gods.

came a housekeeper who made him think of an unwholesome, surfeited worm that had eaten its nut to a hollow shell and now sought to fill the vacancy with edible lodgers.

5   He asked if there was a room to let.

"Come in," said the housekeeper. Her voice came from her throat; her throat seemed lined with fur. "I have the third floor back, vacant since a week back. Should you wish to look at it?"

The young man followed her up the stairs. A faint light from no particular source mitigated the shadows of the halls. They trod noiselessly upon a stair carpet that its own loom would have forsworn. It seemed to have become vegetable; to have degenerated in that rank, sunless air to lush lichen or spreading moss that grew in patches to the staircase and was viscid under the foot like organic matter. At each turn of the stairs were vacant niches in the wall. Perhaps plants had once been set within them. If so, they had died in that foul and tainted air. It may be that statues of the saints had stood there, but it was not difficult to conceive that imps and devils had dragged them forth in the darkness and down to the unholy depths of some furnished pit below.

"This is the room," said the housekeeper, from her furry throat. "It's a nice room. It ain't often vacant. I had some most elegant people in it last summer—no trouble at all, and paid in advance to the minute. The water's at the end of the hall. Sprowls and Mooney kept it three months. They done a vaudeville sketch. Miss B'retta Sprowls—you may have heard of her—Oh, that was just the stage names—right there over the dresser is where the marriage certificate hung, framed. The gas is here, and you see there is plenty of closet room. It's a room everybody likes. It never stays idle long."

"Do you have many theatrical people rooming here?" asked the young man.

10   "They comes and goes. A good proportion of my lodgers is connected with the theaters. Yes, sir, this is the theatrical district. Actor people never stays long anywhere. I get my share.

Chapter One

Yes, they comes and they goes."

He engaged the room, paying for a week in advance. He was tired, he said, and would take possession at once. He counted out the money. The room had been made ready, she said, even to towels and water. As the housekeeper moved away he put, for the thousandth time, the question that he carried at the end of his tongue.

"A young girl—Miss Vashner—Miss Eloise Vashner—do you remember such a one among your lodgers? She would be singing on the stage, most likely. A fair girl, of medium height and slender, with reddish, gold hair and a dark mole near her left eyebrow."

"No, I don't remember the name. Them stage people has names they change as often as their rooms. They comes and they goes. No, I don't call that one to mind."

No. Always no. Five months of ceaseless interrogation and the inevitable negative. So much time spent by day in questioning managers, agents, schools and choruses; by night among the audiences of theaters from all-star casts down to music halls so low that he dreaded to find what he most hoped for. He who had loved her best had tried to find her. He was sure that since her disappearance from home this great, water-girt city held her somewhere, but it was like a monstrous quicksand, shifting its particles constantly, with no foundation, its upper granules of today buried tomorrow in ooze and slime.

15 The furnished room received its latest guest with a first glow of pseudo-hospitality, a hectic, haggard, perfunctory welcome like the specious smile of a demirep. The sophistical comfort came in reflected gleams from the decayed furniture, the ragged brocade upholstery of a couch and two chairs, a foot-wide cheap pier glass between the two windows, from one or two gilt picture frames and a brass bedstead in a corner.

The guest reclined, inert, upon a chair, while the room, confused in speech as though it were an apartment in Babel, tried to discourse to him of its divers tenantry.

A polychromatic rug like some brilliant-flowered rectangular, tropical islet lay surrounded by a billowy sea of soiled matting. Upon the gray-papered wall were those pictures that pursue the homeless one from house to house—The Huguenot Lovers, The First Quarrel, The Wedding Breakfast, Psyche at the Fountain. The mantel's chastely severe outline was ingloriously veiled behind some pert drapery drawn rakishly askew like the sashes of the Amazonian ballet. Upon it was some desolate flotsam cast aside by the room's marooned when a lucky sail had borne them to a fresh port—a trifling vase or two, pictures of actresses, a medicine bottle, some stray cards out of a deck.

One by one, as the characters of a cryptograph become explicit, the little signs left by the furnished room's procession of guests developed a significance. The threadbare space in the rug in front of the dresser told that lovely woman had marched in the throng. The tiny finger prints on the wall spoke of little prisoners trying to feel their way to sun and air. A splattered stain, raying like the shadow of a bursting bomb, witnessed where a hurled glass or bottle had splintered with its contents against the wall. Across the pier glass had been scrawled with a diamond in staggering letters the name "Marie." It seemed that the succession of dwellers in the furnished room had turned in fury—perhaps tempted beyond forbearance by its garish coldness—and wreaked upon it their passions. The furniture was chipped and bruised; the couch, distorted by bursting springs, seemed a horrible monster that had been slain during the stress of some grotesque convulsion. Some more potent upheaval had cloven a great slice from the marble mantel. Each plank in the floor owned its particular cant and shriek as from a separate and individual agony. It seemed incredible that all this malice and injury had been wrought upon the room by those who had called it for a time their home; and yet it may have been the cheated home instinct surviving blindly, the resentful rage at false household gods that had kindled their wrath. A hut that is our own we can sweep and adorn and cherish.

Chapter One

The young tenant in the chair allowed these thoughts to file, softshod, through his mind, while there drifted into the room furnished sounds and furnished scents. He heard in one room a tittering and incontinent, slack laughter; in others the monologue of a scold, the rattling of dice, a lullaby, and one crying dully; above him a banjo tinkled with spirit. Doors banged somewhere; the elevated trains roared intermittently; a cat yowled miserably upon a back fence. And he breathed the breath of the house—a dank savor rather than a smell—a cold, musty effluvium as from underground vaults mingled with the reeking exhalations of linoleum and mildewed and rotten woodwork.

20 Then, suddenly, as he rested there, the room was filled with the strong, sweet odor of mignonette. It came as upon a single buffet of wind with such sureness and fragrance and emphasis that it almost seemed a living visitant. And the man cried aloud: "What, dear?" as if he had been called, and sprang up and faced about. The rich odor clung to him and wrapped him around. He reached out his arms for it, all his senses for the time confused and commingled. How could one be peremptorily called by an odor? Surely it must have been a sound. But, was it not the sound that had touched, that had caressed him?

"She has been in this room," he cried, and he sprang to wrest from it a token, for he knew he would recognize the smallest thing that had belonged to her or that she had touched. This enveloping scent of mignonette, the odor that she had loved and made her own—whence came it?

The room had been but carelessly set in order. Scattered upon the flimsy dresser scarf were half a dozen hairpins—those discreet, indistinguishable friends of womankind, feminine of gender, infinite of mood and uncommunicative of tense. These he ignored, conscious of their triumphant lack of identity. Ransacking the drawers of the dresser, he came upon a discarded, tiny, ragged handkerchief. He pressed it to his face. It was racy and insolent with heliotrope; he hurled it to the floor. In another drawer he found odd buttons, a theater program, a pawnbroker's card, two lost marshmallows, a book on the divination of dreams. In the last was a woman's black satin hairbow, which halted him, poised between ice and fire. But the black satin hairbow also is femininity's demure, impersonal, common ornament, and tells no tales.

And then he traversed the room like a hound on the scent, skimming the walls, considering the corners of the bulging matting on his hands and knees, rummaging mantel and tables, the curtains and hangings, the drunken cabinet in the corner, for a visible sign, unable to perceive that she was there beside, around, against, within, above him, clinging to him, wooing him, calling him so poignantly through the finer senses that even his grosser ones became cognizant of the call. Once again he answered loudly: "Yes, dear!" and turned, wildeyed, to gaze on vacancy, for he could not yet discern form and color and love and outstretched arms in the odor of mignonette. Oh, God! whence that odor, and since when have odors had a voice to call? Thus he groped.

He burrowed in crevices and corners, and found corks and cigarettes. These he passed in passive contempt. But once he found in a fold of the matting a half-smoked cigar, and this he ground beneath his heel with a green and trenchant oath. He sifted the room from end to end. He found dreary and ignoble small records of many a peripatetic tenant; but of her whom he sought, and who may have lodged there, and whose spirit seemed to hover there, he found no trace.

25 And then he thought of the housekeeper.

He ran from the haunted room downstairs and to a door that showed a crack of light. She came out to his knock. He smothered his excitement as best he could.

"Will you tell me, madam," he besought her, "who occupied the room I have before I came?"

"Yes, sir. I can tell you again. 'Twas Sprowls and Mooney, as I said. Miss B'retta Sprowls it was in the theaters, but Missis Mooney she was. My house is well known for respectability. The

Chapter One

marriage certificate hung, framed, on a nail over—"

"What kind of a lady was Miss Sprowls—in looks, I mean?"

30 Why, black-haired, sir, short, and stout, with a comical face. They left a week ago Tuesday."

"And before they occupied it?"

"Why, there was a single gentleman connected with the draying business. He left owing me a week. Before him was Missis Crowder and her two children that stayed four months; and back of them was old Mr. Doyle, whose sons paid for him. He kept the room six months. That goes back a year, sir, and further I do not remember."

He thanked her and crept back to his room. The room was dead. The essence that had vivified it was gone. The perfume of mignonette had departed. In its place was the old, stale odor of moldy house furniture, of atmosphere in storage.

The ebbing of his hope drained his faith. He sat staring at the yellow, singing gaslight. Soon he walked to the bed and began to tear the sheets into strips. With the blade of his knife he drove them tightly into every crevice around windows and door. When all was snug and taut, he turned out the light, turned the gas full on again, and laid himself gratefully upon the bed.

35 It was Mrs. McCool's night to go with the can for beer. So she fetched it and sat with Mrs. Purdy in one of those subterranean retreats where housekeepers foregather and the worm dieth seldom.

"I rented out my third floor, back, this evening," said Mrs. Purdy, across a fine circle of foam. "A young man took it. He went up to bed two hours ago."

"Now, did ye, Mrs. Purdy, ma'am?" said Mrs. McCool, with intense admiration. "You do be a wonder for rentin' rooms of that kind. And did ye tell him, then?" she concluded in a husky whisper laden with mystery.

"Rooms," said Mrs. Purdy, in her furriest tones, "are furnished for to rent. I did not tell him, Mrs. McCool."

"'Tis right ye are, ma'am; 'tis by rentin' rooms we kape[1] alive. Ye have the rale[2] sense for business, ma'am. There be many people will rayjict[3] the rentin' of a room if they be tould[4] a suicide has been after dyin' in the bed of it."

40 "As you say, we has our living to be making," remarked Mrs. Purdy.

"Yis, ma'am; 'tis true. 'Tis just one wake[5] ago this day I helped ye lay out the third floor, back. A pretty slip of a colleen[6] she was to be killin' herself wid[7] the gas—a swate little face she had, Mrs. Purdy, ma'am."

"She'd a-been called handsome, as you say," said Mrs. Purdy, assenting but critical, "but for that mole she had a-growin' by her left eyebrow. Do fill up your glass again, Mrs. McCool."

Discussion

This story is obviously divided into two parts. The first part, which ends with the death of the lodger, concerns his failure in the search for his sweetheart, the odor of mignonette, the lie of the landlady, and the suicide; the second part concerns the revelation, by the landlady to her crony, that his sweetheart had, a week earlier, committed suicide in the same room. What accounts for the fact that O. Henry felt it necessary to treat the story in this fashion? What holds the two parts of the story together? What is the central meaning of this plot?

---

[1] *kape*: keep.
[2] *rale*: real.
[3] *rayjict*: reject.
[4] *tould*: told.
[5] *wake*: week.
[6] *colleen*: girl.
[7] *wid*: with.

Chapter One

The most interesting question has to do with the young man's motivation. In one sense, O. Henry has deliberately made the problem of his motivation more difficult by withholding the information that the young man does not know that his sweetheart is dead; indeed, in the room, he gets, with the scent of mignonette, a renewed hope. Why then, under these circumstances does he commit suicide? Presumably, the explanation is this: he has been searching fruitlessly for five months; he is, we are told, tired — and, we assume, not only momentarily tired physically, but spiritually weary. Indeed, we are told: "He was sure that since her disappearance from home this great, water-girt city held her somewhere, but it was like a monstrous quicksand, shifting its particles constantly, with no foundation, its upper granules of today buried tomorrow in ooze and slime." But we are not supposed to believe, even so, that he would have necessarily turned on the gas this particular evening, except in despair at the loss of hope raised by the scent of mignonette. This is the author's account of the motivation of the suicide.

But is the motivation, as presented, really convincing? That will depend on the character of the man. What sort of man is he? Actually, O. Henry tells us very little about him except that he is young, has searched for his sweetheart for five months, and is tired. Especially does the question of the man's character, and state of mind, come up in the incident in which he notices the odor of mignonette. Did he really smell it? Did he merely imagine that he smelled it? "And he breathed the breath of the house... a cold, musty effluvium... mingled with the reeking exhalations of linoleum and mildewed and rotten woodwork. Then, suddenly, as he rested there, the room was filled with the strong, sweet odor of mignonette. It came as upon a single buffet of wind."

The suddenness with which he notices the odor, the fact that he can find no source for the odor, and finally the complete disappearance of the odor, all tend to imply that he merely imagines it. But over against this view, we have the testimony of the landlady that the sweetheart had actually occupied the room. This question is crucial for the young man's lapse into acute despair. If the odor is real, the author must convince his reader that it exists; if it is imaginary, the author must convince his reader that the psychological condition of the young man will account for its apparent existence. These are the tests the reader must apply to the situation. We have already pointed out that there is some evidence on both sides of the question. The reader must, of course, decide for himself which explanation must be taken, and more important, whether the explanation is convincing, and renders the action credible. The author, perhaps, weighs the evidence toward the presence of the real odor. If this is the case, how are we to account for the fact that the search reveals no source of it, especially since the odor is so overpoweringly strong? Or, perhaps the author has in mind some idea that the odor provokes a mystical communion between the two lovers. But this does not relieve the fiction writer from the necessity for furnishing some sort of specific clue to his meaning. (Moreover, if we are to take the whole experience as an hallucination, the author is certainly not relieved from providing some clear motivation for the event.) In other words, the author is playing with his reader — "mystifying him."

To sum up: it is obvious enough, from the detailed description of the room, that O. Henry is trying to suggest a ground for the man's experience in the nature of the room itself. That is, the room in its disorder, its squalor, its musty smell, its rubbish and debris of nameless lives, reflects the great city, in which his sweetheart has been lost, and in which all humanity seems to become degraded and brutalized. O. Henry wants to suggest the contrast between what the sordid surroundings mean to the hero and what the odor of mignonette means to him. As the girl is lost somewhere in the great city, so the odor is lost somewhere in the room. After the young man is told that the girl has not been there, and after he has been unable to find the source of the odor, the room itself is supposed to become a sort of overwhelming symbol for the futility of his effort. This intention on the part of the author may be sound enough, but the fact that we see what the intention is does not mean that the intention has been carried out. The whole effect of the story depends on the incident of the odor, and we have seen that the handling of this detail is confused. What we have is a faintly symbolic suggestion that the sourceless odor, standing for the young man's finally thwarted hope, is in contrast to the sordidness of the room, and the contrast is too much for him.

Such is the psychological frailty of the story. But resting upon his rather thin and sketchy characterization of the young man, the author chooses to give a turn to the plot by a last-minute surprise. In the second part of the story the landlady tells her crony that she has lied to the young man about the girl.

What is the effect of this revelation? It is intended, obviously, to underline the "irony of fate," to illustrate the hardheartedness of the city in which the young man finds himself, to justify the young man's overwhelming sense that the girl has been in the room, and, all in all, to pull the story together. For the sympathetic reader this conclusion is supposed to suggest that the bonds of love stretch across the confusion and squalor of the great city, and that, in a sense, the young man has finally succeeded in his search, for the lovers are at last united in death. The young man finds, as it were, the proper room in the great city in which to die.

But is the story really pulled together? The end of the story depends on the lie. But are the lives of the lovers altered by the lie? Does the lie cause the death of the young man? It is conceivable that, had the landlady told the truth, the shock of the information might have saved the young man from suicide, but this is the merest speculation. The character, as given in the story, commits suicide in despair when the landlady tells him that the girl has not been there; the landlady's telling him that the girl is irretrievably lost, is dead, would presumably have had the same effect. Or would that fact have saved him?

Actually, is there any point in the lie except to trick the reader

— to provide the illusion of a meaningful ending? Whatever irony lies in the ending is based on a farfetched coincidence, and does not depend on the fact that the woman said one thing rather than another. (Readers who are inclined to accept the conclusion of the story as meaningful might try reconstructing the story with the young man's calling at the door, finding with horror that his sweetheart has committed suicide there a week before, renting the room, and turning on the gas. We would then still have the ironical coincidence and a sort of union of the lovers, but the story would seem very tame and flat.) O. Henry, by withholding certain information and thus surprising us with it at the end, has simply tried to give the reader the illusion that the information was meaningful. The irony, in the story as we have it, simply resides in a trick played on the reader rather than in a trick that fate has played on the young man.

Readers who feel that the end of this story is a shabby trick will be able to point out other symptoms of cheapness: the general thinness of characterization, the cluttered and sometimes mawkish description, the wheedling tone taken by the author, and the obvious play for emotional sympathy in such writing as the following: "Oh, God! whence that odor, and since when have odors had a voice to call?" In other words, we can readily surmise that the trickery involved in the surprise ending may be an attempt to compensate for defects within the body of the story itself. The straining to stir the emotions of the reader, the mawkish and wheedling tone — all are attempts to make up for a lack of logic, a lack of coherence, in the story itself. *Sentimentality* often springs from such a lack of coherence — emotionalism without reference to a reasonable occasion for it.

A trick of plot does not make a story. A surprise ending may appear in a very good story, but only if the surprise has been prepared for, so that, upon second thought, the reader realizes that it is, after all, a logical and meaningful development from what has gone before, and not merely a device employed by the

Chapter One

author to give him an easy way out of his difficulties. The same principle applies to *coincidence* in general. Coincidences do occur in real life, sometimes quite startling ones, and in one sense every story is based on a coincidence — namely, that the particular events happen to occur together, that such and such characters happen to meet, for example, at such and such a moment under such and such circumstances. But since fiction is concerned with a logic of character and action, coincidence, insofar as it is purely illogical, has little place in fiction. Truth can afford to be stranger than fiction, because truth is "true" — is acceptable on its own merits — but the happenings of fiction, as we have seen, must justify themselves in terms of logical connection with other elements in fiction and in terms of meaningfulness. Certainly coincidence is never acceptable when it is used to solve the problem of a story — to bail the author out of his difficulties.

(Cleanth Brooks and Robert Penn Warren)

Questions

1. Can you think of a more honest and effective way for these basic materials to be turned into a story? Do not write a new version; simply mull over the possibilities.
2. Sometimes writers surprise us at the ending of a story. A **surprise ending** is an unexpected twist at the end of a story that you did not predict. It depends on an unexpected resolution of the main conflict. Even though an ending is a surprise, it must be believable. Writers make surprise endings believable by giving you a few hints about the ending without giving it away. O. Henry is known for startling his readers with surprise endings. How does the story really end? What clues does the author plant that lead to this ending? How did you think this story would end when reading it? Which clues led you to expect this ending?

A Rose for Emily
by William Faulkner, 1931

I

When Miss Emily Grierson died, our whole town went to her funeral: the men through a sort of respectful affection for a fallen monument, the women mostly out of curiosity to see the inside of her house, which no one save an old manservant—a combined gardener and cook—had seen in at least ten years.

It was a big, squarish frame house that had once been white, decorated with cupolas and spires and scrolled balconies in the heavily lightsome style of the seventies, set on what had once been our most select street. But garages and cotton gins had encroached and obliterated even the august names of that neighborhood; only Miss Emily's house was left, lifting its stubborn and coquettish decay above the cotton wagons and the gasoline pumps—an eyesore among eyesores. And now Miss Emily had gone to join the representatives of those august names where they lay in the cedarbemused cemetery among the ranked and anonymous graves of Union and Confederate soldiers who fell at the battle of Jefferson.

Alive, Miss Emily had been a tradition, a duty, and a care; a sort of hereditary obligation upon the town, dating from that day in 1894 when Colonel Sartoris, the mayor—he who fathered the edict that no Negro woman should appear on the streets without an apron—remitted her taxes, the dispensation dating from the death of her father on into perpetuity. Not that Miss Emily would have accepted charity. Colonel Sartoris invented an involved tale to the effect that Miss Emily's father had loaned money to the town, which the town, as a matter of business, preferred this way of repaying. Only a man of Colonel Sartoris' generation and thought

Chapter One

could have invented it, and only a woman could have believed it.

When the next generation, with its more modern ideas, became mayors and aldermen, this arrangement created some little dissatisfaction. On the first of the year they mailed her a tax notice. February came, and there was no reply. They wrote her a formal letter, asking her to call at the sheriff's office at her convenience. A week later the mayor wrote her himself, offering to call or to send his car for her, and received in reply a note on paper of an archaic shape, in a thin, flowing calligraphy in faded ink, to the effect that she no longer went out at all. The tax notice was also enclosed, without comment.

5   They called a special meeting of the Board of Aldermen. A deputation waited upon her, knocked at the door through which no visitor had passed since she ceased giving china-painting lessons eight or ten years earlier. They were admitted by the old Negro into a dim hall from which a stairway mounted into still more shadow. It smelled of dust and disuse—a close, dank smell. The Negro led them into the parlor. It was furnished in heavy, leather-covered furniture. When the Negro opened the blinds of one window, they could see that the leather was cracked; and when they sat down, a faint dust rose sluggishly about their thighs, spinning with slow motes in the single sun-ray. On a tarnished gilt easel before the fireplace stood a crayon portrait of Miss Emily's father.

They rose when she entered—a small, fat woman in black, with a thin gold chain descending to her waist and vanishing into her belt, leaning on an ebony cane with a tarnished gold head. Her skeleton was small and spare; perhaps that was why what would have been merely plumpness in another was obesity in her. She looked bloated, like a body long submerged in motionless water, and of that pallid hue. Her eyes, lost in the fatty ridges of her face, looked like two small pieces of coal pressed into a lump of dough as they moved from one face to another while the visitors stated their errand.

She did not ask them to sit. She just stood in the door and

listened quietly until the spokesman came to a stumbling halt. Then they could hear the invisible watch ticking at the end of the gold chain.

Her voice was dry and cold. "I have no taxes in Jefferson. Colonel Sartoris explained it to me. Perhaps one of you can gain access to the city records and satisfy yourselves."

"But we have. We are the city authorities, Miss Emily. Didn't you get a notice from the sheriff, signed by him?"

10 "I received a paper, yes," Miss Emily said. "Perhaps he considers himself the sheriff... I have no taxes in Jefferson."

"But there is nothing on the books to show that, you see. We must go by the—"

"See Colonel Sartoris. I have no taxes in Jefferson."

"But, Miss Emily—"

"See Colonel Sartoris." (Colonel Sartoris had been dead almost ten years.) "I have no taxes in Jefferson. Tobe!" The Negro appeared. "Show these gentlemen out."

II

15 So she vanquished them, horse and foot, just as she had vanquished their fathers thirty years before about the smell. That was two years after her father's death and a short time after her sweetheart—the one we believed would marry her—had deserted her. After her father's death she went out very little; after her sweetheart went away, people hardly saw her at all. A few of the ladies had the temerity to call, but were not received, and the only sign of life about the place was the Negro man—a young man then—going in and out with a market basket.

"Just as if a man—any man—could keep a kitchen properly," the ladies said; so they were not surprised when the smell developed. It was another link between the gross, teeming world and the high and mighty Griersons.

A neighbor, a woman, complained to the mayor, Judge Stevens, eighty years old.

Chapter One

"But what will you have me do about it, madam?" he said.

"Why, send her word to stop it," the woman said. "Isn't there a law?"

20 "I'm sure that won't be necessary," Judge Stevens said. "It's probably just a snake or a rat that nigger of hers killed in the yard. I'll speak to him about it."

The next day he received two more complaints, one from a man who came in diffident deprecation. "We really must do something about it, Judge. I'd be the last one in the world to bother Miss Emily, but we've got to do something." That night the Board of Aldermen met—three graybeards and one younger man, a member of the rising generation.

"It's simple enough," he said. "Send her word to have her place cleaned up. Give her a certain time to do it in, and if she don't..."

"Dammit, sir," Judge Stevens said, "will you accuse a lady to her face of smelling bad?"

So the next night, after midnight, four men crossed Miss Emily's lawn and slunk about the house like burglars, sniffing along the base of the brickwork and at the cellar openings while one of them performed a regular sowing motion with his hand out of a sack slung from his shoulder. They broke open the cellar door and sprinkled lime there, and in all the outbuildings. As they recrossed the lawn, a window that had been dark was lighted and Miss Emily sat in it, the light behind her, and her upright torso motionless as that of an idol. They crept quietly across the lawn and into the shadow of the locusts that lined the street. After a week or two the smell went away.

25 That was when people had begun to feel really sorry for her. People in our town, remembering how old lady Wyatt, her greataunt, had gone completely crazy at last, believed that the Griersons held themselves a little too high for what they really were. None of the young men were quite good enough for Miss Emily and such. We had long thought of them as a tableau, Miss Emily a slender

figure in white in the background, her father a spraddled silhouette in the foreground, his back to her and clutching a horsewhip, the two of them framed by the back-flung front door. So when she got to be thirty and was still single, we were not pleased exactly, but vindicated; even with insanity in the family she wouldn't have turned down all of her chances if they had really materialized.

When her father died, it got about that the house was all that was left to her; and in a way, people were glad. At last they could pity Miss Emily. Being left alone, and a pauper, she had become humanized. Now she too would know the old thrill and the old despair of a penny more or less.

The day after his death all the ladies prepared to call at the house and offer condolence and aid, as is our custom. Miss Emily met them at the door, dressed as usual and with no trace of grief on her face. She told them that her father was not dead. She did that for three days, with the ministers calling on her, and the doctors, trying to persuade her to let them dispose of the body. Just as they were about to resort to law and force, she broke down, and they buried her father quickly.

We did not say she was crazy then. We believed she had to do that. We remembered all the young men her father had driven away, and we knew that with nothing left, she would have to cling to that which had robbed her, as people will.

III

She was sick for a long time. When we saw her again, her hair was cut short, making her look like a girl, with a vague resemblance to those angels in colored church windows—sort of tragic and serene.

30　The town had just let the contracts for paving the sidewalks, and in the summer after her father's death they began the work. The construction company came with niggers and mules and machinery, and a foreman named Homer Barron, a Yankee—a big, dark, ready man, with a big voice and eyes lighter than his face.

Chapter One

The little boys would follow in groups to hear him cuss the niggers, and the niggers singing in time to the rise and fall of picks. Pretty soon he knew everybody in town. Whenever you heard a lot of laughing anywhere about the square, Homer Barron would be in the center of the group. Presently we began to see him and Miss Emily on Sunday afternoons driving in the yellow-wheeled buggy and the matched team of bays from the livery stable.

At first we were glad that Miss Emily would have an interest, because the ladies all said, "Of course a Grierson would not think seriously of a Northerner, a day laborer." But there were still others, older people, who said that even grief could not cause a real lady to forget *noblesse oblige*[1]—without calling it *noblesse oblige*. They just said, "Poor Emily. Her kinsfolk should come to her." She had some kin in Alabama; but years ago her father had fallen out with them over the estate of old lady Wyatt, the crazy woman, and there was no communication between the two families. They had not even been represented at the funeral.

And as soon as the old people said, "Poor Emily," the whispering began. "Do you suppose it's really so?" they said to one another. "Of course it is. What else could..." This behind their hands; rustling of craned silk and satin behind jalousies closed upon the sun of Sunday afternoon as the thin, swift clop-clop-clop of the matched team passed: "Poor Emily."

She carried her head high enough—even when we believed that she was fallen. It was as if she demanded more than ever the recognition of her dignity as the last Grierson; as if it had wanted that touch of earthiness to reaffirm her imperviousness. Like when she bought the rat poison, the arsenic. That was over a year after they had begun to say "Poor Emily," and while the two female cousins were visiting her.

"I want some poison," she said to the druggist. She was over thirty then, still a slight woman, though thinner than usual, with

---

[1] *noblesse oblige*: the obligation of a member of the nobility to behave with honor and dignity.

cold, haughty black eyes in a face the flesh of which was strained across the temples and about the eye-sockets as you imagine a lighthouse-keeper's face ought to look. "I want some poison," she said.
35 "Yes, Miss Emily. What kind? For rats and such? I'd recom—"
"I want the best you have. I dont't care what kind."
The druggist named several. "They'll kill anything up to an elephant. But what you want is—"
"Arsenic," Miss Emily said. "Is that a good one?"
"Is... arsenic? Yes, ma'am. But what you want—"
40 "I want arsenic."
The druggist looked down at her. She looked back at him, erect, her face like a strained flag. "Why, of course," the druggist said. "If that's what you want. But the law requires you to tell what you are going to use it for."
Miss Emily just stared at him, her head tilted back in order to look him eye for eye, until he looked away and went and got the arsenic and wrapped it up. The Negro delivery boy brought her the package; the druggist didn't come back. When she opened the package at home there was written on the box, under the skull and bones: "For rats."

IV

So the next day we all said, "She will kill herself"; and we said it would be the best thing. When she had first begun to be seen with Homer Barron, we had said, "She will marry him." Then we said, "She will persuade him yet," because Homer himself had remarked—he liked men, and it was known that he drank with the younger men in the Elks' Club—that he was not a marrying man. Later we said, "Poor Emily," behind the jalousies as they passed on Sunday afternoon in the glittering buggy, Miss Emily with her head high and Homer Barron with his hat cocked and a cigar in his teeth, reins and whip in a yellow glove.

Chapter One

Then some of the ladies began to say that it was a disgrace to the town and a bad example to the young people. The men did not want to interfere, but at last the ladies forced the Baptist minister—Miss Emily's people were Episcopal—to call upon her. He would never divulge what happened during that interview, but he refused to go back again. The next Sunday they again drove about the streets, and the following day the minister's wife wrote to Miss Emily's relations in Alabama.

45 So she had blood-kin under her roof again and we sat back to watch developments. At first nothing happened. Then we were sure that they were to be married. We learned that Miss Emily had been to the jeweler's and ordered a man's toilet set in silver, with the letters H. B. on each piece. Two days later we learned that she had bought a complete outfit of men's clothing, including a nightshirt, and we said, "They are married." We were really glad. We were glad because the two female cousins were even more Grierson than Miss Emily had ever been.

So we were not surprised when Homer Barron—the streets had been finished some time since—was gone. We were a little disappointed that there was not a public blowing-off, but we believed that he had gone on to prepare for Miss Emily's coming, or to give her a chance to get rid of the cousins. (By that time it was a cabal, and we were all Miss Emily's allies to help circumvent the cousins.) Sure enough, after another week they departed. And, as we had expected all along, within three days Homer Barron was back in town. A neighbor saw the Negro man admit him at the kitchen door at dusk one evening.

And that was the last we saw of Homer Barron. And of Miss Emily for some time. The Negro man went in and out with the market basket, but the front door remained closed. Now and then we would see her at a window for a moment, as the men did that night when they sprinkled the lime, but for almost six months she did not appear on the streets. Then we knew that this was to be expected too; as if that quality of her father which had thwarted her women's life so many times had been too virulent and too furious to die.

When we next saw Miss Emily, she had grown fat and her hair was turning gray. During the next few years it grew grayer and grayer until it attained an even pepper-and-salt iron-gray, when it ceased turning. Up to the day of her death at seventy-four it was still that vigorous iron-gray, like the hair of an active man.

From that time on her front door remained closed, save for a period of six or seven years, when she was about forty, during which she gave lessons in china-painting. She fitted up a studio in one of the downstairs rooms, where the daughters and granddaughters of Colonel Sartoris' contemporaries were sent to her with the same regularity and in the same spirit that they were sent to church on Sundays with a twenty-five-cent piece for the collection plate. Meanwhile her taxes had been remitted.

50   Then the newer generation became the backbone and the spirit of the town, and the painting pupils grew up and fell away and did not send their children to her with boxes of color and tedious brushes and pictures cut from the ladies' magazines. The front door closed upon the last one and remained closed for good. When the town got free postal delivery, Miss Emily alone refused to let them fasten the metal numbers above her door and attach a mailbox to it. She would not listen to them.

Daily, monthly, yearly we watched the Negro grow grayer and more stooped, going in and out with the market basket. Each December we sent her a tax notice, which would be returned by the post office a week later, unclaimed. Now and then we would see her in one of the downstairs windows—she had evidently shut up the top floor of the house—like the carven torso of an idol in a niche, looking or not looking at us, we could never tell which. Thus she passed from generation to generation—dear, inescapable, impervious, tranquil, and perverse.

And so she died. Fell ill in the house filled with dust and shadows, with only a doddering Negro man to wait on her. We did not even know she was sick; we had long since given up trying to get any information from the Negro. He talked to no one, probably not even to her, for his voice had grown harsh and rusty, as if from disuse.

She died in one of the downstairs rooms, in a heavy walnut bed with a curtain, her gray head propped on a pillow yellow and moldy with age and lack of sunlight.

V

The Negro met the first of the ladies at the front door and let them in, with their hushed, sibilant voices and their quick, curious glances, and then he disappeared. He walked right through the house and out the back and was not seen again.

The two female cousins came at once. They held the funeral on the second day, with the town coming to look at Miss Emily beneath a mass of bought flowers, with the crayon face of her father musing profoundly above the bier and the ladies sibilant and macabre; and the very old men—some in their brushed Confederate uniforms—on the porch and the lawn, talking of Miss Emily as if she had been a contemporary of theirs, believing that they had danced with her and courted her perhaps, confusing time with its mathematical progression, as the old do, to whom all the past is not a diminishing road but, instead, a huge meadow which no winter ever quite touches, divided from them now by the narrow bottleneck of the most recent decade of years.

Already we knew that there was one room in that region above stairs which no one had seen in forty years, and which would have to be forced. They waited until Miss Emily was decently in the ground before they opened it.

The violence of breaking down the door seemed to fill this room with pervading dust. A thin, acrid pall as of the tomb seemed to lie everywhere upon this room decked and furnished as for a bridal: upon the valance curtains of faded rose color, upon the rose-shaded lights, upon the dressing table, upon the delicate array of crystal and the man's toilet things backed with tarnished silver, silver so tarnished that the monogram was obscured. Among them lay collar and tie, as if they had just been removed, which, lifted, left upon the surface a pale crescent in the dust. Upon a chair hung the suit, carefully folded; beneath it the two mute shoes and the discarded socks.

The man himself lay in the bed.

For a long while we just stood there, looking down at the profound and fleshless grin. The body had apparently once lain in the attitude of an embrace, but now the long sleep that outlasts love, that conquers even the grimace of love, had cuckolded him. What was left of him, rotted beneath what was left of the nightshirt, had become inextricable from the bed in which he lay; and upon him and upon the pillow beside him lay that even coating of the patient and biding dust.

60 Then we noticed that in the second pillow was the indentation of a head. One of us lifted something from it, and leaning forward, that faint and invisible dust dry and acrid in the nostrils, we saw a long strand of iron-gray hair.

Discussion

This is a story of horror. We have a decaying mansion in which the protagonist, shut away from the world, grows into something monstrous, and becomes as divorced from humanity as some fungus growing in the dark on a damp wall. Miss Emily Grierson remains in voluntary isolation (or perhaps fettered by some inner compulsion) away from the bustle and dust and sunshine of the human world of normal affairs, and what in the end is found in the upstairs room gives perhaps a sense of penetrating and gruesome horror.

Has this sense of horror been conjured up for its own sake? If not, then why has the author contrived to insert so much of the monstrous into the story? In other words, does the horror contribute to the theme of Faulkner's story? Is the horror meaningful?

In order to answer this question, we shall have to examine rather carefully some of the items earlier in the story. In the first place, why does Miss Emily commit her monstrous act? Is she supplied with a proper motivation? Faulkner has, we can see, been rather careful to prepare for his denouement. Miss Emily, it becomes obvious fairly early in the story, is one of those persons for whom the distinction between reality and illusion has blurred. For example, she refuses to admit that she owes any taxes. When the mayor protests, she does not recognize him as mayor. Instead, she refers the committee to Colonel Sartoris, who, as the reader is told, has been dead for nearly ten years. For Miss Emily, apparently, Colonel Sartoris is still alive. Most specific preparation of all, when her father dies, she denies to the townspeople for three days that he is dead: "Just as they were about to resort to law and force, she broke down, and they buried her father quickly."

Miss Emily is obviously a pathological case. The narrator indicates plainly enough that people felt that she was crazy. All of this explanation prepares us for what Miss Emily does in order to hold her lover — the dead lover is in one sense still alive for her — the realms of reality and appearance merge. But having said this, we have got no nearer to justifying the story: for, if Faulkner is merely interested in relating a case history of abnormal psychology, the story lacks meaning and justification as a story and we are back to fiction as "clinical report." If the story is to be justified, there must be what may be called a moral significance, a meaning in moral terms — not merely psychological terms.

Incidentally, it is very easy to misread the story as merely a horrible case history, presented in order to titillate the reader. Faulkner has been frequently judged to be doing nothing more than this in his work.

The lapse of the distinction between illusion and reality,

between life and death, is important, therefore, in helping to account for Miss Emily's motivation, but merely to note this lapse is not fully to account for the theme of the story.

  Suppose we approach the motivation again in terms of character. What is Miss Emily like? What are the mainsprings of her character? What causes the distinction between illusion and reality to blur for her? She is obviously a woman of tremendous firmness of will. In the matter of the taxes, crazed though she is, she is never at a loss. She is utterly composed. She dominates the rather frightened committee of officers who see her. In the matter of her purchase of the poison, she completely overawes the clerk. She makes no pretense. She refuses to tell him what she wants the poison for. And yet this firmness of will and this iron pride have not kept her from being thwarted and hurt. Her father has run off the young men who came to call upon her, and the townspeople think of Miss Emily and her father as a tableau: "Miss Emily a slender figure in white in the background, her father a spraddled silhouette in the foreground, his back to her and clutching a horsewhip, the two of them framed by the backflung front door." Whether the picture is a remembered scene, or merely a symbolical construct, this is the picture that remains in the storyteller's mind.

  Miss Emily's pride is connected with her contempt for public opinion. This comes to the fore, of course, when she rides around about the town with the foreman whom everybody believes is beneath her. And it is her proud refusal to admit an external set of codes, or conventions, or other wills in contradiction to her own, that makes her capable at the end of keeping her lover from going away. Confronted with his jilting her, she tries to override not only his will and the opinion of other people but the laws of death and decay themselves.

  But this, still, hardly gives the meaning of the story. For in all that has been said thus far, we are still merely accounting for a psychological aberration — we are still merely dealing with a case

Chapter One

history in abnormal psychology. In order to make a case for the story as "meaningful," we shall have to tie Miss Emily's thoughts and actions back into the normal life of the community, and establish some sort of relationship between them. And just here one pervasive element in the narration suggests a clue. The story is told by one of the townspeople. And in it, as a constant factor, is the reference to what the community thought of Miss Emily. Continually through the story it is what "we" said, and then what "we" did, and what seemed true to "us," and so on. The narrator puts the matter even more sharply still. It is said, in the course of the story, that to the community Miss Emily seemed "dear, inescapable, impervious, tranquil, and perverse." Each of the adjectives is important and meaningful. In a sense, Miss Emily because of her very fact of isolation and perversity belongs to the whole community. She is even something treasured by it. Ironically, because of Emily's perversion of an aristocratic independence of mores and because of her contempt for "what people say," her life is public, even communal. And various phrases used by the narrator underline this view of her position. For example, her face looks "as you imagine a lighthouse-keeper's face ought to look," like the face of a person who lives in the kind of isolation imposed on a lighthouse-keeper, who looks out into the blackness and whose light serves a public function. Or, again, after her father's death, she becomes very ill, and when she appears after the illness, she had "a vague resemblance to those angels in colored church windows — sort of tragic and serene." Whatever we make of these descriptions, certainly the author is trying to suggest a kind of calm and dignity that is supermundane, unearthly, or "over-earthly," such as an angel might possess.

  Miss Emily, then, is a combination of idol and scapegoat for the community. On the one hand, the community feels admiration for Miss Emily — she represents something in the past of the community that the community is proud of. They feel a sort of awe of her, as is illustrated by the behavior of the mayor and the committee in her presence. On the other hand, her queerness, the fact that she cannot compete with them in their ordinary life, the fact that she is hopelessly out of touch with the modern world — all of these things make them feel superior to her, and also to the past that she represents. It is, then, Miss Emily's complete detachment that gives her actions their special meaning for the community.

Miss Emily, since she is the conscious aristocrat, since she is consciously "better" than other people, since she is above and outside their canons of behavior, can, at the same time, be worse than other people; and she *is* worse, horribly so. She is worse than other people, but at the same time, as the narrator implies, she remains somehow admirable. This raises a fundamental question: why is this true?

Perhaps the horrible and the admirable aspects of Miss Emily's final deed arise from the same basic fact of her character: she insists on meeting the world on her own terms. She never cringes, she never begs for sympathy, she refuses to shrink into an amiable old maid, she never accepts the community's ordinary judgments or values. This independence of spirit and pride can, and does in her case, twist the individual into a sort of monster, but, at the same time, this refusal to accept the herd values carries with it a dignity and courage. The community senses this, as we gather from the fact that the community carries out the decencies of the funeral before breaking in the door of the upper room. There is, as it were, a kind of secret understanding that she has won her right of privacy, until she herself has entered history. Furthermore, despite the fact that, as the narrator says, "already we knew that there was one room in that region above stairs which no one had seen in forty years, and which would have to be forced," her funeral is something of a state occasion, with "the very old men — some in their brushed Confederate uniforms — on the porch and the lawn, talking of Miss Emily as if she had been a contemporary of theirs, believing that they had danced with her and courted her

Chapter One

perhaps." In other words, the community accepts her into its honored history. All of this works as a kind of tacit recognition of Miss Emily's triumph of will. The community, we are told earlier, had wanted to pity Miss Emily when she had lost her money, just as they had wanted to commiserate over her when they believed that she had actually become a fallen woman, but she had triumphed over their pity and commiseration and condemnation, just as she had triumphed over all their other attitudes.

But, still, it may be said that Miss Emily is mad. This may be true, but there are two things to consider in this connection. First, one must consider the special terms that her "madness" takes. Her madness is simply a development of her pride and her refusal to submit to ordinary standards of behavior. So, because of this fact, her "madness" is meaningful after all. It involves issues that in themselves are really important and have to do with the world of conscious moral choice. Second, the community interprets her "madness" as meaningful. They admire her, even if they are disappointed by her refusals to let herself be pitied, and the narrator, who is a spokesman for the commumty, recognizes the last grim revelation as an instance of her having carried ner own values to their ultimate conclusion. She would marry the common laborer, Homer Barron, let the community think what it would. She would not be jilted. And she would hold him as a lover. But it would all be on her own terms. She remains completely dominant, and contemptuous of the day-to-day world.

It has been suggested by many critics that tragedy implies a hero who is completely himself, who insists on meeting the world on his own terms, who wants something so intensely, or lives so intensely, that he cannot accept any compromise. It cannot be maintained that this story is comparable to any of the great tragedies, such as *Hamlet* or *King Lear*, but it can be pointed out that this story, in its own way, involves some of the same basic elements. Certainly, Miss Emily's pride, isolation, and independence remind us of aspects in the character of the typical tragic hero. And it can be pointed out that, just as the horror of her deed lies outside the ordinary life of the community, so the magnificence of her independence lies outside its ordinary virtues.

(Cleanth Brooks and Robert Penn Warren)

Questions

1. What is meaningful in the final detail that the strand of hair on the second pillow is iron-gray?
2. What foreshadowings of the discovery of the body of Homer Barron are we given earlier in the story? Share your experience in reading "A Rose for Emily": did the foreshadowings give away the ending for you? Did they heighten your interest?
3. What contrast does the narrator draw between the changing reality and Emily's refusal or inability to recognize the change?
4. How do the character and background of Emily Grierson differ from those of Homer Barron? What general observations about the society that the author depicts can be made from the portraits of these two characters and from his account of the life in the Mississippi town?
5. Who is the narrator? (See Chapter Two for a brief discussion.) For whom does he profess to be speaking? Compare the story with John Updike's "A & P," what advantages does this form of narration have for this story?
6. What do you infer to be the author's attitude towards Emily Grierson? Is she simply a murderous madwoman? Why do you suppose Faulkner calls his story "A Rose..."?

Chapter Two

Point of View

As we know, an event may be recounted by one person or another, such as a person who is involved in the event, a spectator who just stands by and watches what happens, or a person who has heard it from someone else. It is the same in a story. A story is always a narrative in some way or another, and thus it always involves an agent who narrates what happens in the story. Sometimes the author may assume the role of the person who recounts the story himself or herself (as in Henry Fielding's *Tom Jones* and Goerge Eliot's *Middlemarch*). But generally the author will not tell the story. In stead, he/she will arrange another agent to recount what happens in the story. For instance, at the very beginning of *Adventures of Huckleberry Finn*, Mark Twain, the author, carefully separates himself from the main character who is to tell the story:

> You don't know about me, without you have read a book by the name of *The Adventures of Tom Sawyer*, but that ain't no matter. That book was made by Mr. Mark Twain...

Mark Twain wrote the novel, but the speaker or the narrator is Huck, the one from whose perspective the story is told. Obviously, the narrator of the story in *Huckleberry Finn* is not the same person as the "real-life" author. The **narrator** is the speaker or the voice of the literary text, the agent who does the narration.

The narrator, like any character in fiction, only exists in a narrative, and he cannot be identified with anything of the real-life author of a literary work. In employing Huck as the narrator, Mark Twain selects a special angle of vision: a vision of a resourceful boy moving through the thick of events, with a mind at times shrewd and at other times innocent, and through his eyes the reader sees the diseases of the world. The author does not appear in the novel in any form. He does not have a voice, neither any direct way of communication, but he silently guides the reader through his complete design of the novel. It is the narrator that represents the principles of judgment: he either conceals or reveals the thoughts and feelings of characters, enabling the reader to be aware of his psychological opinion about them; he chooses whether to make the character speak directly or to relate the narrative from another one's mouth; he makes the decision whether to employ description, exposition, comment, or narration in his manipulation of a certain event; and he also decides to narrate an event in accord with chronological sequence or intentionally reverse the order. Gerard Genette clarifies five functions of a narrator (*Narrative Discourse*, 1980): narrating function (the telling of the story as such); directing function (metalinguistic, internal organization of the narrative); function of communication (similar to Roman Jakobson's phatic and conative functions, e.g. conveying of message aiming at opening and maintaining the channel of communication and at seeking to affect the behaviour of the addressee), testimonial function (similar to Roman Jakobson's emotive function, e.g. aiming at an expression of the narrator's attitude towards what he is speaking about); and ideological function (a didactic form of an authorized commentary on the action). Therefore it is generally through his manipulation of the narrator that the author expresses his/her attitude and ideas.

In *Adventures of Huckleberry Finn*, Huck Finn, the leading character, is the narrator. He employs "I," the first person singular form, to tell the story. This is a traditional way to narrate fiction. Daniel Defoe, Jonathan Swift, Henry Fielding, Laurence

Chapter Two

Sterne, Charles Dickens, and many other novelists have employed the first person "I" narrator in their works. Some such narrators, as Huck Finn, are the main characters in the stories, but there are those who play only minor parts in the stories they tell. The use of the "I" narrator has its advantages. For instance, it enables the author to enter the protagonist's mind quite naturally and thus reveal his/her most secret thoughts and feelings to the reader through interior monologue, stream of consciousness (See page 88 for a brief discussion), and other techniques. But similarly, its disadvantage is that the psychological life of other characters in the story will remain less clear to the reader.

However, the most frequently and naturally employed narrative is the third person narrative, in which the narrator remains outside the story. The narrator refers directly to the characters by their names or by personal pronoun (they/them, he/him, she/her) respectively, as we have seen in the short story at the beginning of the introduction of this book. Most novelists employ this form of narrative since it can endow them with the privilege of omniscience: the narrator, unlike the first person narrator who can only reveal his/her own mind and feeling to the public, can enter the mind and reveal the thoughts and feelings of any character and make any comment on them as he/she likes. But in modern times many novelists and storytellers have begun to employ a narrator who seems so impartial and aloof that she/he limits him/herself to reporting only overheard conversation and to describing, without comment or opinion, the surface appearances of things. In the view of Wayne C. Booth, such distant narrators can be dispensed with in dealing with an impersonal "fly-on-the-wall" story, containing no editorializing and confined to the presentation of surface. (*The Rhetoric of Fiction*, 1961) Evidently, narrators greatly differ in kind.

To identify the narrator of a story, describing any part he/she plays in the events and any limits placed upon his/her knowledge, is to identify the story's **point of view**: the way in which the reader is presented with the materials of the story, and the vantage point from which the author presents the actions of the story. In a short story, it is usual for the author to maintain one point of view from beginning to end, but there is nothing to stop him/her from introducing other points of view as well. In a novel, it is quite common for the author to shift from one point of view to another. For instance, in his panoramic novel *War and Peace*, Leo Tolstoy freely shifts the point of view in and out of the minds of many characters, among them Napoleon himself.

One of the earliest critics who proposed the idea of point of view is Percy Lubbock (*The Craft of Fiction*, 1957. The notion is credited to Henry James, *The Art of the Novel*, 1934). Lubbock thinks that all techniques of the novel are bound to be adjusted by point of view, that is, "Who speaks?" and "Who sees?" The term has two senses. First, it resembles the point of vision in visual arts, namely, from which angle and at which position the spectator looks at an object under observation. Similarly, in a literary work, the author regulates the positions of the reader in accordance with what he/she expresses or what he/she intends to express. This regulation includes both spacial and temporal location: the author may place the narrator as far as a thousand miles away or as near as in front of the reader. The author may arrange the narrator as a historical figure or as a witness of a current event. The second sense of point of view lies in the attitude towards the presented objects. A narrative text is always composed of language, and language does not allow us to talk about something without expressing our attitude towards it. Therefore the point of view the narrator adopts in his/her narration of an event or in his/her description of a character or an object is a cue for the reader to discern his/her attitude. Wallace Martin clarifies four aspects of point of view: (1) point of view is a prescribed characteristic of narrative, that is, where there is narrative, there is point of view, and it is regarded as an important aspect of communication from the author to the reader; (2) the term refers generally to all the aspects concerning the relationship between the narrator and the reader, including details of attention, distance, angle of vision, voice, and focalization; (3) point of view is not something subsidiary added to, say, plot, but in contrary, it is point of view that creates interest, conflict, suspense, and even plot itself in most modern narrative works; and (4) point of view constitutes a person's attitude towards, opinion about, and concern for the world (*Recent Theories of Narrative*, 1986).

Theoretically, a great many points of view are possible. Writers may select a unique point of view to fit his/her special observation of life and understanding of the world. For instance, in *Flush*, a fictional biography of Elizabeth Barrett Browning, Virginia Woolf employs the poet's pet spaniel as the narrator; in "The Circular Valley," a short story by Paul Bowles, a man and a woman are watched by a sinister spirit trying to take possession of them, and we see the human characters through the spirit's vague consciousness; and Michel Butor in his *Second Thoughts* skillfully uses the second person "you" point of view. It is not uncommon for an author to try more than one point of view in a work. For instance, Salinger deliberately uses two kinds of narrator in his "For Esme—With Love and Squalor" to achieve a desired effect. However, in reading fiction we often encounter familiar points of view. Here is a list (made by Kennedy and Gioia, *Literature*, 1995) of them, which may provide a few frequently used terms with which to discuss the stories we read and to describe their points of view:

The first person narrator (a participant):
1. a major character
2. a minor character

The third person narrator (a nonparticipant in the story):
3. all-knowing (seeing into any of the characters)
4. seeing into one major character
5. seeing into one minor character
6. objective (not seeing into any character)

When the first person singular "I" enacts the narrative in the story, the narrator is a participant in the events of the story. Such a narrator may be the protagonist or may be a minor character, perhaps merely an observer standing a little to one side and watching a story unfold that mainly involves someone else.

When the narrator is a nonparticipant, he does not appear in the story as a character. He recounts what happens in the story even without the reader's notice of his existence, choosing to make a brief summary or a detailed description at his will with respect to different characters and incidents. When all-knowing (or **omniscient**), the narrator sees into the minds of all (or some) of the characters, revealing their thoughts and feelings whenever he believes necessary. For example, in the short story at the beginning of the introduction of this book, the narrator is omniscient: he enters the mind of the woman, the only character, telling us what she *knows* about the world. Sometimes he makes a comment or adds his opinion. In this case, the narrator is said to show **editorial omniscience** (as we see in the remark "and there was a world of meaning in this simple comment" in Nathaniel Hawthorne's "Young Goodman Brown"). But when he only presents the thoughts and feelings and actions of the characters but does not judge them or comment on them, he is said to show **impartial omniscience.** Such a point of view is characterized by a freedom in shifting from the exterior world to the inner selves of the characters, in movement in both time and place, and in making comment on the meaning of actions.

When a nonparticipant narrator sees events through the eyes of a single character, whether a major character or a minor one, the author is using a **limited point of view**, sometimes called **selective omniscience** or **limited omniscience.** In William Faulkner's "Barn Burning," for instance, the narrator is almost entirely confined to knowing the thoughts and perceptions of a boy, and the reader sometimes sees the world through the eyes of the boy, the central character. (Some critics think that the first person narrative also belongs to this category since the point of view is confined to what the first person narrator knows and experiences.) The author, of course, selects the character through whom to see. Henry James calls such a character his "focus," "mirror," or "center of consciousness" (*The Art of the Novel*, 1934). Here is another example. In the early part of Gustave Flaubert's *Madame Bovary*, the narrator tells of the first time a young country doctor, Charles Bovary, meets Emma, the woman to become his wife later. The doctor has been summoned late at night to set the broken leg of Emma's father:

> A young woman wearing a blue merino dress with three flounces came to the door of the house to greet Monsieur Bovary, and she ushered him into the kitchen, where a big open fire was blazing. Around its edges the farm hands' breakfast was bubbling in small pits of assorted sizes. Damp clothes were drying inside the vast chimney-opening. The fire shovel, the tongs, and the nose of the bellow, all of colossal proportions, shone like polished steel; and along the walls hung a lavish array of kitchen utensils, glimmering in the bright light of the fire and in the first rays of the sun that were now beginning to come in through the window-panes.
>
> Charles went upstairs to see the patient. He found him in bed, sweating under blankets, his nightcap lying where he had flung it. He was a stocky little man of fifty, fair-skinned, blue-eyed, bald in front and wearing earrings. On a chair beside him was a big decanter of brandy: he had been pouring himself drinks to keep up his courage. But as soon as he saw the doctor he dropped his bluster, and instead of cursing as he had been doing for the past twelve hours he began to groan weakly.
>
> The fracture was a simple one, without complications of any kind. Charles couldn't have wished for anything easier. Then he recalled his teachers' bedside manner in accident cases, and proceeded to cheer up his patient with all kinds of facetious remarks—a truly surgical attention, like the oiling

of a scalpel. For splints, they sent someone to bring a bundle of laths from the carriage shed. Charles selected one, cut it into lengths and smoothed it down with a piece of broken window glass, while the maidservant tore sheets for bandages and Mademoiselle Emma tried to sew some pads. She was a long time finding her workbox, and her father showed his impatience. She made no reply, but as she sewed she kept pricking her fingers and raising them to her mouth to suck.

Charles was surprised by the whiteness of her fingernails. They were almond-shaped, tapering, as polished and shining as Dieppe ivories. Her hands, however, were not pretty—not pale enough, perhaps, a little rough at the knuckles; and they were too long, without softness of line. The finest thing about her was her eyes. They were brown, but seemed black under the long eyelashes; and she had an open gaze that met yours with fearless candor.

In this passage, evidently, it is the narrator who is recounting the first meeting between Doctor Bovary and Emma in a farmhouse, but it is Charles Bovary who is beholding objects and people in a natural sequence, and similarly it is through the eyes of Charles Bovary that the reader sees people and objects in this scene. On entering the house, Mr. Bovary notices the dress of the woman coming to greet him, paying little attention to the woman herself. Then he sees the fire, breakfast, damp clothes, utensils and so on in the kitchen. When coming upstairs, he sees the patient (Notice the narrator's selection of expression here: "He *found* him in bed...") and has the first impression about his age, skin, eyes and other characteristics. When he is waiting for some pads for the patient's splints after the surgery, the doctor notices Emma's hands sewing them. Then he observes her face, her fascinating eyes. While recounting the event, the narrator frequently enters the mind of Doctor Bovary, revealing to the reader what he is thinking and how he is feeling (Notice the words "wished," "recalled" and "surprised" when the narrator tells of Doctor Bovary). In addition, the narrative occasionally sounds as if Doctor Bovary is speaking; notice the word "yours" in the last sentence of the passage; it is as if Doctor Bovary is speaking directly to the reader and asking the reader to share his perception of Emma's open gaze. Thus we can see that this point of view is frequently confined to the limitations of one character's psychology and visual perspective. What the narrator relates is all or mostly or limited to what this character sees and thinks, as if the narrator sees everything through the character's eyes, or as if he is standing by the side of the character as an invisible witness.

When the narrator does not see into the mind of any character, nor makes any comment on any action or character, but only describes or accounts the events of the story from the outside, the author employs the objective point of view. In this case, the reader reads a story as if he/she is watching the performance of a play in which there is no soliloquy, nor aside; the narrator merely retells what the characters say and how they act objectively, leaving the reader to infer their thoughts and feelings. So inconspicuous is the narrator that this point of view is compared to **"the fly on the wall"** and the reader hardly notices the existence of the narrator. The metaphor assumes a fly with an acute gaze, who keenly observes every act and every move of the characters and selects whichever details to communicate the meaning. (Some critics call this mode of narrative **"dramatic presentation."**) Here is a passage from *The Maltese Falcon* by Dashiell Hammett, describing the private detective Sam Spade when he has been roused from bed in the middle of the night by a phone call telling him that his partner has been murdered:

> Spade's thick fingers made a cigarette with deliberate care, sifting a measured quantity of tan flakes down into curved paper, spreading the flakes so that they lay equal at the ends with a slight depression in the middle, thumbs rolling

the paper's inner edge down and up under the outer edge as forefingers pressed it over, thumb and fingers sliding to the paper cylinder's ends to hold it even while tongue licked the flap, left forefinger and thumb pinching their ends while right forefinger and thumb smoothed the damp seam, right forefinger and thumb twisting their end and lifting the other to Spade's mouth.

The author deliberately refrains from applying adjectives to describe this moment of crisis but only presents the details of the movement of Spade's hands and fingers with a cigarette, suggesting the stress Spade is in and his cool, efficient, and thoughtful character. The author also avoids exercising editorial omniscience. The objective point of view leaves a large room for the reader's intelligence and judgment.

Only by identifying the point of view of a story are we likely to discern the attitude and opinion of the narrator, which is helpful to a deep understanding of the story. However, the attitude and opinion of the narrator are not necessarily those of the author, though the author may choose to communicate his or her own opinions through the mouth of the narrator. A story may be told by an **innocent narrator** or a **naïve narrator**, who does not comprehend all the complexities and complications of the outer world or who fails to understand all or some of the implications of the story. Huckleberry Finn is such an innocent narrator (despite his sometimes shrewd perceptions). The author certainly does not hold the same attitude towards slavery as Huck and the reader is not supposed to agree with Huck's acceptance of the morality and lawfulness of slavery. Naïve in the extreme is the narrator of one part of William Faulkner's novel *The Sound and Fury*, the idiot Benjy, who, though an adult, has the intellect of a child and thus does not understand the world of the grown-ups at all. Frequently we notice a lively conflict between what we are told and what we are meant to believe. For instance, in a story told by an **unreliable narrator**, the point of view is that of a person who is deceptive, self-deceptive, deluded, or deranged.

Whether a narrator is reliable or unreliable, according to Wayne Booth depends upon how the narrator argues for, and how near the attitude and opinion of the narrator are to, the moral codes of the work (including those of the author). We distinguish an unreliable narrator by the extent to which he or she diverges from the author's attitude and opinion, and by the violations he commits against the author's moral codes (*The Rhetoric of Fiction*, 1961). Rimmon-Kenan discusses the reliable narrator and the unreliable narrator as a relationship between the narrator and the reader: a reliable narrator is characterized by the fact that his narrative is always regarded by the reader as the authoritative description of fictional truth. An unreliable narrator is characterized by the fact that his description of and/or comment on the story always makes the reader plausibly suspicious, whether because the narrator is limited in his knowledge or he himself is involved in the event or there is something wrong with his value system (*Narrative Fiction*, 1983). However, we may find that in many literary works it is difficult to determine whether their narrators are reliable or unreliable and, of the "reliable" ones, the true degree of their reliability. Modern writers have been particular fond of narrtors of unknown reliability, as though they are attempting to communicate a sense of uncertainty of the modern world.

Antony insisted, in his oration over the dead Caesar, that "Brutus is an honorable man." But the audience detected that the statement contained an imprint of **irony**. This is verbal irony (a distinct feature of the style of a writer which is talked about in Chapter Five in this book), the most familiar kind, in which the actual intent is expressed in words that carry the opposite meaning. **Verbal irony**, then, implies a contrast or discrepancy between what is said literally and what is meant actually. Its presence is marked by a sort of grim humour and unemotional detachment on the part of the speaker, a tone of coolness in expression at a time when the speaker's emotions appear to be really heated. Another famous ironic remark in literature is Job's "No doubt but ye are the people, and wisdom shall die with you." The effectiveness of irony as a literary device is the impression of restraint it gives. Irony, of course, is more easily detected in speech than in writing, since the voice can, through its intonation, easily warn the listener of a double significance. Thus in reading fiction, it is advisable for us to keep an eye upon the "tone" of the speaker, or the narrator, so as to detect any ironic touch. In English literature, it is not uncommon to find writers who frequently employ this form. For example, Oliver Goldsmith, Jane Austen, William Thackeray, Thomas Hardy, and Henry James have made use of irony in one novel or another.

An entire story may be told from an **ironic point of view**. Whenever we sense a sharp distinction between the narrator of a story and the author, irony is likely to occur—especially when the narrator is telling us something that we are clearly expected to doubt or to interpret very differently. Jonathan Swift is one of the masters who have used the ironic point of view in his writings—his *Modest Proposal* for saving a starving Ireland, in which he suggests that the Irish people sell their babies to the English landlords to be eaten, is perhaps the most savagely sustained ironic writing in English literature. Sometimes the author may not employ the same point of view throughout the whole story. When we read Hemingway's "A Clean, Well-Lighted Place," we see that the older waiter gives us a compassionate view of a lonely old man, and we do not doubt that this view is Hemingway's. But in the closing lines of the story, the waiter tries to shrug off the sleepless night ahead of him by finding an excuse to console himself: "After all, it is probably insomnia." The reader, recalling the waiter's bleak monologue on *nada*, nothingness, knows that it is certainly not mere insomnia that keeps him awake but an awareness of life's meaninglessness and a dread of solitude and death. At this crucial moment, Hemingway and the older waiter part company and we perceive an ironic point of view, and a verbal irony (Kennedy and Gioia, *Literature*, 1995).

Writers are sometimes fond of ironic twists of fate—developments of plot that reveal a terrible distance between what people deserve and what they get, between what is and what ought to be. In *Tess of the D'Urbervilles* by Thomas Hardy, an all-important letter, thrust under a door, slides beneath a carpet by chance and is thus not received. In O. Henry's short story "The Gift of the Magi," the young wife sells her beautiful hair to buy her poor husband a watch chain for Christmas without knowing that her husband has sold his watch to buy combs for her hair. Such an irony is sometimes called an irony of fate. It suggests that some malicious fate is deliberately frustrating human efforts, as it frequently happens in reality.

The concern with point of view in modern criticism and the experimentation with point of view by many modern novelists are both very great. Since the flourishing of the work of Joseph Conrad and Henry James, point of view has been considered the important technical aspect of fiction that leads critics most readily into understanding the problems and the meanings of a novel or of a short story. By using a particular point of view, an author not only develops technical expertise but also bears out his/her judicious insight.

The Tell-Tale Heart

by Edgar Allan Poe, 1843

True! —Nervous—very, very dreadfully nervous I had been and am; but why *will* you say that I am mad? The disease had sharpened my senses—not destroyed—not dulled them. Above all was the sense of hearing acute. I heard all things in the heaven and in the earth. I heard many things in hell. How, then, am I mad? Hearken! and observe how healthily—how calmly I can tell you the whole story.

It is impossible to say how first the idea entered my brain; but once conceived, it haunted me day and night. Object there was none. Passion there was none. I loved the old man. He had never wronged me. He had never given me insult. For his gold I had no desire. I think it was his eye! yes, it was this! One of his eyes resembled that of a vulture—a pale blue eye, with a film over it. Whenever it fell upon me, my blood ran cold; and so by degrees—very gradually—I made up my mind to take the life of the old man, and thus rid myself of the eye for ever.

Now this is the point. You fancy me mad. Madmen know nothing. But you should have seen *me*. You should have seen how wisely I proceeded—with what caution—with what foresight—with what dissimulation I went to work! I was never kinder to the old man than during the whole week before I killed him. And every night, about midnight, I turned the latch of his door and opened it—oh, so gently! And then, when I had made an opening sufficient for my head, I put in a dark lantern, all closed, closed, so that no light shone out, and then I thrust in my head. Oh, you would have laughed to see how cunningly I thrust it in! I moved it slowly—very, very slowly, so that I might not disturb the old man's sleep. It took me an hour to place my whole head within the opening so far that I could see him as he lay upon his bed. Ha! — would a madman have been so wise as this? And then, when my head was well in the room, I undid the lantern cautiously—oh, so cautiously—cautiously (for the hinges creaked)—I undid it just so much that a single thin ray fell upon the vulture eye. And this I did for seven long nights—every night just at midnight—but I found the eye always closed; and so it was impossible to do the work; for it was not the old man who vexed me, but his Evil Eye. And every morning, when the day broke, I went boldly into the chamber, and

Chapter Two

spoke courageously to him, calling him by name in a hearty tone, and inquiring how he had passed the night. So you see he would have been a very profound old man, indeed, to suspect that every night, just at twelve, I looked in upon him while he slept.

Upon the eighth night I was more than usually cautious in opening the door. A watch's minute hand moves more quickly than did mine. Never before that night had I *felt* the extent of my own powers—of my sagacity. I could scarcely contain my feelings of triumph. To think that there I was, opening the door, little by little, and he not even to dream of my secret deeds or thoughts. I fairly chuckled at the idea; and perhaps he heard me; for he moved on the bed suddenly, as if startled. Now you may think that I drew back—but no. His room was as black as pitch with the thick darkness (for the shutters were close fastened, through fear of robbers), and so I knew that he could not see the opening of the door, and I kept pushing it on steadily, steadily.

5 I had my head in, and was about to open the lantern, when my thumb slipped upon the tin fastening, and the old man sprang up in the bed, crying out—"Who's there?"

I kept quite still and said nothing. For a whole hour I did not move a muscle, and in the meantime I did not hear him lie down. He was still sitting up in the bed listening;—just as I have done, night after night, hearkening to the death watches[1] in the wall.

Presently I heard a slight groan, and I knew it was the groan of mortal terror. It was not a groan of pain or of grief—oh, no! — it was the low stifled sound that arises from the bottom of the soul when overcharged with awe. I knew the sound very well. Many a night, just at midnight, when all the world slept, it has welled up from my own bosom, deepening, with its dreadful echo, the terrors that distracted me. I say I knew it well. I knew what the old man felt, and pitied him, although I chuckled at heart. I knew that he had been lying awake ever since the first slight noise, when

---

[1] death watches: beetles that infest timbers. Their clicking sound was thought to be an omen of death.

he had turned in the bed. His fears had been ever since growing upon him. He had been trying to fancy them causeless, but could not. He had been saying to himself—"It is nothing but the wind in the chimney—it is only a mouse crossing the floor," or "it is merely a cricket which has made a single chirp." Yes, he had been trying to comfort himself with these suppositions; but he had found all in vain. *All in vain*; because Death, in approaching him, had stalked with his black shadow before him, and enveloped the victim. And it was the mournful influence of the unperceived shadow that caused him to feel—although he neither saw nor heard—to *feel* the presence of my head within the room.

When I had waited a long time, very patiently, without hearing him lie down, I resolved to open a little—a very, very little crevice in the lantern. So I opened it—you cannot imagine how stealthily, stealthily—until, at length, a single dim ray, like the thread of the spider, shot from out the crevice and full upon the vulture eye.

It was open—wide, wide open—and I grew furious as I gazed upon it. I saw it with perfect distinctness—all a dull blue, with a hideous veil over it that chilled the very marrow in my bones; but I could see nothing else of the old man's face or person: for I had directed the ray as if by instinct, precisely upon the damned spot.

10   And now have I not told you that what you mistake for madness is but over-acuteness of the senses? —now, I say, there came to my ears a low, dull, quick sound, such as a watch makes when enveloped in cotton. I knew *that* sound well too. It was the beating of the old man's heart. It increased my fury, as the beating of a drum stimulates the soldier into courage.

But even yet I refrained and kept still. I scarcely breathed. I held the lantern motionless. I tried how steadily I could maintain the ray upon the eye. Meantime the hellish tattoo of the heart increased. It grew quicker and quicker, and louder and louder every instant. The old man's terror *must* have been extreme! It grew louder, I say, louder every moment! —do you mark me well? I

Chapter Two

have told you that I am nervous: so I am. And now at the dead hour of the night, amid the dreadful silence of that old house, so strange a noise as this excited me to uncontrollable terror. Yet, for some minutes longer I refrained and stood still. But the beating grew louder, louder! I thought the heart must burst. And now a new anxiety seized me—the sound would be heard by a neighbor! The old man's hour had come! With a loud yell, I threw open the lantern and leaped into the room. He shrieked once—once only. In an instant I dragged him to the floor, and pulled the heavy bed over him. I then smiled gaily, to find the deed so far done. But, for many minutes, the heart beat on with a muffled sound. This, however, did not vex me; it would not be heard through the wall. At length it ceased. The old man was dead. I removed the bed and examined the corpse. Yes, he was stone, stone dead. I placed my hand upon the heart and held it there many minutes. There was no pulsation. He was stone dead. His eye would trouble me no more.

If still you think me mad, you will think so no longer when I describe the wise precautions I took for the concealment of the body. The night waned, and I worked hastily, but in silence. First of all I dismembered the corpse. I cut off the head and the arms and the legs.

I then took up three planks from the flooring of the chamber, and deposited all between the scantlings. I then replaced the boards so cleverly, so cunningly, that no human eye—not even *his*—could have detected anything wrong. There was nothing to wash out—no stain of any kind—no bloodspot whatever. I had been too wary for that. A tub had caught all—ha! ha!

When I had made an end of these labors, it was four o'clock— still dark as midnight. As the bell sounded the hour, there came a knocking at the street door. I went down to open it with a light heart,—for what had I *now* to fear? There entered three men, who introduced themselves, with perfect suavity, as officers of the police. A shriek had been heard by a neighbor during the night; suspicion of foul play had been aroused; information had been lodged at the police office, and they (the officers) had been deputed to search the premises.

15   I smiled,—for *what* had I to fear? I bade the gentlemen welcome. The shriek, I said, was my own in a dream. The old man, I mentioned, was absent in the country. I took my visitors all over the house. I bade them search—search *well*. I led them, at length, to *his* chamber. I showed them his treasures, secure, undisturbed. In the enthusiasm of my confidence, I brought chairs into the room, and desired them *here* to rest from their fatigues, while I myself, in the wild audacity of my perfect triumph, placed my own seat upon the very spot beneath which reposed the corpse of the victim.

    The officers were satisfied. My *manner* had convinced them. I was singularly at ease. They sat, and while I answered cheerily, they chatted familiar things. But, ere long, I felt myself getting pale and wished them gone. My head ached, and I fancied a ringing in my ears: but still they sat and still chatted. The ringing became more distinct:—it continued and became more distinct: I talked more freely to get rid of the feeling: but it continued and gained definitiveness—until, at length, I found that the noise was *not* within my ears.

    No doubt I now grew *very* pale:—but I talked more fluently, and with a heightened voice. Yet the sound increased—and what could I do? It was *a low, dull, quick sound*—much such a sound as *a watch makes when enveloped in cotton*. I gasped for breath—and yet the officers heard it not. I talked more quickly—more vehemently; but the noise steadily increased. I arose and argued about trifles, in a high key and with violent gesticulations, but the noise steadily increased. Why *would* they not be gone? I paced the floor to and fro with heavy strides, as if excited to fury by the observation of the men—but the noise steadily increased. Oh God! what *could* I do? I foamed—I raved—I swore! I swung the chair upon which I had been sitting, and grated it upon the boards, but the noise arose over all and continually increased. It grew louder—

louder—*louder*! And still the men chatted pleasantly, and smiled. Was it possible they heard not? Almighty God!—no, no! They heard!—they suspected!—they *knew*!—they were making a mockery of my horror!—this I thought, and this I think. But any thing was better than this agony! Any thing was more tolerable than this derision! I could bear those hypocritical smiles no longer! I felt that I must scream or die!—and now—again!—hark! louder! louder! louder! *louder*!—

"Villains!" I shrieked, "dissemble no more! I admit the deed!—tear up the planks!—here, here!—it is the beating of his hideous heart!"

Discussion

"The Tell-Tale Heart" presents the most apparent evidence of Poe's use of the issues of the insanity defense. The characteristic form of the tale is not confession but self-defense, at attempt to provide a rational account of apparently irrational events and behavior. In "The Tell-Tale Heart" there is a good deal of dramatic immediacy to this defense. The narrator addresses a specific but unnamed "you" sometime after his arrest but obviously before his execution (if there is to be one). His aim is to refute "you"'s claim that he is insane, a charge that has apparently been both specific and formal enough for the narrator to feel the necessity of responding in earnest and in detail. From the abrupt opening ("True! — nervous — very, very dreadfully nervous I had been and am; but why *will* you say that I am mad?") to the final dramatic breakdown ("and now — again! — hark! louder! louder! louder! *louder*!") the narration seems more spoken than written, something like a courtroom outburst or final statement of the accused.

The point of suggesting such a context for the tale's telling is to underscore a particular significance of the narrator's insistence on his own sanity. The argument he offers reflects the issues of the insanity-defense controversy, both in the way he measures his own state of mind and in the type of madman he reveals himself to be. His argument echoes the terms by which an eighteenth-century prosetutor, employing the "wild beast" test of insanity, might have differentiated the accused (himself) from the recognizably nonculpable madman. Such madmen, according to the narrator, are mentally defective ("Madmen know nothing"), physically impaired ("senses... destroyed... dulled"), incapable of wisdom or "sagacity" in planning, at the mercy of impulse and passion. He, on the other hand, exhibited unmistakable signs of rational behavior in the way he carried out his crime: note, he repeatedly insists, "how wisely I proceeded — with what caution — with what foresight." He also asks the auditor to "observe how healthily — how calmly" he "can tell you the whole story." Thus, insofar as the narrator is manifestly not a "wild beast," the "prosecutor's argument" succeeds: the narrator is capable of reason and is, therefore, morally and legally responsible for his acts.

Of course, in telling his tale, particularly if imagined as a statement in court, the narrator is also offering clear evidence that he is by contemporary standards partialty insane. Like the many monomaniacs, the narrator has a highly developed intellect, is capable of planning and remembering his actions in great detail, but his intellect and energies are fixed unreasonably on a single goal or "one dominant idea" (the old man's "vulture eye") that rides roughshod over his brain — that haunts him day and night until it is granted. ... However, the most convincing proof of his insanity seems to be the very mask of sanity he purports to wear. Ray argued that "madness is not indicated so much by any particular extravagance of thought or feeling, as by a well-marked change of character or departure from the ordinary habits of thinking, feeling and acting, without any adequate external cause." Thus, the narrator's calmness, deliberateness, and rationality signal insanity insofar as they are at variance with his "normal" state ("very, very dreadfully nervous I had been and am"), particularly as that is revealed in the frenetic last few paragraphs. Even the narrator's insistent denial of the charge of insanity fits the pattern of symptoms of the homicidal maniac, so that the act of the tale's telling and its seld-defensive posture constitute evidence in a determination of partial insanity.

(John Cleman)

 Questions

1. From what point of view is Poe's story told? Why is this point of view particularly effective for "The Tell-Tale Heart"?
2. Do you think anyone but the narrator hears the beating of the old man's heart? Why does he hear it so loudly? What finally drives the speaker to confess?
3. Point to the details in the story that identify its speaker as an unreliable narrator. To whom may he be recounting his tale?
4. How do you account for the police officers' chatting calmly with the murderer instead of reacting to the sound that stirs the narrator into frenzy?
5. **Atmosphere**, or **mood**, is the overall feeling created in a story. Poe builds the atmosphere by the use of words, details, and pictures that allow you to feel what the character feels. In the scene where the old man awakens, for instance, Poe includes these details and pictures: ". . . he moved on the bed suddenly, as if startled," "His room was as black as pitch," and "I kept pushing it in, steadily, steadily. " These details help you to feel the atmosphere of terror. Look at the paragraph that begins with "Presently I heard a slight groan. " List three details that help you to feel what the old man feels at this time. And look at the paragraph that begins with "No doubt I now grew *very* pale. " List three details that create the narrator's mood at this point.

6. To create a particular atmosphere, the author chooses words carefully. For example, notice the word *vulture* in the following sentence: "One of his eyes resembled that of a *vulture*." If the author had written "His eyes resembled those of a *puppy*," a quite different atmosphere would have been created. Find three other words in the story that create an atmosphere.

Araby

by James Joyce, 1905

North Richmond Street, being blind[1], was a quiet street except at the hour when the Christian Brothers' School set the boys free. An uninhabited house of two stories stood at the blind end, detached from its neighbors in a square ground. The other houses of the street, conscious of decent lives within them, gazed at one another with brown imperturbable faces.

The former tenant of our house, a priest, had died in the back drawing-room. Air, musty from having long been enclosed, hung in all the rooms, and the waste room behind the kitchen was littered with old useless papers. Among these I found a few paper-covered books, the pages of which were curled and damp: *The Abbot*, by Walter Scott, *The Devout Communicant* and *The Memoirs of Vidocq*[2]. I liked the last best because its leaves were yellow. The wild garden behind the house contained a central apple-tree and a few straggling bushes under one of which I found the late tenant's rusty bicycle-pump. He had been a very charitable priest: in his will he had left all his money to institutions and the

---

[1] being blind: being a dead-end street.

[2] *The Abbot...Vidocq*: a popular historical romance (1820); a book of pious meditations by an eighteenth-century English Franciscan, Pacificus Baker, and the autobiography of François-Jules Vidocq (1775-1857), a criminal who later turned detective.

Chapter Two

furniture of his house to his sister.

When the short days of winter came dusk fell before we had well eaten our dinners. When we met in the street the houses had grown somber. The space of sky above us was the color of ever-changing violet and towards it the lamps of the street lifted their feeble lanterns. The cold air stung us and we played till our bodies glowed. Our shouts echoed in the silent street. The career of our play brought us through the dark muddy lanes behind the houses where we ran the gantlet of the rough tribes from the cottages, to the back doors of the dark dripping gardens where odors arose from the ashpits, to the dark odorous stables where a coachman smoothed and combed the horse or shook music from the buckled harness. When we returned to the street light from the kitchen windows had filled the areas. If my uncle was seen turning the corner we hid in the shadow until we had seen him safely housed. Or if Mangan's sister[1] came out on the doorstep to call her brother in to his tea we watched her from our shadow peer up and down the street. We waited to see whether she would remain or go in and, if she remained, we left our shadow and walked up to Mangan's steps resignedly. She was waiting for us, her figure defined by the light from the half-opened door. Her brother always teased her before he obeyed and I stood by the railings looking at her. Her dress swung as she moved her body and the soft rope of her hair tossed from side to side.

Every morning I lay on the floor in the front parlor watching her door. The blind was pulled down within an inch of the sash so that I could not be seen. When she came out on the doorstep my heart leaped. I ran to the hall, seized my books and followed her. I kept her brown figure always in my eye and, when we came near the point at which our ways diverged, I quickened my pace and passed her. This happened morning after morning. I had never

---

[1] Mangan's sister: an actual young woman in this story, but the phrase recalls Irish poet James Clarence Mangan (1803-1849) and his best-known poem, "Dark Rosaleen," which personifies Ireland as a beautiful woman for whom the poet yearns.

spoken to her, except for a few casual words, and yet her name was like a summons to all my foolish blood.

5   Her image accompanied me even in places the most hostile to romance. On Saturday evenings when my aunt went marketing I had to go to carry some of the parcels. We walked through the flaring streets, jostled by drunken men and bargaining women, amid the curses of laborers, the shrill litanies of shopboys who stood on guard by the barrels of pigs' cheeks, the nasal chanting of street singers, who sang a *come-all-you* about O'Donovan Rossa[1], or a ballad about the troubles in our native land. These noises converged in a single sensation of life for me: I imagined that I bore my chalice safely through the throng of foes. Her name sprang to my lips at moments in strange prayers and praises which I myself did not understand. My eyes were often full of tears (I could not tell why) and at times a flood from my heart seemed to pour itself out into my bosom. I thought little of the future. I did not know whether I would ever speak to her or not or, if I spoke to her, how I could tell her of my confused adoration. But my body was like a harp and her words and gestures were like fingers running upon the wires.

One evening I went into the back drawing-room in which the priest had died. It was a dark rainy evening and there was no sound in the house. Through one of the broken panes I heard the rain impinge upon the earth, the fine incessant needles of water playing in the sodden beds. Some distant lamp or lighted window gleamed below me. I was thankful that I could see so little. All my senses seemed to desire to veil themselves and, feeling that I was about to slip from them, I pressed the palms of my hands together until they trembled, murmuring: *O love! O love!* many times.

At last she spoke to me. When she addressed the first words

---

[1] come-all-you about O'Donovan Rossa: the street singers earned their living by singing timely songs that usually began, "Come all you gallant Irishmen / And listen to my song." Their subject, also called Dynamite Rossa, was a popular hero jailed by the British for advocating violent rebellion.

Chapter Two

to me I was so confused that I did not know what to answer. She asked me was I going to *Araby*. I forget whether I answered yes or no. It would be a splendid bazaar, she said; she would love to go.

—And why can't you? I asked.

While she spoke she turned a silver bracelet round and round her wrist. She could not go, she said, because there would be a retreat that week in her convent[1]. Her brother and two other boys were fighting for their caps and I was alone at the railings. She held one of the spikes, bowing her head towards me. The light from the lamp opposite our door caught the white curve of her neck, lit up her hair that rested there and, falling, lit up the hand upon the railing. It fell over one side of her dress and caught the white border of a petticoat, just visible as she stood at ease.

10 —It's well for you, she said.

—If I go, I said, I will bring you something.

What innumerable follies laid waste my waking and sleeping thoughts after that evening! I wished to annihilate the tedious intervening days. I chafed against the work of school. At night in my bedroom and by day in the classroom her image came between me and the page I strove to read. The syllables of the word *Araby* were called to me through the silence in which my soul luxuriated and cast an Eastern enchantment over me. I asked for leave to go to the bazaar on Saturday night. My aunt was surprised and hoped it was not some Freemason[2] affair. I answered few questions in class. I watched my master's face pass from amiability to sternness; he hoped I was not beginning to idle. I could not call my wandering thoughts together. I had hardly any patience with the serious work of life which, now that it stood between me and my desire, seemed to me child's play, ugly monotonous child's play.

---

[1] a retreat... in her convent: a week devoted to religious observances more intense than usual, at the convent school Miss Mangan attends; probably she will have to listen to a number of hellfire sermons.

[2] Freemason: Catholics in Ireland viewed the Masonic order as a Protestant conspiracy against them.

On Saturday morning I reminded my uncle that I wished to go to the bazaar in the evening. He was fussing at the hall-stand, looking for the hatbrush, and answered me curtly:

—Yes, boy, I know.

As he was in the hall I could not go into the front parlor and lie at the window. I left the house in bad humor and walked slowly towards the school. The air was pitilessly raw and already my heart misgave me.

When I came home to dinner my uncle had not yet been home. Still it was early. I sat staring at the clock for some time and, when its ticking began to irritate me, I left the room. I mounted the staircase and gained the upper part of the house. The high cold empty gloomy rooms liberated me and I went from room to room singing. From the front window I saw my companions playing below in the street. Their cries reached me weakened and indistinct and, leaning my forehead against the cool glass, I looked over at the dark house where she lived. I may have stood there for an hour, seeing nothing but the brown-clad figure cast by my imagination, touched discreetly by the lamplight at the curved neck, at the hand upon the railings and at the border below the dress.

When I came downstairs again I found Mrs. Mercer sitting at the fire. She was an old garrulous woman, a pawnbroker's widow, who collected used stamps for some pious purpose. I had to endure the gossip of the tea-table. The meal was prolonged beyond an hour and still my uncle did not come. Mrs. Mercer stood up to go: she was sorry she couldn't wait any longer, but it was after eight o'clock and she did not like to be out late, as the night air was bad for her. When she had gone I began to walk up and down the room, clenching my fists. My aunt said:

—I'm afraid you may put off your bazaar for this night of Our Lord.

At nine o'clock I heard my uncle's latchkey in the halldoor. I heard him talking to himself and heard the hall-stand rocking when it had received the weight of his overcoat. I could interpret these

Chapter Two

signs. When he was midway through his dinner I asked him to give me the money to go to the bazaar. He had forgotten.

20   —The people are in bed and after their first sleep now, he said.

I did not smile. My aunt said to him energetically:

—Can't you give him the money and let him go? You've kept him late enough as it is.

My uncle said he was very sorry he had forgotten. He said he believed in the old saying: *All work and no play makes Jack a dull boy*. He asked me where I was going and, when I had told him a second time he asked me did I know *The Arab's Farwell to His Steed*[1]. When I left the kitchen he was about to recite the opening lines of the piece to my aunt.

I held a florin tightly in my hands as I strode down Buckingham Street towards the station. The sight of the streets thronged with buyers and glaring with gas recalled to me the purpose of my journey. I took my seat in a third-class carriage of a deserted train. After an intolerable delay the train moved out of the station slowly. It crept onward among ruinous houses and over the twinking river. At Westland Row Station a crowd of people pressed to the carriage doors; but the porters moved them back, saying that it was a special train for the bazaar. I remained alone in the bare carriage. In a few minutes the train drew up beside an improvised wooden platform. I passed out on to the road and saw by the lighted dial of a clock that it was ten minutes to ten. In front of me was a large building which displayed the magical name.

25   I could not find any sixpenny entrance and, fearing that the bazaar would be closed, I passed in quickly through a turnstile, handing a shilling to a weary-looking man. I found myself in a big hall girdled at half its height by a gallery. Nearly all the stalls were

---

[1] *The Arab's Farewell to His Steed*: This sentimental ballad by a popular poet, Caroline Norton (1808-1877), tells the story of a nomad of the desert who, in a fit of greed, sells his beloved horse, then regrets the loss, flings away the gold he had received, and takes back his horse. Notice the echo of "Araby" in the song title.

closed and the greater part of the hall was in darkness. I recognized a silence like that which pervades a church after a service. I walked into the center of the bazaar timidly. A few people were gathered about the stalls which were still open. Before a curtain, over which the words *Café Chantant*[1] were written in colored lamps, two men were counting money on a salver[2]. I listened to the fall of the coins.

  Remembering with difficulty why I had come I went over to one of the stalls and examined porcelain vases and flowered tea-sets. At the door of the stall a young lady was talking and laughing with two young gentlemen. I remarked their English accents and listened vaguely to their conversation.

  —O, I never said such a thing!

  —O, but you did!

  —O, but I didn't!

30   —Didn't she say that!

  —Yes. I heard her.

  —O, there's a...fib!

  Observing me the young lady came over and asked me did I wish to buy anything. The tone of her voice was not encouraging; she seemed to have spoken to me out of a sense of duty. I looked humbly at the great jars that stood like eastern guards at either side of the dark entrance to the stall and murmured:

  —No, thank you.

35   The young lady changed the position of one of the vases and went back to the two young men. They began to talk of the same subject. Once or twice the young lady glanced at me over her shoulder.

  I lingered before her stall, though I knew my stay was useless, to make my interest in her wares seem the more real. Then I turned away slowly and walked down the middle of the bazaar. I allowed the two pennies to fall against the six-pence in my

---

 [1] *Café Chantant*: name for a Paris nightspot featuring topical songs.
 [2] salver: a tray like that used in serving Holy Communion.

pocket. I heard a voice call from one end of the gallery that the light was out. The upper part of the hall was now completely dark.

Gazing up into the darkness I saw myself as a creature driven and derided by vanity; and my eyes burned with anguish and anger.

 Discussion

On what may be called the simplest level this is a story of a boy's disappointment. A great part of the story, however, does not directly concern itself with the boy's love affair, but with the world in which he lives — the description of his street, the information about the dead priest and the priest's abandoned belongings, the relations with the aunt and uncle. These matters seem to come very naturally into the story; that is, they may be justified individually in the story on realistic grounds. If such elements served *merely* as "setting" or *only* as atmosphere, then the story would be overloaded with nonfunctional material. Obviously, however, for any reader except the most casual, these items do have a function. If we find in what way these apparently irrelevant iterns in "Araby" are related to each other and to the disappointment of the boy, we shall have defined the theme of the story.

What, then, is the relation of the boy's disappointment to such matters as the belongings of the dead priest, the fact that he stands apart talking to the girl while his friends are quarreling over the cap, the gossip over the tea table, the uncle's lateness, and so on? One thing that is immediately suggested by the mention of these things is the boy's growing sense of isolation, the lack of sympathy between him and his friends, teachers, and family. He says, "I imagined that I bore my chalice safely through a throng of foes." For instance, when the uncle is standing in the hall, the boy could not go into the front parlor and lie at the window; or at school his ordinary occupations began to seem "ugly monotonous child's play." But this sense of isolation has, also, moments that are almost triumphant. The porters at the station wave the crowds back, "saying that it was a special train for the bazaar" and was not for them. The boy is left alone in the bare carriage, but he is going to "Araby," moving triumphantly toward some romantic and exotic fulfillment. The metaphor of the chalice implies the same kind of precious secret triumph. It is not only the ordinary surrounding world, however, from which he is cruelly or triumphantly isolated. He is also isolated from the girl herself. He talks to her only once, and then is so confused that he does not know how to answer her. But the present he hopes to bring her from Araby would somehow serve as a means of communicating his feelings to her, a symbol for their relationship in the midst of the inimical world.

In the last scene at the bazaar, there is a systematic, though subtle, preparation for the final realization on the part of the boy. There is the "improvised wooden platform" in contrast with the "magical name" displayed above the building. Inside, most of the stalls are closed. The "young lady" and young men who talk together are important in the preparation. They pay the boy no mind, except insofar as the "young lady" is compelled by her position as clerk to ask him what he wants. But her tone is "not encouraging." She, too, belongs to the inimical world. But she, also, belongs to a world he is trying to penetrate: she and her admirers are on terms of easy intimacy — an intimacy in contrast to his relation to Mangan's sister. It is an exotic, rich world into which he cannot penetrate: he can only look "humbly at the great jars that stood like eastern guards at either side of the dark entrance to the stall." Ironically, the "young lady" and her admirers, far from realizing that they are on holy, guarded ground, indulge in trivial, easy banter, which seems to defile and cheapen the secret world from which the boy is barred. How do we know this? It is not stated, but the contrast between the conversation of the young lady and her admirers, and the tone of the sentence about the "great jars" indicates such an interpretation.

Such scenes, then, help to point up and particularize the general sense of isolation suggested by the earlier descriptive materials, and thereby to prepare for the last sentence of the story, in which, under the sudden darkness of the cheap barnlike bazaar, the boy sees himself as "a creature driven and derided by vanity," while his eyes burn with "anguish and anger."

We have seen how the apparently casual incidents and items of description do function in the story to build up the boy's sense of intolerable isolation, his sense of being isolated from the common world in so sacred a precinct. But this is only part of the function of this material. The careful reader will have noticed how many references, direct or indirect, there are to religion and the ritual of the church. We have the dead priest, the Christian Brothers' School, the aunt's hope that the bazaar is not "some Freemason affair," her mention, when the uncle has been delayed, of "this night of Our Lord." At one level, these references merely indicate the type of community in which the impressionable boy is growing up. But there are other, less obvious, references, which relate more intimately to the boy's experience. Even the cries of the shop boys for him are "shrill litanies." He imagines that he bears a "chalice safely through a throng of foes." When he is alone the name of Mangan's sister springs to his lips "in strange prayers and praises." For this reason, when he speaks of his "confused adoration," we see that the love of the girl takes on, for him, something of the nature of a mystic, religious experience. The use of the very word *confused* hints of the fact that romantic love and religious love are mixed up in his mind.

The boy is isolated from a world that seems ignorant of, and even hostile to, his love. In a sense he knows that his aunt and uncle are good and kind, but they do not understand him. He had once found satisfaction in the society of his companions and in his schoolwork, but he has become impatient with both. But there is also a sense in which he accepts his isolation and is even proud of it. The world not only does not understand his secret but would cheapen and contaminate it. The metaphor of the chalice borne through a throng of foes, supported as it is by the body of the story, suggests a sort of consecration like that of the religious devotee. The implications of the references to religion, then, help define the boy's attitude and indicate why, for him, so much is staked upon the journey to the bazaar. It is interesting to note, therefore, that the first overt indication of his disillusionment and disappointment is expressed in a metaphor involving a church: "Nearly all the stalls were closed and the greater part of the hall was in darkness. I recognized a silence like that which pervades a church after a service.... Two men were counting money on a salver. I listened to the fall of the coins." And this episode, of course, is an echo of the money-changers in the Temple at Jerusalem (Mark 11: 15); so here we have the idea that the contamination of the world has invaded the very temple of love. (The question may arise as to whether this is not reading too much into the passage. But whatever interpretation is to be made of the particular incident, it is by just such suggestion and implication that closely wrought stories, such as this one, are controlled by their authors and embody their fundamental meaning.)

  Is this a sentimental story? It is about an adolescent love affair, about "puppy love," which is usually not taken seriously and is often an occasion for amusement. The boy of the story is obviously investing casual incidents with a meaning they do not deserve; he himself admits, in the end, that he has fallen into self-deception. How does the author avoid the charge that he has taken the matter overseriously?

  The answer to this question would involve a consideration of the point of view from which the story is told. It is told by the hero himself, but after a long lapse of time, after he has reached maturity. This fact, it is true, is not stated in the story, but the style itself is not that of an adolescent boy. It is a formal and complicated style, rich in subtle implications. In other words, the man is looking back upon the boy, detached and judicial. For instance, the boy, in the throes of the experience, would never have said of himself: "I had never spoken to her, except for a few casual words, and yet her name was like a summons to all my foolish blood." The man knows, as it were, that the behavior of the boy was, in a sense, foolish. The emotions of the boy are confused. He has unraveled the confusion long after, knows that it existed and why it existed.

If the man has unraveled the confusions of the boy, why is the event still significant to him? Is he merely dwelling on the pathos of adolescent experience? It seems, rather, that he sees in the event, as he looks back on it, a foreshadowing of a problem that has run through later experience. The discrepancy between the real and the ideal scarcely exists for the child, but it is a constant problem, in all sorts of terms, for the adult. This story is about a boy's first confrontation of that problem — that is, about his growing up. The man may have made adjustments to this problem, and may have worked out certain provisional solutions, but, looking back, he still recognizes it as a problem, and an important one. The sense of isolation and disillusion that sprang from the boy's experience — though it may seem trivial — becomes not less but more aggravated and fundamental in the adult's experience. So, the story is not merely an account of a stage in the process of growing up; it does not merely represent a clinical interest in the psychology of growing up. It is a symbolic rendering of a central conflict in mature experience.

(Cleanth Brooks and Robert Penn Warren)

 Questions

1. What images does the name of the bazaar conjure up for the boy? What ironic discrepancies appear between his dream of Araby and the reality? What is significance of the religious background of the story? For instance, consider that the

atmosphere of the bazaar is like that of a church.
2. The story is told by the first person narrator. What is gained by using the first person narrator? Can we say that "Araby" is told from an ironic point of view? Why? Does the narrator of the story seem a boy—a naïve or innocent narrator—or a mature man looking back through a boy's eyes? Can you connect the style (See Chapter Five for a brief discussion of style) of the story with the fact of the first person narrator?
3. Who besides the boy seems to be the other central character (See Chapter Three for a brief discussion of character) in the story? How do you know that the boy's view of this character is not exactly the author's view? (Refer to the narrator's descriptions of the other major character, and of his own feelings.)
4. At what moments in the story does the boy project an air of enchantment upon things?
5. How does the time of day matter to this story? What is meaningful or suggestive about the fall of night in the end?
6. In general, how would you describe the physical setting (See Chapter Four for a brief discussion on setting) of "Araby" as James Joyce details it in the first five paragraphs? Does he make Dublin seem a beautiful metropolis, a merry town, an ugly backwater, or what? What do you make of the detail, in the opening sentence, that the boy's street has a dead end?
7. Can we say this story is one of epiphany—a showing forth, a revelation? If yes, what is the epiphany here? Does the story make a comment merely on the befuddlements and disappointments of puppy love? Or is the comment projected into adult experiences? Connect this question with the style and method of the first person narration.

Chapter Three

Character

In the introduction we have said that fiction is an image of people in action, moving towards an undeclared end. Thus character is always involved in fiction, even in the story of the simplest action. (In the short story we read at the beginning of the introduction, the action is psychological.) Sometimes character is at the centre of our interest because in character we may see many facets of the people we meet in our daily life and even of ourselves. Fictional character is always character in action and the character gets into action because it is caught in a situation of conflict and he/she is always provided with **motivation**; he/she has sufficient reasons to act or behave as he/she does. The character is doing something and the reader while reading fiction wants to know the "why" as well as the "what" of the affairs. (Sometimes a character's motive for an action is not explained on acceptable grounds, for example, the villain in Adgar Allan Poe's story "The Tell-Tall Heart," and thus the reader feels cheated. In this case, the writer of detective fiction who makes the criminal a mere lunatic has cheated the reader by avoiding the problem of motive.) And generally, the action itself is humanly significant and it ends usually in a shift in or clarification of human values, as we have seen in John Updike's "A & P," and the motivation of a character in a story—one of the answers to the question "why"—is of fundamental importance.

A **character**, then, is presumably an imagined person who inhabits a story—although this simple definition may admit to a few exceptions. For example, the chief role (to borrow a term from drama) in George Stewart's novel *Storm* is the wind. However, the term "character" involves both the imagined person and the specific features of personality of that person in fiction. In Aristotle's *Poetics*, character is a concept secondary and subject to action. For Aristotle, there might be a story without character but never a story without action. With the influence of Aristotle, character withdrew to the background as only the agent of action. Later, character was endowed with a firm psychological basis and became a living individual with abundant physical and psychological entities, even if he/she did nothing. The concept of action, thus, was also enriched: the character in fiction is in action psychologically as well as physically. A character always presents a kind of psychological spectrum from the very beginning, even before he/she takes any action.

  Character in fiction is always an imitation of the people in reality under realism. Realists tend to treat characters in their works as our neighbors or colleagues or friends but they represent them in different degrees. E. M. Foster (*Aspects of the Novel*, 1927) suggests that the roles in a story are always human beings or human beings who call themselves such. Although they are fictional and merely exist in the work they inhabit, they are all characters whose private and secret life is visible to or can be seen by others. In contrast, we are human beings whose private and secret life is generally invisible to others. Realists also tend to see different types of characters according to their specific personalities or to the manner in which they act consistently. Sometimes characters become so stereotyped that we can easily recognize them by some outstanding trait or traits: the bragging soldier, the charming prince, the mad scientist, the greedy explorer, the nagging wife, the clown, the miser, the coward, the absent-minded professor and the man whose life is always beset with misfortune. They are often known as **stock characters**. However, a writer of creative originality tends to create characters who strike the reader not as stereotypes but as unique individuals. Falstaff was the outstanding example of the braggart soldier and Ebeneezer Scrooge in Dickens's *A Christmas Carol* was the supreme instance of the miser.

According to E. M. Foster, characters in fiction are either flat or round, depending upon whether the writer sketches or sculptures them. (*Aspects of the Novel*, 1927) A **flat character** generally has only one ostensible trait or feature, or at most a few distinct marks. A flat character seldom surprises the reader, is immediately recognizable, and can usually be represented by a single sentence, as "I never will desert Mr. Micawber" (Charles Dickens, *David Copperfield*), which, Foster asserts, is Mrs. Micawber and is all she is. Such a character is generally created in term of a single concept or quality and can be summed up by one word. Flat characters tend to stay the same throughout a story and the variety of environments will project the stability of their personality. A **round character**, however, presents us with many facets and is generally drawn with sufficient complexity to be able to surprise the reader without losing credibility. For instance, Becky Sharp in W. M. Thackeray's *Vanity Fair* can hardly be summed up in one sentence. She seems to change with the changes of the situation and to reveal many facets of her character with the development of the plot, and she has the incalculability of life about her. Such a round character may appear to the reader as he/she appears to the other characters in the story. If their views of him/her differ, the reader will see him/her from different angles. (Some critics call a fixed character **static;** and a changing one, **dynamic.**) This is not to say that a flat character is an inferior work of art. In most fiction—even the greatest—minor characters tend to be flat rather than round. Flat characters reflect a writer's different observations of human life. Characters in Dickens's writings are almost all flat but nearly every one touches the deep part of human nature. Wallace Martin exemplifies the significance of flat character in Huckleberry Finn. He points out that Huck, due to his simplicity, is fairly regarded as a flat character, but it is exactly through Huck's innocent eye that we see the bias, violence, incredibility, and even cruelty of the world he lives in; it is his innocent eye that deprives "civilization" of its conventions so as to reveal what we civilized readers would otherwise see but neglect. If Huck were a round character, American literature would perhaps have a more interesting character but would lose a world (*Recent Theories of Narrative*, 1986). Northrop Frye also thinks that flat character will not weaken the value of a character and cannot be taken as a criterion to judge the writer's observation of life as shallow while round character may merely embrace the principle that this character is the central character in a novel (*Anatomy of Criticism*, 1957). The classification of characters as flat or round by E. M. Foster is really of great importance in our reading of fiction, but it is not exempt from weakness. Firstly, the term "flat" seems always in contrast with the term "round" and thus imposes a sense of lack of vitality. In fact, many flat characters are filled with vitality and impress the reader deeply—for instance, flat characters under Charles Dicken. Secondly, the dichotomy is simplistic, taking differences in extent and scope of characterization into little or no consideration. And thirdly, the dichotomy seems to confuse the two criteria, which are dynamic rather than static (Rimmon-Kenan, *Narrative Fiction*, 1983). According to Foster, a flat character is simple and unchanging while a round one, complex and changing. Although the two criteria are compatible, in fact we find in narrative fiction that some fictional characters are complex but unchanging (Bloom in James Joyce's *Ulysses*, for instance) and some, simple but changing (Everyman in fables, for instance). Nevertheless, a character, round or flat, dynamic or static, gains the realization of his/her real features of human nature only after the reader can experience his/her actions.

"A character, first of all, is the noise of his name," says novelist William Gass (*Fiction and the Figures of Life*, 1970). Serious writers are careful about naming their characters since a good name often reveals the character of the character. A simple illustration is Becky Sharp, suggesting the unscrupulous nature of this character. Charles Dickens, a vigorous and richly suggestive writer, names a cheerful rogue Mr. Jingle, suggesting something jingly, light, and superficially pleasant; a couple of shyster lawyers Dodgeson and Fogg, suggesting dodging evasiveness and foglike obfuscation (*The Pickwick Papers*); and names a loveless stepmother Miss Murdstone, suggesting the harsh and cruel nature of this character (*David Copperfield*). Henry James, who was so fond of names that he kept lists of them for his fictional characters, chooses the name of Mrs. Bread for a down-to-earth, benevolent woman (*The American*) and the name of Lambert Strether for a sensitive, cultured gentleman (*The Ambassadors*). In addition, sometimes a character is given a descriptive name to suggest his/her identity or job, such as Mr. Hammerdown, the auctioneer in Thackeray's *Vanity Fair*. Sometimes the name of a character may make an **allusion**: a reference to some specific person, place, or thing in history, in classical writings, in other fiction, or in actuality. For instance, Herman Melville names his tragic, domineering Ahab after a Biblical tyrant, and his wandering narrator Ishmael after a Biblical outcast (*Moby-Dick*). Occasionally the choice of a character's name may carry a symbolic significance. Sammy Mountjoy, in William Golding's *Free Fall*, has fallen from the grace of heaven, the mount of joy, by an act of volition that the title makes clear. The eponym of *Doctor Zhivago* is so called because his name, meaning "the living," carries powerful religious overtones. How a writer names his/her characters depends upon how the writer plans to characterize them.

The creation of the characters in fiction so that they exist for the reader as life-like is called **characterization.** The ability to characterize is a primary attribute of a good writer. There are three fundamental methods of characterization in fiction. (1) explicit presentation of the character by the author through direct exposition, either in an introductory block or more often piecemeal throughout the work, illustrated by action; (2) presentation of the character in action, with little or no explicit comment by the author, in the expectation that the reader will be able to deduce the traits of the character from the actions; and (3) representation from within a character, without comment on the character by the author, of the impact of actions and emotions on the character's inner self, with the expectation that the reader will come to a clear understanding of the traits of the character (Holman and Harman, *A Handbook to Literature*, 1986).

If we try to distinguish these methods of characterization when we read a fiction, it is helpful that we discuss them in terms of narrative point of view. Usually the explicit presentation results when the story is told by a first-person narrator, such as Dickens's *David Copperfield* and Sterne's *Tristram Shandy*, or by an omniscient narrator, such as the one in *Tom Jones* or in *Vanity Fair*. The presentation of characters through actions is essentially the dramatic method. For instance, we get to know Hamlet through what he says and does; his true character as Shakespeare intended it will be a forever unanswerable riddle. Many modern novelists and storytellers have adopted the dramatic technique by making objective presentations of their characters in action without authorial comment. The presentation of the impact of external events and emotions on the major character's inward self begins with the novels of Henry James, whose *The Ambassadors* is an excellent example, and continues into the stream-of-consciousness novel, (See Chapter Eight for a brief discussion) where, through interior monologues, the subconscious or unconscious mind of the character is presented, as in James Joyce's *Ulysses* and William Faulkner's *The Sound and the Fury*.

Nevertheless, whatever method an author may use in his/her characterization, the author has his/her reason(s) for choosing to concentrate on a dominant trait to the exclusion of other aspects of personality, or for attempting to present a fully rounded creation. Ultimately every successful character represents a fusion of the universal and the particular and becomes an example of the **concrete**

universal: an expression of the universal through a concrete or particular instance. It is in this particularization of the typical and the universal that one of the essences of characterization is to be found. In reading fiction, it is our emotions that give the aesthetic response, and they ultimately respond to the personal, the particular, and the concrete. This is why a novel speaks to us more durably than a book of, say, philosophy or sociology.

    There is always a chief character (sometimes more than one, especially in longer novels) in a story, which traditionally we call hero (or heroine, if a female one). We call the chief character **hero** since he is generally endowed with the usual respectful attributes such as bravery, skill, idealism, sense of responsibility, etc. However, with the development of the writer's insight into the modern world, many a story and novel have featured an **antihero**: a character conspicuously lacking the usual attributes of a traditional hero. (Thus we borrow the Greek term "**protagonist**," meaning the "first" actor in Greek drama, to refer to both the hero and the antihero in fiction.) The antihero is an ordinary twentieth-century citizen, usually drawn as someone "groping, puzzled, cross, mocking, frustrated, and isolated". (Sean O'Faolain, *The Vanishing Hero*, 1957) Antiheroes tend to be loners, without aims of life, sometimes just barely able to survive; they lack "character." An excellent example is Leopold Bloom, antihero of James Joyce's novel *Ulysses*, who is a parody of Ulysses, hero of the Greek *Odyssey*. In Homer's epic, Ulysses wanders the Mediterranean, battling monsters and overcoming enchantments; in Joyce's novel, Bloom wanders the littered streets of Dublin, peddling advertising space. Mersault, the protagonist of Albert Camus' novel *The Stranger*, is so alienated from his own life that he is unmoved at the news of his mother's death. Character almost entirely disappears in Franz Kafka's *The Castle*, whose protagonist has no work, no home, no family, no definite appearance—not even a name, just the initial K. Modern writers' attempt to decharacterize is perhaps another method of characterization. Still, many writers of fiction go on portraying characters traditionally.

  Some radical critics of modern times think that characteristics of character in fiction are linguistic rather than representative or substantial. Especially in semiotic criticism, character loses its privilege and clear definition. This does not mean that character becomes something inanimate; it is completely textualized. It is, as a mode of repetition, merely something contextual subjected to the formation of themes. Textualized character is thus generally seen as (1) structural element, (2) action, (3) naming, and (4) sign. Russian Formalists believe that character is the animate agent for the various motifs in fiction and that characterization is a common and effective method of connecting these motifs. They look upon character as an element of the whole structure of a story or a novel. (Tomashevsky, "Thematics," 1925) For them, characters play the role in collecting and then classifying and arranging the motifs in a fiction. The French Structuralists explicitly assert that character in fiction is used as a structural element: the existence of events and objects in a fictional work depends upon the characters, and it is through their relations with the characters that they are endowed with the coherence and plausibility that make them meaningful. The tendency that analyzes character from the perspective of action can be traced to Aristotle. But in modern times this tendency does not reduce characters to simple types based on their psychologies: the classification of characters in fiction is based upon the unity of the action with which the narrative work endows the characters. (Roland Barthes, "Introduction to the Structural Analysis of Narratives," 1966) Consequently, various characters in fiction are reduced to several scopes of action, for example, invaders, givers, princesses and fathers, heroes and quasi-heroes and so on, or to elements of action, which may be realized in a particular character or more than one particular character because of their functions in the basic structure of the story. (A. J. Greimas "Narrative

Grammar," 1971) Some critics also attempt to ground their character classification on the levels of action. With regard to the third tendency, Todorov's analysis of narrative sees a narrative text as a sentence, and in this text that can be analyzed syntactically character becomes the subject of the narrative clause: character is the subject, expressed by a special name in order to remove abstractness (*The Poetics of Prose*, 1971). In his analysis, Todorov tends to regard characters as nouns, their characteristics as adjectives, and treat their actions as verbs. Thus such a "sentence" is the whole of character. Roland Barthes (*S/Z*, 1974) suggests that special names plus attributes of personalities constitute the whole of character. He says that character is an adjective, an attributive, a predicate, an assembly of such elements of personality so that these special names enable that person in the story to exist by himself/herself. Once a special name appears, it is the subject, and the elements of personality become the predicate. Those critics who tend to regard character as a sign actually select a point of observation of this object, taking character as a constituent of communication instead of as "human" as in traditional criticism. Generally speaking, all the four tendencies have one thing in common: they seem to indicate that character in fiction is nothing but a fragment of words loosely brought together by special names.

There are also some other critics in modern times who try to reconcile the traditional concept of character with the radical one, taking character as both a common human being and a constituent of literary structure. Rimmon-Kenan (*Narrative Fiction*, 1983) says that these two stances involve two different aspects of fiction. In text, character is the conjunction of structure of words, and in story it is an abstract entity of non-language or pre-language. The existence of a character largely depends upon the reader's concept about ordinary human beings, and thus character in fiction is similar to human beings in life.

The Jilting of Granny Weatherall
by Katherine Anne Porter, 1930

She flicked her wrist neatly out of Doctor Harry's pudgy careful fingers and pulled the sheet up to her chin. The brat ought to be in knee breeches. Doctoring around the country with spectacles on his nose! "Get along now, take your schoolbooks and go. There's nothing wrong with me."

Doctor Harry spread a warm paw like a cushion on her forehead where the forked green vein danced and made her eyelids twitch. "Now, now, be a good girl, and we'll have you up in no time."

"That's no way to speak to a woman nearly eighty years old just because she's down. I'd have you respect your elders, young man."

"Well, Missy, excuse me." Doctor Harry patted her cheek. "But I've got to warn you, haven't I? You're a marvel, but you must be careful or you're going to be good and sorry."

5 "Don't tell me what I'm going to be. I'm on my feet now, morally speaking. It's Cornelia. I had to go to bed to get rid of her."

Her bones felt loose, and floated around in her skin, and Doctor Harry floated like a balloon around the foot of the bed. He floated and pulled down his waistcoat and swung his glasses on a cord. "Well, stay where you are, it certainly can't hurt you."

"Get along and doctor your sick," said Granny Weatherall. "Leave a well woman alone. I'll call for you when I want you.... Where were you forty years ago when I pulled through milk leg and double pneumonia? You weren't even born. Don't let Cornelia lead you on," she shouted, because Doctor Harry appeared to float up to the ceiling and out. "I pay my own bills, and I don't throw my money away on nonsense!"

She meant to wave good-by, but it was too much trouble. Her

Chapter Three

eyes closed of themselves, it was like a dark curtain drawn around the bed. The pillow rose and floated under her, pleasant as a hammock in a light wind. She listened to the leaves rustling outside the window. No, somebody was swishing newspapers: no, Cornelia and Doctor Harry were whispering together. She leaped broad awake, thinking they whispered in her ear.

"She was never like this, *never* like this!" "Well, what can we expect?" "Yes, eighty years old...."

Well, and what if she was? She still had ears. It was like Cornelia to whisper around doors. She always kept things secret in such a public way. She was always being tactful and kind. Cornelia was dutiful; that was the trouble with her. Dutiful and good: "So good and dutiful," said Granny, "that I'd like to spank her." She saw herself spanking Cornelia and making a fine job of it.

"What'd you say, Mother?"

Granny felt her face tying up in hard knots.

"Can't a body think, I'd like to know?"

"I thought you might want something."

"I do. I want a lot of things. First off, go away and don't whisper."

She lay and drowsed, hoping in her sleep that the children would keep out and let her rest a minute. It had been a long day. Not that she was tired. It was always pleasant to snatch a minute now and then. There was always so much to be done, let me see: tomorrow.

Tomorrow was far away and there was nothing to trouble about. Things were finished somehow when the time came; thank God there was always a little margin over for peace: then a person could spread out the plan of life and tuck in the edges orderly. It was good to have everything clean and folded away, with the hair brushes and tonic bottles sitting straight on the white embroidered linen: the day started without fuss and the pantry shelves laid out with rows of jelly glasses and brown jugs and white stone-china jars with blue whirligigs and words painted on them: coffee, tea, sugar, ginger, cinnamon, allspice; and the bronze clock with the lion on top nicely dusted off. The dust that lion could collect in twenty-four hours! The box in the attic with all those letters tied up, well, she'd have to go through that tomorrow. All those letters—George's letters and John's letters and her letters to them both—lying around for the children to find afterwards made her uneasy. Yes, that would be tomorrow's business. No use to let them know how silly she had been once.

While she was rummaging around she found death in her mind and it felt clammy and unfamiliar. She had spent so much time preparing for death there was no need for bringing it up again. Let it take care of itself now. When she was sixty she had felt very old, finished, and went around making farewell trips to see her children and grandchildren, with a secret in her mind: This is the very last of your mother, children! Then she made her will and came down with a long fever. That was all just a notion like a lot of other things, but it was lucky too, for she had once for all got over the idea of dying for a long time. Now she couldn't be worried. She hoped she had better sense now. Her father had lived to be one hundred and two years old and had drunk a noggin of strong hot toddy on his last birthday. He told the reporters it was his daily habit, and he owed his long life to it. He had made quite a scandal and was very pleased about it. She believed she'd just plague Cornelia a little.

"Cornelia! Cornelia!" No footsteps, but a sudden hand on her cheek. "Bless you, where have you been?"

"Here, Mother."

"Well, Cornelia, I want a noggin of hot toddy."

"Are you cold, darling?"

"I'm chilly, Cornelia. Lying in bed stops the circulation. I must have told you that a thousand times."

Well, she could just hear Cornelia telling her husband that Mother was getting a little childish and they'd have to humor her. The thing that most annoyed her was that Cornelia thought she

Chapter Three

was deaf, dumb, and blind. Little hasty glances and tiny gestures tossed around her and over her head saying, "Don't cross her, let her have her way, she's eighty years old," and she sitting there as if she lived in a thin glass cage. Sometimes Granny almost made up her mind to pack up and move back to her own house where nobody could remind her every minute that she was old. Wait, wait, Cornelia, till your own children whisper behind your back!

25　　In her day she had kept a better house and had got more work done. She wasn't too old yet for Lydia to be driving eighty miles for advice when one of the children jumped the track, and Jimmy still dropped in and talked things over: "Now, Mammy, you've a good business head, I want to know what you think of this?..." Old. Cornelia couldn't change the furniture around without asking. Little things, little things! They had been so sweet when they were little. Granny wished the old days were back again with the children young and everything to be done over. It had been a hard pull, but not too much for her. When she thought of all the food she had cooked, and all the clothes she had cut and sewed, and all the gardens she had made—well, the children showed it. There they were, made out of her, and they couldn't get away from that. Sometimes she wanted to see John again and point to them and say, Well, I didn't do so badly, did I? But that would have to wait. That was for tomorrow. She used to think of him as a man, but now all the children were older than their father, and he would be a child beside her if she saw him now. It seemed strange and there was something wrong in the idea. Why, he couldn't possibly recognize her. She had fenced in a hundred acres once, digging the post holes herself and clamping the wires with just a negro boy to help. That changed a woman. John would be looking for a young woman with the peaked Spanish comb in her hair and the painted fan. Digging post holes changed a woman. Riding country roads in the winter when women had their babies was another thing: sitting up nights with sick horses and sick negroes and sick children and hardly ever losing one. John, I hardly ever lost one of them! John

— 97 —

would see that in a minute, that would be something he could understand, she wouldn't have to explain anything!

It made her feel like rolling up her sleeves and putting the whole place to rights again. No matter if Cornelia was determined to be everywhere at once, there were a great many things left undone on this place. She would start tomorrow and do them. It was good to be strong enough for everything, even if all you made melted and changed and slipped under your hands, so that by the time you finished you almost forgot what you were working for. What was it I set out to do? she asked herself intently, but she could not remember. A fog rose over the valley, she saw it marching across the creek swallowing the trees and moving up the hill like an army of ghosts. Soon it would be at the near edge of the orchard, and then it was time to go in and light the lamps. Come in, children, don't stay out in the night air.

Lighting the lamps had been beautiful. The children huddled up to her and breathed like little calves waiting at the bars in the twilight. Their eyes followed the match and watched the flame rise and settle in a blue curve, then they moved away from her. The lamp was lit, they didn't have to be scared and hang on to mother any more. Never, never, never more. God, for all my life I thank Thee. Without Thee, my God, I could never have done it. Hail, Mary, full of grace.

I want you to pick all the fruit this year and see that nothing is wasted. There's always someone who can use it. Don't let good things rot for want of using. You waste life when you waste good food. Don't let things get lost. It's bitter to lose things. Now, don't let me get to thinking, not when I am tired and taking a little nap before supper....

The pillow rose about her shoulders and pressed against her heart and the memory was being squeezed out of it: oh, push down the pillow, somebody: it would smother her if she tried to hold it. Such a fresh breeze blowing and such a green day with no threats in it. But he had not come, just the same. What does a woman do

Chapter Three

when she has put on the white veil and set out the white cake for a man and he doesn't come? She tried to remember. No, I swear he never harmed me but in that. He never harmed me but in that... and what if he did? There was the day, the day, but a whirl of dark smoke rose and covered it, crept up and over into the bright field where everything was planted so carefully in orderly rows. That was hell, she knew hell when she saw it. For sixty years she had prayed against remembering him and against losing her soul in the deep pit of hell, and now the two things were mingled in one and the thought of him was a smoky cloud from hell that moved and crept in her head when she had just got rid of Doctor Harry and was trying to rest a minute. Wounded vanity, Ellen, said a sharp voice in the top of her mind. Don't let your wounded vanity get the upper hand of you. Plenty of girls get jilted. You were jilted, weren't you? Then stand up to it. Her eyelids wavered and let in streamers of blue-gray light like tissue paper over her eyes. She must get up and pull the shades down or she'd never sleep. She was in bed again and the shades were not down. How could that happen? Better turn over, hide from the light, sleeping in the light gave you nightmares. "Mother, how do you feel now?" and a stinging wetness on her forehead. But I don't like having my face washed in cold water!

30 Hapsy? George? Lydia? Jimmy? No, Cornelia, and her features were swollen and full of little puddles. "They're coming, darling, they'll all be here soon." Go wash your face, child, you look funny.

Instead of obeying, Cornelia knelt down and put her head on the pillow. She seemed to be talking but there was no sound. "Well, are you tongue-tied? Whose birthday is it? Are you going to give a party?"

Cornelia's mouth moved urgently in strange shapes. "Don't do that, you bother me, daughter."

"Oh, no, Mother. Oh, no...."

Nonsense. It was strange about children. They disputed your

every word. "No what, Cornelia?"

35   "Here's Doctor Harry."

"I won't see that boy again. He just left three minutes ago."

"That was this morning, Mother. It's night now. Here's the nurse."

"This is Doctor Harry, Mrs. Weatherall. I never saw you look so young and happy!"

"Ah, I'll never be young again—but I'd be happy if they'd let me lie in peace and get rested."

40   She thought she spoke up loudly, but no one answered. A warm weight on her forehead, a warm bracelet on her wrist, and a breeze went on whispering, trying to tell her something. A shuffle of leaves in the everlasting hand of God. He blew on them and they danced and rattled. "Mother, don't mind, we're going to give you a little hypodermic." "Look here, daughter, how do ants get in this bed? I saw sugar ants yesterday." Did you send for Hapsy too?

It was Hapsy she really wanted. She had to go a long way back through a great many rooms to find Hapsy standing with a baby on her arm. She seemed to herself to be Hapsy also, and the baby on Hapsy's arm was Hapsy and himself and herself, all at once, and there was no surprise in the meeting. Then Hapsy melted from within and turned flimsy as gray gauze and the baby was a gauzy shadow, and Hapsy came up close and said, "I thought you'd never come," and looked at her very searchingly and said, "You haven't changed a bit!" They leaned forward to kiss, when Cornelia began whispering from a long way off, "Oh, is there anything you want to tell me? Is there anything I can do for you?"

Yes, she had changed her mind after sixty years and she would like to see George. I want you to find George. Find him and be sure to tell him I forgot him. I want him to know I had my husband just the same and my children and my house like any other woman. A good house too and a good husband that I loved and fine children out of him. Better than I hoped for even. Tell him I was given back everything he took away and more. Oh, no, oh, God, no, there

Chapter Three

was something else besides the house and the man and the children. Oh, surely they were not all? What was it? Something not given back.... Her breath crowded down under her ribs and grew into a monstrous frightening shape with cutting edges; it bored up into her head, and the agony was unbelievable: Yes, John, get the Doctor now, no more talk, my time has come.

When this one was born it should be the last. The last. It should have been born first, for it was the one she had truly wanted. Everything came in good time. Nothing left out, left over. She was strong, in three days she would be as well as ever. Better. A woman needed milk in her to have her full health.

"Mother, do you hear me?"

"I've been telling you—"

"Mother, Father Connolly's here."

"I went to Holy Communion only last week. Tell him I'm not so sinful as all that."

"Father just wants to speak to you."

He could speak as much as he pleased. It was like him to drop in and inquire about her soul as if it were a teething baby, and then stay for a cup of tea and a round of cards and gossip. He always had a funny story of some sort, usually about an Irishman who made his little mistakes and confessed them, and the point lay in some absurd thing he would blurt out in the confessional showing his struggles between native piety and original sin. Granny felt easy about her soul. Cornelia, where are your manners? Give Father Connolly a chair. She had her secret comfortable understanding with a few favorite saints who cleared a straight road to God for her. All as surely signed and sealed as the papers for the new Forty Acres. Forever... heirs and assigns forever. Since the day the wedding cake was not cut, but thrown out and wasted. The whole bottom dropped out of the world, and there she was blind and sweating with nothing under her feet and walls falling away. His hand had caught her under the breast, she had not fallen, there was the freshly polished floor with the green rug on it, just as before. He had cursed like a sailor's parrot and said, "I'll kill him for you." Don't lay a hand on him, for my sake leave something to God. "Now, Ellen, you must believe what I tell you...."

So there was nothing, nothing to worry about any more, except sometimes in the night one of the children screamed in a nightmare, and they both hustled out shaking and hunting for the matches and calling, "There, wait a minute, here we are!" John, get the doctor now, Hapsy's time has come. But there was Hapsy standing by the bed in a white cap. "Cornelia, tell Hapsy to take off her cap. I can't see her plain."

Her eyes opened very wide and the room stood out like a picture she had seen somewhere. Dark colors with the shadows rising towards the ceiling in long angles. The tall black dresser gleamed with nothing on it but John's picture, enlarged from a little one, with John's eyes very black when they should have been blue. You never saw him, so how do you know how he looked? But the man insisted the copy was perfect, it was very rich and handsome. For a picture, yes, but it's not my husband. The table by the bed had a linen cover and a candle and a crucifix. The light was blue from Cornelia's silk lampshades. No sort of light at all, just frippery. You had to live forty years with kerosene lamps to appreciate honest electricity. She felt very strong and she saw Doctor Harry with a rosy nimbus around him.

"You look like a saint, Doctor Harry, and I vow that's as near as you'll ever come to it."

"She's saying something."

"I heard you, Cornelia. What's all this carrying-on?"

"Father Connolly's saying—"

Cornelia's voice staggered and bumped like a cart in a bad road. It rounded corners and turned back again and arrived nowhere. Granny stepped up in the cart very lightly and reached for the reins, but a man sat beside her and she knew him by his hands, driving the cart. She did not look in his face, for she knew without seeing, but looked instead down the road where the trees

Chapter Three

leaned over and bowed to each other and a thousand birds were singing a Mass. She felt like singing too, but she put her hand in the bosom of her dress and pulled out a rosary, and Father Connolly murmured Latin in a very solemn voice and tickled her feet. My God, will you stop that nonsense? I'm a married woman. What if he did run away and leave me to face the priest by myself? I found another a whole world better. I wouldn't have exchanged my husband for anybody except St. Michael himself, and you may tell him that for me with a thank you in the bargain.

Light flashed on her closed eyelids, and a deep roaring shook her. Cornelia, is that lightning? I hear thunder. There's going to be a storm. Close all the windows. Call the children in.... "Mother, here we are, all of us." "Is that you, Hapsy?" "Oh, no, I'm Lydia. We drove as fast as we could." Their faces drifted above her, drifted away. The rosary fell out of her hands and Lydia put it back. Jimmy tried to help, their hands fumbled together, and Granny closed two fingers around Jimmy's thumb. Beads wouldn't do, it must be something alive. She was so amazed her thoughts ran round and round. So, my dear Lord, this is my death and I wasn't even thinking about it. My children have come to see me die. But I can't, it's not time. Oh, I always hated surprises. I wanted to give Cornelia the amethyst set—Cornelia, you're to have the amethyst set, but Hapsy's to wear it when she wants, and, Doctor Harry, do shut up. Nobody sent for you. Oh, my dear Lord, do wait a minute. I meant to do something about the Forty Acres, Jimmy doesn't need it and Lydia will later on, with that worthless husband of hers. I meant to finish the altar cloth and send six bottles of wine to Sister Borgia for her dyspepsia. I want to send six bottles of wine to Sister Borgia, Father Connolly, now don't let me forget.

Cornelia's voice made short turns and tilted over and crashed, "Oh, Mother, oh, Mother, oh, Mother...."

"I'm not going, Cornelia. I'm taken by surprise. I can't go."

You'll see Hapsy again. What about her? "I thought you'd never come." Granny made a long journey outward, looking for

Hapsy. What if I don't find her? What then? Her heart sank down and down, there was no bottom to death, she couldn't come to the end of it. The blue light from Cornelia's lampshade drew into a tiny point in the center of her brain, it flickered and winked like an eye, quietly it fluttered and dwindled. Granny lay curled down within herself, amazed and watchful, staring at the point of light that was herself; her body was now only a deeper mass of shadow in an endless darkness and this darkness would curl around the light and swallow it up. God, give a sign!

For the second time there was no sign. Again no bridegroom and the priest in the house. She could not remember any other sorrow because this grief wiped them all away. Oh, no, there's nothing more cruel than this—I'll never forgive it. She stretched herself with a deep breath and blew out the light.

Discussion

In telling the story of Granny Weatherall, Porter relied, for the most part, on the techniques of stream-of-consciousness, flashback, ambiguity, and epiphany. Once students understand that this stream of thoughts is what the term *stream-of-consciousness* means, they will see that Porter uses this technique throughout. Instead of the usual short story elements of plot such as exposition, rising action, climax, and denouement, Porter skillfully uses stream-of-consciousness not merely to delineate the character of Granny Weatherall but to tell her life's story as well.

Most students will be familiar with the term *flashback*. By carefully noting the series of stream-of-consciousness episodes in which Porter shifts from the past to Granny's present condition, one in which she weaves in and out of consciousness, students will see a portrait of a dominating, matriarchal woman who tried to engineer every detail of her life. As she lies dying, Granny considers Dr. Harry, the attending physician, as a brat, a mere school boy and gives him the peremptory command to get along with his schoolbooks and leave her alone.

How desperately ill Granny is becomes apparent early in the story in her reflection that "her bones felt loose and floated around in her skin" and that she does not have enough energy to wave goodbye to Dr. Harry. Her antagonism toward Cornelia is apparent from the outset. To Granny, a forthright, outspoken, headstrong woman, Cornelia's tact, her tiptoeing around, and her whispering are irritating, Granny emerges as a person who ordered every detail of her life from "hair brushes and tonic bottles sitting straight on the white embroidered linen" to "the bronze clock with the lion on top nicely dusted off."

In her reminiscences, Granny recalls a box of letters in the attic, something not tidied up, something left undone. This box contains "George's letters and John's letters and her letters to them both." Recollecting the hidden letters. Granny feels uneasy, not wanting her children to "know how silly she had been once."

The letters represent one of the puzzling ambiguities of the story. Students need to understand that a writer uses ambiguity to allow multiple interpretations. Ambiguity deliberately employed by a writer indicates that no clear answers are intended and opens up the way for the reader to explore various interpretations merely hinted at. Given a woman of Granny's meticulous habits, the letters seem enigmatic.

What is Porter's purpose in telling the reader that Granny has "George's letters and John's letters and her letters to them both?" Since John is her husband, it is understandable that she may have kept his letters over the years. But why, after sixty years, does she have letters from the man who jilted her? The story makes no further reference to the letters, but Granny's reference to them suggests several possibilities; she saved George's letters of sixty years ago because she has not really gotten over him or George has written to her during the intervening years. If the latter is true, it's possible that George may have written to offer some explanation of the jilting or tried to communicate with her after John's death.

Even more provocative is her statement that she has her letters to George and John. Although she might have her husband's letters because he had kept them, why should she fear her children's finding them? Has she cloaked herself with the image of the iron-willed, resolute woman who spurns the thought of having her children see that she was vulnerable to love? A woman who clings to letters over many decades may be a woman who is incapable of closing out the early chapters of her life. The most enigmatic phrase is that she has her letters to George. Granny has not seen George in sixty years, but perhaps she would like to see him now that she is dying to assure him that she has forgotten him. Clearly, Granny has not forgotten George.

The fact that Granny has her letters to George can only mean that she has written letters to him that she has never sent. The contents of these letters remain ambiguous. Was Granny pregnant when she was jilted? Did this circumstance increase the pain of the jilting? Is Cornelia, in fact, George's child? Since she repeatedly claims she had her husband, her family, her home, in spite of George, this does not seem likely, but the hint is there. The letters are surely another clue to Granny's vulnerability to love, to an emotional wound that has never healed. Does Granny worry about the letters because of their disclosure of human frailty which contradicts the image she has forged for herself as a strong, indomitable woman in full command of her life? The ambiguity of the letters and their contents points to some unrevealed disclosures.

Hapsy represents another of the ambiguities in the story. In her reverie, Granny confuses the pain of her death agony with the pain of childbearing, and, more precisely, with the birth of Hapsy. Throughout the story Hapsy remains somewhat of an enigma with the implication that she is much loved but also the source of pain. The story contains some irrefutable clues. Hapsy is the youngest daughter, the one whom Granny says she wanted most, the one for whom Granny searches unsuccessfully throughout the story.

When she thinks about Hapsy's birth, Granny reflects that the child shoud have been born first, for this was the "one she had truly wanted." In her reverie, she calls on John to get the doctor at Hapsy's birth, a proof that John had not died quite as young as the story otherwise implies. As she prepares for the birth of Hapsy, she reflects that she will be well in three days. But this did not happen. In the opening of the story, when Granny dismisses Dr. Harry, she taunts him with his youth saying. "Where were you forty years ago when I pulled throught milk leg and double pneumonia?" Since milk leg is a disease associated with child bearing, this illness must have followed Hapsy's birth, for we know that Hapsy is the last child. In their zeal for intrigue, students frequently suggest Hapsy is George's child, and this is the reason she was the one Granny truly wanted. But this interpretation has no foundation in fact since Granny has not seen George in sixty years.

In her reverie, Granny tells John to get the doctor since her time has come, and later she says Hapsy's time has come. Although the latter statement might be interpreted to mean Hapsy's giving birth, it seems rather to be a reference to Granny's giving birth to Hapsy. Since the story states that John died at a relatively young age, he would not have been alive whe Hapsy was of child-bearing age. Both references seem to be to Hapsy's birth. A moment later Granny sees Hapsy at her bed with a white cap on. With her failing senses. Granny has mistaken the nurse for Hapsy. After Granny goes back through a great many rooms to find Hapsy, Porter says she finds Hapsy holding a baby and follows with the ambiguous statement, "She seemed to herself to be Hapsy also, and the baby in Hapsy's arm was Hapsy, and himself and herself, all at once, and there was no surprise in the meeting."

In the story Granny never meets Hapsy except in a kind of reverie or in a vision of life to come. Although the *himself* in the above quotation has been interpreted to mean George, it is more likely that the *himself* is John. Although the character of Hapsy is ambiguous, it seems reasonable to suppose that given the facts of Granny's illness at Hapsy's birth, her preference for Hapsy, the pet name Hapsy. Granny's going back through "many rooms" to find Hapsy, and the shadowy elusiveness of Hapsy throughout the story, she is Granny's last child lost in childbirth. Just as Granny cannot destroy her letters or forget George, she cannot forget Hapsy, a child dead forty years. Since Hapsy and John are both dead, she links the two in the statement "the baby in Hapsy's arm was Hapsy and himself and herself, all at once," with the implication that she and John in the bond of marriage are one and that Hapsy is the fruit of that love.

  Another of the much-disputed ambiguities in the story is Ellen Weatherall's relation to George. After all those years, she has not forgotten the wound of the first jilting. The dark smoke of that memory clouds "the bright field where everything was planted so carefully in orderly rows." That painful memory casts a dark shadow over the bright, careful order she had tried to establish in he life. She recalls that "for sixty years she had prayed against remembering him and against losing her soul in the deep pit of hell." She chides herself not to let this wounded vanity from the past triumph and to accept the reality of her jilting. A little later she demands that Cornelia find George so she can tell him that she had everything his jilting would have denied her — a home, a husband, children. But suddenly there comes to Granny the realization that something was missing in her life.

  "Oh no, oh, God, no, there was something else beside the house and the man and the children. Oh, surely they were not all? What was it? Something not given back." Again, this agonized statement is open to speculation. Some critics have coupled Granny's bitter memories of the jilting by George with the jilting of the heavenly bridegroom at the end of the story and have interpreted the story to mean that Granny is damned to hell for clinging to the memory of George and her inability to forgive him.

  This interpretation is contrary to the Roman Catholic theology of sin and punishment on which the story is based. In Catholic teaching, people are condemned to hell only if they knowingly and willingly commit a grievous sin and refuse to repent. Temptation is not sin. As long as temptation is resisted, even though it recurs, a person is not guilty of grievous sin and is not deserving of hell. In the course of her reverie, Granny says, "God for all of my life. I thank thee. Without Thee, my God, I could never have done it." Note here that Granny thanks God for "all of her life," a phrase that includes the jilting. She acknowledges that only God's grace has sustained her, has enabled her to resist the recurring temptation. In her perparation for death, she has observed the traditional practices of the church, has gone to confession, and received the last rites. Porter says Granny felt "easy" about her soul.

  As Death, symbolized as a man driving a cart, comes to fetch Granny, it seems to her as she begins her journey, that "the trees leaned over and bowed to each other and a thousand birds were singing a Mass." This description implies an entrance to Paradise, not a plunge into eternal perdition. She recalls that even though George jilted her, she found "another a whole world better."

  As death draws closer, Granny's peace explodes into a storm as she bears thunder and sees the flash of lightning. At this moment, Porter uses a sudden moment of revelation, as Granny understands in a flash that "her time" has really come, and she is not ready in spite of all her preparations. At this point, the student will need to be familar with the Joycean technique of the *epiphany*, the sudden understanding in which characters understand some fundamental truth about themselves or their situations. Although the technique is frequently used in the modern short story, most students will not be familiar with it. As this moment comes to Granny, her mind runs hurriedly through a litany of intended bequests as she attempts to make final arrangements. She searches frantically for Hapsy but does not find her. As she lies there "amazed and watchful," she pleads, "God, give a sign," but no sign is forthcoming as Granny stretches herself with a deep breath and blows out the light of her life. Once again, the bridegroom does not appear. Granny is jilted by the heavenly bridegroom who does not appear at her death to receive her soul.

The second jilting has been the subject of conjecture. In the light of Catholic theology and the lifelong temptation that Granny resisted, the jilting can scarcely mean condemnation to hell. Recalling the careful delineation of Ellen Weatherall as a woman who plotted and planned every detail of her life, who weathered a jilting and made a new life with John, who according to her own words wouldn't have exchanged him for anybody but St. Michael, the moment of revelation reveals to her that in spite of all her planning death is taking her by surprise. That moment pinpoints the basic truth of the mystery of life and death, a mystery that even the most resourceful planner cannot forestall or anticipate. Death maintains for everyone an element of surprise; it remains for all the ultimate mystery.

(Eleanore M. Britton)

Questions

1. What does the writer tell us about Granny Weatherall in the first paragragh?
2. What does the name of Weatherall have to do with Granny's character (or her life story)? What other qualities or traits do you find in her?
3. "She lay and drowsed, hoping in her sleep that the children would keep out and let her rest a minute. It had been a long day. Not that she was tired. It was always pleasant to snatch a minute now and then. There was always so much to be done, let me see: tomorrow" (paragraph 16). What do you understand from this statement? By what other remarks does the writer indicate Granny's conditions? At what other moments in the story does Granny fail to understand what is happening, or confusing the present with the past?

4. Exactly what happened to Ellen Weatherall sixty years earlier? What effects did this event have on her?
5. Why doesn't Granny's last child Hapsy come to her mother's deathbed?
6. Would you call the character of Doctor Harry "flat" or "round"? Why is his flatness (or roundness) appropriate to the story?
7. How is this the story of another "jilting"? What is similar between that fateful day of sixty years ago and the moment when Granny is dying?
8. Virginia Woolf compared life to "a luminous halo, a semitransparent envelop surrounding us from the beginning of consciousness to the end" ("Modern Fiction" in *Collected Essays*). To capture such a reality, modern writers of fiction have employed many strategies. One experimental technique of writing is called **stream of consciousness,** a phrase coined by psychologist Williams James in *Principles of Psychology* (1890) to describe the procession of thoughts passing through the mind. In fiction, the stream of consciousness is the presentation of thoughts and feelings in the form of a flow of sensations, thoughts, memories, associations and reflections, and if the exact content of the mind ("consciousness") is to be described at any moment, then these varied, disjointed, and illogical elements must find expression in a flow of words, images, and ideas similar to the unorganized flow of mind (See a brief discussion about the stream-of-consciousness novel in Chapter Eight). Would you call "The Jilting of Granny Weatherall" a stream-of-consciousness story? Refer to the story in your reply.

Tickets, Please
by D. H. Lawrence, 1922

There is in the Midlands a single-line tramway system which

boldly leaves the county town and plunges off into the black, industrial countryside, up hill and down dale, through the long, ugly villages of workmen's houses, over canals and railways, past churches perched high and nobly over the smoke and shadows, through stark, grimy, cold little market-places, tilting away in a rush past cinemas and shops down to the hollow where the collieries are, then up again, past a little rural church, under the ash trees, on in a rush to the terminus, the last little ugly place of industry, the cold little town that shivers on the edge of the wild, gloomy country beyond. There the green and creamy colored tram-car seems to pause and purr with curious satisfaction. But in a few minutes — the clock on the turret of the Co-operative Wholesale Society's Shops gives the time — away it starts once more on the adventure. Again there are the reckless swoops downhill, bouncing the loops: again the chilly wait in the hill-top market-place: again the breathless slithering round the precipitous drop under the church: again the patient halts at the loops, waiting for the outcoming car: so on and on, for two long hours, till at last the city looms beyond the fat gas-works, the narrow factories draw near, we are in the sordid streets of the great town, once more we sidle to a standstill at our terminus, abashed by the great crimson and cream-coloured city cars, but still perky, jaunty, somewhat dare-devil, green as a jaunty sprig of parsley out of a black colliery garden.

　　To ride on these cars is always an adventure. Since we are in war-time, the drivers are men unfit for active service: cripples and hunchbacks. So they have the spirit of the devil in them. The ride becomes a steeple-chase. Hurray! we have leapt in a clear jump over the canal bridges — now for the four-lane corner. With a shriek and a trail of sparks we are clear again. To be sure, a tram often leaps the rails — but what matter! It sits in a ditch till other trams come to haul it out. It is quite common for a car, packed with one solid mass of living people, to come to a dead halt in the midst of unbroken blackness, the heart of nowhere on a dark night, and for the driver and the girl conductor to call, "All get off

Chapter Three

— car's on fire!" Instead, however, of rushing out in a panic, the passengers stolidly reply: "Get on — get on! We're not coming out. We're stopping where we are. Push on, George." So till flames actually appear.

The reason for this reluctance to dismount is that the nights are howlingly cold, black, and windswept, and a car is a haven of refuge. From village to village the miners travel, for a change of cinema, of girl, of pub. The trams are desperately packed. Who is going to risk himself in the black gulf outside, to wait perhaps an hour for another tram, then to see the forlorn notice "Depot Only", because there is something wrong! or to greet a unit of three bright cars all so tight with people that they sail past with a howl of derision. Trams that pass in the night.

This, the most dangerous tram-service in England, as the authorities themselves declare, with pride, is entirely conducted by girls, and driven by rash young men, a little crippled, or by delicate young men, who creep forward in terror. The girls are fearless young hussies. In their ugly blue uniform, skirts up to their knees, shapeless old peaked caps on their heads, they have all the sang-froid of an old non-commissioned officer. With a tram packed with howling colliers, roaring hymns downstairs and a sort of antiphony of obscenities upstairs, the lasses are perfectly at their ease. They pounce on the youths who try to evade their ticket-machine. They push off the men at the end of their distance. They are not going to be done in the eye — not they. They fear nobody — and everybody fears them.

"Hello, Annie!"

"Hello, Ted!"

"Oh, mind my corn, Miss Stone. It's my belief you've got a heart of stone, for you've trod on it again."

"You should keep it in your pocket," replies Miss Stone, and she goes sturdily upstairs in her high boots.

"Tickets, please."

She is peremptory, suspicious, and ready to hit first. She can hold her own against ten thousand. The step of that tram-car is her Thermopylae.

Therefore, there is a certain wild romance aboard these cars — and in the sturdy bosom of Annie herself. The time for soft romance is in the morning, between ten o'clock and one, when things are rather slack: that is, except market-day and Saturday. Thus Annie has time to look about her. Then she often hops off her car and into a shop where she has spied something, while the driver chats in the main road. There is very good feeling between the girls and the drivers. Are they not companions in peril, shipments aboard this careering vessel of a tram-car, for ever rocking on the waves of a stormy land?

Then, also, during the easy hours, the inspectors are most in evidence. For some reason, everybody employed in this tram-service is young: there are no grey heads. It would not do. Therefore the inspectors are of the right age, and one, the chief, is also good-looking. See him stand on a wet, gloomy morning, in his long oilskin, his peaked cap well down over his eyes, waiting to board a car. His face is ruddy, his small brown moustache is weathered, he has a faint impudent smile. Fairly tall and agile, even in his waterproof, he springs aboard a car and greets Annie.

"Hello, Annie! Keeping the wet out?"

"Trying to."

15   There are only two people in the car. Inspecting is soon over. Then for a long and impudent chat on the footboard, a good, easy, twelve-mile chat.

The inspector's name is John Thomas Raynor — always called John Thomas, except sometimes, in malice, Coddy. His face sets in fury when he is addressed, from a distance, with this abbreviation. There is considerable scandal about John Thomas in half a dozen villages. He flirts with the girl conductors in the morning and walks out with them in the dark night, when they leave their tram-car at the depot. Of course, the girls quit the service frequently. Then he flirts and walks out with the

Chapter Three

newcomer: always providing she is sufficiently attractive, and that she will consent to walk. It is remarkable, however, that most of the girls are quite comely, they are all young, and this roving life aboard the car gives them a sailor's dash and recklessness. What matter how they behave when the ship is in port. Tomorrow they will be aboard again.

Annie, however, was something of a Tartar, and her sharp tongue had kept John Thomas at arm's length for many months. Perhaps, therefore, she liked him all the more: for he always came up smiling, with impudence. She watched him vanquish one girl, then another. She could tell by the movement of his mouth and eyes, when he flirted with her in the morning, that he had been walking out with this lass, or the other, the night before. A fine cock-of-the-walk he was. She could sum him up pretty well.

In this subtle antagonism they knew each other like old friends, they were as shrewd with one another almost as man and wife. But Annie had always kept him sufficiently at arm's length. Besides, she had a boy of her own.

The Statutes fair, however, came in November, at Bestwood. It happened that Annie had the Monday night off. It was a drizzling ugly night, yet she dressed herself up and went to the fair ground. She was alone, but she expected soon to find a pal of some sort.

The roundabouts were veering round and grinding out their music, the side shows were making as much commotion as possible. In the cocoanut shies there were no cocoanuts, but artificial war-time substitutes, which the lads declared were fastened into the irons. There was a sad decline in brilliance and luxury. None the less, the ground was muddy as ever, there was the same crush, the press of faces lighted up by the flares and the electric lights, the same smell of naphtha and a few fried potatoes, and of electricity.

Who should be the first to greet Miss Annie, on the show ground but John Thomas. He had a black overcoat buttoned up to his chin, and a tweed cap pulled down over his brows, his face between was ruddy and smiling and handy as ever. She knew so well the way his mouth moved.

She was very glad to have a "boy". To be at the Statutes without a fellow was no fun. Instantly, like the gallant he was, he took her on the dragons, grim-toothed, roundabout switchbacks. It was not nearly so exciting as a tram-car actually. But, then, to be seated in a shaking green dragon, uplifted above the sea of bubble faces, careering in a rickety fashion in the lower heavens, whilst John Thomas leaned over her, his cigarette in his mouth, was after all the right style. She was a plump, quick, alive little creature. So she was quite excited and happy.

John Thomas made her stay on for the next round. And therefore she could hardly for shame repulse him when he put his arm round her and drew her a little nearer to him, in a very warm and cuddly manner. Besides, he was fairly discreet, he kept his movement as hidden as possible. She looked down and saw that his red, clean hand was out of sight of the crowd. And they knew each other so well. So they warmed up to the fair.

After the dragons they went on the horses. John Thomas paid each time, so she could but be complaisant. He, of course, sat astride on the outer horse — named "Black Bess" — and she sat sideways, towards him, on the inner horse — named "Wildfire." But of course John Thomas was not going to sit discreetly on "Black Bess," holding the brass bar. Round they spun and heaved, in the light. And round he swung on his wooden steed, flinging one leg across her mount, and perilously tipping up and down, across the space, half lying back, laughing at her. He was perfectly happy; she was afraid her hat was on one side, but she was excited.

25　　He threw quoits on a table, and won for her two large, pale-blue hatpins. And then, hearing the noise of the cinemas, announcing another performance, they climbed the boards and went in.

Of course, during these performances pitch darkness falls from time to time, when the machine goes wrong. Then there is a wild

Chapter Three

whooping, and a loud smacking of simulated kisses. In these moments John Thomas drew Annie towards him. After all, he had a wonderfully warm, cosy way of holding a girl with his arm, he seemed to make such a nice fit. And after all, it was pleasant to be so held: so very comforting and cosy and nice. He leaned over her and she felt his breath on her hair; she knew he wanted to kiss her on the lips. And after all, he was so warm and she fitted in to him so softly. After all, she wanted him to touch her lips.

But the light sprang up; she also started electrically, and put her hat straight. He left his arm lying nonchalantly behind her. Well, it was fun, it was exciting to be at the Statutes with John Thomas.

When the cinema was over they went for a walk across the dark, damp fields. He had all the arts of love-making. He was especially good at holding a girl, when he sat with her on a stile in the black, drizzling darkness. He seemed to be holding her in space, against his own warmth and gratification. And his kisses were soft and slow and searching.

So Annie walked out with John Thomas, though she kept her own boy dangling in the distance. Some of the tram-girls chose to be huffy. But there, you must take things as you find them, in this life.

There was no mistake about it, Annie liked John Thomas a good deal. She felt so rich and warm in herself whenever he was near. And John Thomas really liked Annie more than usual. The soft, melting way in which she could flow into a fellow, as if she melted into his very bones, was something rare and good. He fully appreciated this.

But with a developing acquaintance there began a developing intimacy. Annie wanted to consider him a person, a man; she wanted to take an intelligent interest in him, and to have an intelligent response. She did not want a mere nocturnal presence, which was what he was so far. And she prided herself that he could not leave her.

Here she made a mistake. John Thomas intended to remain a nocturnal presence; he had no idea of becoming an all-round individual to her. When she started to take an intelligent interest in him and his life and his character, he sheered off. He hated intelligent interest. And he knew that the only way to stop it was to avoid it. The possessive female was aroused in Annie. So he left her.

It is no use saying she was not surprised. She was at first startled, thrown out of her count. For she had been so *very* sure of holding him. For a while she was staggered, and everything became uncertain to her. Then she wept with fury, indignation, desolation, and misery. Then she had a spasm of despair. And then, when he came, still impudently, on to her car, still familiar, but letting her see by the movement of his head that he had gone away to somebody else for the time being and was enjoying pastures new, then she determined to have her own back.

She had a very shrewd idea what girls John Thomas had taken out. She went to Nora Purdy. Nora was a tall, rather pale, but well-built girl, with beautiful yellow hair. She was rather secretive.

"Hey!" said Annie, accosting her, then softly, "Who's John Thomas on with now?"

35 "I don't know," said Nora.

"Why tha does," said Annie, ironically lapsing into dialect. "Tha knows as well as I do."

"Well, I do, then," said Nora. "It isn't me, so don't bother."

"It's Cissy Meakin, isn't it?"

"It is, for all I know."

40 "Hasn't he got a face on him!" said Annie. "I don't half like his cheek. I could knock him off the footboard when he comes round at me."

"He'll get dropped-on one of these days," said Nora.

"Ay, he will, when somebody makes up their mind to drop it

on him. I should like to see him taken down a peg or two, shouldn't you?"

"I shouldn't mind," said Nora.

"You've got quite as much cause to as I have," said Annie. "But we'll drop on him one of these days, my girl. What? Don't you want to?"

45   "I don't mind," said Nora.

But as a matter of fact, Nora was much more vindictive than Annie.

One by one Annie went the round of the old flames. It so happened that Cissy Meakin left the tramway service in quite a short time. Her mother made her leave. Then John Thomas was on the qui-vive. He cast his eyes over his old flock. And his eyes lighted on Annie. He thought she would be safe now. Besides, he liked her.

She arranged to walk home with him on Sunday night. It so happened that her car would be in the depot at half past nine: the last car would come in at ten-fifteen. So John Thomas was to wait for her there.

At the depot the girls had a little waiting-room of their own. It was quite rough, but cosy, with a fire and an oven and a mirror, and table and wooden chairs. The half dozen girls who knew John Thomas only too well had arranged to take service this Sunday afternoon. So, as the cars began to come in, early, the girls dropped into the waiting-room. And instead of hurrying off home, they sat around the fire and had a cup of tea. Outside was the darkness and lawlessness of war-time.

50   John Thomas came on the car after Annie, at about a quarter to ten. He poked his head easily into the girls' waiting-room.

"Prayer-meeting?" he asked.

"Ay," said Laura Sharp. "Ladies only."

"That's me!" said John Thomas. It was one of his favourite exclamations.

"Shut the door, boy," said Muriel Baggaley.

"On which side of me?" said John Thomas.

"Which tha likes," said Polly Birkin.

He had come in and closed the door behind him. The girls moved in their circle, to make a place for him near the fire. He took off his greatcoat and pushed back his hat.

"Who handles the teapot?" he said.

Nora Purdy silently poured him out a cup of tea.

"Want a bit o' my bread and drippin'?" said Muriel Baggaley to him.

"Ay, give us a bit."

And he began to eat his piece of bread.

"There's no place like home, girls," he said.

They all looked at him as he uttered this piece of impudence. He seemed to be sunning himself in the presence of so many damsels.

"Especially if you're not afraid to go home in the dark," said Laura Sharp.

"Me! By myself I am."

They sat till they heard the last tram come in. In a few minutes Emma Houselay entered.

"Come on, my old duck!" cried Polly Birkin.

"It *is* perishing," said Emma, holding her fingers to the fire.

"But — I'm afraid to, go home in, the dark," sang Laura Sharp, the tune having got into her mind.

"Who're you going with tonight, John Thomas?" asked Muriel Baggaley, coolly.

"Tonight?" said John Thomas. "Oh, I'm going home by myself tonight — all on my lonely-O."

"That's me!" said Nora Purdy, using his own ejaculation.

The girls laughed shrilly.

"Me as well, Nora," said John Thomas.

"Don't know what you mean," said Laura.

"Yes, I'm toddling," said he, rising and reaching for his overcoat.

Chapter Three

"Nay," said Polly. "We're all here waiting for you."

"We've got to be up in good time in the morning," he said in the benevolent official manner.

80　　They all laughed.

"Nay," said Muriel. "Don't leave us all lonely, John Thomas. Take one!"

"I'll take the lot, if you like," he responded gallantly.

"That you won't either," said Muriel, "Two's company; seven's too much of a good thing."

"Nay — take one," said Laura. "Fair and square, all above board, and say which."

85　　"Ay," cried Annie, speaking for the first time. "Pick, John Thomas; let's hear thee."

"Nay," he said. "I'm going home quiet tonight. Feeling good, for once."

"Whereabouts?" said Annie. "Take a good un, then. But tha's got to take one of us!"

"Nay, how can I take one," he said, laughing uneasily. "I don't want to make enemies."

"You'd only make *one*," said Annie.

90　　"The chosen *one*," added Laura.

"Oh, my! Who said girls!" exclaimed John Thomas, again turning, as if to escape. "Well — good-night."

"Nay, you've got to make your pick," said Muriel. "Turn your face to the wall and say which one touches you. Go on — we shall only just touch your back — one of us. Go on — turn your face to the wall, and don't look, and say which one touches you."

He was uneasy, mistrusting them. Yet he had not the courage to break away. They pushed him to a wall and stood him there with his face to it. Behind his back they all grimaced, tittering. He looked so comical. He looked around uneasily.

"Go on!" he cried.

95　　"You're looking — you're looking!" they shouted.

He turned his head away. And suddenly, with a movement

— *121* —

like a swift cat, Annie went forward and fetched him a box on the side of the head that sent his cap flying, and himself staggering. He started round.

But at Annie's signal they all flew at him, slapping him, pinching him, pulling his hair, though more in fun than in spite or anger. He, however, saw red. His blue eyes flamed with strange fear as well as fury, and he butted through the girls to the door. It was locked. He wrenched at it. Roused, alert, the girls stood round and looked at him. He faced them, at bay. At that moment they were rather horrifying to him, as they stood in their short uniforms. He was distinctly afraid.

"Come on, John Thomas! Come on! Choose!" said Annie.

"What are you after? Open the door," he said.

100 "We shan't — not till you've chosen!" said Muriel.

"Chosen what?" he said.

"Chosen the one you're going to marry," she replied.

He hesitated a moment.

"Open the blasted door," he said, "and get back to your senses." He spoke with official authority.

105 "You've got to choose!" cried the girls.

"Come on!" cried Annie, looking him in the eye. " Come on! Come on!"

He went forward, rather vaguely. She had taken off her belt, and swinging it, she fetched him a sharp blow over the head with the buckle end. He sprang and seized her. But immediately the other girls rushed upon him, pulling and tearing and beating him. Their blood was now thoroughly up. He was their sport now. They were going to have their own back, out of him. Strange, wild creatures, they hung on him and rushed at him to bear him down. His tunic was torn right up the back, Nora had hold at the back of his collar, and was actually strangling him. Luckily the button burst. He struggled in a wild frenzy of fury and terror, almost mad terror. His tunic was simply torn off his back, his shirtsleeves were torn away, his arms were naked. The girls rushed at him,

Chapter Three

clenched their hands on him and pulled at him; or they rushed at him and pushed him, butted him with all their might; or they struck him wild blows. He ducked and cringed and struck sideways. They became more intense.

At last he was down. They rushed on him, kneeling on him. He had neither breath nor strength to move. His face was bleeding with a long scratch, his brow was bruised.

Annie knelt on him, the other girls knelt and hung on to him. Their faces were flushed, their hair wild, their eyes were all glittering strangely. He lay at last quite still, with face averted, as an animal lies when it is defeated and at the mercy of the captor. Sometimes his eye glanced back at the wild faces of the girls. His breast rose heavily, his wrists were torn.

110   "Now, then, my fellow!" gasped Annie at length. "Now then — now — "

At the sound of her terrifying, cold triumph, he suddenly started to struggle as an animal might, but the girls threw themselves upon him with unnatural strength and power, forcing him down.

"Yes — now, then!" gasped Annie at length.

And there was a dead silence, in which the thud of heart-beating was to be heard. It was a suspense of pure silence in every soul.

"Now you know where you are," said Annie.

115   The sight of his white, bare arm maddened the girls. He lay in a kind of trance of fear and antagonism. They felt themselves filled with supernatural strength.

Suddenly Polly started to laugh — to giggle wildly — helplessly — and Emma and Muriel joined in. But Annie and Nora and Laura remained the same, tense, watchful, with gleaming eyes. He winced away from these eyes.

"Yes," said Annie, in a curious low tone, secret and deadly. "Yes! You've got it now! You know what you've done, don't you? You know what you've done."

He made no sound nor sign, but lay with bright, averted eyes, and averted, bleeding face.

"You ought to be *killed*, that's what you ought," said Annie tensely. "You ought to be *killed*." And there was a terrifying lust in her voice.

120   Polly was ceasing to laugh, and giving long-drawn Oh-h-hs and sighs as she came to herself.

"He's got to choose," she said vaguely.

"Oh, yes, he has," said Laura, with vindictive decision.

"Do you hear — do you hear?" said Annie. And with a sharp movement that made him wince, she turned his face to her.

"Do you hear?" she repeated, shaking him.

125   But he was quite dumb. She fetched him a sharp slap on the face. He started, and his eyes widened. Then his face darkened with defiance, after all.

"Do you hear?" she repeated.

He only looked at her with hostile eyes.

"Speak!" she said, putting her face devilishly near his.

"What?" he said, almost overcome.

130   "You've got to *choose*!" she cried, as if it were some terrible menace, and as if it hurt her that she could not exact more.

"What?" he said in fear.

"Choose your girl, Coddy. You've got to choose her now. And you'll get your neck broken if you play any more of your tricks, my boy. You're settled now."

There was a pause. Again he averted his face. He was cunning in his overthrow. He did not give in to them really — no, not if they tore him to bits.

"All right, then," he said, "I choose Annie." His voice was strange and full of malice. Annie let go of him as if he had been a hot coal.

135   "He's chosen Annie!" said the girls in chorus.

"Me!" cried Annie. She was still kneeling, but away from him. He was still lying prostrate, with averted face. The girls grouped uneasily around.

"Me!" repeated Annie, with a terrible bitter accent.

Then she got up, drawing away from him with strange disgust and bitterness.

"I wouldn't touch him," she said.

But her face quivered with a kind of agony, she seemed as if she would fall. The other girls turned aside. He remained lying on the floor, with his torn clothes and bleeding, averted face.

140 "Oh, if he's chosen — " said Polly.

"I don't want him — he can choose again," said Annie, with the same rather bitter hopelessness.

"Get up," said Polly, lifting his shoulder. "Get up."

He rose slowly, a strange, ragged, dazed creature. The girls eyed him from a distance, curiously, furtively, dangerously.

"Who wants him?" cried Laura, roughly.

145 "Nobody," they answered, with contempt. Yet each one of them waited for him to look at her, hoped he would look at her. All except Annie, and something was broken in her.

He, however, kept his face closed and averted from them all. There was a silence of the end. He picked up the torn pieces of his tunic, without knowing what to do with them. The girls stood about uneasily, flushed, panting, tidying their hair and their dress unconsciously, and watching him. He looked at none of them. He espied his cap in a corner and went and picked it up. He put it on his head, and one of the girls burst into a shrill, hysteric laugh at the sight he presented. He, however, took no heed, but went straight to where his overcoat hung on a peg. The girls moved away from contact with him as if he had been an electric wire. He put on his coat and buttoned it down. Then he rolled his tunicrags into a bundle, and stood before the locked door, dumbly.

"Open the door, somebody," said Laura.

"Annie's got the key," said one.

Annie silently offered the key to the girls. Nora unlocked the door.

150　　"Tit for tat, old man," she said. "Show yourself a man, and don't bear a grudge."

　　　But without a word or sign he had opened the door and gone, his face closed, his head dropped.

　　　"That'll learn him," said Laura.

　　　"Coddy!" said Nora.

　　　"Shut up, for God's sake!" cried Annie fiercely, as if in torture.

155　　"Well, I'm about ready to go, Polly. Look sharp!" said Muriel.

　　　The girls were all anxious to be off. They were tidying themselves hurriedly, with mute, stupefied faces.

Discussion

　　　The plot of this story is quite simple. One of the young inspectors of the tram line, John Thomas, begins to go out with Annie, one of the girl conductors. He drops her when he realizes that she is taking his attentions seriously. Annie arranges a meeting with the other girls whom he has treated in this fashion, and they join her in roughing him up. They do not seriously hurt him, though they get in some blows and they tear his tunic. John Thomas leaves, and the girls find themselves nonplussed at what they have done, a little dazed, and even a little frightened.

　　　Though the story presents a good deal of action, even violent action, not very much has been resolved. Presumably John Thomas and Annie will continue to go their separate ways. Indeed, the story ends on a note of uneasy irresolution. The superficial reader may even be baffled by the ending of the story and so dismiss it.

　　　Other readers, however, may feel that the internal action is important. Indeed, the very debacle of the ending points toward an exciting psychological development. The girls have got in over their depth and find that their emotions toward John Thomas are in excess of, and indeed widely different from, the rather tomboyish triumph of their revenge. As the author tells us in the last sentence, after John Thomas's departure, the girls wear "mute, stupified faces."

The story derives much of its richness from the fact that it succeeds in dramatizing what may be called the "doubleness" of love — its strange mixture of aggressiveness and passivity, of cruelty and tenderness, of possessiveness and surrender. All the characters in the story experience something of these contradictory feelings, but the author has properly kept the focus upon one particular character, Annie, who is more deeply involved than the others, and who therefore not only feels the experience more intensely but is also the more intensely subject to the contradictory impulses within the experience.

What is it that Annie wants from the trick to be played on John Thomas? On the conscious level, presumably no more than the humiliation that he will suffer at facing all the girls together and the taunts that they mean to hurl at him. But unconsciously Annie must have wanted much more — if we are to judge from what actually happens in the latter part of the story. Certainly she must have wanted the specific confrontation with him — including the physical contact. She must also have wanted a chance to pour out some of her feelings of hurt and anger; the prank will afford her a kind of justification for doing so. Secretly, perhaps she wanted to hear him name her as his choice — if only to have the chance to tell him she has no interest in him. But it is plain that neither Annie nor the rest of the girls have really thought out just what they expect the prank to accomplish or to mean.

The last point comes out clearly when we see that nobody knows just how to end the joke. Once they have got into it, their actions are emotional and compulsive, sexual in fact, and sexual in a way that puzzles and even frightens the girls. They have worked themselves in a wild frenzy that they cannot understand and that might conceivably end in extreme violence. Annie gives John Thomas a box on the side of the head that is probably much harder than she had first meant to strike. At this signal the girls fly at John Thomas "more in fun than in spite or anger." But soon they have their "blood... up" and are attacking in frenzy. When John Thomas stops resisting, the girls find themselves waiting for something to happen, not knowing what to do next, and repeating illogically and "vaguely" that he has "got to choose." Indeed, some of the girls, beginning "to giggle wildly," are obviously on the verge of hysteria.

There is, of course, no way for the episode to end satisfactorily for any of the girls — least of all for the leader of the prank, Annie, whose relation to John Thomas is so emotionally ambiguous. The only satisfactory ending for such a mixture of feelings — and of feelings waked to such intensity by the physical struggle — is possession and marriage. But this is the solution that the tomboy prank has made impossible. (To Annie at least it will now *seem* so.) It is as if Annie's revenge has made John Thomas more desirable, and yet the forcing of his admission that, having to choose, he would indeed choose her, has made that choice in fact impossible. The very frustration of the prank she has engineered has revealed to her things about herself that she had not surmised.

(Cleanth Brooks and Robert Penn Warren)

Questions

1. Why is it with "bitter hopelessness" that Annie says "I don't want him"?
2. What is meant by the author's saying of Annie that "something was broken in her"?
3. What are Annie's feelings toward John Thomas at the end of the story?
4. What are John Thomas's feelings toward Annie?

5. Has the author put too much emphasis upon John Thomas's emotions, particulariy in the last half of the story? Or too little emphasis?
6. Note that the author is constantly telling us what the characters think and what certain of their actions mean: for example, "He was uneasy, mistrusting them" and "yet each one of them... hoped he would look at her." Even so, the story is vivid in its presentation and remains "dramatic." Why don't the author's comments and interpretations kill the immediacy of this story?
7. Observe the tone of the story for the first several pages. The effect in describing the course of the tram is harum-scarum and comic. In fact, until John Thomas drops Annie, the general effect is comic, or at least detached, as is even the beginning of the get-even scene. What is implied in the sudden shift at this point? How is the shift of tone central to the meaning of the story? Is the event one that any individual girl might have imagined possible? Is there an element of self-discovery, even a frightening one, that comes out of the episode?

Chapter Four

Setting

By the **setting** of a story, we simply mean its place and time, the physical, and sometimes spiritual, background against which the action of a narrative takes place. Even a story as short as the one at the beginning of the introduction must be *set* in a certain place and time: we have an "old, shuttered house" and the present tense suggests time (though the present tense indicates much more than time itself in the story). The elements making up a setting are generally (1) the actual geographical location, its topography, scenery, and such physical arrangements as the location of the windows and doors in a room; (2) the occupations and daily manner of living of the characters; (3) the time or period in which the action takes place, for example, the late eighteenth century in history or winter of the year; (4) the general environment of the characters, for example, religious, mental, moral, social, and emotional conditions through which characters in the story move. (Holman and Harman, *A Handbook to Literature*, 1986) But often, in an effective story, setting may figure as more than mere background. It can make things happen. It can prompt characters to act, bring them to realizations, or cause them to reveal their innermost natures, as we shall see in Kate Chopin's short story "The Storm."

First, as we have said, the idea of setting includes the physical environment of a story: a region, a landscape, a city, a village, a street, a house—a particular place or a series of places where a story occurs. (Where a story takes place is sometimes called its

Chapter Four

locale.) Places in fiction not only provide a location for an action or an event of the story but also provoke feelings in us. A sight of a green field dotted with fluttering daffodils affects us very differently from a sight of a dingy alley, a tropical jungle, or a small house crowded with furniture. In addition to a sense of beauty or ugliness, we usually build up certain associations when we put ourselves in such a scene. We are depressed by a dingy alley, not only because it is ugly, but because it may arouse a feeling, perhaps sometimes unconsciously, of poverty, misery, violence, viciousness, and the struggles of human beings who have to live under such conditions. A tropical jungle, for example, in Joseph Conrad's *Heart of Darkness*, might involve a complicated analysis: the pleasure of the colours and forms of vegetation, the discomfort of humidity, heat, and insects, a sense of mystery, horror, etc. The popularity of Sir Walter Scott's "Waverley" novels is due in part to their evocation of a romantic mood of Scotland. The English novelist Graham Greene apparently needed to visit a fresh scene in order to write a fresh novel. His ability to encapsulate the essence of an exotic setting in a single book is exemplified in *The Heart of the Matter*; his contemporary Evelyn Waugh stated that the West Africa of that book replaced the true remembered West Africa of his own experience. Such power is not uncommon: the Yorkshire moors have been romanticized because Emily Brontë wrote of them in *Wuthering Heights*, and literary tourists have visited Stoke-on-Trent in northern England because it comprises the "Five Towns" of Arnold Bennett's novels of the early twentieth century. Thus, a reader's reaction to a place is not merely based upon the way it looks, but upon the potentialities of action suggested by it (Cleanth Brooks et al, *An Approach to Literature*, 1964). Places matter greatly to many writers. For instance, the French novelist Balzac placed so much importance on physical places that sometimes, before writing a story set in a town, he would go and visit that town, select a few lanes and houses, and describe them in detail, down to their very smells. In his view the place in which an event occurs was of equal moment with the event itself, and it has a part to play (Henry James, *The Art of the Novel*, 1934). Another example is Thomas Hardy, under whom the presentation of setting assumes an unusual importance. His "Wessex" villages cast intangibly such a spell upon the villagers that once they leave their hometowns they will inevitably suffer from disasters, and the farther they are away from their hometowns, the more terrible their disasters will be. For example, in the *Tess of the D'Urbervilles*, the Vale of Blakemore was the place where Tess was born and her life was to unfold. Every contour of the surrounding hills was as personal to her as that of her relatives' faces; she loved the place and was loved in the place. The vale, far from the madding crowd of the civilized city, was as serene and pure as the inhabitants. Tess, imbued deeply with the natural hue of the vale and bound closely to this world of simplicity and seclusion, experienced her own delight and happiness though her family was poor. It was, to some extent, her departure from her native place that led to her tragedy. In *The Return of the Native*, the atmosphere of Egdon Heath prevails over the whole book; as an environment, it absorbs some and repels others of the characters: those who are absorbed achieve a somber integration with it, but those who are repelled and rebel suffer disaster.

  Sometimes an environment serves as more than a mere place to set the story. Often, it is inextricably entangled with the protagonist, and even carries strong symbolic meanings. Cathy as an image of the feminine personality, for example, in Emily Brontë's *Wuthering Heights*, is not supposed to possess the "wilderness" characteristic of masculinity and symbolized by the locales of Heathcliff and Wuthering Heights. William Faulkner, at the beginning of "A Rose for Emily," depicts Emily's house, once handsome but now "an eyesore among eyesores" amongst the surrounding gas stations. Still standing and refusing to yield its old-time splendor to the age of automobiles, the house in "its stubborn and coquettish decay" embodies the character of its owner. In some fiction,

Chapter Four

setting is closely bound with theme. In *The Scarlet Letter*, even small details afford powerful hints at the theme of the story. At the start of the story, the narrator describes a colonial jailhouse:

> Before this ugly edifice, and between it and the wheel-track of the street, was a grass-plot, much overgrown with burdock, pigweed, apple-peru, and such unsightly vegetation, which evidently found something congenial in the soil that had so early borne the black flower of civilized society, a prison. But, on one side of the portal, and rooted almost at the threshold, was a wild rosebush, covered, in this month of June, with its delicate gems, which might be imagined to offer their fragrance and fragile beauty to the prisoner as he went in, and to the condemned criminal as he came forth to his doom, in token that the deep heart of Nature could pity and be kind to him.

Apparently, the author makes a contrast between the ugly jailhouse with a tangled grass-plot overgrown with burdock and pigweed and something as beautiful as a wild rose. As the story unfolds, he will further suggest that secret sin and a pretty child may go together like pigweed and wild roses. In this artfully crafted novel, setting is intimately blended with characters, symbolism, and theme.

In addition to place, setting may crucially involve the time of the story—century, year, or even specific hour. It may matter greatly that a story takes place in the morning or at noon. The medieval background informs us differently from the twentieth century. Kennedy and Gioia note that, in *The Scarlet Letter*, the nineteenth-century author Nathaniel Hawthorne utilizes a long introduction and a vivid description of the scene at a prison door to inform us that the events in the story took place in the Puritan community of Boston of the earlier seventeenth century. (*Literature*, 1995) This setting, to which Hawthorne pays so much attention, together with our schemata concerning Puritan practice, helps us understand what happens in the novel. We can understand to some extent the agitation in the town when a woman is accused of adultery, for adultery was a flagrant defiance of church for the God-fearing New England Puritan community, and an illegitimate child was evidence of sin. Without information about the seventeenth-century Puritan back ground, a reader today may be perplexed at the agitation of the community and he/she will make no sense of the novel. The fact that the story in Hawthorne's novel took place in a time remote from our own leads us to expect different attitudes and customs, and the setting of the story, including the beliefs and assumptions of the characters, is strongly suggestive of the whole society, which is crucial to an essential understanding of *The Scarlet Letter* as a whole.

Besides place and time, setting may also include the weather, which, indeed, may be crucial in some stories, as it is in the story "The Storm" we are going to read here. In John Steinbeck's " The Chrysanthemums" (Chapter Seven), the story begins with a fog that has sealed off a valley from the rest of the world. At the very beginning of Dostoevsky's *Crime and Punishment*, the story unfolds on a "hot evening at the beginning of July," one of the "White Nights" of the year that virtually make people in St Petersburg wakeful and restless. Climate seems as substantial as any character in William Faulkner's "Dry September. " After sixty-two rainless days, a long-unbroken spell of late-summer heat has frayed every nerve in a small town and caused a hotheaded supremacist, the main character, to feel more and more irritated. And when a false report circulates that a woman has been raped by a black man, the rumor, like a match flung into a dry field, ignites explosive rage among the community. It provokes a lynching, as the weather, someone remarks, is "enough to make a man do anything. " Evidently, to understand the story, we have to recognize its locale, a small town in Mississippi, and the time, the 1930s. However, the infernal heat wave matters, too. To make a full sense of Faulkner's story, we have to take in

Chapter Four

the setting in its entirety.

When setting dominates, or when a piece of fiction is written largely to present the manners and customs of a locality, the writing is often called **local colour writing** or **regionalism** and the writer, **a regional writer**. A regional writer usually sets his/her stories in one geographic area and tries to bring it alive to readers everywhere. Thomas Hardy, in his portrayal of life in Wessex, wrote regional novels. Arnold Bennett's novels of the "Five Towns" are markedly regional. William Faulkner, known as a distinguished regional writer, almost always set his novels and stories in his native Mississippi. Kate Chopin, though born in St. Louis, became known for writing about Louisiana in many of her short stories and in her novel *The Awakening*. The sequence of four novels that Hugh Walpole began with *Rogue Herries* was the result of his desire to do homage to Cumberland in England, where he had elected to live. In addition, the work of Willa Cather, Ellen Glasgow, and Robert Penn Warren also merit distinction. However, there is often something arbitrary in calling an author a regional writer. The label generally has a political tinge. In a sense, we might think of James Joyce as a regional writer, since all his fiction takes place in the city of Dublin, but we usually call him an Irish writer.

The setting of a novel is not always drawn from a real-life locale. Literary artists sometimes prefer to create the totality of their fiction—the setting as well as characters and their actions. The future envisaged in H. G. Wells's novels and in Aldous Huxley's *Brave New World* are recognized in an age that the authors did not live to see. In the Russian expatriate Vladimir Nabokov's *Ada*, there is an entirely new space-time continuum. J. R. R. Tolkien in his *Lord of the Rings* created an "alternative world" that appeals greatly to many who are not satisfied with the existing one. The creation of setting can be a magical fictional gift in a novelist or storyteller. But whatever the setting of his/her work, a true novelist is concerned with making an environment credible for his/her characters and their actions and in accord with the development of the plot.

In some stories, a writer seems to draw a setting mainly to evoke atmosphere. In such a story, setting starts us feeling whatever the storyteller would have us feel. Thus atmosphere is a metaphor for a feeling or an impression which we cannot, perhaps, readily attach to some tangible cause. We say that an old farmhouse set among large maples, on a green lawn, has an atmosphere of peace. Here what we mean is that the house, by reason of the look of quietness and by reason of a number of pleasant associations we have with the kind of life lived there, stirs a certain reaction in us which we do not attach to any single incident or object, but generally to the whole scene. In the same way we may say that the setting of a story contributes to defining its atmosphere. For instance, in "The Tell-Tale Heart," Poe's setting the action in an old, dark, lantern-lit house greatly contributes to the reader's sense of unease, and so helps to build the story's effectiveness. Another example is Lawrence's "The Horse Dealer's Daughter," the description at the beginning of which contributes much to the atmosphere of the story.

But it is a mistake to say that the atmosphere of a piece of fiction depends on the setting alone. (As illustrated in Shakespeare's *Hamlet*, the dialogue at the very beginning of the play helps powerfully to establish the atmosphere of uncertainty, in addition to the setting—the cold midnight castle.) The vocabulary, the figures of speech, and the rhythm of the sentence also help define the general atmosphere, for by these factors the writer manages to control the kind of associations that come to the reader's mind. Atmosphere also depends on character and action. In short, we may say that the **atmosphere** of fiction is the pervasive, general feeling, generated by a number of factors (setting, character, action, and style) that is characteristic of a given story or novel (Cleanth Brooks et al, *An Approach to Literature*, 1964).

Chapter Four

The Storm

by Kate Chopin, 1898

I

The leaves were so still that even Bibi thought it was going to rain. Bobinôt, who was accustomed to converse on terms of perfect equality with his little son, called the child's attention to certain somber clouds that were rolling with sinister intention from the west, accompanied by a sullen, threatening roar. They were at Friedheimer's store and decided to remain there till the storm had passed. They sat within the door on two empty kegs. Bibi was four years old and looked very wise.

"Mama'll be 'fraid, yes," he suggested with blinking eyes.

"She'll shut the house. Maybe she got Sylvie helpin' her this evenin'," Bobinôt responded reassuringly.

"No; she ent got Sylvie. Sylvie was helpin' her yistiday," piped Bibi.

Bobinôt arose and going across to the counter purchased a can of shrimps, of which Calixta was very fond. Then he returned to his perch on the keg and sat stolidly holding the can of shrimps while the storm burst. It shook the wooden store and seemed to be ripping great furrows in the distant field. Bibi laid his little hand on his father's knee and was not afraid.

II

Calixta, at home, felt no uneasiness for their safety. She sat at a side window sewing furiously on a sewing machine. She was greatly occupied and did not notice the approaching storm. But she felt very warm and often stopped to mop her face on which the perspiration gathered in beads. She unfastened her white sacque at the throat. It began to grow dark, and suddenly realizing the situation she got up hurriedly and went about closing windows and doors.

Out on the small front gallery she had hung Bobinôt's Sunday clothes to air and she hastened out to gather them before the rain fell. As she stepped outside, Alcée Laballière rode in at the gate. She had not seen him very often since her marriage, and never alone. She stood there with Bobinôt's coat in her hands, and the big rain drops began to fall. Alcée rode his horse under the shelter of a side projection where the chickens had huddled and there were plows and a harrow piled up in the corner.

"May I come and wait on your gallery till the storm is over, Calixta?" he asked.

"Come 'long in, M'sieur Alcée."

10   His voice and her own startled her as if from a trance, and she seized Bobinôt's vest. Alcée, mounting to the porch, grabbed the trousers and snatched Bibi's braided jacket that was about to be carried away by a sudden gust of wind. He expressed an intention to remain outside, but it was soon apparent that he might as well have been out in the open: the water beat in upon the boards in driving sheets, and he went inside, closing the door after him. It was even necessary to put something beneath the door to keep the water out.

"My! what a rain! It's good two years sence it rain like that," exclaimed Calixta as she rolled up a piece of bagging and Alcée helped her to thrust it beneath the crack.

She was a little fuller of figure than five years before when she married; but she had lost nothing of her vivacity. Her blue eyes still retained their melting quality; and her yellow hair, dishevelled by the wind and rain, kinked more stubbornly than ever about her ears and temples.

The rain beat upon the low, shingled roof with a force and clatter that threatened to break an entrance and deluge them there. They were in the dining room—the sitting room—the general utility room. Adjoining was her bed room, with Bibi's couch along

Chapter Four

side her own. The door stood open, and the room with its white, monumental bed, its closed shutters, looked dim and mysterious.

Alcée flung himself into a rocker and Calixta nervously began to gather up from the floor the lengths of a cotton sheet which she had been sewing.

15 "If this keeps up, *Dieu sait*[1] if the levees goin' to stan' it!" she exclaimed.

"What have you got to do with the levees?"

"I got enough to do! An' there's Bobinôt with Bibi out in that storm—if he only didn' left Friedheimer's!"

"Let us hope, Calixta, that Bobinôt's got sense enough to come in out of a cyclone."

She went and stood at the window with a greatly disturbed look on her face. She wiped the frame that was clouded with moisture. It was stiflingly hot. Alcée got up and joined her at the window, looking over her shoulder. The rain was coming down in sheets obscuring the view of far-off cabins and enveloping the distant wood in a gray mist. The playing of the lightning was incessant. A bolt struck a tall chinaberry tree at the edge of the field. It filled all visible space with a blinding glare and the crash seemed to invade the very boards they stood upon.

20 Calixta put her hands to her eyes, and with a cry, staggered backward. Alcée's arm encircled her, and for an instant he drew her close and spasmodically to him.

"*Bonté*![2]" she cried, releasing herself from his encircling arm and retreating from the window, "the house'll go next! If I only knew w'ere Bibi was!" She would not compose herself; she would not be seated. Alcée clasped her shoulders and looked into her face. The contact of her warm, palpitating body when he had unthinkingly drawn her into his arms, had aroused all the old-time infatuation and desire for her flesh.

"Calixta," he said, "don't be frightened. Nothing can

---

[1] Dieu sait: God only knows.
[2] Bonté!: Heavens!

happen. The house is too low to be struck, with so many tall trees standing about. There! aren't you going to be quiet? say, aren't you?" He pushed her hair back from her face that was warm and steaming. Her lips were as red and moist as pomegranate seed. Her white neck and a glimpse of her full, firm bosom disturbed him powerfully. As she glanced up at him the fear in her liquid blue eyes had given place to a drowsy gleam that unconsciously betrayed a sensuous desire. He looked down into her eyes and there was nothing for him to do but gather her lips in a kiss. It reminded him of Assumption[1].

"Do you remember—in Assumption, Calixta?" he asked in a low voice broken by passion. Oh! she remembered; for in Assumption he had kissed her and kissed and kissed her; until his senses would well nigh fail, and to save her he would resort to a desperate flight. If she was not an immaculate dove in those days, she was still inviolate; a passionate creature whose very defenselessness had made her defense, against which his honor forbade him to prevail. Now—well, now—her lips seemed in a manner free to be tasted, as well as her round, white throat and her whiter breasts.

They did not heed the crashing torrents, and the roar of the elements made her laugh as she lay in his arms. She was a revelation in that dim, mysterious chamber; as white as the couch she lay upon. Her firm, elastic flesh that was knowing for the first time its birthright, was like a creamy lily that the sun invites to contribute its breath and perfume to the undying life of the world.

25   The generous abundance of her passion, without guile or trickery, was like a white flame which penetrated and found response in depths of his own sensuous nature that had never yet been reached.

  When he touched her breasts they gave themselves up in quivering ecstasy, inviting his lips. Her mouth was a fountain of

---

[1] Assumption: a parish west of New Orleans.

delight. And when he possessed her, they seemed to swoon together at the very borderland of life's mystery.

He stayed cushioned upon her, breathless, dazed, enervated, with his heart beating like a hammer upon her. With one hand she clasped his head, her lips lightly touching his forehead. The other hand stroked with a soothing rhythm his muscular shoulders.

The growl of the thunder was distant and passing away. The rain beat softly upon the shingles, inviting them to drowsiness and sleep. But they dared not yield.

The rain was over; and the sun was turning the glistening green world into a palace of gems. Calixta, on the gallery, watched Alcée ride away. He turned and smiled at her with a beaming face; and she lifted her pretty chin in the air and laughed aloud.

III

Bobinôt and Bibi, trudging home, stopped without at the cistern to make themselves presentable.

"My! Bibi, w'at will yo'mama say! You ought to be ashame'. You oughtn' put on those good pants. Look at 'em! An' that mud on yo' collar! How you got that mud on yo' collar, Bibi? I never saw such a boy!" Bibi was the picture of pathetic resignation. Bobinôt was the embodiment of serious solicitude as he strove to remove from his own person and his son's the signs of their tramp over heavy roads and through wet fields. He scraped the mud off Bibi's bare legs and feet with a stick and carefully removed all traces from his heavy brogans. Then, prepared for the worst—the meeting with an overscrupulous housewife, they entered cautiously at the back door.

Calixta was preparing supper. She had set the table and was dripping coffee at the hearth. She sprang up as they came in.

"Oh, Bobinôt! You back! My! but I was uneasy. W'ere you been during the rain? An' Bibi? he ain't wet? he ain't hurt?" She had clasped Bibi and was kissing him effusively. Bobinôt's explanations and apologies which he had been composing all along the way, died on his lips as Calixta felt him to see if he were dry, and seemed to express nothing but satisfaction at their safe return.

"I brought you some shrimps, Calixta," offered Bobinôt, hauling the can from his ample side pocket and laying it on the table.

35 "Shrimps! Oh, Bobinôt! you too good fo' anything!" and she gave him a smacking kiss on the cheek that resounded. "*J'vous reponds*[1], we'll have feas' to night! umph-umph!"

Bobinôt and Bibi began to relax and enjoy themselves, and when the three seated themselves at table they laughed much and so loud that anyone might have heard them as far away as Laballière's.

IV

Alcée Laballière wrote to his wife, Clarisse, that night. It was a loving letter, full of tender solicitude. He told her not to hurry back, but if she and the babies liked it at Biloxi, to stay a month longer. He was getting on nicely; and though he missed them, he was willing to bear the separation a while longer—realizing that their health and pleasure were the first things to be considered.

V

As for Clarisse, she was charmed upon receiving her husband's letter. She and the babies were doing well. The society was agreeable; many of her old friends and acquaintances were at the bay. And the first free breath since her marriage seemed to restore the pleasant liberty of her maiden days. Devoted as she was to her husband, their intimate conjugal life was something which she was more than willing to forego for a while.

So the storm passed and everyone was happy.

---

[1] *J'vous reponds*: Let me tell you.

Chapter Four

 Discussion

Reading Mrs. Chopin's stories one recognizes the range and depth of Mrs. Chopin's perception, her compassion, and her remarkable ability to create a scene, a person, an emotion with deft verbal economy. "The Storm" is an exquisitely carved cameo, as much to be admired for the artistry of its restraint as for the boldness (and chuckling good humor) of its glimpse into what Mrs. Chopin describes as a "generous abundance" of adulterous passion, during which Alcée's hand "touched [Calixta's] breasts" which "gave themselves up in quivering ecstasy, inviting his lips," while, passion spent, she "stroked with a soothing rhythm his muscular shoulders," Calixta's "mouth was a fountain of delight," and so is this brief tale of a storm which blew perilously hard, but "passed and every one was happy." There is no moral, no theme, just a fleeting glimpse of something which perhaps should not have been, but was.

Truth was not single to Kate Chopin: it expressed itself in myriad guises. "Story-telling," she explained, " — at least to me — is the spontaneous expression of impressions gathered goodness knows where." No attempt to describe her as programmatic finally succeeds: "consistency," she once wrote, "is a pompous and wearisome burden to bear." It is correct enough and perhaps necessary to say that she was in revolt against tradition and authority, that she saw sex as something which could or could not be conjoined with love and/or marriage. and that she daringly — how daringly for her time and place! — "undertook to give the unsparing truth about woman's submerged life" (the whole truth and nothing but?). That however does not seem enough. Programs are too often what people of a later generation superimpose on artists. When Mrs. Chopin becomes tendentious, as she sometimes does, she loses much of her charm, her controlled skill. When she tells of people doing things that people do, she is a compelling advocate — not of the things done, but of people.

She was feminine to the core, a wife, a mother, and a protester. But she was too complete a human being to be activist. The liberation she sought was only incidentally and symbolically sexual. That was something here to stay. It stood for and emphasized differences at the same time that it pointed toward one experience that men and women could share, in ecstasy leading toward joy or distress.

(Lewis Leary)

Questions

1. An **inference** is a judgment of conclusion based on evidence. Not all information about the setting of a story is stated directly by the author. You must also make inference about the setting from the clues given by the author just as you do about the other elements of a story. Exactly where does this story take place? How can you tell?
2. What circumstances introduced in Part I turn out to have a profound effect on events in the story?
3. What details in the story emphasize the fact that Bobinôt loves his wife? What details reveal that he comprehend her nature imperfectly?
4. What meaning do you find in the title "the Storm"?
5. In the story as a whole, how do setting and plot reinforce each other?
6. What general attitudes towards love, marriage, and sex does Chopin imply? Cite evidence to support your answer. If you are informed that this story was written about a hundred years ago, does this have any effect on your understanding of the story?

Chapter Four

The Three Strangers
by Thomas Hardy, 1883

    Among the few features of agricultural England which retain an appearance but little modified by the lapse of centuries may be reckoned the high, grassy and furzy downs, coombs, or eweleases, as they are indifferently called, that fill a large area of certain counties in the south and southwest. If any mark of human occupation is met with hereon, it usually takes the form of the solitary cottage of some shepherd.

    Fifty years ago such a lonely cottage stood on such a down, and may possibly be standing there now. In spite of its loneliness, however, the spot, by actual measurement, was not more than five miles from a county-town. Yet that affected it little. Five miles of irregular upland, during the long inimical seasons, with their sleets, snows, rains, and mists, afford withdrawing space enough to isolate a Timon or a Nebuchadnezzar; much less, in fair weather, to please that less repellent tribe, the poets, philosophers, artists, and others who "conceive and meditate of pleasant things."

    Some old earthen camp or barrow, some clump of trees, at least some starved fragment of ancient hedge is usually taken advantage of in the erection of these forlorn dwellings. But, in the present case, such a kind of shelter had been disregarded. Higher Crowstairs, as the house was called, stood quite detached and undefended. The only reason for its precise situation seemed to be the crossing of two footpaths at right angles hard by, which may have crossed there and thus for a good five hundred years. Hence the house was exposed to the elements on all sides. But, though the wind up here blew unmistakably when it did blow, and the rain hit hard whenever it fell, the various weathers of the winter season were not quite so formidable on the coomb as they were imagined to be by dwellers on low ground. The raw rimes were not so pernicious as in the hollows, and the frosts were scarcely so severe. When the shepherd and his family who tenanted the house were pitied for their sufferings from the exposure, they said that upon the whole they were less inconvenienced by "wuzzes and flames" (hoarses and phlegms) than when they had lived by the stream of a snug neighboring valley.

The night of March 28, 182- was precisely one of the nights that were wont to call forth these expressions of commiseration. The level rainstorm smote walls, slopes, and hedges like the clothyard shafts of Senlac and Crecy. Such sheep and outdoor animals as had no shelter stood with their buttocks to the winds; while the tails of little birds trying to roost on some scraggy thorn were blown inside-out like umbrellas. The gable-end of the cottage was stained with wet, and the eavesdroppings flapped against the wall. Yet never was commiseration for the shepherd more misplaced. For that cheerful rustic was entertaining a large party in glorification of the christening of his second girl.

5 The guests had arrived before the rain began to fall, and they were all now assembled in the chief or living room of the dwelling. A glance into the apartment at eight o'clock on this eventful evening would have resulted in the opinion that it was as cozy and comfortable a nook as could be wished for in boisterous weather. The calling of its inhabitant was proclaimed by a number of highly polished sheep-crooks without stems that were hung ornamentally over the fireplace, the curl of each shining crook varying from the antiquated type engraved in the patriarchal pictures of old family Bibles to the most approved fashion of the last local sheep-fair. The room was lighted by half-a-dozen candles, having wicks only a trifle smaller than the grease which enveloped them, in candle-sticks that were never used but at high-days, holy-days, and family feasts. The lights were scattered about the room, two of them standing on the chimney-piece. This position of candles was in itself significant. Candles on the chimney-piece always meant a party.

On the hearth, in front of a back-brand to give substance, blazed a fire of thorns, that crackled "like the laughter of the fool."

Nineteen persons were gathered here. Of these, five women, wearing gowns of various bright hues, sat in chairs along the wall;

Chapter Four

girls shy and not shy filled the window-bench; four men, including Charley Jake the hedge-carpenter, Elijah New the parish-clerk, and John Pitcher, a neighboring dairyman, the shepherd's father-in-law, lolled in the settle; a young man and maid, who were blushing over tentative *pourparlers*[1] on a life-companionship, sat beneath the corner-cupboard; and an elderly engaged man of fifty or upward moved restlessly about from spots where his betrothed was not to the spot where she was. Enjoyment was pretty general, and so much the more prevailed in being unhampered by conventional restrictions. Absolute confidence in each other's good opinion begat perfect ease, while the finishing stroke of manner, amounting to a truly princely serenity, was lent to the majority by the absence of any expression or trait denoting that they wished to get on in the world, enlarge their minds, or do any eclipsing thing whatever—which nowadays so generally nips the bloom and *bonhomie*[2] of all except the two extremes of the social scale.

Shepherd Fennel had married well, his wife being a dairyman's daughter from a vale at a distance, who brought fifty guineas in her pocket—and kept them there, till they should be required for ministering to the needs of a coming family. This frugal woman had been somewhat exercised as to the character that should be given to the gathering. A sit-still party had its advantages; but an undisturbed position of ease in chairs and settles was apt to lead on the men to such an unconscionable deal of toping that they would sometimes fairly drink the house dry. A dancing-party was the alternative; but this, while avoiding the foregoing objection on the score of good drink, had a counterbalancing disadvantage in the matter of good victuals, the ravenous appetites engendered by the exercise causing immense havoc in the buttery. Shepherdess Fennel fell back upon the intermediate plan of mingling short dances with short periods of talk and singing, so as to hinder any ungovernable rage in either. But this scheme was entirely confined to her own

---

[1] pourparler: an informal preliminary discussion.
[2] bonhomie: good nature.

gentle mind; the shepherd himself was in the mood to exhibit the most reckless phases of hospitality.

The fiddler was a boy of those parts, about twelve years of age, who had a wonderful dexterity in jigs and reels, though his fingers were so small and short as to necessitate a constant shifting for the high notes, from which he scrambled back to the first position with sounds not of unmixed purity of tone. At seven the shrill tweedle-dee of this youngster had begun, accompanied by a booming ground-bass from Elijah New, the parish-clerk, who had thoughtfully brought with him his favorite musical instrument, the serpent. Dancing was instantaneous, Mrs. Fennel privately enjoining the players on no account to let the dance exceed the length of a quarter of an hour.

10 But Elijah and the boy, in the excitement of their position, quite forgot the injunction. Moreover, Oliver Giles, a man of seventeen, one of the dancers, who was enamored of his partner, a fair girl of thirty-three rolling years, had recklessly handed a new crown-piece to the musicians, as a bribe to keep going as long as they had muscle and wind. Mrs. Fennel, seeing the steam begin to generate on the countenances of her guests, crossed over and touched the fiddler's elbow and put her hand on the serpent's mouth. But they took no notice, and fearing she might lose her character of genial hostess if she were to interfere too markedly, she retired and sat down helpless. And so the dance whizzed on with cumulative fury, the performers moving in their planet-like courses, direct and retrograde, from apogee to perigee, till the hand of the well-kicked clock at the bottom of the room had traveled over the circumference of an hour.

While these cheerful events were in course of enactment within Fennel's pastoral dwelling, an incident having considerable bearing on the party had occurred in the gloomy night without. Mrs. Fennel's concern about the growing fierceness of the dance corresponded in point of time with the ascent of a human figure to the solitary hill of Higher Crowstairs from the direction of the distant town. This personage strode on through the rain without a pause, following the little-worn path which, further on in its course, skirted the shepherd's cottage.

It was nearly the time of full moon, and on this account, though the sky was lined with a uniform sheet of dripping cloud, ordinary objects out of doors were readily visible. The sad wan light revealed the lonely pedestrian to be a man of supple frame; his gait suggested that he had somewhat passed the period of perfect and instinctive agility, though not so far as to be otherwise than rapid of motion when occasion required. At a rough guess, he might have been about forty years of age. He appeared tall, but a recruiting sergeant, or other person accustomed to the judging of men's heights by the eye, would have discerned that this was chiefly owing to his gauntness, and that he was not more than five-feet-eight or nine.

Notwithstanding the regularity of his tread, there was caution in it, as in that of one who mentally feels his way; and despite the fact that it was not a black coat nor a dark garment of any sort that he wore, there was something about him which suggested that he naturally belonged to the black-coated tribes of men. His clothes were of fustian, and his boots hobnailed, yet in his progress he showed not the mud-accustomed bearing of hobnailed and fustianed peasantry.

By the time that he had arrived abreast of the shepherd's premises the rain came down, or rather came along, with yet more determined violence. The outskirts of the little settlement partially broke the force of wind and rain, and this induced him to stand still. The most salient of the shepherd's domestic erections was an empty sty at the forward corner of his hedgeless garden, for in these latitudes the principle of masking the homelier features of your establishment by a conventional frontage was unknown. The traveler's eye was attracted to this small building by the pallid shine of the wet slates that covered it. He turned aside, and, finding it empty, stood under the pent-roof for shelter.

15   While he stood, the boom of the serpent within the adjacent house, and the lesser strains of the fiddler, reached the spot as an

accompaniment to the surging hiss of the flying rain on the sod, its louder beating on the cabbage-leaves of the garden on the eight or the beehives just discernible by the path, and its dripping from the eaves into a row of buckets and pans that had been placed under the walls of the cottage. For at Higher Crowstairs, as at all such elevated domiciles, the grand difficulty of housekeeping was an insufficiency of water; and a casual rainfall was utilized by turning out, as catchers, every utensil that the house contained. Some queer stories might be told of the contrivances for economy in suds and dishwaters that are absolutely necessitated in upland habitations during the droughts of summer. But at this season there were no such exigencies; a mere acceptance of what the skies bestowed was sufficient for an abundant store.

At last the notes of the serpent ceased and the house was silent. This cessation of activity aroused the solitary pedestrian from the reverie into which he had lapsed, and, emerging from the shed, with an apparently new intention, he walked up the path to the house-door. Arrived here, his first act was to kneel down on a large stone beside the row of vessels, and to drink a copious draught from one of them. Having quenched his thirst he rose and lifted his hand to knock, but paused with his eye upon the panel. Since the dark surface of the wood revealed absolutely nothing, it was evident that he must be mentally looking through the door, as if he wished to measure thereby all the possibilities that a house of this sort might include, and how they might bear upon the question of his entry.

In his indecision he turned and surveyed the scene around. Not a soul was anywhere visible. The garden-path stretched downward from his feet, gleaming like the track of a snail; the roof of the little well (mostly dry), the well-cover, the top rail of the gardengate, were varnished with the same dull liquid glaze; while, far away in the vale, a faint whiteness of more than usual extent showed that the rivers were high in the meads. Beyond all this winked a few bleared lamplights through the beating drops—lights

Chapter Four

that denoted the situation of the county-town from which he had appeared to come. The absence of all notes of life in that direction seemed to clinch his intentions, and he knocked at the door.

Within, a desultory chat had taken the place of movement and musical sound. The hedge-carpenter was suggesting a song to the company, which nobody just then was inclined to undertake, so that the knock afforded a not unwelcome diversion.

"Walk in!" said the shepherd promptly.

The latch clicked upward, and out of the night our pedestrian appeared upon the doormat. The shepherd arose, snuffed two of the nearest candles, and turned to look at him.

Their light disclosed that the stranger was dark in complexion and not unprepossessing as to feature. His hat, which for a moment he did not remove, hung low over his eyes, without concealing that they were large, open, and determined, moving with a flash rather than a glance round the room. He seemed pleased with his survey, and, baring his shaggy head, said, in a rich deep voice, "The rain is so heavy, friends, that I ask leave to come in and rest awhile."

"To be sure, stranger," said the shepherd. "And faith, you've been lucky in choosing your time, for we are having a bit of a fling for a glad cause—though, to be sure, a man could hardly wish that glad cause to happen more than once a year."

"Nor less," spoke up a woman. "For 'tis best to get your family over and done with, as soon as you can, so as to be all the earlier out of the fag o't."

"And what may be this glad cause?" asked the stranger.

"A birth and christening," said the shepherd.

The stranger hoped his host might not be made unhappy, either by too many or too few of such episodes, and being invited by a gesture to a pull at the mug, he readily acquiesced. His manner, which, before entering, had been so dubious, was now altogether that of a careless and candid man.

"Late to be traipsing athwart this coomb—hey?" said the

engaged man of fifty.

"Late it is, master, as you say. —I'll take a seat in the chimney-corner, if you have nothing to urge against it, ma'am; for I am a little moist on the side that was next the rain."

Mrs. Shepherd Fennel assented, and made room for the selfinvited comer, who, having got completely inside the chimneycorner, stretched out his legs and his arms with the expansiveness of a person quite at home.

30 "Yes, I am rather cracked in the vamp," he said freely, seeing that the eyes of the shep-herd's wife fell upon his boots, "and I am not well fitted either. I have had some rough times lately, and have been forced to pick up what I can get in the way of wearing, but I must find a suit better fit for working-days when I reach home."

"One of hereabouts?" she inquired.

"Not quite that—further up the country."

"I thought so. And so be I; and by your tongue you come from my neighborhood."

"But you would hardly have heard of me," he said quickly. "My time would be long before yours, ma'am, you see."

35 This testimony to the youthfulness of his hostess had the effect of stopping her cross-examination.

"There is only one thing more wanted to make me happy," continued the new-comer. "And that is a little baccy, which I am sorry to say I am out of."

"I'll fill your pipe," said the shepherd.

"I must ask you to lend me a pipe likewise."

"A smoke, and no pipe about 'ee?"

40 "I have dropped it somewhere on the road."

The shepherd filled and handed him a new clay pipe, saying, as he did so, "Hand me your baccy-box—I'll fill that too, now I am about it."

The man went through the movement of searching his pockets.

"Lost that too?" said his entertainer, with some surprise.

Chapter Four

"I am afraid so," said the man with some confusion. "Give it to me in a screw of paper." Lighting his pipe at the candle with a suction that drew the whole flame into the bowl, he resettled himself in the corner and bent his looks upon the faint steam from his damp legs, as if he wished to say no more.

45　　　Meanwhile the general body of guests had been taking little notice of this visitor by reason of an absorbing discussion in which they were engaged with the band about a tune for the next dance. The matter being settled, they were about to stand up when an interruption came in the shape of another knock at the door.

At sound of the same the man in the chimney-corner took up the poker and began stirring the brands as if doing it thoroughly were the one aim of his existence; and a second time the shepherd said, "Walk in!" In a moment another man stood upon the straw-woven doormat. He too was a stranger.

This individual was one of a type radically different from the first. There was more of the commonplace in his manner, and a certain jovial cosmopolitanism sat upon his features. He was several years older than the first arrival, his hair being slightly frosted, his eyebrows bristly, and his whiskers cut back from his cheeks. His face was rather full and flabby, and yet it was not altogether a face without power. A few grog-blossoms marked the neigh-borhood of his nose. He flung back his long drab greatcoat, reveal-ing that beneath it he wore a suit of cinder-gray shade throughout, large heavy seals, of some metal or other that would take a polish, dangling from his fob as his only personal ornament. Shaking the water-drops from his low-crowned glazed hat, he said, "I must ask for a few minutes' shelter, comrades, or I shall be wetted to my skin before I get to Casterbridge."

"Make yourself at home, master," said the shepherd, perhaps a trifle less heartily than on the first occasion. Not that Fennel had the least tinge of niggardliness in his composition; but the room was far from large, spare chairs were not numerous, and damp companions were not altogether desirable at close quarters for the women and girls in their bright-colored gowns.

However, the second comer, after taking off his greatcoat, and hanging his hat on a nail in one of the ceiling-beams as if he had been specially invited to put it there, advanced and sat down at the table. This had been pushed so closely into the chimney-corner, to give all available room to the dancers, that its inner edge grazed the elbow of the man who had ensconced himself by the fire; and thus the two strangers were brought into close companionship. They nodded to each other by way of breaking the ice of unacquaintance, and the first stranger handed his neighbor the family mug—a huge vessel of brown ware, having its upper edge worn away like a threshold by the rub of whole generations of thirsty lips that had gone the way of all flesh, and bearing the following inscription burnt upon its rotund side in yellow letters:

THERE IS NO FUN UNTILL I CUM

The other man, nothing loth, raised the mug to his lips, and drank on, and on, and on—till a curious blueness overspread the countenance of the shepherd's wife, who had regarded with no little surprise the first stranger's free offer to the second of what did not belong to him to dispense.

"I knew it!" said the toper to the shepherd with much satisfaction. "When I walked up your garden before coming in, and saw the hives all of a row, I said to myself, 'Where there's bees there's honey, and where there's honey there's mead.' But mead of such a truly comfortable sort as this I really didn't expect to meet in my older days." He took yet another pull at the mug, till it assumed an ominous elevation.

"Glad you enjoy it!" said the shepherd warmly.

"It is goodish mead," assented Mrs. Fennel, with an absence of enthusiasm which seemed to say that it was possible to buy praise for one's cellar at too heavy a price. "It is trouble enough to make—and really I hardly think we shall make any more. For honey

Chapter Four

sells well, and we ourselves can make shift with a drop o' small mead and metheglin for common use from the comb-washings."

"O, but you'll never have the heart!" reproachfully cried the stranger in cinder-gray, after taking up the mug a third time and setting it down empty. "I love mead, when 'tis old like this, as I love to go to church o' Sundays, or to relieve the needy any day of the week."

"Ha, ha, ha!" said the man in the chimney-corner, who, in spite of the taciturnity induced by the pipe of tobacco, could not or would not refrain from this slight testimony to his comrade's humor.

55　　Now the old mead of those days, brewed of the purest first year or maiden honey, four pounds to the gallon—with its due complement of white of eggs, cinnamon, ginger, cloves, mace, rosemary, yeast, and processes of working, bottling and cellaring— tasted remarkably strong; but it did not taste so strong as it actually was. Hence, presently, the stranger in cinder-gray at the table, moved by its creeping influence, unbuttoned his waistcoat, threw himself back in his chair, spread his legs, and made his presence felt in various ways.

"Well, well, as I say," he resumed, "I am going to Casterbridge, and to Casterbridge I must go. I should have been almost there by this time; but the rain drove me into your dwelling, and I'm not sorry for it."

"You don't live in Casterbridge?" said the shepherd.

"Not as yet; though I shortly mean to move there."

"Going to set up in trade, perhaps?"

60　　"No, no," said the shepherd's wife. "It is easy to see that the gentleman is rich, and don't want to work at anything."

The cinder-gray stranger paused, as if to consider whether he would accept that definition of himself. He presently rejected it by answering, "Rich is not quite the word for me, dame. I do work, and I must work. And even if I only get to Casterbridge by midnight I must begin work there at eight tomorrow morning.

— 155 —

Yes, het or wet, blow or snow, famine or sword, my day's work tomorrow must be done."

"Poor man! Then, in spite o' seeming, you be worse off than we?" replied the shepherd's wife.

"'Tis the nature of my trade, men and maidens. 'Tis the nature of my trade more than my poverty.... But really and truly I must up and off, or I shan't get a lodging in the town." However, the speaker did not move, and directly added, "There's time for one more draught of friendship before I go; and I'd perform it at once if the mug were not dry."

"Here's a mug o' small," said Mrs. Fennel. "Small, we call it, though to be sure 'tis only the first wash o' the combs."

"No," said the stranger disdainfully. "I won't spoil your first kindness by partaking o' your second."

"Certainly not." broke in Fennel. "We don't increase and multiply every day, and I'll fill the mug again." He went away to the dark place under the stairs where the barrel stood. The shepherdess followed him.

"Why should you do this?" she said reproachfully, as soon as they were alone. "He's emptied it once, though it held enough for ten people; and now he's not contented wi' the small, but must needs call for more o' the strong! And a stranger unbeknown to any of us. For my part, I don't like the look o' the man at all."

"But he's in the house, my honey; and 'tis a wet night, and a christening. Daze it, what's a cup of mead more or less? There'll be plenty more next bee-burning."

"Very well—this time, then," she answered, looking wistfully at the barrel. "But what is the man's calling, and where is he one of, that he should come in and join us like this?"

"I don't know. I'll ask him again."

The catastrophe of having the mug drained dry at one pull by the stranger in cinder-gray was effectually guarded against this time by Mrs. Fennel. She poured out his allowance in a small cup, keeping the large one at a discreet distance from him. When he had

Chapter Four

tossed off his portion the shepherd renewed his inquiry about the stranger's occupation.

The latter did not immediately reply, and the man in the chimney-corner, with sudden demonstrativeness, said, "Anybody may know my trade—I'm a wheelwright."

"A very good trade for these parts," said the shepherd.

"And anybody may know mine—if they've the sense to find it out," said the stranger in cinder-gray.

"You may generally tell what a man is by his claws," observed the hedge-carpenter, looking at his own hands. "My fingers be as full of thorns as an old pincushion is of pins."

The hands of the man in the chimney-corner instinctively sought the shade, and he gazed into the fire as he resumed his pipe. The man at the table took up the hedge-carpenter's remark, and added smartly, "True; but the oddity of my trade is that, instead of setting a mark upon me, it sets a mark upon my customers."

No observation being offered by anybody in elucidation of this enigma, the shepherd's wife once more called for a song. The same obstacles presented themselves as at the former time—one had no voice, another had forgotten the first verse. The stranger at the table, whose soul had now risen to a good working temperature, relieved the difficulty by exclaiming that, to start the company, he would sing himself. Thrusting one thumb into the arm-hole of his waistcoat, he waved the other hand in the air, and, with an extemporizing gaze at the shining sheep-crooks above the mantelpiece, began:

> *O my trade it is the rarest one,*
>   *Simple shepherds all—*
> *For my customers I tie, and take them up on high,*
>   *And waft 'em to a far countree!*

The room was silent when he had finished the verse—with one exception, that of the man in the chimney-corner, who, at the singer's word, "Chorus!" joined him in a deep bass voice of musical relish:

  And waft 'em to a far countree!

  Oliver Giles, John Pitcher the dairyman, the parish-clerk, the engaged man of fifty, the row of young women against the wall, seemed lost in thought not of the gayest kind. The shepherd looked meditatively on the ground, the shepherdess gazed keenly at the singer, and with some suspicion; she was doubting whether this stranger were merely singing an old song from recollection, or was composing one there and then for the occasion. All were as perplexed at the obscure revelation as the guests at Belshazzar's Feast, except the man in the chimney-corner, who quietly said, "Second verse, stranger," and smoked on.

  The singer thoroughly moistened himself from his lips inwards, and went on with the next stanza as requested:

  My tools are but common ones,
          Simple shepherds all—
  My tools are no sight to see:
A little hempen string, and a post whereon to swing
  Are implements enough for me!

  Shepherd Fennel glanced round. There was no longer any doubt that the stranger was answering his question rhythmically. The guests one and all started back with suppressed exclamations. The young woman engaged to the man of fifty fainted half-way, and would have proceeded, but finding him wanting in alacrity for catching her she sat down trembling.

  "O, he's the—!" whispered the people in the background, mentioning the name of an ominous public officer. "He's come to do it! 'Tis to be at Casterbridge jail tomorrow—the man for sheep-stealing—the poor clock-maker we heard of, who used to live away at Shottsford and had no work to do—Timothy Summers, whose family were a-starving, and so he went out of Shottsford by the high-road, and took a sheep in open daylight, defying the farmer and the farmer's wife and the farmer's lad, and every man jack among 'em. He" (and they nodded towards the stranger of the deadly trade) "is come from up the country to do it because there's not enough to do in his own county-town, and he's got the place here now our own county man's dead; he's going to live in the same cottage under the prison wall."

80 The stranger in cinder-gray took no notice of this whispered string of observations, but again wetted his lips. Seeing that his friend in the chimney-corner was the only one who reciprocated his joviality in any way, he held out his cup towards that appreciative comrade, who also held out his own. They clinked together, the eyes of the rest of the room hanging upon the singer's actions. He parted his lips for the third verse; but at that moment another knock was audible upon the door. This time the knock was faint and hesitating.

The company seemed scared; the shepherd looked with consternation towards the entrance, and it was with some effort that he resisted his alarmed wife's deprecatory glance, and uttered for the third time the welcoming words, "Walk in!"

The door was gently opened, and another man stood upon the mat. He, like those who had preceded him, was a stranger. This time it was a short, small personage, of fair complexion, and dressed in a decent suit of dark clothes.

"Can you tell me the way to—?" he began: when, gazing round the room to observe the nature of the company amongst whom he had fallen, his eyes lighted on the stranger in cindergray. It was just at the instant when the latter, who had thrown his mind into his song with such a will that he scarcely heeded the interruption, silenced all whispers and inquiries by bursting into his third verse.

Tomorrow is my working day,

   Simple shepherds all—
Tomorrow is a working day for me:
For the farmer's sheep is slain, and the lad who did it ta'en,
   And on his soul may God ha' merc-y!

The stranger in the chimney-corner, waving cups with the singer so heartily that his mead splashed over on the hearth, repeated in his bass voice as before:

   And on his soul may God ha' merc-y!

All this time the third stranger had been standing in the doorway. Finding now that he did not come forward or go on speaking, the guests particularly regarded him. They noticed to their surprise that he stood before them the picture of abject terror—his knees trembling, his hand shaking so violently that the door-latch by which he supported himself rattled audibly: his white lips were parted, and his eyes fixed on the merry officer of justice in the middle of the room. A moment more and he had turned, closed the door, and fled.

"What a man can it be?" said the shepherd.

The rest, between the awfulness of their late discovery and the odd conduct of this third visitor, looked as if they knew not what to think, and said nothing. Instinctively they withdrew further and further from the grim gentleman in their midst, whom some of them seemed to take for the Prince of Darkness[1] himself, till they formed a remote circle, and empty space of floor being left between them and him:

   ...circulus, cujus centrum diabolus[2].

---

[1] Prince of Darkness: the Devil
[2] circulus, cujus centrum diabolus: a circle of a hundred devils.

Chapter Four

The room was so silent—though there were more than twenty people in it—that nothing could be heard but the patter of the rain against the window-shutters, accompanied by the occasional hiss of a stray drop that fell down the chimney into the fire, and the steady puffing of the man in the corner, who had now resumed his pipe of long clay.

The stillness was unexpectedly broken. The distant sound of a gun reverberated through the air—apparently from the direction of the county-town.

"Be jiggered!" cried the stranger who had sung the song, jumping up.

"What does that mean?" asked several.

"A prisoner escaped from the jail—that's what it means."

90　　All listened. The sound was repeated, and none of them spoke but the man in the chimney-corner, who said quietly, "I've often been told that in this county they fire a gun at such times; but I never heard it till now."

"I wonder if it is *my* man?" murmured the personage in cindergray.

"Surely it is!" said the shepherd involuntarily. "And surely we've zeed[1] him! That little man who looked in at the door by now, and quivered like a leaf when he zeed ye and heard your song!"

"His teeth chattered, and the breath went out of his body," said the dairyman.

"And his heart seemed to sink within him like a stone," said Oliver Giles.

95　　"And he bolted as if he'd been shot at," said the hedgecarpenter.

"True—his teeth chattered, and his heart seemed to sink; and he bolted as if he'd been shot at," slowly summed up the man in the chimney-corner.

---

[1] zeed: seen; saw.

"I didn't notice it," remarked the hangman.

"We were all a-wondering what made him run off in such a fright," faltered one of the women against the wall, "and now 'tis explained!"

The firing of the alarm-gun went on at intervals, low and sullenly, and their suspicions became a certainty. The sinister gentleman in cinder-gray roused himself. "Is there a constable here?" he asked, in thick tones. "If so, let him step forward."

100 The engaged man of fifty stepped quavering out from the wall, his betrothed beginning to sob on the back of the chair.

"You are a sworn constable?"

"I be, sir."

"Then pursue the criminal at once, with assistance, and bring him back here. He can't have gone far."

"I will, sir, I will—when I've got my staff. I'll go home and get it, and come sharp here, and start in a body."

105 "Staff!—never mind your staff; the man'll be gone!"

"But I can't do nothing without my staff—can I, William, and John, and Charles Jake? No; for there's the king's royal crown a painted on en in yaller[1] and gold, and the lion and the unicorn, so as when I raise en up and hit my prisoner, 'tis made a lawful blow thereby. I wouldn't 'tempt to take up a man without my staff—no, not I. If I hadn't the law to gie[2] me courage, why, instead o' my taking up him he might take up me!"

"Now, I'm a king's man, myself, and can give you authority enough for this," said the formidable officer in gray. "Now then, all of ye, be ready. Have ye any lanterns?"

"Yes—have ye any lanterns?—I demand it!" said the constable.

"And the rest of you able-bodied—"

110 "Able-bodied men—yes—the rest of ye!" said the constable.

---

[1] yaller: yellow.

[2] gie: give.

Chapter Four

"Have you some good stout staves and pitchforks—"

"Staves and pitchforks—in the name o' the law! And take 'em in yer hands and go in quest, and do as we in authority tell ye!"

Thus aroused, the men prepared to give chase. The evidence was, indeed, though circumstantial, so convincing, that but little argument was needed to show the shepherd's guests that after what they had seen it would look very much like connivance if they did not instantly pursue the unhappy third stranger who could not as yet have gone more than a few hundred yards over such uneven country.

A shepherd is always well provided with lanterns; and, lighting these hastily, and with hurdle-staves in their hands, they poured out of the door, taking a direction along the crest of the hill, away from the town, the rain having fortunately a little abated.

115 Disturbed by the noise, or possibly by unpleasant dreams of her baptism, the child who had been christened began to cry heartbrokenly in the room overhead. These notes of grief came down through the chinks of the floor to the ears of the women below, who jumped up one by one, and seemed glad of the excuse to ascend and comfort the baby, for the incidents of the last half-hour greatly oppressed them. Thus in the space of two or three minutes the room on the ground-floor was deserted quite.

But it was not for long. Hardly had the sound of footsteps died away when a man returned round the corner of the house from the direction the pursuers had taken. Peeping in at the door, and seeing nobody there, he entered leisurely. It was the stranger of the chimney-corner, who had gone out with the rest. The motive of his return was shown by his helping himself to a cut piece of skimmer-cake that lay on a ledge beside where he had sat, and which he had apparently forgotten to take with him. He also poured out half a cup more mead from the quantity that remained, ravenously eating and drinking these as he stood. He had not finished when another figure came in just as quietly—his friend in cinder-gray.

"O—you here?" said the latter, smiling. "I thought you had gone to help in the capture." And this speaker also revealed the object of his return by looking solicitously round for the fascinating mug of old mead.

"And I thought you had gone," said the other, continuing his skimmer-cake with some effort.

"Well, on second thoughts, I felt there were enough without me," said the first confidentially, "and such a night as it is, too. Besides, 'tis the business o' the Government to take care of its criminals—not mine."

120　　"True; so it is. And I felt as you did, that there were enough without me."

"I don't want to break my limbs running over the humps and hollows of this wild country."

"Nor I neither, between you and me."

"These shepherd-people are used to it—simple-minded souls, you know, stirred up to anything in a moment. They'll have him ready for me before morning, and no trouble to me at all."

"They'll have him, and we shall have saved ourselves all labor in the matter."

125　　"True, true, Well, my way is to Casterbridge; and 'tis as much as my legs will do to take me that far. Going the same way?"

"No, I am sorry to say! I have to get home over there"(he nodded indefinitely to the right), "and I feel as you do, that it is quite enough for my legs to do before bedtime."

The other had by this time finished the mead in the mug, after which, shaking hands heartily at the door, and wishing each other well, they went their several ways.

In the meantime the company of pursuers had reached the end of the hog's-back elevation which dominated this part of the down. They had decided on no particular plan of action; and, finding that the man of the baleful trade was no longer in their company, they seemed quite unable to form any such plan now. They descended in all directions down the hill, and straightway several of the party fell into the snare set by Nature for all misguided midnight ramblers over this part of the cretaceous formation. The "lanchets," or flint slopes, which belted the escarpment at intervals of a dozen yards, took the less cautious ones unawares, and losing their footing on the rubbly steep they slid sharply downwards, the lanterns rolling from their hands to the bottom, and there lying on their sides till the horn was scorched through.

When they had again gathered themselves together, the shepherd, as the man who knew the country best, took the lead, and guided them round these treacherous inclines. The lanterns, which seemed rather to dazzle their eyes and warn the fugitive than to assist them in the exploration, were extinguished, due silence was observed; and in this more rational order they plunged into the vale. It was a grassy, briery, moist defile, affording some shelter to any person who had sought it; but the party perambulated it in vain, and ascended on the other side. Here they wandered apart, and after an interval closed together again to report progress. At the second time of closing in they found themselves near a lonely ash, the single tree on this part of the coomb, probably sown there by a passing bird some fifty years before. And here, standing a little to one side of the trunk, as motionless as the trunk itself, appeared the man they were in quest of, his outline being well defined against the sky beyond. The band noiselessly drew up and faced him.

130 "Your money or your life!" said the constable sternly to the still figure.

"No, no," whispered John Pitcher. " 'Tisn't our side ought to say that. That's the doctrine of vagabonds like him, and we be on the side of the law."

"Well, well," replied the constable impatiently; "I must say something, mustn't I? and if you had all the weight o' this undertaking upon your mind, perhaps you'd say the wrong thing too! — Prisoner at the bar, surrender, in the name of the

Father—the Crown, I mane[1]!"

The man under the tree seemed now to notice them for the first time, and, giving them no opportunity whatever for exhibiting their courage, he strolled slowly towards them. He was, indeed, the little man, the third stranger; but his trepidation had in a great measure gone.

"Well, travelers," he said, "did I hear ye speak to me?"

"You did: you've got to come and be our prisoner at once!" said the constable. "We arrest 'ee on the charge of not biding in Casterbridge jail in a decent proper manner to be hung tomorrow morning. Neighbors, do your duty, and seize the culpet[2]!"

On hearing the charge, the man seemed enlightened, and, saying not another word, resigned himself with preternatural civility to the search-party, who, with their staves in their hands, surrounded him on all sides, and marched him back towards the shepherd's cottage.

It was eleven o'clock by the time they arrived. The light shining from the open door, a sound of men's voices within, proclaimed to them as they approached the house that some new events had arisen in their absence. On entering they discovered the shepherd's living room to be invaded by two officers from the Casterbridge jail, and a well-known magistrate who lived at the nearest county-seat, intelligence of the escape having become generally circulated.

"Gentlemen," said the constable, "I have brought back your man—not without risk and danger; but every one must do his duty! He is inside this circle of able-bodied persons, who have lent me useful aid, considering their ignorance of Crown work. Men, bring forward your prisoner!" And the third stranger was led to the light.

"Who is this?" said one of the officials.

"The man," said the constable.

---

[1] mane: mean.
[2] culpet: culprit.

Chapter Four

"Certainly not," said the turnkey; and the first corroborated his statement.

"But how can it be otherwise?" asked the constable. "Or why was he so terrified at sight o' the singing instrument of the law who sat there?" Here he related the strange behavior of the third stranger on entering the house during the hangman's song.

"Can't understand it," said the officer coolly. "All I know is that it is not the condemned man. He's quite a different character from this one; a gauntish[1] fellow, with dark hair and eyes, rather good-looking, and with a musical bass voice that if you heard it once you'd never mistake as long as you lived."

"Why, souls—'twas the man in the chimney-corner!"

"Hey—what?" said the magistrate, coming forward after inquiring particulars from the shepherd in the background. "Haven't you got the man after all?"

"Well, sir," said the constable, "he's the man we were in search of, that's true; and yet he's not the man we were in search of. For the man we were in search of was not the man we wanted, sir, if you understand my every-day way; for 'twas the man in the chimney-corner!"

"A pretty kettle of fish altogether!" said the magistrate. "You had better start for the other man at once."

The prisoner now spoke for the first time. The mention of the man in the chimney-corner seemed to have moved him as nothing else could do. "Sir," he said, stepping forward to the magistrate, "take no more trouble about me. The time is come when I may as well speak. I have done nothing; my crime is that the condemned man is my brother. Early this afternoon I left home at Shottsford to tramp it all the way to Casterbridge jail to bid him farewell. I was benighted, and called here to rest and ask the way. When I opened the door I saw before me the very man, my brother, that I thought to see in the condemned cell at Casterbridge. He was in

---

[1] gauntish: gaunt.

this chimney-corner; and jammed close to him, so that he could not have got out if he had tried, was the executioner who'd come to take his life, singing a song about it and not knowing that it was his victim who was close by, joining in to save appearances. My brother looked a glance of agony at me, and I knew he meant, 'Don't reveal what you see; my life depends on it.' I was so terror-struck that I could hardly stand, and, not knowing what I did, I turned and hurried away."

The narrator's manner and tone had the stamp of truth, and his story made a great impression on all around. "And do you know where your brother is at the present time?" asked the magistrate.

150 "I do not. I have never seen him since I closed this door."

"I can testify to that, for we've been between ye ever since," said the constable.

"Where does he think to fly to? —what is his occupation?"

"He's a watch-and-clock-maker, sir."

" 'A said 'a was a wheelwright—a wicked rogue," said the constable.

155 "The wheels of clocks and watches he meant, no doubt," said Shepherd Fennel. "I thought his hands were palish for's trade."

"Well, it appears to me that nothing can be gained by retaining this poor man in custody," said the magistrate; "your business lies with the other, unquestionably."

And so the little man was released off-hand; but he looked nothing the less sad on that account, it being beyond the power of magistrate or constable to raze out the written troubles in his brain, for they concerned another whom he regarded with more solicitude than himself. When this was done, and the man had gone his way, the night was found to be so far advanced that it was deemed useless to renew the search before the next morning.

Next day, accordingly, the quest for the clever sheep-stealer became general and keen, to all appearance at least. But the intended punishment was cruelly disproportioned to the transgression, and the sympathy of a great many country-folk in that district was strongly on the side of the fugitive. Moreover, his marvelous coolness and daring in hob-and-nobbing with the hangman, under the unprecedented circumstances of the shepherd's party, won their admiration. So that it may be questioned if all those who ostensibly made themselves so busy in exploring woods and fields and lanes were quite so thorough when it came to the private examination of their own lofts and outhouses. Stories were afloat of a mysterious figure being occasionally seen in some overgrown trackway or other, remote from turnpike roads; but when a search was instituted in any of these suspected quarters nobody was found. Thus the days and weeks passed without tidings.

In brief, the bass-voiced man of the chimney-corner was never recaptured. Some said that he went across the sea, others that he did not, but buried himself in the depths of a populous city. At any rate, the gentleman in cinder-gray never did his morning's work at Casterbridge, nor met anywhere at all, for business purposes, the genial comrade with whom he had passed an hour of relaxation in the lonely house on the coomb.

160   The grass has long been green on the graves of Shepherd Fennel and his frugal wife; the guests who made up the christening party have mainly followed their entertainers to the tomb; the baby in whose honor they all had met is a matron in the sere and yellow leaf. But the arrival of the three strangers at the shepherd's that night, and the details connected therewith, is a story as well known as ever in the country about Higher Crowstairs.

 Discussion

If the plot element in "The Three Strangers" is separated from the total story it appears to be a rather poor and mechanical contrivance. The coincidence may seem strained and the whole action, finally, rather pointless. Does Hardy's method of presentation mitigate these criticisms? Does it, in fact, give point to the story?

In the first place, Hardy does give a picture of a way of life which in itself holds some interest for the reader. The careful description of the countryside and of the cottage, the presentation of the manners and customs of the isolated community, appeal to the interest that many readers have in such details of "local color" for themselves. The main persons, the hangman and the condemned, are rendered rather fully, at least in regard to appearance and in hints of character, as in the conversation between them and in the sudden flight of the third stranger. But granting the competence of much of this treatment, the reader may still have the feeling that many of the details do not bear directly on the action, that the story is filled with much irrelevant descriptive matter, and that the general organization is very loose.

In the course of the story, we may come to see that some of this material is relevant, and that, in its special way, the organization is effective. For instance, the fact that the shepherd's cottage is located at the crossing of the paths helps to make more plausible the coincidental arrival of the several men there; or the fact that one of the strangers is without pipe and tobacco and borrows from the shepherd comes to have a real significance when we learn that he is a fugitive. Even such a detail as the fact that Shepherd Fennel's wife is proud of the quality of her mead, yet is anxious to husband it, though it does not bear a relation to the series of events unfolding here, may have a function.

We shall miss much of the point of the story if we consider that Hardy is merely taking the occasion to present some of the quaint customs of Wessex or a picture of pleasant rural simplicity. Actually, the total effect of the background and atmosphere of the story is not to emphasize the quaint peculiarities of the people, but to affirm the elemental humanity of these people, the qualities which they share with, let us say, an Irish peasant or a Tennessee mountaineer. Their world is a simple world. Their life is constantly related to the necessity for getting food and shelter, and is tied to the natural routine of the seasons. The occasion for the celebration described in the story is one of the universal human occasions for rejoicing, but even in the midst of the celebration the shepherd's wife can count the cups of mead. This emphasis on the nature of the life of these people will be seen to be integral in the story. At the very end of the story Hardy writes: "But the arrival of the three strangers at the shepherd's that night, and the details connected therewith, is a story as well known as ever in the country about Higher Crowstairs." In other words, Hardy has defined the little world where the event, which in itself may seem so bare and mechanical, came to be perpetuated in a "tale," a legend.

But what would make the event significant? To these people, who had gathered to celebrate a birth and a christening, there enter the condemned man and the hangman, who participate in the celebration; and this accidental juxtaposition between birth and death provides the basic ironical situation of the story. But it is not merely natural death, but death decreed by society, legalistically and mechanically, for the infraction of a code which has been broken for the most "natural" of reasons—to secure food for a hungry family. In other words, the situation is a little two-fold parable of the essential circumstances of the human being's condition in this world. First, the parable involves the natural unpredictability of fate, the natural association—here so accidentally and ironically arrived at—of death with life, sorrow with joy. The neighbors who have turned out to celebrate the birth find themselves, before the evening is over, hunting for the condemned man who is to be punished by death; and this fact suggests an ironical commentary concerning the kind of world into which the human being is born. Second, the parable involves a contrast between the warm, spontaneous quality of the average person when he is allowed to approach another without the restrictions and considerations which society would impose upon him, and the cold, mechanical, dehumanized quality of the codes and conventions by which society necessarily operates: even the hangman's humanity triumphs over his dehumanized and dehumanizing profession so that he can join in the spirit of the occasion. Hardy expresses a similar contrast in one of his poems, "The Man He Killed," the last stanza of which is quoted here:

  Yes: quaint and curious war is!
  You shoot a fellow down
  You'd treat if met where any bar is,
  Or help to half-a-crown.

  Hardy never actually states the point in the story as he states it in the poem; none of the characters moralizes the situation as does the soldier in the poem. And undoubtedly the oddity of the coincidence itself, and the coolness of the condemned man, which makes possible his escape, help make the incident immediately memorable, but these matters alone do not account for the incident's becoming a legend. Another consideration operated: whether the shepherd folk realized it or not, the incident became a legend because it dramatized a fundamental insight into human circumstance.

  If this account of the theme of the story is correct, then it will be seen that Hardy has *not been building toward* a coincidence—has not been depending upon a coincidence to solve a problem of plot and structure—but *has worked from* the coincidence as an essential part of the situation which he undertook to interpret as a story. But this does not completely answer the possible charge of implausibility which may be brought against the coincidence as such. Why is the coincidence here relatively easy to accept? The answer may lie in the particular approach which Hardy has taken to the material. He sets the situation up as a tale, a legend, an event which, presumably, really happened, and which found its way, because of its striking quality, into the consciousness of the simple world of the shepherds to be "told" and retold. His strategy is to imply that he takes no responsibility for the events of the story but only for the imaginative reconstruction of the incident, for the presentation of the world which preserved its memory, for the interpretation which made memorable the event.

(Cleanth Brooks)

 Questions

1. Discuss the "local colour" of the story. How does it help to establish the major theme of the story?
2. What does the title of the story suggest to your understanding of the story?
3. In what way(s) does the setting contribute to characterization?
4. The utility of the rather elaborate background helps much in interpreting the legend of the story and in giving it plausibility. But some of the details have other functions. For example, the incident of the girl's decision not to faint because her betrothed was, apparently, not prepared to catch her. The incident has a humorous quality, though it comes at the very moment when the profession of the hangman is revealed. The element of humour helps to prevent "life-death" contrast from appearing oversolemn, stagy, and mechanical. What are the functions of various other details in the story?

Chapter Five

Style

"Proper words in proper places, makes the true definition of a style." Jonathan Swift's remarks lead us generally to thinking of modes of expression of a piece of fiction as the most characteristic of the author's style. Thus **style** generally refers to how the author uses language in his/her work: to the author's particular ways of managing words that we come to recognize as habitual or customary. A distinctive style marks the work of a fine writer: we can tell his or her work from that of anyone else. This is argued by the Latin expression: *Stilus virus arguit* ("The style proclaims the man"), and for this matter we are familiar with the experience of trying to guess the author of a piece of writing on the evidence of his/her language. Actually, style is a combination of two elements, the idea to be expressed and the linguistic traits or characteristics of the author. It is, as J. R. Lowell said, "the establishment of a perfect mutual understanding between the worker and his material" (Holman and Harman, *A Handbook to Literature*, 1986).

However, there has never been an agreement on the exact meaning of style in the history of literary criticism, and the further narrowing of its meaning brings us on to more controversial ground, where different definitions of style involve even conflicting views of the use of language in literature. There is a strong tradition of thought which restricts style to choices of manner rather than matter, of expression rather than content. Such separation between form and meaning is implied in the common definition of style as a "way of writing" or a "mode of expression."

Chapter Five

There is equally a strong literary tradition that emphasizes the inseparability between style and content; in Flaubert's words: "It is like body and soul; form and content to me are one" (From a letter of December 12, 1857).

The distinction between what a writer wants to say and how it is presented to the reader underlies one of the early and persistent concepts of style: style as the "dress of thought," as Wesley put it:

> Style is the dress of thought; a modest dress,
> Neat, but not gaudy, will true critics please.

This metaphor resonates with Renaissance and Neo-Classicist pronouncements on style. For example, the idea that style is merely the "adornment" or "covering" of thought or meaning is clearly expressed in the very beginning of John Lyly's *Eupheus*, which can be plausibly taken as the first novel in English:

> There dwelt in Athens a young gentleman of great patrimony, and of so comely a personage.... This young gallant, of more *w*it than *w*ealth, and yet of more *w*ealth than *w*isdom, seeing himself inferior to none in pleasant conceits, THOUGHT himself superior to all in honest conditions, insomuch that he deemed himself so apt in all things, that he gave himself almost to nothing, but practicing of those things commonly which are incident to these sharp wits, fine phrases, smooth quipping, merry taunting, using jesting without *m*ean, and abusing *m*irth without *m*easure. As therefore the sweetest rose hath his prickle, the *f*inest velvet his *b*rack, the *f*airest *f*lower his *b*ran, so the sharpest *w*it HATH his *w*anton *w*ill and the *h*oliest *h*ead his *w*icked *w*ay.

We can see clearly the elaborate parallelistic structure of the three sentences, and the parallelisms are reinforced by frequent uses of alliteration (indicated by italics). As Leech and Short analyze

(*Style in Fiction*, 1981), the architecture of parallelism is to some extent in counterpoint with the grammatical structure of the sentence so that the main verb (shown in capitals) occurs in mid-parallelism and forms a concealed centre of gravity, balancing subject against predicate. It is obviously the aesthetics of form that tends to attract the reader's attention here rather than the meaning. We might plausibly say that Lyly has embroidered an elaborate garment round the simple idea "Eupheus was a young dandy." If "adornment" is to be identified in linguistic patterns which have little semantic function, we can point to the alliterations clustered in the end of the third sentence. We can also point to grammatical parallelisms which, though not devoid of content, seem merely to play a role of embellishment, providing further examples of a concept already expressed: "The sweetest rose hath his prickle" already conveys the meaning "even the best things are alloyed with bad," and thus the repetition of the pattern in "the finest velvet his brack, the fairest flower his bran" is redundant. Lyly might not have, then, added the last piece of pattern unless he had elaborated on the alliterative function of "holiest head" and "wicked way." However, the elaboration of form will inevitably bring an elaboration of meaning. The repetition of parallel of examples from different experience ("rose ... velvet ... flower ... wit ... head") spurs our association with the generality of a didactic principle which is otherwise seen to be particular. The repetition in "wit ... wealth ... wisdom" is not mere repetition but a progression implying an increasing weightiness of the qualities listed. The parallelism of "inferior to none in pleasant conceits" and "superior to all in honest conditions" gives a schematic balance to the image of something light ("pleasant conceits") being weighed against something heavy ("honest conditions"), underlining the faulty logic of Eupheus's youthful mind. So the schematism of form aims at the ideas being presented.

A more general and tenable definition of style is the "manner of expression": every writer necessarily makes choices of expression, and it is in these choices, in his/her "way of putting

Chapter Five

things," that style resides. This definition of style abides by the belief that there can be different ways of conveying the same content and draws parallels with other art forms such as music, painting and architecture, and to varied activities such as playing the piano or playing tennis for elucidation. In such activities, there are some invariant rules that must be followed, but there are also variant ways in which the individual may perform them. Such an analogy is employed by Richard Ohmann:

> A style is a way of writing.... In general, [style] applies to human action that is partly invariant and partly variable.... Now this picture leads to few complications if the action is playing the piano or playing tennis.... But the relevant division between fixed and variable components in literature is by no means so obvious. What is content, and what is form, or style? The attack on a dichotomy of form and content has been persistent in modern criticism; to change so much as a word, the argument runs, is to change the meaning as well. This austere doctrine has a certain theoretical appeal.... Yet at the same time this doctrine leads to the altogether counterintuitive conclusion that there can be no such thing as style, or that style is simply a part of content.
>
> To put the problem more concretely, the idea of style implies that the words on page might have been different, or differently arranged, without a corresponding difference in substance. ("Generative Grammars and the Concept of Literary Style", 1964)

To back up his argument that there are different ways of saying the same thing, Ohmann offers the following paraphrases of "After dinner, the senator made a speech":

(1) When dinner was over, the senator made a speech.
(2) A speech was made by the senator after dinner.

(3) The senator made a postprandial oration.

and points out that these are variants of the original in a sense which is not true of, say, "Columbus was brave" or "Columbus was nautical." The differences among (1)-(3) are chiefly grammatical; and the grammatical, rather than lexical, aspect of style is the one on which Ohmann concentrates. Thus in the analysis of a writer's style in a work of fiction, we should study what the writer has written against the background of what he/she might have written; we should search for some significance, which we may call **stylistic value**, in the writer's choice to express his/her sense in *this* rather than *that* way.

The above notion of style as "dress of thought" or as "manner of expression" consists in the assumption that there is some basic sense that can be preserved in different renderings of words or sentence structures. This is not likely to be challenged in everyday uses of language. But in literature, particularly in poetry, paraphrasing becomes problematic. For example, the metaphor in "Come, seeling night, / Scarf the tender eye of pitiful day" (Macbeth, III. ii. 46-47) denies us a paraphrase in either a literal sense or a hidden meaning. Any paraphrase would devoid it of its richness of implications that induces us to find interpretations beyond the meanings captured by paraphrasing. Such a metaphor, as Terence Hawkes says, "is not fanciful embroidery of the facts. It is a way of experiencing the facts" (*Metaphor*, 1972). Literary devices, in addition to metaphor, such as irony, ambiguity, pun, and even images, generally become multivalued and their sense loses its primacy in poetry. With deliberate consideration of this fact, some theorists, especially the New Critics, reject the form-meaning dichotomy and they tend to see sense and style as one thing, as Wimsatt asserts:

> It is hardly necessary to adduce proof that the doctrine of identity of style and meaning is today firmly established. The doctrine is, I take it, **one**[emphasis mine] from which a

modern theorist can hardly escape, or hardly wishes to. (*The Prose Style of Samuel Johnson*, 1941)

It is to be noted that the emphasis upon the artistic integrity and inviolability of their works is echoed not only in poets but also in many prose writers, and we can find an articulation in Tolstoy's words: "This is indeed one of the significant facts about a true work of art—that its content in its entirety can be expressed only by itself." Critics holding such an idea about style tend to look at a work of fiction as a verbal artifact. They believe that in such a verbal artifact there can be no separation of the author's creation of the plot, character, social and moral life, from the language in which they are portrayed. As David Lodge puts it: "The novelist's medium is language; whatever he does, *qua* novelist, he does in and through language." (*Language in Fiction*, 1966) Thus in his practice of criticism, Lodge is ready to see no difference between the kind of choice a writer makes in calling a character "dark-haired" or "fair," since all the choices a writer makes are a matter of language. Lodge also argues that there is no essential difference between poetry and prose and that the following tenets apply to both:

(1) It is impossible to paraphrase literary writing;
(2) It is impossible to translate a literary work;
(3) It is impossible to divorce the general appreciation of a literary work from the appreciation of its style.

Perhaps Lodge's statements sound rather arbitrary since we do have a great number of translated literary works in various languages, including poems, in which the essential artistry remains (though something must have been lost), and paraphrasing sometimes can be said to be one of important methods for a basic understanding and appreciation of the essential literariness of a literary work and is often employed in the teaching of literature.

Whatever notion a person may have towards style, it is important to understand that language in fiction is the focus in our analysis of style. At the same time language is used to project a world beyond language itself, and our analysis of language can never exclude our general knowledge and understanding of the real world.

Therefore, a linguistic approach to style is frequently employed in stylistic studies. Among such practices, critics generally try to determine the features of style, or **style markers**, the linguistic items that only appear or are typical or most or least frequent in a work of fiction. We thus need to make comparisons and contrasts so as to find out the differences between the normal frequency of a feature and its frequency in the text or corpus. Of course, features can register on a reader's mind in his/her recognition of style, and doubtlessly the degree to his/her recognition of these features as they are salient will vary, and the degree to which the reader responds to these features in a given reading will also vary according to a number of factors, such as his/her attentiveness, sensitivity to style markers and previous reading experience (Leech and Short, *Style in Fiction*, 1981).

Foregrounding, artistically motivated deviation or defamiliarrization of language or structure or other basic elements, according to Russian Formalists, makes a literary work literary. By determining what is foregrounded or defamiliarized we can distinguish a work or a writer's writing from others. With regard to style, foregrounding may be qualitative, —a breach of some rule or convention of English such as the present tense of the link verb "be" in Jesus words in the Authorized Version of St John's Gospel: "Before Abraham was, I am" and the use of "now" in a sentence of past tense in the beginning paragraph of Hemingway's "A Clean, Well-Lighted Place": "... and now at night it was quiet..."—or it may be simply quantitative, i. e. deviation from some expected frequency, for instance, the repetition of "nada" in the older waiter's monologue in Hemingway's "A Clean, Well-Lighted Place." And quantitative foregrounding of a prominent pattern of choice within the code may shade into qualitative foregrounding which changes the code itself. For example, the quantitative foregrounding of long compound sentences (clause plus clause plus clause) of simple words, sometimes joined with "and," in Hemingway's narrative produces the effect of listening to speech, which is a mark of qualitative foregrounding in Hemingway's writing. Thus what is foregrounded may soundly be taken as a distinctive feature of style of a piece of fiction.

As the foregrounding of language in a story is concerned, it may be useful to make a checklist of features which may be significant in a given text, though the features which recommend themselves to the attention in one text will not necessarily be important in another text by the same or different author. Leech and Short (*Style in Fiction*, 1981) list four headings of stylistic categories, which may be helpful in our analysis of the style of a story:

I. Lexical

1. General: Is the vocabulary simple or complex? Formal or colloquial? Descriptive or evaluative? General or specific? How far does the author make use of the emotive or other associations of words, as opposed to their referential meanings? Does the text contain idiomatic usages, and if so, with what kind of register (language variation beyond dialectical differences, such as differences between polite and familiar language; spoken and written language; scientific, religious, legal language, etc.) are these idioms associated? Is there any use of rare or specialized vocabulary? Are any particular morphological categories noteworthy (*eg* rare compound words, words with particular suffixes)?
2. Nouns: Are the nouns abstract or concrete? What kinds of abstract nouns (*eg* nouns referring to events, perceptions, processes, moral qualities, social qualities) are used? Why do proper names occur? Collective nouns?

3. Adjectives: To what degree of frequency are the adjectives used? To what kinds of attributes do the adjectives refer (*eg* physical, psychological, visual, auditory, colour, referential, emotive, evaluative, etc)? Are the adjectives restrictive or non-restrictive? Attributive or predictive?
4. Verbs: Do the verbs carry an important part of the meaning? Do they refer to movements, physical acts, speech acts (roughly utterances in the language which can be used to perform acts, or in which the speaker can be seen to have performed some act; for example "I name the ship the *Queen Elizabeth*."), psychological states or activities, perceptions, etc? Are they transitive, intransitive, linking, etc? Are they stative (describing states) or dynamic (describing actions)?
5. Adverbs: Are the adverbs frequently used in the text? What semantic functions do they perform (manner, place, direction, time, degree, etc)? Is there any significant use of sentence adverbs (such as "therefore", "however"; "obviously", "frankly")?

II. Grammatical

1. Sentence type: Does the author use only statements, or does he/she also use questions, commands, exclamations, or sentence fragments (such as sentences with no verbs)? If other types of sentence are used, what is their function?
2. Sentence complexity: Do sentences on the whole have a simple or a complex structure? What is the average sentence length? What is the ratio of dependent to independent clauses? Does complexity vary strikingly from one sentence to another? Is complexity mainly due to (i) coordination, (ii) subordination, (iii) juxtaposition of clauses or of other equivalent structures? In what parts of the text does complexity tend to occur?
3. Clause types: What types of clauses are favoured—relative clauses, adverbial clauses, or different types of nominal clauses?

Are non-finite forms commonly used, and if so, of what types are they (infinitive, *-ing* form, *-ed* form, verbless structure)? What is their function?
4. Clause structure: Is there anything significant about clause elements (*eg* frequency of objects, adverbials, complements; of transitive or intransitive verb constructions)? Are there any unusual orderings (initial adverbials, fronting of object or complement, etc)? Do special kinds of clause construction occur (such as those with preparatory *it* or *there*)?
5. Noun phrases: Are they relatively simple or complex? Where does the complexity lie (in premodification by adjectives, nouns, etc, or in postmodification by prepositional phrases, relative clauses, etc)?
6. Verb phrases: Are there any significant departures from the use of the simple past tense? For example, notice occurrences and functions of the present tense, of the progressive aspect, of the perfect aspect, of modal auxiliaries.
7. Other phrase types: Is there anything to be said about other phrases types, such as prepositional phrases, adverb phrases, adjective phrases?
8. Word classes: Having already considered major word classes, we may consider minor word classes (*eg* functional words), such as prepositions, conjunctions, pronouns, determiners, auxiliaries, interjections. Are particular words of these types used for particular effect (*eg* demonstratives such as *this* and *that*, negatives such as *not*, *nothing*)?
9. General: Note whether any general types of grammatical construction are used to special effect (*eg* comparative or superlative constructions, coordinative or listing constructions, parenthetical constructions, interjections and afterthoughts as occur in casual speech). And see to the number of lists and coordinations.

III. Figures of Speech

Here we consider the features which are foregrounded by

virtue of departing in some way from general norms of communication by means of the language code, for example, exploitation of deviations from the linguistic code.
1. Grammatical and lexical schemes (foregrounded repetitions of expression): Are there any cases of formal and structural repetition (anaphora, parallelism, etc) or of mirror-image patterns (chiasmus)? Is the rhetorical effect of these one of antithesis, reinforcement, climax, anticlimax, etc?
2. Phonological schemes: Are there any phonological patterns of rhyme, alliteration, assonance, consonance, etc? Are there any salient rhythmical patterns? Do vowels and consonant sounds pattern or cluster in particular ways? How do these phonological features interact with meaning?
3. Tropes (foregrounded irregularities of content): Are there any obvious violations of or departure from the linguistic code? For example, are there any neologisms (such as "Americanly"), deviant lexical collocations (such as "portentous infants")? Are there any semantic, syntactic, phonological, or graphological deviations? Such deviations are often the clue to special interpretations associated with traditional figures of speech such as metaphor, metonymy, synecdoche, paradox, and irony. If such tropes occur, what kind of special interpretation is involved (for example, metaphor can be classified as personifying, animalizing, concretizing, synaesthetic, etc)?

IV. Context and Cohesion

Here we take a look at features which are generally fully dealt with in discourse analysis. Under **cohesion** ways in which one part of a text is linked to another are considered; for instance, the ways sentences are connected. This is the internal organization of a text. Under **context**, roughly the material, mental, personal, interactional, social, institutional, cultural, and historical situation in which the discourse is made, we consider the external relations of the literary text or a part of the text, seeing it as a discourse presupposing a social relation between its participants (author and reader, character and character, character and reader, etc), and a sharing of knowledge and assumptions by participants.

1. Cohesion: Does the text contain logical or other links between sentences (*eg* coordinating conjunctions, linking adverbials), or does it tend to rely on implicit connections of meaning? What sort of use is made of cross-reference by pronouns (*she*, *it*, *they*, etc), by substitute forms (*do*, *so*, etc), or ellipsis? Is there any use made of **elegant variation**—the avoidance of repetition by substitution of a descriptive phrase (as "the old lawyer" substitutes for the repetition of an earlier "Mr Jones")? Are meaning connections reinforced by repetition of words and phrases, or by repeatedly using words from the same semantic field?

2. Context: Does the writer address the reader directly, or through the words or thoughts of some fictional character? What linguistic clues (*eg* first person pronouns *I*, *me*, *my*, *mine*) are there of the addresser-addressee relationship? What attitude does the author imply towards his/her subject? If a character's words or thoughts are represented, is this done by direct quotation, or by some other method (*eg* indirect speech, free indirect speech)? Are there significant changes of style with respect to different persons (narrator or character) who is supposedly speaking or thinking the words on the page? What is the point of view of the story? Are there frequent shifts of point view? If so, in whose voice is the narrator speaking?

A Clean, Well-Lighted Place
by Ernest Hemingway, 1933

It was late and every one had left the café except an old man who sat in the shadow the leaves of the tree made against the electric light. In the day time the street was dusty, but at night the dew settled the dust and the old man liked to sit late because he was deaf and now at night it was quiet and he felt the difference. The two waiters inside the café knew that the old man was a little drunk, and while he was a good client they knew that if he became too drunk he would leave without paying, so they kept watch on him.

"Last week he tried to commit suicide," one waiter said.

"Why?"

"He was in despair."

5   "What about?"

"Nothing."

"How do you know it was nothing?"

"He has plenty of money."

They sat together at a table that was close against the wall near the door of the café and looked at the terrace where the tables were all empty except where the old man sat in the shadow of the leaves of the tree that moved slightly in the wind. A girl and a soldier went by in the street. The street light shone on the brass number on his collar. The girl wore no head covering and hurried beside him.

10   "The guard will pick him up," one waiter said.

"What does it matter if he gets what he's after?"

"He had better get off the street now. The guard will get him. They went by five minutes ago."

The old man sitting in the shadow rapped on his saucer with his glass. The younger waiter went over to him.

"What do you want?"

15   The old man looked at him. "Another brandy," he said.

"You'll be drunk," the waiter said. The old man looked at him. The waiter went away.

"He'll stay all night," he said to his colleague. "I'm sleepy now. I never get into bed before three o'clock. He should have killed himself last week."

Chapter Five

The waiter took the brandy bottle and another saucer from the counter inside the café and marched out to the old man's table. He put down the saucer and poured the glass full of brandy.

"You should have killed yourself last week," he said to the deaf man. The old man motioned with his finger. "A little more," he said. The waiter poured on into the glass so that the brandy slopped over and ran down the stem into the top saucer of the pile. "Thank you," the old man said. The waiter took the bottle back inside the café. He sat down at the table with his colleague again.

"He's drunk now," he said.

"He's drunk every night."[1]

"What did he want to kill himself for?"

"How should I know?"

"How did he do it?"

"He hung himself with a rope."

"Who cut him down?"

"His niece."

"Why did they do it?"

"Fear for his soul."

"How much money has he got?"

"He's got plenty."

"He must be eighty years old."

"Anyway I should say he was eighty."[2]

"I wish he would go home. I never get to bed before three o'clock. What kind of hour is that to go to bed?"

"He stays up because he likes it."

"He's lonely. I'm not lonely. I have a wife waiting in bed for me."

---

[1] "He's drunk now," he said. "He's drunk every night.": The younger waiter says both these lines. A device of Hemingway's style is sometimes to have a character pause, then speak again—as often happens in actual speech.

[2] "He must be eighty years old." "Anyway I should say he was eighty.": Is this another instance of the same character's speaking twice? Clearly, it is the younger waiter who says the next line, "I wish he would go home."

"He had a wife once too."

"A wife would be no good to him now."

"You can't tell. He might be better with a wife."

40 "His niece looks after him."

"I know. You said she cut him down."

"I wouldn't want to be that old. An old man is a nasty thing."

"Not always. This old man is clean. He drinks without spilling. Even now, drunk. Look at him."

"I don't want to look at him. I wish he would go home. He has no regard for those who must work."

45 The old man looked from his glass across the square, then over at the waiters.

"Another brandy," he said, pointing to his glass. The waiter who was in a hurry came over.

"Finished," he said, speaking with that omission of syntax stupid people employ when talking to drunken people or foreigners. "No more tonight. Close now."

"Another," said the old man.

"No. Finished." The waiter wiped the edge of the table with a towel and shook his head.

50 The old man stood up, slowly counted the saucers, took a leather coin purse from his pocket and paid for the drinks, leaving half a peseta tip.

The waiter watched him go down the street, a very old man walking unsteadily but with dignity.

"Why didn't you let him stay and drink?" the unhurried waiter asked. They were putting up the shutters. "It is not half-past two."

"I want to go home to bed."

"What is an hour?"

55 "More to me than to him."

"An hour is the same."

"You talk like an old man yourself. He can buy a bottle and

Chapter Five

drink at home."

"It's not the same."

"No, it is not," agreed the waiter with a wife. He did not wish to be unjust. He was only in a hurry.

60   "And you? You have no fear of going home before the usual hour?"

"Are you trying to insult me?"

"No, hombre, only to make a joke."

"No," the waiter who was in a hurry said, rising from pulling down the metal shutters. "I have confidence. I am all confidence."

"You have youth, confidence, and a job," the older waiter said. "You have everything."

65   "And what do you lack?"

"Everything but work."

"You have everything I have."

"No. I have never had confidence and I am not young."

"Come on. Stop talking nonsense and lock up."

70   "I am of those who like to stay late at the café," the older waiter said. "With all those who do not want to go to bed. With all those who need a light for the night."

"I want to go home and into bed."

"We are of two different kinds," the older waiter said. He was not dressed to go home. "It is not only a question of youth and confidence although those things are very beautiful. Each night I am reluctant to close up because there may be some one who needs the café."

"Hombre, there are bodegas[1] open all night long."

"You do not understand. This is a clean and pleasant café. It is well lighted. The light is very good and also, now, there are shadows of the leaves."

75   "Good night," said the younger waiter.

"Good night," the other said. Turning off the electric light he

---

[1] bodegas: wineshops.

continued the conversation with himself. It is the light of course but it is necessary that the place be clean and pleasant. You do not want music. Certainly you do not want music. Nor can you stand before a bar with dignity although that is all that is provided for these hours. What did he fear? It was not fear or dread. It was a nothing that he knew too well. It was all a nothing and a man was nothing too. It was only that and light was all it needed and a certain cleanness and order. Some lived in it and never felt it but he knew it all was nada y pues nada y nada y pues nada[1]. Our nada who art in nada, nada be thy name thy kingdom nada thy will be nada in nada as it is in nada. Give us this nada our daily nada and nada us our nada as we nada our nadas and nada us not into nada but deliver us from nada; pues nada. Hail nothing full of nothing, nothing is with thee. He smiled and stood before a bar with a shining steam pressure coffee machine.

"What's yours?" asked the barman.

"Nada."

"Otro loco más[2]," said the barman and turned away.

80 "A little cup," said the waiter.

The barman poured it for him.

"The light is very bright and pleasant but the bar is unpolished," the waiter said.

The barman looked at him but did not answer. It was too late at night for conversation.

"You want another copita[3]?" the barman asked.

85 "No, thank you," said the waiter and went out. He disliked bars and bodegas. A clean, well-lighted café was a very different thing. Now, without thinking further, he would go home to his room. He would lie in the bed and finally, with daylight, he would go to sleep. After all, he said to himself, it is probably only insomnia. Many must have it.

---

[1] nada y pues... nada: nothing and then nothing and nothing and then nothing.

[2] Otro loco más: another lunatic.

[3] copita: little cup.

Chapter Five

 Discussion

The problem here, as found in so many Hemingway stories, is to discover how he manages to make apparently so little come to so much. A basic concern of every literary artist is to devise a technique, a literary form, to fashion the meaning of the situation he is exploring. No modern writer has worked more diligently to develop such a literary technique than Hemingway.

Ralph Ellison, author of the story "King of the Bingo Game" and the celebrated novel *Invisible Man* (1952), says about Hemingway: "In the end ... it is the quality of his art which is primary.... And it was through this struggle with form that he became the master, the culture hero, whom we have come to know and admire." In a letter (February 4, 1930) to one of the editors of this book Hemingway comments on that struggle: "I have some 40 drafts of the last chapter [of *A Farewell to Arms*]—may have destroyed others. This process proves nothing as far as I know except that I worked over and over it to get it right.... This process of transmitting your sensations and imagination, etc. from yourself, complete, to the person reading is what constitutes the discipline of prose."

What disciplines has Hemingway used to create "A Clean, Well-Lighted Place," one of the shortest stories in the English language and one of Hemingway's favorites? On the surface level we have a simple tale with three principal characters, but its implications, like those in Hemingway's *The Old Man and the Sea* (1952), can be as profound as the reader has insight. The scene is a Spanish café very late at night where an old man is having a drink while an old waiter and a young one discuss him. Except when the old waiter closes the café and goes to a bar for a drink, there is no action, much less suspense, whatever.

The story is a triumph of meaning expressed through dramatic tone and symbolism [See Chapter Seven for a brief discussion on symbol and symbolism]. Hemingway uses the dramatic method to permit the characters to present themselves. The story is actually a little one-act play with the author comment almost totally absent. Further, most of the customary exposition and author comment are embodied in the dialogue (for which Hemingway is justly famous), and the key facts are merely touched upon, rarely accented. The story is highly compressed: hardly a wasted word and every word counts. All this means that the reader participates in a drama which requires him to contribute to its understanding. Whatever tension the story possesses is created by the conflict between the old and young waiter as they regard the old man drinking in his loneliness. The symbolism? Each character represents a value system, a basic attitude toward life, and the word *nada*, or *nothing*, finally becomes the basic symbol upon which the meaning of the story turns.

It is easy to say, as one critic has said, "The story is about nothing, and we know that from the start...the style itself tells us that there is no meaning in life." But this preemptive judgment hardly considers the importance of the café as a substitute for home as understood by the old waiter. And he understands even more: the value of affection, of communication among men, and that love is necessary to self-realization and simple dignity to the end. These things are precisely what the young waiter does not understand, and the old waiter's *ironic* prayer makes perfectly clear that the story is about something very important to sensitive men and women. How else account for the final paragraph where the old man says to himself, "After all...it is probably only insomnia. Many must have it." Insomnia? Surely, an ironic name for loneliness and loss of identity, as Hemingway means it to be.

(K. L. Knickerbocker and H. Willard Reninger)

Questions

1. What besides insomnia makes the older waiter reluctant to go to

Chapter Five

bed? Comment especially on his meditation with its nada refrain. Why does he so well understand the old man's need for a café? What does the café represent for the two of them?
2. Compare the younger waiter and the older waiter in their attitudes towards the old man. Whose attitude do you take to be closer to that of the author? Even though Hemingway does not editorially state his own feelings, how does he make them clear to us?
3. Point to sentences that establish the style of the story. What is distinctive in them? What repetitions of words or phrases seem particularly effective? Why do you think Hemingway favours a simple vocabulary?
4. What is the story's point of view? Discuss its appropriateness.
5. What does "insomnia" symbolize?
6. What do you think is the main idea of the story?

Barn Burning
by William Faulkner, 1939

  The store in which the Justice of the Peace's court was sitting smelled of cheese. The boy, crouched on his nail keg at the back of the crowded room, knew he smelled cheese, and more: from where he sat he could see the ranked shelves close-packed with the solid, squat, dynamic shapes of tin cans whose labels his stomach read, not from the lettering which meant nothing to his mind but from the scarlet devils and the silver curve of fish—this, the cheese which he knew he smelled and the hermetic meat which his intestines believed he smelled coming in intermittent gusts momentary and brief between the other constant one, the smell and sense just a little of fear because mostly of despair and grief, the old fierce pull of blood. He could not see the table where the Justice sat and before which his father and his father's enemy (*our enemy* he thought in that despair: *ourn! mine and hisn both!*

He's my father!) stood, but he could hear them, the two of them that is, because his father had said no word yet:

"But what proof have you, Mr. Harris?"

"I told you. The hog got into my corn. I caught it up and sent it back to him. He had no fence that would hold it. I told him so, warned him. The next time I put the hog in my pen. When he came to get it I gave him enough wire to patch up his pen. The next time I put the hog up and kept it. I rode down to his house and saw the wire I gave him still rolled on to the spool in his yard. I told him he could have the hog when he paid me a dollar pound fee. That evening a nigger came with the dollar and got the hog. He was a strange nigger. He said, 'He say to tell you wood and hay kin burn.' I said, 'What?' 'That whut he say to tell you,' the nigger said. 'Wood and hay kin burn.' That night my barn burned. I got the stock out but I lost the barn."

"Where's the nigger? Have you got him?"

"He was a strange nigger, I tell you. I don't know what became of him."

"But that's not proof. Don't you see that's not proof?"

"Get that boy up here. He knows." For a moment the boy thought too that the man meant his older brother until Harris said, "Not him. The little one. The boy," and, crouching, small for his age, small and wiry like his father, in patched and faded jeans even too small for him, with straight, uncombed, brown hair and eyes gray and wild as storm scud, he saw the men between himself and the table part and become a lane of grim faces, at the end of which he saw the Justice, a shabby, collarless, graying man in spectacles, beckoning him. He felt no floor under his bare feet; he seemed to walk beneath the palpable weight of the grim turning faces. His father, still in his black Sunday coat donned not for the trial but for the moving, did not even look at him. *He aims for me to lie*, he thought, again with that frantic grief and despair. *And I will have to do hit*[1].

---

[1] hit: it.

Chapter Five

"What's your name, boy?" the Justice said.

"Colonel Sartoris Snopes," the boy whispered.

10 "Hey?" the Justice said. "Talk louder. Colonel Sartoris? I reckon anybody named for Colonel Sartoris in this country can't help but tell the truth, can they?" The boy said nothing. *Enemy! Enemy!* he thought; for a moment he could not even see, could not see that the Justice's face was kindly nor discern that his voice was troubled when he spoke to the man named Harris: "Do you want me to question this boy?" But he could hear, and during those subsequent long seconds while there was absolutely no sound in the crowded little room save that of quiet and intent breathing it was as if he had swung outward at the end of a grape vine, over a ravine, and at the top of the swing had been caught in a prolonged instant of mesmerized gravity, weightless in time.

"No!" Harris said violently, explosively. "Damnation! Send him out of here!" Now time, the fluid world, rushed beneath him again, the voices coming to him again through the smell of cheese and sealed meat, the fear and despair and the old grief of blood:

"This case is closed. I can't find against you, Snopes, but I can give you advice. Leave this country and don't come back to it."

His father spoke for the first time, his voice cold and harsh, level, without emphasis: "I aim to. I don't figure to stay in a country among people who..." he said something unprintable and vile, addressed to no one.

"That'll do," the Justice said. "Take your wagon and get out of this country before dark. Case dismissed."

15 His father turned, and he followed the stiff black coat, the wiry figure walking a little stiffly from where a Confederate provost's man's musket ball had taken him in the heel on a stolen horse thirty years ago, followed the two backs now, since his older brother had appeared from somewhere in the crowd, no taller than the father but thicker, chewing tobacco steadily, between the two lines of grimfaced men and out of the store and across the worn

gallery and down the sagging steps and among the dogs and half-grown boys in the mild May dust, where as he passed a voice hissed:

"Barn burner!"

Again he could not see, whirling; there was a face in a red haze, moonlike, bigger than the full moon, the owner of it half again his size, he leaping in the red haze toward the face, feeling no blow, feeling no shock when his head struck the earth, scrabbling up and leaping again, feeling no blow this time either and tasting no blood, scrabbling up to see the other boy in full flight and himself already leaping into pursuit as his father's hand jerked him back, the harsh, cold voice speaking above him: "Go get in the wagon."

It stood in a grove of locusts and mulberries across the road. His two hulking sisters in their Sunday dresses and his mother and her sister in calico and sunbonnets were already in it, sitting on and among the sorry residue of the dozen and more movings which even the boy could remember—the battered stove, the broken beds and chairs, the clock inlaid with mother-of-pearl, which would not run, stopped at some fourteen minutes past two o'clock of a dead and forgotten day and time, which had been his mother's dowry. She was crying, though when she saw him she drew her sleeve across her face and began to descend from the wagon. "Get back," the father said.

"He's hurt. I got to get some water and wash his..."

"Get back in the wagon," his father said. He got in too, over the tail-gate. His father mounted to the seat where the older brother already sat and struck the gaunt mules two savage blows with the peeled willow, but without heat. It was not even sadistic; it was exactly that same quality which in later years would cause his descendants to over-run the engine before putting a motor car into motion, striking and reining back in the same movement. The wagon went on, the store with its quiet crowd of grimly watching men dropped behind; a curve in the road hid it. *Forever* he

Chapter Five

thought. *Maybe he's done satisfied now, now that he has...* stopping himself, not to say it aloud even to himself. His mother's hand touched his shoulder.

"Does hit hurt?" she said.

"Naw," he said. "Hit don't hurt. Lemme be."

"Can't you wipe some of the blood off before hit dries?"

"I'll wash to-night," he said. "Lemme be, I tell you."

25   The wagon went on. He did not know where they were going. None of them ever did or ever asked, because it was always somewhere, always a house of sorts waiting for them a day or two days or even three days away. Likely his father had already arranged to make a crop on another farm before he... Again he had to stop himself. He (the father) always did. There was something about his wolflike independence and even courage when the advantage was at least neutral which impressed strangers, as if they got from his latent ravening ferocity not so much a sense of dependability as a feeling that his ferocious conviction in the rightness of his own actions would be of advantage to all whose interest lay with his.

That night they camped, in a grove of oaks and beeches where a spring ran. The nights were still cool and they had a fire against it, of a rail lifted from a nearby fence and cut into lengths—a small fire, neat, niggard almost, a shrewd fire; such fires were his father's habit and custom always, even in freezing weather. Older, the boy might have remarked this and wondered why not a big one; why should not a man who had not only seen the waste and extravagance of war, but who had in his blood an inherent voracious prodigality with material not his own, have burned everything in sight? Then he might have gone a step farther and thought that that was the reason: that niggard blaze was the living fruit of nights passed during those four years in the woods hiding from all men, blue and gray, with his strings of horses (captured horses, he called them). And older still, he might have divined the true reason: that the element of fire spoke to some deep mainspring of his father's being, as the element of steel or of powder spoke to other men, as the one weapon for the preservation of integrity, else breath were not worth the breathing, and hence to be regarded with respect and used with discretion.

But he did not think this now and he had seen those same niggard blazes all his life. He merely ate his supper beside it and was already half asleep over his iron plate when his father called him, and once more he followed the stiff back, the stiff and ruthless limp, up the slope and on to the starlit road where, turning, he could see his father against the stars but without face or depth—a shape black, flat, and bloodless as though cut from tin in the iron folds of the frockcoat which had not been made for him, the voice harsh like tin and without heat like tin:

"You were fixing to tell them. You would have told him."

He didn't answer. His father struck him with the flat of his hand on the side of the head, hard but without heat, exactly as he had struck the two mules at the store, exactly as he would strike either of them with any stick in order to kill a horse fly, his voice without heat or anger: "You're getting to be a man. You got to learn. You got to learn to stick to your own blood or you ain't going to have any blood to stick to you. Do you think either of them, any man there this morning, would? Don't you know all they wanted was a chance to get at me because they knew I had them beat? Eh?" Later, twenty years later, he was to tell himself, "If I had said they wanted only truth, justice, he would have hit me again." But now he said nothing. He was not crying. He just stood there. "Answer me," his father said.

"Yes," he whispered. His father turned.

"Get on to bed. We'll be there tomorrow."

Tomorrow they were there. In the early afternoon the wagon stopped before a paintless two-room house identical almost with the dozen others it had stopped before even in the boy's ten years, and again, as on the other dozen occasions, his mother and aunt got down and began to unload the wagon, although his two sisters and

Chapter Five

his father and brother had not moved.

"Likely hit ain't fitten for hawgs[1]," one of the sisters said.

"Nevertheless, fit it will and you'll hog it and like it," his father said. "Get out of them chairs and help your Ma unload."

35   The two sisters got down, big, bovine, in a flutter of cheap ribbons; one of them drew from the jumbled wagon bed a battered lantern, the other a worn broom. His father handed the reins to the older son and began to climb stiffly over the wheel. "When they get unloaded, take the team to the barn and feed them." Then he said, and at first the boy thought he was still speaking to his brother: "Come with me."

"Me?" he said.

"Yes," his father said. "You."

"Abner," his mother said. His father paused and looked back—the harsh level stare beneath the shaggy, graying, irascible brows.

"I reckon I'll have a word with the man that aims to begin tomorrow owning me body and soul for the next eight months."

40   They went back up the road. A week ago—or before last night, that is—he would have asked where they were going, but not now. His father had struck him before last night but never before had he paused afterward to explain why; it was as if the blow and the following calm, outrageous voice still rang, repercussed, divulging nothing to him save the terrible handicap of being young, the light weight of his few years, just heavy enough to prevent his soaring free of the world as it seemed to be ordered but not heavy enough to keep him footed solid in it, to resist it and try to change the course of its events.

Presently he could see the grove of oaks and cedars and the other flowering trees and shrubs where the house would be, though not the house yet. They walked beside a fence massed with honeysuckle and Cherokee roses and came to a gate swinging open

---

[1] hit ain't fitten for hawgs: it isn't fit for hogs.

between two brick pillars, and now, beyond a sweep of drive, he saw the house for the first time and at that instant he forgot his father and the terror and despair both, and even when he remembered his father again(who had not stopped) the terror and despair did not return. Because, for all the twelve movings, they had sojourned until now in a poor country, a land of small farms and fields and houses, and he had never seen a house like this before. *Hit's big as a courthouse* he thought quietly, with a surge of peace and joy whose reason he could not have thought into words, being too young for that: *They are safe from him. People whose lives are a part of this peace and dignity are beyond his touch, he no more to them than a buzzing wasp: capable of stinging for a little moment but that's all; the spell of this peace and dignity rendering even the barns and stable and cribs which belong to it impervious to the puny flames he might contrive...* this, the peace and joy, ebbing for an instant as he looked again at the stiff black back, the stiff and implacable limp of the figure which was not dwarfed by the house, for the reason that it had never looked big anywhere and which now, against the serene columned backdrop, had more than ever that impervious quality of something cut ruthlessly from tin, depthless, as though, sidewise to the sun, it would cast no shadow. Watching him, the boy remarked the absolutely undeviating course which his father held and saw the stiff foot come squarely down in a pile of fresh droppings where a horse had stood in the drive and which his father could have avoided by a simple change of stride. But it ebbed only a moment, though he could not have thought this into words either, walking on in the spell of the house, which he could even want but without envy, without sorrow, certainly never with that ravening and jealous rage which unknown to him walked in the ironlike black coat before him: *Maybe he will feel it too. Maybe it will even change him now from what maybe he couldn't help but be.*

They crossed the portico. Now he could hear his father's stiff foot as it came down on the boards with clocklike finality, a sound

Chapter Five

out of all proportion to the displacement of the body it bore and which was not dwarfed either by the white door before it, as though it had attained to a sort of vicious and ravening minimum not to be dwarfed by anything—the flat, wide, black hat, the formal coat of broadcloth which had once been black but which had now that friction-glazed greenish cast of the bodies of old house flies, the lifted sleeve which was too large, the lifted hand like a curled claw. The door opened so promptly that the boy knew the Negro must have been watching them all the time, an old man with neat grizzled hair, in a linen jacket, who stood barring the door with his body, saying, "Wipe yo foots, white man, fo you come in here. Major ain't home nohow."

"Get out of my way, nigger," his father said, without heat too, flinging the door back and the Negro also and entering, his hat still on his head. And now the boy saw the prints of the stiff foot on the doorjamb and saw them appear on the pale rug behind the machinelike deliberation of the foot which seemed to bear (or transmit) twice the weight which the body compassed. The Negro was shouting "Miss Lula! Miss Lula!" somewhere behind them, then the boy, deluged as though by a warm wave by a suave turn of the carpeted stair and a pendant glitter of chandeliers and a mute gleam of gold frames, heard the swift feet and saw her too, a lady—perhaps he had never seen her like before either—in a gray, smooth gown with lace at the throat and an apron tied at the waist and the sleeves turned back, wiping cake or biscuit dough from her hands with a towel as she came up the hall, looking not at his father at all but at the tracks on the blond rug with an expression of incredulous amazement.

"I tried," the Negro cried. "I tole him to..."

45   "Will you please go away?" she said in a shaking voice. "Major de Spain is not at home. Will you please go away?"

His father had not spoken again. He did not speak again. He did not even look at her. He just stood stiff in the center of the rug, in his hat, the shaggy iron-gray brows twitching slightly above the pebble-colored eyes as he appeared to examine the house with brief deliberation. Then with the same deliberation he turned; the boy watched him pivot on the good leg and saw the stiff foot drag around the arc of the turning, leaving a final long and fading smear. His father never looked at it, he never once looked down at the rug. The Negro held the door. It closed behind them, upon the hysteric and indistinguishable woman-wail. His father stopped at the top of the steps and scraped his boot clean on the edge of it. At the gate he stopped again. He stood for a moment, planted stiffly on the stiff foot, looking back at the house. "Pretty and white, ain't it?" he said. "That's sweat. Nigger sweat. Maybe it ain't white enough yet to suit him. Maybe he wants to mix some white sweat with it."

  Two hours later the boy was chopping wood behind the house within which his mother and aunt and the two sisters (the mother and aunt, not the two girls, he knew that; even at this distance and muffled by walls the flat loud voices of the two girls emanated an incorrigible idle inertia) were setting up the stove to prepare a meal, when he heard the hooves and saw the linen-clad man on a fine sorrel mare, whom he recognized even before he saw the rolled rug in front of the Negro youth following on a fat bay carriage horse—a suffused, angry face vanishing, still at full gallop, beyond the corner of the house where his father and brother were sitting in the two tilted chairs; and a moment later, almost before he could have put the axe down, he heard the hooves again and watched the sorrel mare go back out of the yard, already galloping again. Then his father began to shout one of the sisters' names, who presently emerged backward from the kitchen door dragging the rolled rug along the ground by one end while the other sister walked behind it.

  "If you ain't going to tote, go on and set up the wash pot," the first said.

  "You, Sarty!" the second shouted. "Set up the wash pot!" His father appeared at the door, framed against that shabbiness, as he had been against that other bland perfection, impervious to either, the mother's anxious face at his shoulder.

50 "Go on," the father said. "Pick it up." The two sisters stooped, broad, lethargic; stooping, they presented an incredible expanse of pale cloth and a flutter of tawdry ribbons.

"If I thought enough of a rug to have to git hit[1] all the way from France I wouldn't keep hit where folks coming in would have to tromp on hit," the first said. They raised the rug.

"Abner," the mother said. "Let me do it."

"You go back and git dinner," his father said. "I'll tend to this."

From the woodpile through the rest of the afternoon the boy watched them, the rug spread flat in the dust beside the bubbling wash pot, the two sisters stooping over it with that profound and lethargic reluctance, while the father stood over them in turn, implacable and grim, driving them though never raising his voice again. He could smell the harsh homemade lye they were using; he saw his mother come to the door once and look toward them with an expression not anxious now but very like despair; he saw his father turn, and he fell to with the axe and saw from the corner of his eye his father raise from the ground a flattish fragment of field stone and examine it and return to the pot, and this time his mother actually spoke: "Abner. Abner. Please don't. Please, Abner."

55 Then he was done too. It was dusk; the whippoorwills had already begun. He could smell coffee from the room where they would presently eat the cold food remaining from the mid-afternoon meal, though when he entered the house he realized they were having coffee again probably because there was a fire on the hearth, before which the rug now lay spread over the backs of the two chairs. The tracks of his father's foot were gone. Where they had been were now long, water-cloudy scoriations resembling the sporadic course of a lilliputian mowing machine.

---

[1] git hit: get it.

It still hung there while they ate the cold food and then went to bed, scattered without order or claim up and down the two rooms, his mother in one bed, where his father would later lie, the older brother in the other, himself, the aunt, and the two sisters on pallets on the floor. But his father was not in bed yet. The last thing the boy remembered was the depthless, harsh silhouette of the hat and coat bending over the rug and it seemed to him that he had not even closed his eyes when the silhouette was standing over him, the fire almost dead behind it, the stiff foot prodding him awake. "Catch up the mule," his father said.

When he returned with the mule his father was standing in the back door, the rolled rug over his shoulder. "Ain't you going to ride?" he said.

"No. Give me your foot."

He bent his knee into his father's hand, the wiry, surprising power flowed smoothly, rising, he rising with it, on to the mule's bare back (they had owned a saddle once; the boy could remember it though not when or where) and with the same effortlessness his father swung the rug up in front of him. Now in the starlight they retraced the afternoon's path, up the dusty road rife with honey-suckle, through the gate and up the black tunnel of the drive to the lightless house, where he sat on the mule and felt the rough warp of the rug drag across his thighs and vanish.

"Don't you want me to help?" he whispered. His father did not answer and now he heard again that stiff foot striking the hollow portico with that wooden and clocklike deliberation, that outrageous overstatement of the weight it carried. The rug, hunched, not flung (the boy could tell that even in the darkness) from his father's shoulder struck the angle of wall and floor with a sound unbelievably loud, thunderous, then the foot again, unhurried and enormous; a light came on in the house and the boy sat, tense, breathing steadily and quietly and just a little fast, though the foot itself did not increase its beat at all, descending the steps now; now the boy could see him.

Chapter Five

"Don't you want to ride now?" he whispered. "We kin both ride now," the light within the house altering now, flaring up and sinking. *He's coming down the stairs now*, he thought. He had already ridden the mule up beside the horse block; presently his father was up behind him and he doubled the reins over and slashed the mule across the neck, but before the animal could begin to trot the hard, thin arm came around him, the hard, knotted hand jerking the mule back to a walk.

In the first red rays of the sun they were in the lot, putting plow gear on the mules. This time the sorrel mare was in the lot before he heard it at all, the rider collarless and even bareheaded, trembling, speaking in a shaking voice as the woman in the house had done, his father merely looking up once before stooping again to the hame he was buckling, so that the man on the mare spoke to his stooping back:

"You must realize you have ruined that rug. Wasn't there anybody here, any of your women..." he ceased, shaking, the boy watching him, the older brother leaning now in the stable door, chewing, blinking slowly and steadily at nothing apparently. "It cost a hundred dollars. But you never had a hundred dollars. You never will. So I'm going to charge you twenty bushels of corn against your crop. I'll add it in your contract and when you come to the commissary you can sign it. That won't keep Mrs. de Spain quiet but maybe it will teach you to wipe your feet off before you enter her house again."

Then he was gone. The boy looked at his father, who still had not spoken or even looked up again, who was now adjusting the logger-head in the hame.

"Pap," he said. His father looked at him—the inscrutable face, the shaggy brows beneath where the gray eyes glinted coldly. Suddenly the boy went toward him, fast, stopping as suddenly. "You done the best you could!" he cried. "If he wanted hit done different why didn't he wait and tell you how? He won't git no twenty bushels! He won't git none! We'll gather hit and hide hit!

I kin watch...."

"Did you put the cutter back in that straight stock like I told you?"

"No, sir," he said.

"Then go do it."

That was Wednesday. During the rest of that week he worked steadily, at what was within his scope and some which was beyond it, with an industry that did not need to be driven nor even commanded twice; he had this from his mother, with the difference that some at least of what he did he liked to do, such as splitting wood with the half-size axe which his mother and aunt had earned, or saved money somehow, to present him with at Christmas. In company with the two older women (and on one afternoon, even one of the sisters), he built pens for the shoat and the cow which were a part of his father's contract with the landlord, and one afternoon, his father being absent, gone somewhere on one of the mules, he went to the field.

They were running a middle buster now, his brother holding the plow straight while he handled the reins, and walking beside the straining mule, the rich black soil shearing cool and damp against his bare ankles, he thought *Maybe this is the end of it. Maybe even that twenty bushels that seems hard to have to pay for just a rug will be a cheap price for him to stop forever and always from being what he used to be*; thinking, dreaming now, so that his brother had to speak sharply to him to mind the mule: *Maybe he even won't collect the twenty bushels. Maybe it will all add up and balance and vanish—corn, rug, fire; the terror and grief; the being pulled two ways like between two teams of horses—gone, done with for ever and ever.*

Then it was Saturday; he looked up from beneath the mule he was harnessing and saw his father in the black coat and hat. "Not that," his father said. "The wagon gear." And then, two hours later, sitting in the wagon bed behind his father and brother on the seat, the wagon accomplished a final curve, and he saw the weathered paintless store with its tattered tobacco and patent-medicine posters and the tethered wagons and saddle animals below the gallery. He mounted the gnawed steps behind his father and brother, and there again was the lane of quiet, watching faces for the three of them to walk through. He saw the man in spectacles sitting at the plank table and he did not need to be told this was a Justice of the Peace; he sent one glare of fierce, exultant, partisan defiance at the man in collar and cravat now, whom he had seen but twice before in his life, and that on a galloping horse, who now wore on his face an expression not of rage but of amazed unbelief which the boy could not have known was at the incredible circumstance of being sued by one of his own tenants, and came and stood against his father and cried at the Justice:"He ain't done it! He ain't burnt..."

"Go back to the wagon," his father said.

"Burnt?" the Justice said. "Do I understand this rug was burned too?"

"Does anybody here claim it was?" his father said. "Go back to the wagon." But he did not, he merely retreated to the rear of the room, crowded as that other had been, but not to sit down this time, instead, to stand pressing among the motionless bodies, listening to the voices:

"And you claim twenty bushels of corn is too high for the damage you did to the rug?"

"He brought the rug to me and said he wanted the tracks washed out of it. I washed the tracks out and took the rug back to him."

"But you didn't carry the rug back to him in the same condition it was in before you made the tracks on it."

His father did not answer, and now for perhaps half a minute there was no sound at all save that of breathing, the faint, steady suspiration of complete and intent listening.

"You decline to answer that, Mr. Snopes?" Again his father did not answer. "I'm going to find against you, Mr. Snopes. I'm going to find that you were responsible for the injury to Major de Spain's rug and hold you liable for it. But twenty bushels of corn seems a little high for a man in your circumstances to have to pay. Major de Spain claims it cost a hundred dollars. October corn will be worth about fifty cents. I figure that if Major de Spain can stand a ninety-five dollar loss on something he paid cash for, you can stand a five-dollar loss you haven't earned yet. I hold you in damages to Major de Spain to the amount of ten bushels of corn over and above your contract with him, to be paid to him out of your crop at gathering time. Court adjourned."

80 It had taken no time hardly, the morning was but half begun. He thought they would return home and perhaps back to the field, since they were late, far behind all other farmers. But instead his father passed on behind the wagon, merely indicating with his hand for the older brother to follow with it, and crossed the road toward the blacksmith shop opposite, pressing on after his father, overtaking him, speaking, whispering up at the harsh, calm face beneath the weathered hat: "He won't git no ten bushels either. He won't git one. We'll..." until his father glanced for an instant down at him, the face absolutely calm, the grizzled eyebrows tangled above the cold eyes, the voice almost pleasant, almost gentle:

"You think so? Well, we'll wait till October anyway."

The matter of the wagon—the setting of a spoke or two and the tightening of the tires—did not take long either, the business of the tires accomplished by driving the wagon into the spring branch behind the shop and letting it stand there, the mules nuzzling into the water from time to time, and the boy on the seat with the idle reins, looking up the slope and through the sooty tunnel of the shed where the slow hammer rang and where his father sat on an upended cypress bolt, easily, either talking or listening, still sitting there when the boy brought the dripping wagon up out of the branch and halted it before the door.

"Take them on to the shade and hitch," his father said. He did so and returned. His father and the smith and a third man

Chapter Five

squatting on his heels inside the door were talking, about crops and animals; the boy, squatting too in the ammoniac dust and hoofparings and scales of rust, heard his father tell a long and unhurried story out of the time before the birth of the older brother even when he had been a professional horsetrader. And then his father came up beside him where he stood before a tattered last year's circus poster on the other side of the store, gazing rapt and quiet at the scarlet horses, the incredible poisings and convulsions of tulle and tights and the painted leers of comedians, and said, "It's time to eat."

But not at home. Squatting beside his brother against the front wall, he watched his father emerge from the store and produce from a paper sack a segment of cheese and divide it carefully and deliberately into three with his pocket knife and produce crackers from the same sack. They all three squatted on the gallery and ate, slowly, without talking; then in the store again, they drank from a tin dipper tepid water smelling of the cedar bucket and of living beech trees. And still they did not go home. It was a horse lot this time, a tall rail fence upon and along which men stood and sat and out of which one by one horses were led, to be walked and trotted and then cantered back and forth along the road while the slow swapping and buying went on and the sun began to slant westward, they—the three of them—watching and listening, the older brother with his muddy eyes and his steady, inevitable tobacco, the father commenting now and then on certain of the animals, to no one in particular.

85　　It was after sundown when they reached home. They ate supper by lamp-light, then, sitting on the doorstep, the boy watched the night fully accomplish, listening to the whippoorwills and the frogs, when he heard his mother's voice: "Abner! No! No! Oh, God. Oh, God. Abner!" and he rose, whirled, and saw the altered light through the door where a candle stub now burned in a bottle neck on the table and his father, still in the hat and coat, at once formal and burlesque as though dressed carefully for some shabby and ceremonial violence, emptying the reservoir of the lamp back into the five-gallon kerosene can from which it had been filled, while the mother tugged at his arm until he shifted the lamp to the other hand and flung her back, not savagely or viciously, just hard, into the wall, her hands flung out against the wall for balance, her mouth open and in her face the same quality of hopeless despair as had been in her voice. Then his father saw him standing in the door.

"Go to the barn and get that can of oil we were oiling the wagon with," he said. The boy did not move. Then he could speak.

"What..." he cried. "What are you..."

"Go get that oil," his father said. "Go."

Then he was moving, running, outside the house, toward the stable: this the old habit, the old blood which he had not been permitted to choose for himself, which had been bequeathed him willy nilly and which had run for so long (and who knew where, batten-ing on what of outrage and savagery and lust) before it came to him. *I could keep on*, he thought. *I could run on and on and never look back, never need to see his face again. Only I can't. I can't*, the rusted can in his hand now, the liquid sploshing in it as he ran back to the house and into it, into the sound of his mother's weeping in the next room, and handed the can to his father.

"Ain't you going to even send a nigger?" he cried. "At least you sent a nigger before!"

This time his father didn't strike him. The hand came even faster than the blow had, the same hand which had set the can on the table with almost excruciating care flashing from the can toward him too quick for him to follow it, gripping him by the back of his shirt and on to tiptoe before he had seen it quit the can, the face stooping at him in breathless and frozen ferocity, the cold, dead voice speaking over him to the older brother who leaned against the table, chewing with that steady, curious, sidewise motion of cows:

"Empty the can into the big one and go on. I'll catch up with

Chapter Five

you."

"Better tie him up to the bedpost," the brother said.

"Do like I told you," the father said. Then the boy was moving, his bunched shirt and the hard, bony hand between his shoulder-blades, his toes just touching the floor, across the room and into the other one, past the sisters sitting with spread heavy thighs in the two chairs over the cold hearth, and to where his mother and aunt sat side by side on the bed, the aunt's arm about his mother's shoulders.

95   "Hold him," the father said. The aunt made a startled movement. "Not you," the father said. "Lennie. Take hold of him. I want to see you do it." His mother took him by the wrist. "You'll hold him better than that. If he gets loose don't you know what he is going to do? He will go up yonder." He jerked his head toward the road. "Maybe I'd better tie him."

"I'll hold him," his mother whispered.

"See you do then." Then his father was gone, the stiff foot heavy and measured upon the boards, ceasing at last.

Then he began to struggle. His mother caught him in both arms, he jerking and wrenching at them. He would be stronger in the end, he knew that. But he had no time to wait for it. "Lemme go!" he cried. "I don't want to have to hit you!"

"Let him go!" the aunt said. "If he don't go, before God, I am going up there myself!"

100   "Don't you see I can't?" his mother cried. "Sarty! Sarty! No! No! Help me, Lizzie!"

Then he was free. His aunt grasped at him but it was too late. He whirled, running, his mother stumbled forward on to her knees behind him, crying to the nearer sister: "Catch him, Net! Catch him!" But that was too late too, the sister (the sisters were twins, born at the same time, yet either of them now gave the impression of being, encompassing as much living meat and volume and weight as any other two of the family) not yet having begun to rise from the chair, her head, face, alone merely turned, presenting to him in the flying instant an astonishing expanse of young female features untroubled by any surprise even, wearing only an expression of bovine interest. Then he was out of the room, out of the house, in the mild dust of the starlit road and the heavy rifeness of honeysuckle, the pale ribbon unspooling with terrific slowness under his running feet, reaching the gate at last and turning in, running, his heart and lungs drumming, on up the drive toward the lighted house, the lighted door. He did not knock, he burst in, sobbing for breath, incapable for the moment of speech; he saw the astonished face of the Negro in the linen jacket without knowing when the Negro had appeared.

"De Spain!" he cried, panted. "Where's..." then he saw the white man too emerging from a white door down the hall. "Barn!" he cried. "Barn!"

"What?" the white man said. "Barn?"

"Yes!" the boy cried. "Barn!"

"Catch him!" the white man shouted.

But it was too late this time too. The Negro grasped his shirt, but the entire sleeve, rotten with washing, carried away, and he was out that door too and in the drive again, and had actually never ceased to run even while he was screaming into the white man's face.

Behind him the white man was shouting. "My horse! Fetch my horse!" and he thought for an instant of cutting across the park and climbing the fence into the road, but he did not know the park nor how the vine-massed fence might be and he dared not risk it. So he ran on down the drive, blood and breath roaring; presently he was in the road again though he could not see it. He could not hear either: the galloping mare was almost upon him before he heard her, and even then he held his course, as if the very urgency of his wild grief and need must in a moment more find him wings, waiting until the ultimate instant to hurl himself aside and into the weed-choked roadside ditch as the horse thundered past and on, for an instant in furious silhouette against the stars, the tranquil early

Chapter Five

summer night sky which, even before the shape of the horse and rider vanished, stained abruptly and violently upward: a long, swirling roar incredible and soundless, blotting the stars, and he springing up and into the road again, running again, knowing it was too late yet still running even after he heard the shot and an instant later, two shots, pausing now without knowing he had ceased to run, crying, "Pap! Pap!", running again before he knew he had begun to run, stumbling, tripping over something and scrabbling up again without ceasing to run, looking backward over his shoulder at the glare as he got up, running on among the invisible trees, panting, sobbing, "Father! Father!"

At midnight he was sitting on the crest of a hill. He did not know it was midnight and he did not know how far he had come. But there was no glare behind him now and he sat now, his back toward what he had called home for four days anyhow, his face toward the dark woods which he would enter when breath was strong again, small, shaking steadily in the chill darkness, hugging himself into the remainder of his thin, rotten shirt, the grief and despair now no longer terror and fear but just grief and despair. *Father. My father,* he thought. "He was brave!" he cried suddenly, aloud but not loud, no more than a whisper. "He was! He was in the war! He was in Colonel Sartoris' cav'ry!" not knowing that his father had gone to that war a private in the fine old European sense, wearing no uniform, admitting the authority of and giving fidelity to no man or army or flag, going to war as Malbrouck[1] himself did: for booty—it meant nothing and less than nothing to him if it were enemy booty or his own.

The slow constellations wheeled on. It would be dawn and then sun-up after a while and he would be hungry. But that would be tomorrow and now he was only cold, and walking would cure that. His breathing was easier now and he decided to get up and go

---

[1] Malbrouck: John Churchill, Duke of Marlborough (1650-1722), English general victorious in the Battle of Blenheim (1704), which triumph drove the French army out of Germany. The French called him Malbrouck, a name they found easier to pronounce.

on, and then he found that he had been asleep because he knew it was almost dawn, the night almost over. He could tell that from the whippoorwills. They were everywhere now among the dark trees below him, constant and inflectioned and ceaseless, so that, as the instant for giving over to the day birds drew nearer and nearer, there was no interval at all between them. He got up. He was a little stiff, but walking would cure that too as it would the cold, and soon there would be the sun. He went on down the hill, toward the dark woods within which the liquid silver voices of the birds called unceasing—the rapid and urgent beating of the urgent and quiring heart of the late spring night. He did not look back.

Discussion

A convenient starting place occurs near the beginning of the story. When the Snopes family makes camp the evening of the day of the first trial, Ab Snopes, as is his "habit and custom always," builds "a small fire, neat, niggard almost, a shrewd fire." Then, in a passage that deserves to be quoted at length, the narrator presents a hypothetical scenario for how Sarty Snopes might react to the size of his father's fire at subsequent stages in his development. "Older," the narrator says,

> the boy might have remarked this and wondered why not a big one; why should not a man who had not only seen the waste and extravagance of war, but who had in his blood an inherent voracious prodigality with material not his own, have burned everything in sight? Then he might have gone a step farther and thought that that was the reason: that niggard blaze was the living fruit of nights passed during those four years in the woods hiding from all men, blue or gray.... And older still, he

might have divined the true reason: that the element of fire spoke to some deep mainspring of his father's being... as the one weapon for the preservation of integrity, else breath were not worth the breathing, and hence to be regarded with respect and used with discretion.

This passage often receives commentary in formal terms, as an example of the extreme plasticity of Faulkner's approach to point of view. A moment's reflection should convince us that the passage is also important thematically, for it adumbrates the story's central action of Sarty's development into intellectual and moral adulthood. This development does not consist, as we might at first expect, of a three-stage movement from passive acceptance, to questioning, to insight. Faulkner instead subdivides the third stage, so that the moment of true insight is preceded by a moment of false but plausible insight. As the narrator's shift from "thought" to "divined" suggests, the distinction between the false and true moments of insight implies a larger distinction, evident throughout Faulkner's fiction, between a positivistic, probabilistic, external understanding of human behavior and an anti-rational, intuitive, internal one. The first, false explanation Sarty is imagined to provide derives from the external qualities of his father's history. It is plausible for the same reason it is false: because it can apply with equal likelihood to anyone who had endured four years of hiding during wartime. By comparison, the second explanation is true for an exactly opposite reason: because it moves past probability to an intuitive understanding of "the deep mainspring of [Sarty's] father's being."

The revelation of the nature of this "deep mainspring" is a central concern of the story as a whole. At first glance, the mainspring can be said to consist of two qualities of Ab's personality: his "ravening and jealous rage", which produces his gratuitous acts of provocation and revenge, and his tyranny, which produces his attempts to control the mind and emotions of his son. The attempts that the second of these qualities produces — in almost fairy-tale fashion, there are three of them — are central to the story of Sarty's development. If approached in the interrogative spirit of the developmental scenario, the three can be construed as a trio of questions: 1) Why does Ab take Sarty to the de Spain house the first time? 2) Why does he take Sarty the second time? and 3) Why does he refuse to tie Sarty to the bed, as his other son suggests, before leaving to burn de Spain's barn?

  Sarty's groping engagement with these three questions enacts the journey outlined in the developmental scenario. During the first trip to the de Spain house, Sarty exhibits the passivity characteristic of the first of the four stages of his hypothetical development. But his quiescence is fragile, a merely temporary retreat from the second stage, already begun, of his process of growth. It is only because his father "paused... to explain why" after striking him the night before that Sarty does not ask where they are going. Hence it is understandable that the second trip to the de Spain house should entail more active questioning on his part, and that the character of his questions should show Sarty fumbling toward a third-stage — that is, a plausible but incorrect — understanding of his father's motives. "Ain't you going to ride?" he says, and "Don't you want me to help," in attempts to explain in probabilistic ways why his father has had him "catch up" the mule and come along on the journey. "Don't you want to ride now... We kin both ride now", he says after Ab has placed the rug on de Spain's porch, yet again desperately seeking a rational, external explanation for his father's actions.

  Sarty's enactment of the story's script for development reaches its culmination in the third question-producing episode. This climactic scene depicts only implicitly Sarty's arrival at the divinatory fourth stage of insight. Instead, the scene depicts a stage beyond the fourth stage, where Sarty's struggle to understand his father's motives recedes into unimportance. When Sarty sees the de Spain house for the first time, with its promise of

Chapter Five

a life more peaceful and dignified than any he has known, the narrator says that "he forgot his father and the terror and despair both, and even when he remembered his father again... the terror and despair did not return". The father forgotten here (and throughout the story) is not the real father of flesh and blood but the minimalized, caricatured image of the father as principle of prohibitive authority resident within Sarty's mind. In the novel's imagistic economy, this process of forgetting, or of symbolic slaying, takes the form of a loosening of constraints on Sarty's physical movement. Forced to walk behind "the stiff black back, the stiff and implacable limp," and to feel himself "not heavy enough to [be] footed solid in the [world]", Sarty gradually comes into a "footedness" of his own, a process that culminates in his breaking out of the circle of his mother's arms, rushing out to warn de Spain, and, the next morning, walking "down the hill, toward the dark woods within which the liquid silver voices of the birds called unceasing."

The sketch just provided barely samples the richness of detail that can be elicited by a developmental reading of "Barn Burning." One thinks, for example, of Sarty's refusal to wipe away his blood after the fight with the boy who hisses "barn burner," a refusal that resonates against his struggle to define himself in relation to blood ties. Yet tempting as the prospect may be, remaining inside an exclusively developmental reading radically foreshortens the story's significance. This is so because a developmental reading limits our capacities as readers to those exhibited by Sarty himself: it allows us to see with Sarty, but not beyond him. The story invites us not so to limit ourselves, for it provides, in the long passage quoted above, a model not only for Sarty's development but for our performance as readers of Faulkner's fiction.

(Karl F. Zender)

Questions

1. What do you understand to be Faulkner's attitude towards Abner Snopes? Point to details in the story that convey attitudes.
2. After delivering his warning to Major de Spain, the boy Snopes does not actually witness what happens to his father and brother, nor what happens to the Major's barn. What do you assume does happen? What evidence is given in the story?
3. Suppose that Faulkner has written another story told by Abner Snopes in the first person. Why would such a story need a style different from that of "Barn Burning"? (Suggestion: Notice Faulkner's descriptions of Abner Snopes's voice.)
4. How would you like to describe the character of the father?
5. Although "Barn Burning" takes place some thirty years after the Civil War, how does the war figure in it?
6. What symbols do you find in the story? What symbolic acts?
7. Comparing with Hemingway's "A Clean, Well-Lighted Place," how will you sum up Faulkner's style in "Barn Burning"?
8. The author's choice of details, words, characters, and of events may lead us to infer his/her attitude, mood, and moral outlook in his/her work; even, perhaps, the way his personality pervades the work. Whatever leads us to infer the author's attitude, mood, moral outlook, and/or personality is commonly called **tone**. Like a tone of voice, the tone of a story may communicate amusement, anger, affection, sorrow, contempt, etc. Which adjective(s) best describe(s) the general tone of the story: calm, amused, disinterested, scornful, excited, impassioned? Point out passages that may be so described.

Chapter Six

Theme

Aristotle in *Poetics* lists six basic elements of tragedy. *Melody* (song) and *diction* (language) fall in the general category of style, and *spectacle* is relevant to setting in our discussion of fiction. The other three aspects are *mythos* or plot, *ethos* or character, and *dianoia*, which we generally translate into "thought" in English. According to Aristotle, plot is the "soul" or shaping principle of fiction, and characters exist primarily as functions of the plot. In most of the stories in the previous chapters, plot plays the role of principal structure of the story. But, as Northrop Frye points out, besides the internal fiction of the character and his/her society, there is an external fiction consisting of a relation between the writer and the writer's society (*Anatomy of Criticism*, 1957). We indeed have literary works by the likes of Shakespeare and Homer in which artistry is completely absorbed in their internal characters and we can hardly perceive the existence of the author. However, as soon as the author's personality appears on the horizon, a relation with the reader is established, and sometimes there seems no story at all apart from what the author is conveying to his/her reader. In this case, the primary interest is in *dianoia*, the idea or thought that the reader gets from the writer, which in modern criticism we generally call "theme."

The **theme** of a story, then, is whatever general idea or insight the entire story reveals. In some stories, the theme is rather obvious. For example, in Aesop's fable about the council of the mice that cannot decide who will bell the cat, the theme is stated in the moral at the end: "It is easier to propose a thing than to carry it out." In some novels, the title may offer a suggestion about the main theme. For example, Jane Austen's *Pride and Prejudice* is named after its theme, and the whole story unfolds itself a round that theme. In some novels, the title is not so named but the plot exists primarily to illustrate the theme and it is not very difficult for us to infer what it is. For example, *Uncle Tom's Cabin* by H. B. Stowe and *The Grapes of Wrath* by John Steinbeck voice the themes of slavery and migratory labour respectively. The title of *The Grapes of Wrath* comes from a line in an extremely famous Civil War song, "The Battle Hymn of the Republic." The line is, "He is trampling out the vintage where the Grapes of wrath are stored," which means "an unjust or oppressive situation, action or policy that may inflame desire for vengeance: an explosive condition." The song was written by a famous and influential social activist, Julia Ward Howe.

But in most literary works of fiction, the theme is seldom so obvious. That is, generally a theme is not a moral nor a message, neither is it clearly conveyed in the title. When we finish reading a finely wrought story, it is easier to sum up the plot—to say what happens—than to describe the main idea. To say of James Joyce's "Araby" that it is about a boy who goes to a bazaar to buy a gift for a young woman but arrives too late is to summarize plot, not theme. In many fine short stories, theme is the centre, the moving force, the principle of unity. Clearly, such a theme is something more than the characters and events of the story. Most of the short stories in the previous chapters challenge an easy-come theme. In Hemingway's "A Clean, Well-Lighted Place," as observed by Kennedy and Gioia, the events are rather simple—a younger waiter manages to get rid of the old man from the café and the older waiter stops at a coffee bar on his way home—but while the events themselves seem relatively slight, the story as a whole is full of meaning. (*Literature*, 1995) For a deep understanding of the meaning, we have to look to other elements of the story besides what happens in it: narrative, symbols, tone, the dialogue between the two waiters, the monologue of the older waiter, etc. Evidently the author intends us to pay more attention to the thoughts and feelings of the older waiter, the character whose words echo the author's voice. One try on the theme may be: "The older waiter understands the old man and sympathizes with his need for a clean, well-lighted place." But here we are still talking about what happens in the story, though we are not summing up the plot. A theme is usually stated in general words. Another try sounds like this: "Solitary people need a orderly place where they can drink with dignity." That is a little better. We have indicated that Hemingway's story is more than merely about an old man and two waiters. We remember that at the end the story is entirely confined to the older waiter's thoughts and perceptions. How do we understand his meditation on "nada," nothingness, which bears so much emphasis? No good statement of the theme of the story can leave it out. Then we have still another try: "Solitary people need a place of refuge from their terrible awareness that their life (or perhaps, human life) is essentially meaningless." Neither this nor any other statement of the story's theme is unarguably appropriate, but the statement at least touches one primary idea that Hemingway seems to be driving at. After we read "A Clean, Well-Lighted Place," we feel that there is such a theme, a unifying vision, even though we cannot reduce it to a tag and we may still vary in our opinion about, and statement of, the theme.

  Moral inferences may be drawn from most stories, no doubt, even when an author does not intend his/her story to be read this way. In "A Clean, Well-Lighted Place," we feel that Hemingway is indirectly giving us advice for properly regarding and sympathizing the lonely, the uncertain, and the old. But obviously the story does not set forth a lesson that we are supposed to put into practice. We can say for sure that "A Clean, Well-Lighted Place" contains several themes and other statements could be made to take in Hemingway's view of love, of communication between people, of dignity. Great stories, like great symphonies, frequently have more than one theme.

　　When we say that the title of *Pride and Prejudice* conveys the theme of the novel or that *Uncle Tom's Cabin* and *The Grapes of Wrath* treat the themes of slavery and migratory labour respectively, this is to use theme in a larger and more abstract sense than it is in our discussion of Hemingway's "A Clean, Well-Lighted Place." In this larger sense it is relatively easy to say that Mark Twain's *Huckleberry Finn*, Updike's *A & P*, and Faulkner's *Barn Burning* concern the theme of "initiation into maturity." Such general descriptions of theme can be useful, especially if we want to sort a large number of stories and novels into rough categories, but the fact that they are similar in theme does not mean that they mean the same thing. The attitude towards the theme may be very different: the tone of treatment may be, for example, either comic or tragic, straightforward or ironic. The writer's vision of life is the special underlying fact of a story, and a theme, abstractly stated, is not the same thing as a vision of life. And we suggest anyway that, in the beginning, you look for whatever truth or insight you think the writer of a story intends to reveal. Try to state a theme in a sentence. By doing so, we will find ourselves looking closely at the story. Kennedy and Gioia (*Literature*, 1995) make a helpful suggestion to consider the following points when we think about the theme of a story:

1. Look back once more at the title of the story. What does it indicate in relation to the whole story?
2. Does the main character in any way change in the story? Does this character arrive at any eventual realization or understanding? Are you left with any realization or understanding after finishing reading the story?
3. Does the author (through the narrator) make any general observations about life or human nature? Do the characters make any? (Caution: Characters now and again will utter opinions with which the reader is not necessarily supposed to agree.)

4. Does the story contain any especially curious objects, mysterious flat characters, significant animals, repeated names, special allusions, or whatever, that hint towards meanings larger than such things ordinarily have? In literary stories, such symbols or metaphors may point to central themes. (For a brief discussion of symbol, see Chapter Seven.)
5. When we have worded our statement of theme, have we cast our statement into general language, not just given a plot summary?
6. Does our statement hold true for the story as a whole, not just part of it?

Young Goodman Brown

by Nathaniel Hawthorne, (1829-1835)

  Young Goodman[1] Brown came forth, at sunset, into the street of Salem village[2], but put his head back, after crossing the threshold, to exchange a parting kiss with his young wife. And Faith, as the wife was aptly named, thrust her own pretty head into the street, letting the wind play with the pink ribbons of her cap, while she called to Goodman Brown.
  "Dearest heart," whispered she, softly and rather sadly, when her lips were close to his ear, "pray thee, put off your journey until sunrise, and sleep in your own bed to-night. A lone woman is troubled with such dreams and such thoughts, that she's afraid of herself, sometimes. Pray, tarry with me this night, dear husband, of all nights in the year!"
  "My love and my Faith," replied young Goodman Brown, "of all nights in the year, this one night must I tarry away from thee.

---

 [1] Goodman: title given by Puritans to a male head of a household; a farmer or other ordinary citizen.
 [2] Salem village: in England's Massachusetts Bay Colony.

My journey, as thou callest it, forth and back again, must needs be done 'twixt now and sunrise. What, my sweet, pretty wife, dost thou doubt me already, and we but three months married!"

"Then, God bless you!" said Faith, with the pink ribbons, "and may you find all well, when you come back."

"Amen!" cried Goodman Brown. "Say thy prayers, dear Faith, and go to bed at dusk, and no harm will come to thee."

So they parted; and the young man pursued his way, until, being about to turn the corner by the meeting-house, he looked back, and saw the head of Faith still peeping after him, with a melancholy air, in spite of her pink ribbons.

"Poor little Faith!" thought he, for his heart smote him. "What a wretch am I, to leave her on such an errand! She talks of dreams, too. Methought, as she spoke, there was trouble in her face, as if a dream had warned her what work is to be done tonight. But, no, no! 'twould kill her to think it. Well; she's a blessed angel on earth; and after this one night, I'll cling to her skirts and follow her to Heaven."

With this excellent resolve for the future, Goodman Brown felt himself justified in making more haste on his present evil purpose. He had taken a dreary road, darkened by all the gloomiest trees of the forest, which barely stood aside to let the narrow path creep through, and closed immediately behind. It was all as lonely as could be; and there is this peculiarity in such a solitude, that the traveller knows not who may be concealed by the innumerable trunks and the thick boughs overhead; so that, with lonely footsteps, he may yet be passing through an unseen multitude.

"There may be a devilish Indian behind every tree," said Goodman Brown, to himself; and he glanced fearfully behind him, as he added, "What if the devil himself should be at my very elbow!"

His head being turned back, he passed a crook of the road, and looking forward again, beheld the figure of a man, in grave and decent attire, seated at the foot of an old tree. He arose, at

Chapter Six

Goodman Brown's approach, and walked onward, side by side with him.

"You are late, Goodman Brown," said he. "The clock of the Old South was striking as I came through Boston; and that is full fifteen minutes agone[1]."

"Faith kept me back awhile," replied the young man, with a tremor in his voice, caused by the sudden appearance of his companion, though not wholly unexpected.

It was now deep dusk in the forest, and deepest in that part of it where these two were journeying. As nearly as could be discerned, the second traveller was about fifty years old, apparently in the same rank of life as Goodman Brown, and bearing a considerable resemblance to him, though perhaps more in expression than features. Still, they might have been taken for father and son. And yet, though the elder person was as simply clad as the younger, and as simple in manner too, he had an indescribable air of one who knew the world, and would not have felt abashed at the governor's dinner-table, or in King William's court[2], were it possible that his affairs should call him thither. But the only thing about him, that could be fixed upon as remarkable, was his staff, which bore the likeness of a great black snake, so curiously wrought, that it might almost be seen to twist and wriggle itself, like a living serpent. This, of course, must have been an ocular deception, assisted by the uncertain light.

"Come, Goodman Brown!" cried his fellow-traveller, "this is dull pace for the beginning of a journey. Take my staff, if you are so soon weary."

"Friend," said the other, exchanging his slow pace for a full stop, "having kept covenant by meeting thee here, it is my purpose now to return whence I came. I have scruples, touching the matter

---

[1] full fifteen minutes agone: Apparently this mystery man has traveled in a flash from Boston's Old South Church all the way to the woods beyond Salem—as the crow flies, a good sixteen miles.

[2] King William's court: back in England, where William Ⅲ reigned in 1689-1702.

thou wot'st[1] of."

"Sayest thou so?" replied he of the serpent, smiling apart. "Let us walk on, nevertheless, reasoning as we go, and if I convince thee not, thou shalt turn back. We are but a little way in the forest, yet."

"Too far, too far!" exclaimed the goodman, unconsciously resuming his walk. "My father never went into the woods on such an errand, nor his father before him. We have been a race of honest men and good Christians, since the days of the martyrs[2]. And shall I be the first of the name of Brown, that ever took this path, and kept—"

"Such company, thou wouldst say," observed the elder person, interpreting his pause. "Well said, Goodman Brown! I have been as well acquainted with your family as with ever a one among the Puritans; and that's no trifle to say. I helped your grandfather, the constable, when he lashed the Quaker woman so smartly through the streets of Salem. And it was I that brought your father a pitch-pine knot, kindled at my own hearth, to set fire to an Indian village, in King Philip's war[3]. They were my good friends, both; and many a pleasant walk have we had along this path, and returned merrily after midnight. I would fain be friends with you, for their sake."

"If it be as thou sayest," replied Goodman Brown, "I marvel they never spoke of these matters. Or, verily, I marvel not, seeing that the least rumor of the sort would have driven them from New-England. We are a people of prayer, and good works, to boot, and

---

[1] wot'st: know.

[2] days of the martyrs: a time when many forebears of the New England Puritans had given their lives for their religious convictions—when Mary I (Mary Tudor, nicknamed "Bloody Mary"), queen of England from 1553 to 1558, briefly re-established the Roman Catholic Church in England and launched a campaign of persecution against Protestants.

[3] King Philip's war: Metacomet, or King Philip (as the English called him), chief of the Wampanoag Indians, had led a bitter, widespread uprising of several New England tribes (1675-1678). Metacomet died in the war, as did one out of every ten white male colonists.

Chapter Six

abide no such wickedness."

20 "Wickedness or not," said the traveller with the twisted staff, "I have a very general acquaintance here in New-England. The deacons of many a church have drunk the communion wine with me; the selectmen, of divers towns, make me their chairman; and a majority of the Great and General Court are firm supporters of my interest. The governor and I, too—but these are state-secrets."

"Can this be so!" cried Goodman Brown, with a stare of amazement at his undisturbed companion. "Howbeit, I have nothing to do with the governor and council; they have their own ways, and are no rule for a simple husbandman, like me. But, were I to go on with thee, how should I meet the eye of that good old man, our minister, at Salem village? Oh, his voice would make me tremble, both Sabbath-day and lecture-day[1]!"

Thus far, the elder traveller had listened with due gravity, but now burst into a fit of irrepressible mirth, shaking himself so violently, that his snake-life staff actually seemed to wriggle in sympathy.

"Ha! ha! ha!" shouted he, again and again; then composing himself, "Well, go on, Goodman Brown, go on; but pray thee, don't kill me with laughing!"

"Well, then, to end the matter at once," said Goodman Brown, considerably nettled, "there is my wife, Faith. It would break her dear little heart; and I'd rather break my own!"

25 "Nay, if that be the case," answered the other, "e'en go thy ways, Goodman Brown. I would not, for twenty old women like the one hobbling before us, that Faith should come to any harm."

As he spoke, he pointed his staff at a female figure on the path, in whom Goodman Brown recognized a very pious and exemplary dame, who had taught him his catechism, in youth, and was still his moral and spiritual adviser, jointly with the minister and Deacon Gookin.

---

[1] lecture-day: a weekday when everyone had to go to church to hear a sermon or Bible-reading.

"A marvel, truly, that Goody[1] Cloyse should be so far in the wilderness, at night-fall!" said he. "But, with your leave, friend, I shall take a cut through the woods, until we have left this Christian woman behind. Being a stranger to you, she might ask whom I was consorting with, and whither I was going."

"Be it so," said his fellow-traveller. "Betake you to the woods, and let me keep the path."

Accordingly, the young man turned aside, but took care to watch his companion, who advanced softly along the road, until he had come within a staff's length of the old dame. She, meanwhile, was making the best of her way, with singular speed for so aged a woman, and mumbling some indistinct words, a prayer, doubtless, as she went. The traveller put forth his staff, and touched her withered neck with what seemed the serpent's tail.

"The devil!" screamed the pious old lady.

"Then Goody Cloyse knows her old friend?" observed the traveller, confronting her, and leaning on his writhing stick.

"Ah, forsooth, and is it your worship, indeed?" cried the good dame. "Yea, truly is it, and in the very image of my old gossip[2], Goodman Brown, the grand-father of the silly fellow that now is. But—would your worship believe it?—my broomstick hath strangely disappeared, stolen, as I suspect, by that unhanged witch, Goody Cory, and that, too, when I was all anointed with the juice of smallage and cinquefoil and wolf's bane[3]—"

"Mingled with fine wheat and the fat of a new-born babe," said the shape of old Goodman Brown.

"Ah, your worship knows the receipt," cried the old lady,

---

[1] Goody: short for Goodwife, title for a married woman of ordinary station. In his story, Hawthorne borrows from history the names of two "Goodys"—Goody Cloyse and Goody Cory—and one unmarried woman, Martha Carrier. In 1692 Hawthorne's great-grandfather, John Hawthorne, a judge in the Salem witchcraft trials, had condemned all three to be hanged.

[2] gossip: friend or kinsman.

[3] smallage and cinquefoil and wolf's bane: wild plants—here, ingredients for a witch's brew.

Chapter Six

cackling aloud. "So, as I was saying, being all ready for the meeting, and no horse to ride on, I made up my mind to foot it; for they tell me, there is a nice young man to be taken into communion to-night. But now your good worship will lend me your arm, and we shall be there in a twinkling."

35 "That can hardly be," answered her friend. "I may not spare you my arm, Goody Cloyse, but here is my staff, if you will."

So saying, he threw it down at her feet, where, perhaps, it assumed life, being one of the rods which its owner had formerly lent to the Egyptian Magi[1]. Of this fact, however, Goodman Brown could not take cognizance. He had cast up his eyes in astonishment, and looking down again, beheld neither Goody Cloyse nor the serpentine staff, but his fellow-traveller alone, who waited for him as calmly as if nothing had happened.

"That old woman taught me my catechism!" said the young man; and there was a world of meaning in this simple comment.

They continued to walk onward, while the elder traveller exhorted his companion to make good speed and persevere in the path, discoursing so aptly, that his arguments seemed rather to spring up in the bosom of his auditor, than to be suggested by himself. As they went, he plucked a branch of maple, to serve for a walking-stick, and began to strip it of the twigs and little boughs, which were wet with evening dew. The moment his fingers touched them, they became strangely withered and dried up, as with a week's sunshine. Thus the pair proceeded, at a good free pace, until suddenly, in a gloomy hollow of the road, Goodman Brown sat himself down on the stump of a tree, and refused to go any farther.

"Friend," said he, stubbornly, "my mind is made up. Not another step will I budge on this errand. What if a wretched old woman do choose to go to the devil, when I thought she was going

---

[1] Egyptian Magi: In the Bible, Pharaoh's wise men and sorcerers who by their magical powers changed their rods into live serpents. (This incident, part of the story of Moses and Aaron, is related in Exodus 7:8-12.)

to Heaven! Is that any reason why I should quit my dear Faith, and go after her?"

40 　　"You will think better of this, by-and-by," said his acquaintance, composedly. "Sit here and rest yourself awhile; and when you feel like moving again, there is my staff to help you along."

　　Without more words, he threw his companion the maple stick, and was as speedily out of sight, as if he had vanished into the deepening gloom. The young man sat a few moments, by the roadside, applauding himself greatly, and thinking with how clear a conscience he should meet the minister, in his morning-walk, nor shrink from the eye of good old Deacon Gookin. And what calm sleep would be his, that very night, which was to have been spent so wickedly, but purely and sweetly now, in the arms of Faith! Amidst these pleasant and praiseworthy meditations, Goodman Brown heard the tramp of horses along the road, and deemed it advisable to conceal himself within the verge of the forest, conscious of the guilty purpose that had brought him thither, though now so happily turned from it.

　　On came the hoof-tramps and the voices of the riders, two grave old voices, conversing soberly as they drew near. These mingled sounds appeared to pass along the road, within a few yards of the young man's hiding-place; but owing, doubtless, to the depth of the gloom, at that particular spot, neither the travellers nor their steeds were visible. Though their figures brushed the small boughs by the way-side, it could not be seen that they intercepted, even for a moment, the faint gleam from the strip of bright sky, athwart which they must have passed. Goodman Brown alternately crouched and stood on tip-toe, pulling aside the branches, and thrusting forth his head as far as he durst, without discerning so much as a shadow. It vexed him the more, because he could have sworn, were such a thing possible, that he recognized the voices of the minister and Deacon Gookin, jogging along quietly, as they were wont to do, when bound to some ordination or ecclesiastical council. While yet within hearing, one of the riders stopped to pluck a switch.

"Of the two, reverend Sir," said the voice like the deacon's, "I had rather miss an ordination-dinner than to-night's meeting. They tell me that some of our community are to be here from Falmouth and beyond, and others from Connecticut and Rhode-Island; besides several of the Indian powows[1], who, after their fashion, know almost as much deviltry as the best of us. Moreover, there is a goodly young woman to be taken into communion."

"Mighty well, Deacon Gookin!" replied the solemn old tones of the minister. "Spur up, or we shall be late. Nothing can be done, you know, until I get on the ground."

45　　The hoofs clattered again, and the voices, talking so strangely in the empty air, passed on through the forest, where no church had ever been gathered, nor solitary Christian prayed. Whither, then, could these holy men be journeying, so deep into the heathen wilderness? Young Goodman Brown caught hold of a tree, for support, being ready to sink down on the ground, faint and overburdened with the heavy sickness of his heart. He looked up to the sky, doubting whether there really was a Heaven above him. Yet, there was the blue arch, and the stars brightening in it.

"With Heaven above, and Faith below, I will yet stand firm against the devil!" cried Goodman Brown.

While he still gazed upward, into the deep arch of the firmament, and had lifted his hands to pray, a cloud, though no wind was stirring, hurried across the zenith, and hid the brightening stars. The blue sky was still visible, except directly overhead, where this black mass of cloud was sweeping swiftly northward. Aloft in the air, as if from the depths of the cloud, came a confused and doubtful sound of voices. Once, the listener fancied that he could distinguish the accents of town's-people of his own, men and women, both pious and ungodly, many of whom he

---

[1] powows: Indian priests or medicine men.

had met at the communion-table, and had seen others rioting at the tavern. The next moment, so indistinct were the sounds, he doubted whether he had heard aught but the murmur of the old forest, whispering without a wind. Then came a stronger swell of those familiar tones, heard daily in the sunshine, at Salem village, but never, until now, from a cloud of night. There was one voice, of a young woman, uttering lamentations, yet with an uncertain sorrow, and entreating for some favor, which, perhaps, it would grieve her to obtain. And all the unseen multitude, both saints and sinners, seemed to encourage her onward.

"Faith!" shouted Goodman Brown, in a voice of agony and desperation; and the echoes of the forest mocked him, crying—"Faith! Faith!" as if bewildered wretches were seeking her, all through the wilderness.

The cry of grief, rage, and terror, was yet piercing the night, when the unhappy husband held his breath for a response. There was a scream, drowned immediately in a louder murmur of voices, fading into far-off laughter, as the dark cloud swept away, leaving the clear and silent sky above Goodman Brown. But something fluttered lightly down through the air, and caught on the branch of a tree. The young man seized it, and beheld a pink ribbon.

"My Faith is gone!" cried he, after one stupefied moment. "There is no good on earth; and sin is but a name. Come, devil! for to thee is this world given."

And maddened with despair, so that he laughed loud and long, did Goodman Brown grasp his staff and set forth again, at such a rate, that he seemed to fly along the forest-path, rather than to walk or run. The road grew wilder and drearier, and more faintly traced, and vanished at length, leaving him in the heart of the dark wilderness, still rushing onward, with the instinct that guides mortal man to evil. The whole forest was peopled with frightful sounds; the creaking of the trees, the howling of wild beasts, and the yell of Indians; while, sometimes, the wind tolled like a distant church-bell, and sometimes gave a broad roar around the traveller,

Chapter Six

as if all Nature were laughing him to scorn. But he was himself the chief horror of the scene, and shrank not from its other horrors.

"Ha! ha! ha!" roared Goodman Brown, when the wind laughed at him. "Let us hear which will laugh loudest! Think not to frighten me with your deviltry! Come witch, come wizard, come Indian powow, come devil himself! and here comes Goodman Brown. You may as well fear him as he fear you!"

In truth, all through the haunted forest, there could be nothing more frightful than the figure of Goodman Brown. On he flew, among the black pines, brandishing his staff with frenzied gestures, now giving vent to an inspiration of horrid blasphemy, and now shouting forth such laughter, as set all the echoes of the forest laughing like demons around him. The fiend in his own shape is less hideous, than when he rages in the breast of man. Thus sped the demoniac on his course, until, quivering among the trees, he saw a red light before him, as when the felled trunks and branches of a clearing have been set on fire, and throw up their lurid blaze against the sky, at the hour of midnight. He paused, in a lull of the tempest that had driven him onward, and heard the swell of what seemed a hymn, rolling solemnly from a distance, with the weight of many voices. He knew the tune; it was a familiar one in the choir of the village meeting-house. The verse died heavily away, and was lengthened by a chorus, not of human voices, but of all the sounds of the benighted wilderness, pealing in awful harmony together. Goodman Brown cried out; and his cry was lost to his own ear, by its unison with the cry of the desert.

In the interval of silence, he stole forward, until the light glared full upon his eyes. At one extremity of an open space, hemmed in by the dark wall of the forest, arose a rock, bearing some rude, natural resemblance either to an altar or a pulpit, and surrounded by four blazing pines, their tops aflame, their stems untouched, like candles at an evening meeting. The mass of foliage, that had overgrown the summit of the rock, was all on fire, blazing high into the night, and fitfully illuminating the whole field. Each pendent twig and leafy festoon was in a blaze. As the red light arose and fell, a numerous congregation alternately shone forth, then disappeared in shadow, and again grew, as it were, out of the darkness, peopling the heart of the solitary woods at once.

55   "A grave and dark-clad company!" quoth Goodman Brown.

In truth, they were such. Among them, quivering to-and-fro, between gloom and splendor, appeared faces that would be seen, next day, at the council-board of the province, and others which, Sabbath after Sabbath, looked devoutly heavenward, and benignantly over the crowded pews, from the holiest pulpits in the land. Some affirm that the lady of the governor was there. At least, there were high dames well known to her, and wives of honored husbands, and widows, a great multitude, and ancient maidens, all of excellent repute, and fair young girls, who trembled, lest their mothers should espy them. Either the sudden gleams of light, flashing over the obscure field, bedazzled Goodman Brown, or he recognized a score of the church-members of Salem village, famous for their especial sanctity. Good old Deacon Gookin had arrived, and waited at the skirts of that venerable saint, his revered pastor. But, irreverently consorting with these grave, reputable, and pious people, these elders of the church, these chaste dames and dewy virgins, there were men of dissolute lives and women of spotted fame, wretches given over to all mean and filthy vice, and suspected even of horrid crimes. It was strange to see, that the good shrank not from the wicked, nor were the sinners abashed by the saints. Scattered, also, among their pale-faced enemies, were the Indian priests, or powows, who had often scared their native forest with more hideous incantations than any known to English witchcraft.

"But, where is Faith?" thought Goodman Brown; and, as hope came into his heart, he trembled.

Another verse of the hymn arose, a slow and mournful strain, such as the pious love, but joined to words which expressed all that our nature can conceive of sin, and darkly hinted at far more.

Chapter Six

Unfathomable to mere mortals is the lore of fiends. Verse after verse was sung, and still the chorus of the desert swelled between, like the deepest tone of a mighty organ. And, with the final peal of that dreadful anthem, there came a sound, as if the roaring wind, the rushing streams, the howling beasts, and every other voice of the unconverted wilderness, were mingling and according with the voice of guilty man, in homage to the prince of all. The four blazing pines threw up a loftier flame, and obscurely discovered shapes and visages of horror on the smoke-wreaths, above the impious assembly. At the same moment, the fire on the rock shot redly forth, and formed a glowing arch above its base, where now appeared a figure. With reverence be it spoken, the figure bore no slight similitude, both in garb and manner, to some grave divine of the New-England churches.

"Bring forth the converts!" cried a voice, that echoed through the field and rolled into the forest.

60   At the word, Goodman Brown stepped forth from the shadow of the trees, and approached the congregation, with whom he felt a loathful brotherhood, by the sympathy of all that was wicked in his heart. He could have well nigh sworn, that the shape of his own dead father beckoned him to advance, looking downward from a smoke-wreath, while a woman, with dim features of despair, threw out her hand to warn him back. Was it his mother? But he had no power to retreat one step, nor to resist, even in thought, when the minister and good old Deacon Gookin seized his arms, and led him to the blazing rock. Thither came also the slender form of a veiled female, led between Goody Cloyse, that pious teacher of the catechism, and Martha Carrier, who had received the devil's promise to be queen of hell. A rampant hag was she! And there stood the proselytes[1], beneath the canopy of fire.

"Welcome, my children," said the dark figure, "to the communion of your race! Ye have found, thus young, your nature

---

[1] proselytes: new converts.

and your destiny. My children, look behind you!"

They turned; and flashing forth, as it were, in a sheet of flame, the fiend-worshippers were seen; the smile of welcome gleamed darkly on every visage.

"There," resumed the sable form, "are all whom ye have reverenced from youth. Ye deemed them holier than yourselves, and shrank from your own sin, contrasting it with their lives of righteousness, and prayerful aspirations heavenward. Yet, here are they all, in my worshipping assembly! This night it shall be grant-ed you to know their secret deeds; how hoary-bearded elders of the church have whispered wanton words to the young maids of their households; how many a woman, eager for widow's weeds, has given her husband a drink at bed-time, and let him sleep his last sleep in her bosom; how beardless youths have made haste to inherit their fathers' wealth; and how fair damsels—blush not, sweet ones! —have dug little graves in the garden, and bidden me, the sole guest, to an infant's funeral. By the sympathy of your human hearts for sin, ye shall scent out all the places—whether in church, bed-chamber, street, field, or forest—where crime has been committed, and shall exult to behold the whole earth one stain of guilt, one mighty bloodspot. Far more than this! It shall be yours to penetrate, in every bosom, the deep mystery of sin, the fountain of all wicked arts, and which inexhaustibly supplies more evil impulses than human power—than my power, at its utmost! —can make manifest in deeds. And now, my children, look upon each other."

They did so; and, by the blaze of the hell-kindled torches, the wretched man beheld his Faith, and the wife her husband, trembling before that unhallowed altar.

65 "Lo! there ye stand, my children," said the figure, in a deep and solemn tone, almost sad, with its despairing awfulness, as if his once angelic nature could yet mourn for our miserable race. "Depending upon one another's hearts, ye had still hoped, that virtue were not all a dream. Now are ye undeceived! Evil is the

Chapter Six

nature of mankind. Evil must be your only happiness. Welcome, again, my children, to the communion of your race!"

"Welcome!" repeated the fiend-worshippers, in one cry of despair and triumph.

And there they stood, the only pair, as it seemed, who were yet hesitating on the verge of wickedness, in this dark world. A basin was hollowed, naturally, in the rock. Did it contain water, reddened by the lurid light? or was it blood? or, perchance, a liquid flame? Herein did the Shape of Evil dip his hand, and prepare to lay the mark of baptism upon their foreheads, that they might be partakers of the mystery of sin, more conscious of the secret guilt of others, both in deed and thought, than they could now be of their own. The husband cast one look at his pale wife, and Faith at him. What polluted wretches would the next glance show them to each other, shuddering alike at what they disclosed and what they saw!

"Faith! Faith!" cried the husband. "Look up to Heaven, and resist the Wicked one!"

Whether Faith obeyed, he knew not. Hardly had he spoken, when he found himself amid calm night and solitude, listening to a roar of the wind, which died heavily away through the forest. He staggered against the rock and felt it chill and damp, while a hanging twig, that had been all on fire, besprinkled his cheek with the coldest dew.

The next morning, young Goodman Brown came slowly into the street of Salem village, staring around him like a bewildered man. The good old minister was taking a walk along the graveyard, to get an appetite for breakfast and meditate his sermon, and bestowed a blessing, as he passed, on Goodman Brown. He shrank from the venerable saint, as if to avoid an anathema[1]. Old Deacon Goodkin was at domestic worship, and the holy words of his prayer were heard through the open window. "What God doth the wizard

---

[1] anathema: an official curse, a decree that casts one out of a church and bans him from receiving the sacraments.

pray to?" quoth Goodman Brown. Goody Cloyse, that excellent old Christian, stood in the early sunshine, at her own lattice, catechizing a little girl, who had brought her a pint of morning's milk. Goodman Brown snatched away the child, as from the grasp of the fiend himself. Turning the corner by the meeting-house, he spied the head of Faith, with the pink ribbons, gazing anxiously forth, and bursting into such joy at sight of him, that she skipt along the street, and almost kissed her husband before the whole village. But, Goodman Brown looked sternly and sadly into her face, and passed on without a greeting.

Had Goodman Brown fallen asleep in the forest, and only dreamed a wild dream of a witch-meeting?

Be it so, if you will. But, alas! it was a dream of evil omen for young Goodman Brown. A stern, a sad, a darkly meditative, a distrustful, if not a desperate man, did he become, from the night of that fearful dream. On the Sabbath-day, when the congregation were singing a holy psalm, he could not listen, because an anthem of sin rushed loudly upon his ear, and drowned all the blessed strain. When the minister spoke from the pulpit, with power and fervid eloquence, and, with his hand on the open Bible, of the sacred truths of our religion, and of saint-like lives and triumphant deaths, and of future bliss or misery unutterable, then did Goodman Brown turn pale, dreading, lest the roof should thunder down upon the gray blasphemer and his hearers. Often, awakening suddenly at midnight, he shrank from the bosom of Faith, and at morning or eventide, when the family knelt down at prayer, he scowled, and muttered to himself, and gazed sternly at his wife, and turned away. And when he had lived long, and was borne to his grave, a hoary corpse, followed by Faith, an aged woman, and children and grandchildren, a goodly procession, besides neighbors, not a few, they carved no hopeful verse upon his tombstone; for his dying hour was gloom.

Chapter Six

Discussion

The setting of this story — Salem village in the very late seventeenth century — gives the reader a firm grounding in place and time. The element of witchcraft which seems so odd to the modern reader, was actually a firm belief of the period, and the witch trials (and the names of some of the victims) provide plausibility to the atmosphere of the story.

But in contrast to such historical realism we are early given some hint of the fantastic beyond the beliefs of the period. It is odd, is it not, that Faith has been offered no excuse for her new husband's journey, which will leave her alone, he says, this "of all nights of the year"? And an equally fantastic suggestion has just been found in Faith's statement: "A lone woman is troubled with such dreams and such thoughts that she's afeard of herself sometimes. Pray, tarry with me this night, dear husband, of all nights in the year." What is so special about this night? Further, after the husband has left her, he thinks "Well, she's a blessed angel on earth; and after this one night, I'll cling to her skirts and follow her to heaven."

Clearly, we have left the realm of ordinary realism when young Goodman Brown enters the forest, which early Puritans thought to have been a haunt of natural and supernatural evil. Though they have been presented as a "real" forest and journey, we have hints that they have philosophical or psychological symbolism. When the real devil appears, that is strange enough, but when we realize his resemblance to Brown, and later to Brown's father, we find suggested a "communion" of evil in the blood — a communion that in the end turns out to be universal. The communion with young Goodman Brown is more intimate later, for the devil's arguments seemed rather to spring up in the bosom of the auditor than to be suggested by himself. Can it ever be said that, in a sense, the forest is the inwardness of young Goodman Brown, and that all takes place there?

The journey into the forest toward the great "initiation" into the evil "communion of the race" does have a growth of suspense, as does a story of action, but the suspense is directed at a philosophical point and not toward the resolution of an action. Even Goodman Brown's hesitation and hope of turning back is not, we sense, based on a woman named Faith, but on the other meaning of the word, on Faith as an allegorical figure. That "faith" enables him to let the minister and Deacon Gookin ride on.

For even though his resolution is weakened by the appearance of the minister and the deacon, he catches a glimpse of a patch of blue evening sky and stars, and cries out: "With heaven above and Faith below, I will stand firm against the devil!"

At this moment, however, a cloud sweeps over the blue and a sound of many voices bursts out, many familiar, among them the voice of a young woman uttering a lamentation, which Brown recognizes as that of Faith. Then he cries her name, and the forest echoes "as if bewildered wretches were seeking her all through the wilderness." This, of course, seems to imply that all in the communion of evil seek, after all, only faith. Meanwhile, Faith's pink ribbon has come fluttering down; and grasping it, Brown bursts into maniacal laughter and rushes through the forest toward the spot of fearful initiation. That is to say, the actual woman Faith may also be of the communion of evil — which has already been hinted at in her fear of dreams during her husband's absence.

There, after the blasphemous ritual, the proselytes are presented to the dark figure, who concludes his speech of welcome: "Depending upon one another's hearts, ye had still hoped that virtue was not all a dream. Now are ye undeceived. Evil is the nature of mankind. Welcome again, my children, to the communion of your race." At the climax, Faith is presented for the mark of baptism.

At the sight young Goodman Brown cries out for her to resist, but he cannot know the end, for suddenly he is alone, listening to the roar of wind disappearing into the forest. Next morning he has found his way back to the village, where all lead their lives as before, the virtuous and unvirtuous, those in truth and those in deception.

The story is left as a question. Had it been merely a dream? In any case, young Goodman Brown has lost his confidence in life. He continues to live with Faith, though without faith, and dies at a ripe age, with children and grandchildren, but with no sentiment of hope on his tomb. His life has been a meaningless charade.

What is the parable saying? At one level it asks, and does not answer, a fundamental question about human nature, a question that has been asked again and again throughout history. Is man naturally evil — as, for example, in the doctrine of Original Sin? Or is he naturally good, as has been held by various sects, but most notably by the French philosopher Rousseau? Or in one modern version, is virtue the result of good environment, and evil the result of bad environment? Are evil and good merely the results of conditioning? In any case, the story is a parable asking a perennial question, in which each generation answers in its own terms.

Can we say that the story by-passes the question of vice and virtue as absolutes — that human nature is a complex thing and that man must live in the effort to make his own definition by faith? In which case, can we hazard that Goodman Brown is the total idealist who cannot live life as it necessarily is?

(Cleanth Brooks and Robert Penn Warren)

 Questions

1. When we learn in the opening sentence that this story begins in Salem village, what suggestions come to mind from our knowledge of American history? How does Salem make a more appropriate setting than some other colonial American village?

2. Why is Brown's wife Faith "aptly named" (as we are told in the opening paragraph)? Point to details in which the author seems to be punning on her name. What do you understand from them?
3. What do you make of the fact that the strange man in the woods closely resembles Brown himself (paragraphs 13,32)?
4. As Brown and the stranger proceed deeper into the woods, what does Brown find out that troubles him?
5. When the pink ribbon flutters to the ground, as though falling from something airborne (paragraph 49), what does Brown assume? What effect does the event have upon his determination to resist the devil?
6. What is the purpose of the ceremony in the woods? Bring to your understanding of it anything you have heard or read about witchcraft, the witches' Sabbath, and the notion of making pact with the devil.
7. "Evil is the nature of mankind," declares the devil (paragraph 65). Does Hawthorne agree with him? (Exactly what do you find in this story to suggest the author's view?) What is your opinion about human nature?
8. Was Brown's experience in the woods all a dream, or wasn't it? Does the author favour one explanation, or the other? Please illustrate your answer by assembling evidence from the story.
9. How would you state the main theme of the story?
10. In many places "Young Goodman Brown" seems to have been written from the point of view of Brown, in that we frequently move into his consciousness to learn what he is thinking—a perspective we are offered with no other character in the story. But the story is not entirely told from the point of view of Brown—the voice telling the story provides more. What are some of these features that do not seem to be part of Brown's consciousness? Can you clarify them? Think further about the gap between the narrator and Brown, and assess its significance to the way you read the story.

11. Try to retell Brown's experience by a first-person narrator, that is, from his own point of view; from the point of view of a Salem villager (you can use a character in the story or make up one); and from your own point of view. How is the meaning of the story affected by the choice of point of view (and by what is included and left out, stressed and ignored accordingly)?

The Killers

by Ernest Hemingway, 1927

The door of Henry's lunchroom opened and two men came in. They sat down at the counter.

"What's yours?" George asked them.

"I don't know," one of the men said. "What do you want to eat, Al?"

"I don't know," said Al. "I don't know what I want to eat."

Outside it was getting dark. The street light came on outside the window. The two men at the counter read the menu. From the other end of the counter Nick Adams watched them. He had been talking to George when they came in.

"I'll have a roast pork tenderloin with apple sauce and mashed potatoes," the first man said.

"It isn't ready yet."

"What the hell do you put it on the card for?"

"That's the dinner," George explained. "You can get that at six o'clock."

George looked at the clock on the wall behind the counter.

"It's five o'clock."

"The clock says twenty minutes past five," the second man said.

"It's twenty minutes fast."

"Oh, to hell with the clock," the first man said. "What have you got to eat?"

"I can give you any kind of sandwiches," George said. "You can have ham and eggs, bacon and eggs, liver and bacon, or a steak."

"Give me chicken croquettes with green peas and cream sauce and mashed potatoes."

"That's the dinner."

"Everything we want's the dinner, eh? That's the way you work it."

"I can give you ham and eggs, bacon and eggs, liver—"

"I'll take ham and eggs," the man called Al said. He wore a derby hat and a black overcoat buttoned across the chest. His face was small and white and he had tight lips. He wore a silk muffler and gloves.

"Give me bacon and eggs," said the other man. He was about the same size as Al. Their faces were different, but they were dressed like twins. Both wore overcoats too tight for them. They sat leaning forward, their elbows on the counter.

"Got anything to drink?" Al asked.

"Silver beer, bevo, ginger ale," George said.

"I mean you got anything to *drink*?"

"Just those I said."

"This is a hot town," said the other. "What do they call it?"

"Summit."

"Ever hear of it?" Al asked his friend.

"No," said the friend.

"What do you do here nights?" Al asked.

"They eat the dinner," his friend said. "They all come here and eat the big dinner."

"That's right," George said.

"So you think that's right?" Al asked George.

"Sure."

"You're a pretty bright boy, aren't you?"

"Sure," said George.

Chapter Six

"Well, you're not," said the other little man. "Is he, Al?"

"He's dumb," said Al. He turned to Nick. "What's your name?"

"Adams."

"Another bright boy," Al said. "Ain't he a bright boy, Max?"

"The town's full of bright boys," Max said.

George put the two platters, one of ham and eggs, the other of bacon and eggs, on the counter. He set down two side dishes of fried potatoes and closed the wicket into the kitchen.

"Which is yours?" he asked Al.

"Don't you remember?"

"Ham and eggs."

"Just a bright boy," Max said. He leaned forward and took the ham and eggs. Both men ate with their gloves on. George watched them eat.

"What are *you* looking at?" Max looked at George.

"Nothing."

"The hell you were. You were looking at me."

"Maybe the boy meant it for a joke, Max," Al said.

George laughed.

"*You* don't have to laugh," Max said to him. "*You* don't have to laugh at all, see?"

"All right," said George.

"So he thinks it's all right." Max turned to Al. "He thinks it's all right. That's a good one."

"Oh, he's a thinker," Al said. They went on eating.

"What's the bright boy's name down the counter?" Al asked Max.

"Hey, bright boy," Max said to Nick. "You go around on the other side of the counter with your boy friend."

"What's the idea?" Nick asked.

"There isn't any idea."

"You better go around, bright boy," Al said. Nick went

— 245 —

around behind the counter.

"What's the idea?" George asked.

"None of your damn business," Al said. "Who's out in the kitchen?"

"The nigger."

"What do you mean the nigger?"

"The nigger that cooks."

"Tell him to come in."

"What's the idea?"

"Tell him to come in."

"Where do you think you are?"

"We know damn well where we are," the man called Max said. "Do we look silly?"

"You talk silly," Al said to him. "What the hell do you argue with this kid for? Listen," he said to George, "tell the nigger to come out here."

"What are you going to do to him?"

"Nothing. Use your head, bright boy. What would we do to a nigger?"

George opened the slit that opened back into the kitchen. "Sam," he called. "Come in here a minute."

The door to the kitchen opened and the nigger came in. "What was it?" he asked. The two men at the counter took a look at him.

"All right, nigger. You stand right there," Al said.

Sam, the nigger, standing in his apron, looked at the two men sitting at the counter. "Yes, sir," he said. Al got down from his stool.

"I'm going back to the kitchen with the nigger and bright boy," he said. "Go on back to the kitchen, nigger. You go with him, bright boy." The little man walked after Nick and Sam, the cook, back into the kitchen. The door shut after them. The man called Max sat at the counter opposite George. He didn't look at George but looked in the mirror that ran along back of the counter. Henry's had been made over from a saloon into a lunch counter.

Chapter Six

"Well, bright boy," Max said, looking into the mirror, "why don't you say something?"

"What's it all about?"

"Hey, Al," Max called, "bright boy wants to know what it's all about."

"Why don't you tell him?" Al's voice came from the kitchen.

"What do you think it's all about?"

"I don't know."

"What do you think?"

Max looked into the mirror all the time he was talking.

"I wouldn't say."

"Hey, Al, bright boy says he wouldn't say what he thinks it's all about."

"I can hear you, all right," Al said from the kitchen. He had propped open the slit that dishes passed through into the kitchen with a catsup bottle. "Listen, bright boy," he said from the kitchen to George. "Stand a little further along the bar. You move a little to the left, Max." He was like a photographer arranging for a group picture.

"Talk to me, bright boy," Max said. "What do you think's going to happen?"

George did not say anything.

"I'll tell you," Max said. "We're going to kill a Swede. Do you know a big Swede named Ole Anderson?"

"Yes."

"He comes here to eat every night, don't he?"

"Sometimes he comes here."

"He comes here at six o'clock, don't he?"

"If he comes."

"We know all that, bright boy," Max said. "Talk about something else. Ever go to the movies?"

"Once in a while."

"You ought to go to the movies more. The movies are fine for a bright boy like you."

"What are you going to kill Ole Anderson for? What did he ever do to you?"

"He never had a chance to do anything to us. He never even seen us."

"And he's only going to see us once," Al said from the kitchen.

"What are you going to kill him for, then?" George asked.

"We're killing him for a friend. Just to oblige a friend, bright boy."

"Shut up," said Al from the kitchen. "You talk too goddamn much."

"Well, I got to keep bright boy amused. Don't I, bright boy?"

"You talk too damn much," Al said. "The nigger and my bright boy are amused by themselves. I got them tied up like a couple of girl friends in a convent."

"I suppose you were in a convent."

"You never know."

"You were in a kosher convent. That's where you were."

George looked up at the clock.

"If anybody comes in you tell them the cook is off, and if they keep after it, you tell them you'll go back and cook yourself. Do you get that, bright boy?"

"All right," George said. "What you going to do with us afterward?"

"That'll depend," Max said. "That's one of those things you never know at the time."

George looked up at the clock. It was a quarter past six. The door from the street opened. A street-car motorman came in.

"Hello, George," he said. "Can I get supper?"

"Sam's gone out," George said. "He'll be back in about half an hour."

"I'd better go up the street," the motorman said. George looked at the clock. It was twenty minutes past six.

"That was nice, bright boy," Max said. "You're a regular little gentleman." At six-fifty-five George said: "He's not coming."

Two other people had been in the lunchroom. Once George had gone out to the kitchen and made a ham-and-egg sandwich "to go" that a man wanted to take with him. Inside the kitchen he saw Al, his derby hat tipped back, sitting on a stool beside the wicket with the muzzle of a sawed-off shotgun resting on the ledge. Nick and the cook were back to back in the corner, a towel tied in each of their mouths. George had cooked the sandwich, wrapped it up in oiled paper, put it in a bag, brought it in, and the man had paid for it and gone out.

"Bright boy can do everything," Max said. "He can cook and everything. You'd make some girl a nice wife, bright boy."

"Yes?" George said, "Your friend, Ole Anderson, isn't going to come."

"We'll give him ten minutes," Max said.

Max watched the mirror and the clock. The hands of the clock marked seven o'clock, and then five minutes past seven.

"Come on, Al," said Max. "We better go. He's not coming."

"Better give him five minutes," Al said from the kitchen.

In the five minutes a man came in, and George explained that the cook was sick.

"Why the hell don't you get another cook?" the man asked. "Aren't you running a lunch counter?" He went out.

"Come on, Al," Max said.

"What about the two bright boys and the nigger?"

"They're all right."

"You think so?"

"Sure. We're through with it."

"I don't like it," said Al. "It's sloppy. You talk too much."

"Oh, what the hell," said Max. "We got to keep amused, haven't we?"

"You talk too much, all the same," Al said. He came out from the kitchen. The cut-off barrels of the shotgun made a slight bulge under the waist of his too tight-fitting overcoat. He straightened his coat with his gloved hands.

"So long, bright boy," he said to George. "You got a lot of luck."

"That's the truth," Max said. "You ought to play the races, bright boy."

The two of them went out the door. George watched them, through the window, pass under the arc light and cross the street. In their tight overcoats and derby hats they looked like a vaudeville team. George went back through the swinging door into the kitchen and untied Nick and the cook.

"I don't want any more of that," said Sam, the cook. "I don't want any more of that."

Nick stood up. He had never had a towel in his mouth before.

"Say," he said. "What the hell?" He was trying to swagger it off.

"They were going to kill Ole Anderson," George said. "They were going to shoot him when he came in to eat."

"Ole Anderson?"

"Sure."

The cook felt the corners of his mouth with his thumbs.

"They all gone?" he asked.

"Yeah," said George. "They're gone now."

"I don't like it," said the cook. "I don't like any of it at all."

"Listen," George said to Nick. "You better go see Ole Anderson."

"All right."

"You better not have anything to do with it at all," Sam, the cook, said. "You better stay way out of it."

"Don't go if you don't want to," George said.

"Mixing up in this ain't going to get you anywhere," the cook said. "You stay out of it."

"I'll go see him," Nick said to George. "Where does he live?"

The cook turned away.

Chapter Six

"Little boys always know what they want to do," he said.

"He lives up at Hirsch's rooming house," George said to Nick.

"I'll go up there."

Outside the arc light shone through the bare branches of a tree. Nick walked up the street beside the car tracks and turned at the next arc light down a side street. Three houses up the street was Hirsch's rooming house. Nick walked up the two steps and pushed the bell. A woman came to the door.

"Is Ole Anderson here?"

"Do you want to see him?"

"Yes, if he's in."

Nick followed the woman up a flight of stairs and back to the end of a corridor. She knocked on the door.

"Who is it?"

"It's somebody to see you, Mr. Anderson," the woman said.

"It's Nick Adams."

"Come in."

Nick opened the door and went into the room. Ole Anderson was lying on the bed with all his clothes on. He had been a heavyweight prizefighter and he was too long for the bed. He lay with his head on two pillows. He did not look at Nick.

"What was it?" he asked.

"I was up at Henry's," Nick said, "and two fellows came in and tied up me and the cook, and they said they were going to kill you."

It sounded silly when he said it. Ole Anderson said nothing.

"They put us out in the kitchen," Nick went on. "They were going to shoot you when you came in to supper."

Ole Anderson looked at the wall and did not say anything.

"George thought I better come and tell you about it."

"There isn't anything I can do about it," Ole Anderson said.

"I'll tell you what they were like."

"I don't want to know what they were like," Ole Anderson said. He looked at the wall. "Thanks for coming to tell me about it."

"That's all right."

Nick looked at the big man lying on the bed.

"Don't you want me to go and see the police?"

"No," Ole Anderson said. "That wouldn't do any good."

"Isn't there something I could do?"

"No. There ain't anything to do."

"Maybe it was just a bluff."

"No. It ain't just a bluff."

Ole Anderson rolled over toward the wall.

"The only thing is," he said, talking toward the wall, "I just can't make up my mind to go out. I been in here all day."

"Couldn't you get out of town?"

"No," Ole Anderson said. "I'm through with all that running around."

He looked at the wall.

"There ain't anything to do now."

"Couldn't you fix it up some way?"

"No. I got in wrong." He talked in the same flat voice. "There ain't anything to do. After a while I'll make up my mind to go out."

"I better go back and see George," Nick said.

"So long," said Ole Anderson. He did not look toward Nick. "Thanks for coming around."

Nick went out. As he shut the door he saw Ole Anderson with all his clothes on, lying on the bed looking at the wall.

"He's been in his room all day," the landlady said downstairs. "I guess he don't feel well. I said to him: 'Mr. Anderson, you ought to go out and take a walk on a nice fall day like this,' but he didn't feel like it."

"He doesn't want to go out."

"I'm sorry he don't feel well," the woman said. "He's an awfully nice man. He was in the ring, you know."

"I know it."

Chapter Six

"You'd never know it except from the way his face is," the woman said. They stood talking just inside the street door. "He's just as gentle."

"Well, good-night, Mrs. Hirsch," Nick said.

"I'm not Mrs. Hirsch," the woman said. "She owns the place. I just look after it for her. I'm Mrs. Bell."

"Well, good-night, Mrs. Bell," Nick said.

"Good-night," the woman said.

Nick walked up the dark street to the corner under the arc light, and then along the car tracks to Henry's eating house. George was inside, back of the counter.

"Did you see Ole?"

"Yes," said Nick. "He's in his room and he won't go out."

The cook opened the door from the kitchen when he heard Nick's voice.

"I don't even listen to it," he said and shut the door.

"Did you tell him about it?" George asked.

"Sure. I told him but he knows what it's all about."

"What's he going to do?"

"Nothing."

"They'll kill him."

"I guess they will."

"He must have got mixed up in something in Chicago."

"I guess so," said Nick.

"It's a hell of a thing!"

"It's an awful thing," Nick said.

They did not say anything. George reached down for a towel and wiped the counter.

"I wonder what he did?" Nick said.

"Double-crossed somebody. That's what they kill them for."

"I'm going to get out of this town," Nick said.

"Yes," said George. "That's a good thing to do."

"I can't stand to think about him waiting in the room and knowing he's going to get it. It's too damned awful."

"Well," said George, "you better not think about it."

Discussion

There are certain fairly obvious points to be made about the technique of this story. It breaks up into one long scene and three short scenes. Indeed, the method is so thoroughly scenic that not over three or four sentences are required to make the transitions. The focus of narration is objective throughout; practically all information is conveyed in simple realistic dialogue. In the first scene the revelation of the mission of the gangsters is accomplished through a few significant details — the fact that the gangsters eat with gloves (to avoid leaving fingerprints), the fact that they keep their eyes on the mirror behind the bar, the fact that, after Nick and the cook have been tied up, the gangster who has the shotgun at the service window stations his friend and George out front "like a photographer arranging for a group picture" — all of this before the specific nature of their mission is made clear.

Other observations concerning the technique of the story could be made — the cleverness of composition, the subtlety with which the suspense is maintained in the first scene by the banter of the gangsters, and then is transferred to another level in the second scene. But such observations, though they are worth making, do not answer the question that first comes (or should come) to the reader's mind: what is the story about?

The importance of giving an early answer to this question can be seen by considering two readers who have typical but different reactions to the story. One reader, upon first acquaintance with the story, is inclined to feel that it is exhausted in the first scene, and in fact that the first scene itself does not come to focus — does not have a "point." The other reader sees that the first scene, with its lack of resolution, is really being used to "charge" the second scene. He finds his point in Ole Andreson's decision not to try to escape the gangsters — to stop "all that running around." This reader feels that the story should end here. He sees no relevance in the last several pages of the story, and wonders why the author has flattened his effect. The first reader, we may say, feels that "The Killers" is the gangsters' story — a story of action that does not come off. The second and more sophisticated reader interprets it as Andreson's story, though perhaps with some wonder that Andreson's story has been approached so indirectly and is allowed to trail off so irrelevantly.

In other words, the second reader is inclined to transpose the question "What is the story about?" into the question, "Whose story is it?" When he states the question in this way, he confronts the fact that Hemingway has left the story focused not on the gangsters, nor on Andreson, but on the boys at the lunchroom. Consider the last sentences of the story:

> "I'm going to get out of this town," Nick said.
> "Yes," said George. "That's a good thing to do."
> "I can't stand to think about him waiting in the room and knowing he's going to get it. It's too damned awful."
> "well," said George, "you better not think about it."

So, of the two boys, it is obviously Nick on whom the impression has been made. George has managed to come to terms with the situation. By this line of reasoning, it is Nick's story. And the story is about the discovery of evil.

This definition of the theme of the story, even if it appears acceptable, must, of course, be tested against the detailed structure. In evaluating the story, as well as in understanding it, the skill with which the theme has been assimilated must be taken into account. For instance, to put a concrete question: does the last paragraph of the story illuminate for the reader certain details that had, at their first appearance, seemed to be merely casual, realistic items?

If we take the theme to be the boy's discovery of evil, several such details do find their meaning. Nick had been bound and gagged by the gangsters, and has been released by George. To quote: "Nick stood up. He had never had a towel in his mouth before. 'Say,' he said. 'What the hell?' He was trying to swagger it off." Being gagged was something you read about in a thriller and not something that happened to you; and the first effect is one of excitement, almost pleasurable, certainly an excuse for a manly pose. (It may be worth noting in this connection that Hemingway uses the specific word *towel* and not the general word *gag*. It is true that the word *towel* has a certain sensory advantage over the word *gag* — because it suggests the coarseness of the fabric and the unpleasant drying effect on the membranes of the mouth. But this advantage in immediacy is probably overshadowed by another: the towel is sanctified in the thriller as the gag, and here the cliché of the thriller has come true.) The way the whole incident is given — "He had *never* had a towel in his mouth *before*" — charges the apparently realistic detail as a pointer to the final discovery.

Another pointer appears in the gangster's wisecrack about the movies: "You ought to go to the movies more. The movies are fine for a bright boy like you." In one sense, of course, the iterated remarks about the movies, coming just after the gangsters have made their arrangements in the lunchroom, serve as a kind of indirect exposition: the reader knows the standard reason and procedure for gang killings. But at another level, these remarks emphasize the discovery that the unreal clichés of the newspaper and movie have become a reality.

The boy to whom the gangster speaks understands the allusion to the movies, for he immediately asks: "What are you going to kill Ole Andreson for? What did he ever do to you?" "He never had a chance to do anything to us. He never even seen us," the gangster replies.

Chapter Six

The gangster accepts, and even glories a little in, the terms by which he lives — terms that transcend the small-town world. He lives, as it were, by a code, which lifts him above questions of personal likes or personal animosities. This unreal code — unreal because it denies the ordinary personal elements of life — has, like the gag, suddenly been discovered as real. This unreal and theatrical quality is reflected in the description of the gangsters as, after leaving the lunchroom, they go out under the arc light and cross the street: "In their tight overcoats and derby hats they looked like a vaudeville team." It even permeates their dialogue. The dialogue itself has the sleazy quality of mechanized gag and wisecrack, a kind of stereotyped banter that is always *a priori* to the situation and overrides the situation. On this level the comparison to the vaudeville team is a kind of explicit summary of details that have been presented more indirectly and dramatically. On another level, the weary and artificial quality of their wit has a grimmer implication. It is an index to the professional casualness with which they accept a situation that to the boys is shocking. They are contemptuous and even bored, with the contempt and boredom of the initiated when confronted by callow lay observers. This code, which has suddenly been transferred from the artificial world of the movie thriller into reality, is shocking enough, but even more shocking to Nick is the fact that Ole Andreson, the hunted man, accepts the code too. Confronted by the news that Nick brings, he rejects all the responses the boy would consider normal: he will not call the police; he will not regard the thing as a mere bluff; he will not leave town. "Couldn't you fix it up some way?" the boy asks. "No. I got in wrong."

As we observed earlier, for one type of reader this is the high point of the story, and the story should end here. If we are to convince such a reader that the author is right in proceeding, we are obliged to answer his question "What is the significance of the rather tame, and apparently irrelevant, little incident that follows, the conversation with Mrs. Bell?" It is sometimes said that Mrs.

Bell serves to give a bit of delayed exposition or even to point the story by gaining sympathy for Andreson, who is, to her, "an awfully nice man," not at all like her idea of a pugilist. But this is not enough to satisfy the keen reader, and he is right in refusing to be satisfied with this. Mrs. Bell is, really, the Porter at Hell Gate in *Macbeth*. She is the world of normality, which is shocking now from the very fact that life continues to flow on in its usual course. To her, Ole Andreson is just a nice man, despite the fact that he has been in the ring; he ought to go out and take his walk on such a nice day. She points to his ordinary individuality, which is in contrast to the demands of the mechanical code. Even if the unreal horror of the movie thriller has become real, even if the hunted man lies upstairs on his bed trying to make up his mind to go out, Mrs. Bell is still Mrs. Bell. She is not Mrs. Hirsch. Mrs. Hirsch owns the place, she just looks after it for Mrs. Hirsch. She is Mrs. Bell: normal life.

At the door of the rooming house Nick has met Mrs. Bell — normality unconscious of the ironical contrast it presents. Back at the lunchroom, Nick returns to the normal scene, but the normal scene conscious of the impingement of horror. It is the same old lunchroom, with George and the cook going about their business. But they, unlike Mrs. Bell, know what has happened. Yet even they are scarcely deflected from their ordinary routine. George and the cook represent two different levels of response to the situation. The cook, from the first, has wanted no part of it. When he hears Nick's voice, on his return, he says, "I don't even listen to it." And he shuts the door. But George had originally suggested that Nick go see Andreson, telling him, however, "Don't go if you don't want to." After Nick has told his story, George can comment, "It's a hell of a thing." but George, in one sense at least, has accepted the code, too. When Nick says, "I wonder what he did?" George replies, with an echo of the killers' own casualness: "Double-crossed somebody. That's what they kill them for." In other words, the situation is shocking to the cook

Chapter Six

only insofar as it involves his own safety. George is aware of other implications but can dismiss them. Neither of them makes a discovery of evil in the situation. But Nick does, for he has not yet learned to take George's adult advice: "Well, you better not think about it."

Aside from such structural concerns as the relations among incidents and the attitudes of the characters, other interesting questions can be raised. What is Hemingway's attitude toward his material? How does this attitude find its expression?

Perhaps the simplest approach to these questions may be through a consideration of the kinds of situations and characters that Hemingway wrote about. The situations are usually violent ones: the hard-drinking and sexually promiscuous world of the *The Sun Also Rises*; the chaotic and brutal world of war in *A Farewell to Arms*, *For Whom the Bell Tolls*, and "A Way You'll Never Be"; the dangerous and exciting world of the bull ring or the prize ring in *The Sun Also Rises*, *Death in the Afternoon*, "The Undefeated," and "Fifty Grand"; the world of crime in "The Killers," *To Have and to Have Not*, and "The Gambler, the Nun, and the Radio." Hemingway's typical characters are usually tough men, experienced in the hard worlds they inhabit, and apparently insensitive: Lieutenant Henry in *A Farewell to Arms*, the big-game hunter in "The Snows of Kilimanjaro," Robert Jordan in *For Whom the Bell Tolls*, or even Ole Andreson. They are, also, usually defeated men. Out of their practical defeat, however, they have managed to salvage something. And here we come upon Hemingway's basic interest in such situations and such characters. They are not defeated except upon their own terms; some of them have even courted defeat; certainly, they have maintained, even in the practical defeat, an ideal of themselves, formulated or unformulated, by which they have lived.

Hemingway's attitude is, in a sense, like that of Robert Louis Stevenson, as Stevenson states it in one of his essays, "Pulvis et Umbra":

Poor soul, here for so little, cast among so many hardships, filled with desires so incommensurate and so inconsistent, savagely surrounded, savagely descended, irremediably condemned to prey upon his fellow lives: who should have blamed him had he been of a piece with his destiny and a being merely barbarous? And we look and behold him instead filled with imperfect virtues: . . . an ideal of decency, to which he would rise if it were possible; a limit of shame, below which, if it be possible, he will not stoop. . . Man is indeed marked for failure in his efforts to do right. But where the best consistently miscarry, how tenfold more remarkable that all should continue to strive; and surely we should find it both touching and inspiring, that in a field from which success is banished, our race should not cease to labor. . . . It matters not where we look, under what climate we observe him, in what stage of society, in what depth of ignorance, burthened with what erroneous morality; by campfires in Assiniboia, the snow powdering his shoulders, the wind plucking his blanket, as he sits, passing the ceremonial calumet and uttering his grave opinions like a Roman senator; in ships at sea, a man inured to hardship and vile pleasures, his brightest hope a fiddle in a tavern and a bedizened trull who sells herself to rob him, and he for all that, simple, innocent, cheerful, kindly like a child, constant to toil, brave to drown, for others; . . . in the brothel, the discard of society, living mainly on strong drink, fed with affronts, a fool, a thief, the comrade of thieves, and even here keeping the point of honor and the touch of pity, often repaying the world's scorn with service, often standing firm upon a scruple, and at a certain cost, rejecting riches; — everywhere some virtue cherished or affected, everywhere some decency of thought and carriage, everywhere the ensign of man's ineffectual goodness! . . . under every circumstance of failure, without hope, without health, without thanks, still obscurely fighting the lost fight of virtue, still clinging, in the brothel or on the scaffold, to some rag of honor, the poor jewel of their souls! They may seek to escape, and yet they cannot; it is not alone their privilege and glory, but their doom, they are condemned to some nobility...

For Stevenson, the world in which this drama is played out is, objectively considered, a violent and meaningless world: "our rotary island loaded with predatory life and more drenched with blood... than ever mutinied ship, scuds through space." This is Hemingway's world, too. But its characters, at least those whose stories Hemingway cares to tell, make one gallant effort to redeem the incoherence and meaninglessness of this world: they attempt to impose some form upon the disorder of their lives, the technique of the bullfighter or sportsman, the discipline of the soldier, the code of the gangster, which, even though brutal and dehumanizing, has its own ethic. (Ole Andreson is willing to take his medicine without whining. Or the dying Mexican in "The Gambler, the Nun, and the Radio" refuses to squeal, despite the detective's argument: "One can, with honor, denounce one's assailant.") The form is never quite adequate to subdue the world, but the fidelity to it is part of the gallantry of defeat.

We have said that the typical Hemingway hero is tough and, apparently, insensitive. But only apparently, for the fidelity to a code, to a discipline, may be an index to a sensitivity that allows his characters to see, at moments, their true plight. At times, and usually at times of stress, it is the tough man — for Hemingway, the disciplined man — who actually is aware of pathos or tragedy. The individual toughness (which may be taken to be the private discipline demanded by the world), may find itself in conflict with some more natural and spontaneous human emotion; in contrast with this, the discipline may, even, seem to be inhuman; but the Hemingway hero, though he is aware of the claims of this spontaneous human emotion, is afraid to yield to those claims because he has learned that the only way to hold on to "honor," to individuality, to the human order as against the brute chaos of the world, is to live by his code. This is the irony of the situation in which the hero finds himself. Hemingway's heroes are aristocrats in the sense that they are the initiate, and practice a lonely virtue.

Hemingway's heroes utter themselves, not in rant and bombast, but in terms of ironic understatement. This understatement, stemming from the contrast between the toughness and the sensitivity, the violence and the sensitivity, is a constant aspect of Hemingway's method, an aspect that was happily caught in a cartoon in the *New Yorker* some years ago. The cartoonist showed a brawny, hairy forearm and a muscled hand clutching a little rose. The cartoon was entitled "The Soul of Ernest Hemingway." Just as there is a margin of victory in the defeat of the Hemingway characters, so there is a little margin of sensibility in their brutal and violent world.

Ole Andreson, as we have noted, fits into this pattern. Andreson won't whimper. But Ole Andreson's story is buried in the larger story, which is focused on Nick. How does Nick Adams fit into the pattern? Hemingway, as a matter of fact, is accustomed to treat his basic situation at one or the other of two levels. There is the story of the person who is already initiated, who has already adopted his appropriate code, or discipline, in the world that otherwise he cannot code with. (One finds examples in Jake and Brett in *The Sun Also Rises*, Jordan and Pilar in *For Whom the Bell Tolls*, the bullfighter in "The Undefeated," and many other stories.) There is also the story of the process of the initiation, the discovery of evil and disorder, and the first step toward the mastery of the discipline. This is Nick's story. (The same basic situation occurs in many other stories by Hemingway, for example, "Up in Michigan," "Indian Camp." and "The Three-Day Blow.")

Besides being tough and apparently insensitive, the typical Hemingway character is also, usually, simple. The impulse that led Hemingway to the simple character is akin to that that led the

Chapter Six

Romantic poet Wordsworth to the same choice. Wordsworth felt that peasants or children, who are the characters of so many of his poems, were more honest in their responses than the cultivated man, and therefore more poetic. Instead of Wordsworth's typical peasant we find in Hemingway's work the bullfighter, the soldier, the revolutionist, the sportsman, and the gangster; instead of Wordsworth's children, we find young men like Nick. There are, of course, differences between the approach of Wordsworth and that of Hemingway, but there is little difference on the point of marginal sensibility.

The main difference between the two writers depends on the difference in their two worlds. Hemingway's world is a more disordered world, and more violent, than the simple and innocent world of Wordsworth. Therefore, the sensibility of Hemingway's characters is in sharper coutrast to the nature of his world. This creates an irony not found in the work of Wordsworth. Hemingway plays down the sensibility as such, and sheathes it in the code of toughness. Gertrude Stein once wrote of Hemingway: "Hemingway is the shyest and proudest and sweetest-smelling storyteller of my reading." When she refers to his "shyness" she was, apparently, thinking of his use of irony and understatement. The typical character is sensitive, but his sensitivity is never insisted upon; he may be worthy of pity, but he never demands it. The underlying attitude in Hemingway's work may be stated like this: pity is valid only when it is wrung from a man who has been seasoned by experience, and is only earned by a man who never demands it. Therefore, a premium is placed upon the fact of violent experience.

A further question suggests itself. How is Hemingway's style related to his basic fictional concerns? In "The Killers," as in many of his other stories, the style is simple even to the point of monotony. The characteristic sentence is simple, or compound; and if compound, there is no implied subtlety in the coordination of the clauses. The paragraph structure is, characteristically, based on simple sequence. First, we can observe that there is an obvious relation between this style and the characters and situations with which the author is concerned: unsophisticated characters and simple, fundamental situations are rendered in an uncomplicated style.

There is another, and more interesting, aspect of the question of style, involving not the sensibility of the characters but the sensibility of the author himself. The short simple rhythms, the succession of coordinate clauses, and the general lack of subordination — all suggest a dislocated and ununified world. Hemingway Was apparently trying to suggest in his style the direct experience — things as seen and felt, one after another, and not as the mind arranges and analyzes them. A style that involves subordination and complicated shadings of emphasis, a style that tends toward complex sentences with many qualifying clauses and phrases, implies an exercise of critical discrimination — the sifting of experience through the intellect. But Hemingway, apparently, was primarily concerned with giving the immediate impact of experience rather than with analyzing and evaluating it in detail (We can notice, in this connection, that in his work he rarely indulges in any psychological analysis, and is rarely concerned with the detailed development of a character.) His very style, then, seems to imply that the use of the intellect, with its careful discriminations, may blur the rendering of experience and may falsify it; and this style, in connection with his basic concern for the character of marginal sensibility, may be taken as implying a distrust of the intellect in solving man's basic problems. Despite the application of the human intellect to the problems of the world, he seems to be saying, the world is still a disorderly and brutal mess. And it is hard to find any sure scale of values. Therefore, it is well to remember the demands of fundamental situations — those involving sex, love; danger, and death, in which the instinctive life is foremost — because they are frequently glossed over or falsified by social conventions or sterile intellectuality. It is well to remember the simple virtues of courage, honesty, fidelity, discipline.

But is all of this a way of saying that Hemingway is really writing innocently, without calculation, crudely? Now, as a matter of fact, his style is a result of calculation, and is not, strictly speaking, spontaneous and naive at all. His style is, then, a dramatic device, developed because of its appropriateness to the total effect he intends to give. A writer who was in point of fact uninstructed and spontaneous would probably not be able to achieve the impression of spontaneity and immediacy found in Hemingway's best work, the work in which his basic attitude and subject matter can be functionally coordinated.

In our comment on this story we have tried, among other and more obvious concerns, to relate the style of the story to the theme and then to relate the various qualities of this story to the general body of Hemingway's work and his attitude toward his world. Ordinarily we have been studying stories taken individually, but it is time for us to realize that the various (and often quite different) stories done by a good writer always have some fundamental unifying attitudes — for a man can be only himself. Since this is true, we can nearly always enter more deeply into a piece of fiction and understand it more fully when we are prepared to relate it to the writer's other work. A good writer does not offer us, for instance, a glittering variety of themes. He probably treats, over and over, those few themes that seem to him most important in his actual living and observation of life.

(Cleanth Brooks and Robert Penn Warren)

 Questions

1. How do you understand the theme of the story? What does the title suggest to you?
2. After the two men left the restaurant, George suggested to Nick

that he should go and tell Ole Andreson about what had happened. But Sam, the cook, said, "you better not have anything to do with it at all." Why do you think Sam said that?
3. When Nick told Ole Andreson that two men had been trying to kill him, Ole was quite indifferent. How do you understand his indifference? How does this scene add to your interpretation of the theme?
4. The style of the story is an indicator of Hemingway's vision of the world, "a dislocated and ununified world." Please illustrate how Hewingway suggests about this world in his use of rhythms, clauses, and words.

Chapter Seven

Symbol

In F. Scott Fitzgerald's novel *The Great Gatsby*, a huge pair of bespectacled eyes stares across a wildness of ash heaps from a billboard advertising the services of an oculist. Repeatedly appearing in the story, the bespectacled eyes come to mean more than simply the availability of eye examination. A character in the story compares it to the eyes of God; he hints that some sad, compassionate spirit is brooding as it watches the passing procession of humanity. Such an object is a **symbol**: in literature, a symbol is a thing that refers or suggests more than its literal meaning. There are quite a lot of symbols that appear in ordinary life, for the use of symbol is by no means limited to literature and art. For instance, a dove is a symbol of peace, the flag is the symbol of a country, and the cross is the symbol of the Christian religion. These are symbols adopted by a whole society and are recognized by all members of such a society. There are other kinds of symbols, such as the figure 3, which may be called abstract symbols. But symbols in literary works are different from either of the other types. Generally speaking, a literary symbol does not have a common social acceptance, as does the flag; it is, rather, a symbol the poet or the writer adopts for the purpose of his/her work, and it is to be understood only in the context of that work. It differs from the kind of symbol illustrated by the figure 3 because it is concrete and specific. A poet or a writer uses symbols for the same reason he/she uses similes, metaphors, and images, etc: they help to express his/her meaning in a way that will appeal to the senses and to the emotions of the reader. Most symbols, in literature and everyday life as well, possess a tremendous condensing power. Their focusing on the relationships between the visible (audible) and what they suggest can kindle a flame of response from the heat the reader broods and they bring it into a single impact. Of course, in literary works, symbols, unlike those in ordinary life, usually do not "stand for" any one meaning, nor for anything absolutely definite; they point, they hint, or, as Henry James put it, they cast long shadows (Brooks et al, *An Approach to Literature*, 1964).

Symbol is generally acknowledged to be one of the most frequently employed devices in poetry. In works of fiction it is no less frequent and no less important. The fact is that, when a reader reads a work of fiction, his focus is mostly cast upon the plot, the character, and the language used, so that the symbols are automatically backgrounded on the reader's part. But in some novels and stories, the symbolism looms so large that the reader will fail to get a comprehensive understanding of the work without paying special attention to the symbols. *The Scarlet Letter* by Nathaniel Hawthorne is one of such works. The very title points to a double symbol: the scarlet letter *A* worn by Hester conveys a multiple of senses which differ greatly from what it literally stands for, and the work eventually develops into a test and critique of symbols themselves. Thomas Pynchon's *V.* continues along much the same line, testing an alphabetical symbol. Another example is Herman Melville's *Moby-Dick*, in which the huge white whale in the title of the book acquires greater meaning than the literal dictionary-definition of an aquatic mammal. It also suggests more than the devil, to whom some of the characters liken it. The huge whale, as the story unfolds, comes to imply an amplitude of meanings: among them the forces of nature and the whole universe.

Literary symbols are of two broad types: one type includes those embodying universal suggestions of meaning. Flowing water suggests time and eternity, a journey into the underworld and return from it is interpreted as a spiritual experience or a dark night of the soul, and a kind of redemptive odyssey. Such symbols are used widely (and sometimes unconsciously) in western literature. The other type of symbol secures its suggestiveness not from qualities inherent in itself but from the way in which it is used in a given work, in a special context. Thus, in *Moby-Dick* the voyage, the land, and the ocean are objects pregnant with meanings that seem almost independent of the author's use of them in the story; on the other hand, the white whale is invested with different meanings for different crew members through the handling of materials in the novel. Similarly, in Hemingway's *A Farewell to Arms*, rain, which is generally regarded as a symbol of life (especially in spring), and which is a mildly annoying meteorological phenomenon in the opening chapter, is converted into a symbol of death through the uses to which it is put in the work.

Often symbols we meet in fiction are inanimate objects. In William Faulkner's "A Rose for Emily," Miss Emily's invisible but perceptible watch ticking at the end of a golden chain not only indicates the passage of time, but suggests that time passes without even being noticed by the watch's owner. The golden chain to which it is attached carries suggestions of wealth and authority. Other things may also function symbolically. In James Joyce's "Araby," the very name of the bazaar, Araby—the poetic name for Arabia—suggests magic, romance, and *The Arabian Nights*; its syllables, the narrator tells us, "cast an Eastern enchantment over me." Even a locale, or a feature of physical topography, can provide rich symbolic suggestions. The café in Ernest Hemingway's "A Clean, Well-Lighted Place" is not merely a café, but an island of refuge from sleepless night, chaos, loneliness, old age, the meaninglessness of life, and impending death. In some novels and stories, some characters are symbolic. Such characters usually appear briefly and remain slightly mysterious. In Joseph Conrad's *Heart of Darkness*, a steamship company that hires men to work in Congo maintains in its waiting room two women who knit black wool—they symbolize the classical Fates. Such a character is seen as a portrait rather than as a person, at least portraitlike. Faulkner's Miss Emily, twice appears at a window of her house "like the carven torso of an idol in a niche." Though Faulkner invests her with life and vigour, he also clothes her in symbolic hints: she seems almost to personify the vanishing aristocracy of the South, still maintaining a black servant and being ruthless betrayed by a moneymaking Yankee. Sometimes a part of a character's body or an attribute may convey symbolic meaning, for example, a baleful eye in Edgar Allan Poe's "The Tell-Tale Heart."

Another kind of symbol commonly employed in works of fiction is the symbolic act: an act or a gesture with larger significance than its literal meaning. Captain Ahab in Melville's *Moby-Dick* deliberately snaps his tobacco pipe and throws it away before setting out in pursuit of the huge whale, a gesture suggesting that he is determined to take his revenge and will let nothing to distract him from it. Another typical symbolic act is the burning of the barn by the boy's father in Faulkner's "Barn Burning": it is an act of no mere destroying a barn, but an expression of his profound spite and hatred towards that class of people who have driven his family out of his land. His hatred extends to anything he does not possess himself and, beyond that, burning a barn reflects the father's memories of the "waste and extravagance of war" and the "element of fire spoke to some deep mainspring" in his being.

In a broad literary sense, a symbol is such a trope that combines a literal and sensuous quality with an abstract or suggestive aspect. However, in literary criticism it is necessary to distinguish symbol from image, metaphor, and, especially, allegory. An **image** is a literal and concrete representation of a sensory experience or of an object that can be known by one or more of the senses. It is the means by which experience in its richness and emotional complexity is communicated. (Holman and Harmon, *A Handbook to Literature*, 1986) Images may be literal or figurative, a literal image being one that involves no necessary change or extension in the obvious meaning of the words. Prose works are usually full of this kind of image. For example, novels and stories by Conrad and Hemingway are noted for the evocative power of their literal images. A figurative image is one that involves a "turn" on the literary meaning of the words. For example, in the lines "It is a beauteous evening, calm and free; / The holy time is quiet as a nun," the second line is highly figurative while the first line evokes a literal image. We consider an image, whether literal or figurative, to have a concrete referent in the objective world and to function as image when it powerfully evokes that referent; whereas a symbol functions like an image but differs from it in going beyond the evocation of the objective referent by making that referent suggest to the reader a meaning beyond itself. In other words, a symbol is an image that evokes an objective, concrete reality, but then that reality suggests another level of meaning. In other words, the symbol does not "stand for" the meaning directly; it evokes an object that suggests the meaning, with the emphasis being laid on the latter part. As Coleridge said, "It partakes of the reality which it renders intelligible."

  A **metaphor** is an implied analogy imaginatively identifying one object with another and ascribing to the first object one or more of the qualities of the second, or investing the first with emotional or imaginative qualities associated with the second. It is not an uncommon literary device in fiction, though it is more commonly used in poetry while simile is more commonly used in prose. A metaphor emphasizes rich suggestiveness in the differences between the things compared and the recognition of surprising but unsuspected similarities. Cleanth Brooks uses the term "functional metaphor" to describe the way in which the metaphor is able to have "referential" and "emotive" characteristics, and to go beyond those characteristics to become a direct means in itself of representing a truth incommunicable by other means. When a metaphor performs this function, it is behaving as a symbol. But a symbol differs from a metaphor in that a metaphor evokes an object in order to *illustrate* an idea or demonstrate a quality, whereas a symbol *embodies* the idea or the quality.

An **allegory** is a story in which persons, places, actions, and things are equated with meanings that lie outside of the story itself. Thus it represents one thing in the guise of another—an abstraction in the form of a concrete image. A clear example is the old Arab fable of the frog and scorpion, who met one day on the bank of the Nile, which they both wanted to cross. The frog offered to ferry the scorpion over on his back, provided the scorpion promised not to sting him. The scorpion agreed so long as the frog would promise not to drown him. The mutual promise exchanged, they crossed the river. On the far bank the scorpion stung the frog mortally. "Why did you do that?" croaked the frog, as he lay dying. "Why?" replied the scorpion. "We're both Arabs, aren't we?" If we substitute for the frog a "Mr. Goodwill" and for the scorpion "Mr. Treachery" or "Mr. Two-Face", and we make the river any river, and for "We're both Arabs" we substitute "We're both men," we can make the fable into an allegory. In a simple allegory, characters and other ingredients often stand for other definite meanings, which are often abstractions. We have met such a character in the last chapter: Faith in Hawthorne's "Young Goodman Brown." A classical allegory is the medieval play *Everyman*, whose protagonist represents us all, and who, deserted by false friends named Kindred and Goods, faces the judgment of God accompanied only by a faithful friend called Good Deeds. In John Bunyan's *Pilgrim's Progress*, the protagonist, Christian, struggles along the difficult road towards salvation, meeting along the way with such persons as Mr. Worldly Wiseman, who directs him into a comfortable path (a wrong turn), and the residents of a town called Fair Speech, among them a hypocrite named Mr. Facing-both-ways. One modern instance is George Orwell's *Animal Farm*, in which (among its double meanings) barnyard animals stand for human victims and totalitarian oppressors. Allegory attempts to evoke a dual interest, one in the events, characters, and setting presented, and the other in the ideas they are intended to convey or the significance they bear. Symbol differs from allegory, according to Coleridge, in that in allegory the objective referent evoked is without value until it acquires fixed meaning from its own particular structure of ideas, whereas a symbol includes permanent objective value, independent of the meanings that it may suggest.

In a broad sense, all stories are symbolic, that is, the writer lends the characters and their actions some special significance. Of course, this is to think of symbol in an extremely broad and inclusive way. For the usual purpose of reading a story and understanding it, there is probably little point in looking for symbolism in every word, in every stick or stone, in every striking of a match, in every minor character. But to refuse to think about the symbolic meanings would be another way to misread a story. So to be on the alert for symbols when reading fiction is perhaps wiser than to ignore them.

How, then, do we recognize a symbol in fiction when we meet it? Fortunately, the storyteller often gives the symbol particular emphasis. It may be mentioned repeatedly throughout the story; it may even be indicated in the title ("Araby," "Barn Burning," "A Clean, Well-Lighted Place"). At times, a crucial symbol will open a story or end it. Unless an object, act, or character is given some special emphasis and importance, we may generally feel safe in taking it at face value. But an object, an act, or a character is surely symbolic if, when we finish the story, we realize that it was that very item—those gigantic eyes; that clean, well-lighted café; that burning of a barn—which led us to the theme, the essential meaning of the story. (Kennedy and Gioia, *Literature*, 1995)

The Lottery

by Shirley Jackson, 1948

The morning of June 27th was clear and sunny, with the fresh warmth of a full-summer day; the flowers were blossoming profusely and the grass was richly green. The people of the village began to gather in the square, between the post office and the bank, around ten o'clock; in some towns there were so many people that the lottery took two days and had to be started on June 26th, but in this village, where there were only about three hundred people, the whole lottery took less than two hours, so it could begin at ten o'clock in the morning and still be through in time to allow the villagers to get home for noon dinner.

  The children assembled first, of course. School was recently over for the summer, and the feeling of liberty sat uneasily on most of them; they tended to gather together quietly for a while before they broke into boisterous play, and their talk was still of the classroom and the teacher, of books and reprimands. Bobby Martin had already stuffed his pockets full of stones, and the other boys soon followed his example, selecting the smoothest and roundest stones; Bobby and Harry Jones and Dickie Delacroix—the villagers pronounced this name "Dellacroy"—eventually made a great pile of stones in one corner of the square and guarded it against the raids of the other boys. The girls stood aside, talking among themselves, looking over their shoulders at the boys, and the very small children rolled in the dust or clung to the hands of their older brothers or sisters.

  Soon the men began to gather, surveying their own children, speaking of planting and rain, tractors and taxes. They stood together, away from the pile of stones in the corner, and their jokes were quiet and they smiled rather than laughed. The women, wearing faded house dresses and sweaters, came shortly after their menfolk. They greeted one another and exchanged bits of gossip as they went to join their husbands. Soon the women, standing by their husbands, began to call to their children, and the children came reluctantly, having to be called four or five times. Bobby Martin ducked under his mother's grasping hand and ran, laughing, back to the pile of stones. His father spoke up sharply,

Chapter Seven

and Bobby came quickly and took his place between his father and his oldest brother.

The lottery was conducted—as were the square dances, the teenage club, the Halloween program—by Mr. Summers, who had time and energy to devote to civic activities. He was a roundfaced, jovial man and he ran the coal business, and people were sorry for him, because he had no children and his wife was a scold. When he arrived in the square, carrying the black wooden box, there was a murmur of conversation among the villagers and he waved and called, "Little late today, folks." The postmaster, Mr. Graves, followed him, carrying a three-legged stool, and the stool was put in the center of the square and Mr. Summers set the black box down on it. The villagers kept their distance, leaving a space between themselves and the stool, and when Mr. Summers said, "Some of you fellows want to give me a hand?" there was a hesitation before two men, Mr. Martin and his oldest son, Baxter, came forward to hold the box steady on the stool while Mr. Summers stirred up the papers inside it.

5   The original paraphernalia for the lottery had been lost long ago, and the black box now resting on the stool had been put into use even before Old Man Warner, the oldest man in town, was born. Mr. Summers spoke frequently to the villagers about making a new box, but no one liked to upset even as much tradition as was represented by the black box. There was a story that the present box had been made with some pieces of the box that had preceded it, the one that had been constructed when the first people settled down to make a village here. Every year, after the lottery, Mr. Summers began talking again about a new box, but every year the subject was allowed to fade off without anything's being done. The black box grew shabbier each year; by now it was no longer completely black but splintered badly along one side to show the original wood color, and in some places faded or stained.

Mr. Martin and his oldest son, Baxter, held the black box securely on the stool until Mr. Summers had stirred the papers thoroughly with his hand. Because so much of the ritual had been forgotten or discarded, Mr. Summers had been successful in having slips of paper substituted for the chips of wood that had been used for generations. Chips of wood, Mr. Summers had argued, had been all very well when the village was tiny, but now that the population was more than three hundred and likely to keep on growing, it was necessary to use something that would fit more easily into the black box. The night before the lottery, Mr. Summers and Mr. Graves made up the slips of paper and put them in the box, and it was then taken to the safe of Mr. Summers's coal company and locked up until Mr. Summers was ready to take it to the square next morning. The rest of the year, the box was put away, sometimes one place, sometimes another; it had spent one year in Mr. Graves's barn and another year underfoot in the post office, and sometimes it was set on a shelf in the Martin grocery and left there.

There was a great deal of fussing to be done before Mr. Summers declared the lottery open. There were lists to make up—of heads of families, heads of households in each family, members of each household in each family. There was the proper swearing-in of Mr. Summers by the postmaster, as the official of the lottery; at one time, some people remembered, there had been a recital of some sort, performed by the official of the lottery, a perfunctory, tuneless chant that had been rattled off duly each year; some people believed that the official of the lottery used to stand just so when he said or sang it, others believed that he was supposed to walk among the people, but years and years ago this part of the ritual had been allowed to lapse. There had been, also, a ritual salute, which the official of the lottery had had to use in addressing each person who came up to draw from the box, but this also had changed with time, until now it was felt necessary only for the official to speak to each person approaching. Mr. Summers was very good at all this; in his clean white shirt and blue jeans, with one hand resting carelessly on the black box, he seemed very proper and important as he talked interminably to Mr. Graves and the Martins.

Just as Mr. Summers finally left off talking and turned to the assembled villagers, Mrs. Hutchinson came hurriedly along the path to the square, her sweater thrown over her shoulders, and slid into place in the back of the crowd. "Clean forgot what day it was," she said to Mrs. Delacroix, who stood next to her, and they both laughed softly. "Thought my old man was out back stacking wood," Mrs. Hutchinson went on, "and then I looked out the window and the kids were gone, and then I remembered it was the twenty-seventh and came a-running." She dried her hands on her apron, and Mrs. Delacroix said, "You're in time, though. They're still talking away up there."

Mrs. Hutchinson craned her neck to see through the crowd and found her husband and children standing near the front. She tapped Mrs. Delacroix on the arm as a farewell and began to make her way through the crowd. The people separated good-humoredly to let her through; two or three people said, in voices just loud enough to be heard across the crowd, "Here comes your Missus, Hutchinson," and "Bill, she made it after all." Mrs. Hutchinson reached her husband, and Mr. Summers, who had been waiting, said cheerfully, "Thought we were going to have to get on without you, Tessie." Mrs. Hutchinson said, grinning, "Wouldn't have me leave m'dishes in the sink, now would you, Joe?" and soft laughter ran through the crowd as the people stirred back into position after Mrs. Hutchinson's arrival.

10   "Well, now," Mr. Summers said soberly, "guess we better get started, get this over with, so's we can go back to work. Anybody ain't here?"

"Dunbar," several people said. "Dunbar, Dunbar."

Mr. Summers consulted his list. "Clyde Dunbar," he said. "That's right. He's broke his leg, hasn't he? Who's drawing for him?"

"Me, I guess," a woman said, and Mr. Summers turned to

look at her. "Wife draws for her husband," Mr. Summers said. "Don't you have a grown boy to do it for you, Janey?" Although Mr. Summers and everyone else in the village knew the answer perfectly well, it was the business of the official of the lottery to ask such questions formally. Mr. Summers waited with an expression of polite interest while Mrs. Dunbar answered.

"Horace's not but sixteen yet," Mrs. Dunbar said regretfully. "Guess I gotta fill in for the old man this year."

15 "Right," Mr. Summers said. He made a note on the list he was holding. Then he asked, "Watson boy drawing this year?"

A tall boy in the crowd raised his hand. "Here," he said. "I'm drawing for m'mother and me." He blinked his eyes nervously and ducked his head as several voices in the crowd said things like "Good fellow, Jack," and "Glad to see your mother's got a man to do it."

"Well," Mr. Summers said, "guess that's everyone. Old Man Warner make it?"

"Here," a voice said, and Mr. Summers nodded.

A sudden hush fell on the crowd as Mr. Summers cleared his throat and looked at the list. "All ready?" he called. "Now, I'll read the names—heads of families first—and the men come up and take a paper out of the box. Keep the paper folded in your hand without looking at it until everyone has had a turn. Everything clear?"

20 The people had done it so many times that they only half listened to the directions; most of them were quiet, wetting their lips, not looking around. Then Mr. Summers raised one hand high and said, "Adams." A man disengaged himself from the crowd and came forward. "Hi, Steve," Mr. Summers said, and Mr. Adams said, "Hi, Joe." They grinned at one another humorlessly and nervously. Then Mr. Adams reached into the black box and took out a folded paper. He held it firmly by one corner as he turned and went hastily back to his place in the crowd, where he stood a little apart from his family, not looking down at his hand.

Chapter Seven

"Allen," Mr. Summers said. "Anderson.... Bentham."

"Seems like there's no time at all between lotteries any more," Mrs. Delacroix said to Mrs. Graves in the back row. "Seems like we got through with the last one only last week."

"Time sure goes fast," Mrs. Graves said.

"Clark.... Delacroix."

"There goes my old man," Mrs. Delacroix said. She held her breath while her husband went forward.

"Dunbar," Mr. Summers said, and Mrs. Dunbar went steadily to the box while one of the women said, "Go on, Janey," and another said, "There she goes."

"We're next," Mrs. Graves said. She watched while Mr. Graves came around from the side of the box, greeted Mr. Summers gravely, and selected a slip of paper from the box. By now, all through the crowd there were men holding the small folded papers in their large hands, turning them over and over nervously. Mrs. Dunbar and her two sons stood together, Mrs. Dunbar holding the slip of paper.

"Harburt.... Hutchinson."

"Get up there, Bill," Mrs. Hutchinson said, and the people near her laughed.

"Jones."

"They do say," Mr. Adams said to Old Man Warner, who stood next to him, "that over in the north village they're talking of giving up the lottery."

Old Man Warner snorted. "Pack of crazy fools," he said. "Listening to the young folks, nothing's good enough for *them*. Next thing you know, they'll be wanting to go back to living in caves, nobody work any more, live *that* way for a while. Used to be a saying about 'Lottery in June, corn be heavy soon.' First thing you know, we'd all be eating stewed chickweed and acorns. There's *always* been a lottery," he added petulantly. "Bad enough to see young Joe Summers up there joking with everybody."

"Some places have already quit lotteries," Mrs. Adams said.

"Nothing but trouble in *that*," Old Man Warner said stoutly. "Pack of young fools."

35 "Martin." And Bobby Martin watched his father go forward. "Overdyke.... Percy."

"I wish they'd hurry," Mrs. Dunbar said to her older son. "I wish they'd hurry."

"They're almost through," her son said.

"You get ready to run tell Dad," Mrs. Dunbar said.

Mr. Summers called his own name and then stepped forward precisely and selected a slip from the box. Then he called, "Warner."

40 "Seventy-seventh year I been in the lottery," Old Man Warner said as he went through the crowd. "Seventy-seventh time."

"Watson." The tall boy came awkwardly through the crowd. Someone said, "Don't be nervous, Jack," and Mr. Summers said, "Take your time, son."

"Zanini."

After that, there was a long pause, a breathless pause, until Mr. Summers, holding his slip of paper in the air, said, "All right, fellows." For a minute, no one moved, and then all the slips of paper were opened. Suddenly, all women began to speak at once, saying, "Who is it?" "Who's got it?" "Is it the Dunbars?" "Is it the Watsons?" Then the voices began to say, "It's Hutchinson. It's Bill." "Bill Hutchinson's got it."

"Go tell your father," Mrs. Dunbar said to her older son.

45 People began to look around to see the Hutchinsons. Bill Hutchinson was standing quiet, staring down at the paper in his hand. Suddenly, Tessie Hutchinson shouted to Mr. Summers, "You didn't give him time enough to take any paper he wanted. I saw you. It wasn't fair!"

"Be a good sport, Tessie," Mrs. Delacroix called, and Mrs. Graves said, "All of us took the same chance."

"Shut up, Tessie," Bill Hutchinson said.

"Well, everyone," Mr. Summers said, "that was done pretty fast, and now we've got to be hurrying a little more to get done in time." He consulted his next list. "Bill," he said, "you draw for the Hutchinson family. You got any other households in the Hutchinsons?"

"There's Don and Eva," Mrs. Hutchinson yelled. "Make *them* take their chance!"

"Daughters draw with their husband's families, Tessie," Mr. Summers said gently. "You know that as well as anyone else."

"It wasn't fair," Tessie said.

"I guess not, Joe," Bill Hutchinson said regretfully. "My daughter draws with her husband's family, that's only fair. And I've got no other family except the kids."

"Then, as far as drawing for families is concerned, it's you." Mr. Summers said in explanation, "and as far as drawing for households is concerned, that's you, too. Right?"

"Right," Bill Hutchinson said.

"How many kids, Bill?" Mr. Summers asked formally.

"Three," Bill Hutchinson said. "There's Bill, Jr., and Nancy, and little Dave. And Tessie and me."

"All right, then," Mr. Summers said. "Harry, you got their tickets back?"

Mr. Graves nodded and held up the slips of paper. "Put them in the box, then," Mr. Summers directed. "Take Bill's and put it in."

"I think we ought to start over," Mrs. Hutchinson said, as quietly as she could. "I tell you it wasn't *fair*. You didn't give him time enough to choose. *Everybody* saw that."

Mr. Graves had selected the five slips and put them in the box, and he dropped all the papers but those onto the ground, where the breeze caught them and lifted them off.

"Listen, everybody," Mrs. Hutchinson was saying to the people around her.

"Ready, Bill?" Mr. Summers asked, and Bill Hutchinson,

— 281 —

with one quick glance around at his wife and children, nodded.

"Remember," Mr. Summers said, "take the slips and keep them folded until each person has taken one. Harry, you help little Dave." Mr. Graves took the hand of the little boy, who came willingly with him up to the box. "Take a paper out of the box, Davy," Mr. Summers said. Davy put his hand into the box and laughed. "Take just *one* paper," Mr. Summers said. "Harry, you hold it for him." Mr. Graves took the child's hand and removed the folded paper from the tight fist and held it while little Dave stood next to him and looked up at him wonderingly.

"Nancy next," Mr. Summers said. Nancy was twelve, and her school friends breathed heavily as she went forward, switching her skirt, and took a slip daintily from the box. "Bill, Jr.," Mr. Summers said, and Billy, his face red and his feet over-large, nearly knocked the box over as he got a paper out. "Tessie," Mr. Summers said. She hesitated for a minute, looking around defiantly, and then set her lips and went up to the box. She snatched a paper out and held it behind her.

65 "Bill," Mr. Summers said, and Bill Hutchinson reached into the box and felt around, bringing his hand out at last with the slip of paper in it.

The crowd was quiet. A girl whispered, "I hope it's not Nancy," and the sound of the whisper reached the edges of the crowd.

"It's not the way it used to be," Old Man Warner said clearly. "People ain't the way they used to be."

"All right," Mr. Summers said. "Open the papers. Harry, you open little Dave's."

Mr. Graves opened the slip of paper and there was a general sigh through the crowd as he held it up and everyone could see that it was blank. Nancy and Bill, Jr., opened theirs at the same time, and both beamed and laughed, turning around to the crowd and holding their slips of paper above their heads.

70 "Tessie," Mr. Summers said. There was a pause, and then Mr. Summers looked at Bill Hutchinson, and Bill unfolded his

paper and showed it. It was blank.

"It's Tessie," Mr. Summers said, and his voice was hushed. "Show us her paper, Bill."

Bill Hutchinson went over to his wife and forced the slip of paper out of her hand. It had a black spot on it, the black spot Mr. Summers had made the night before with the heavy pencil in the coal-company office. Bill Hutchinson held it up, and there was a stir in the crowd.

"All right, folks," Mr. Summers said, "let's finish quickly."

Although the villagers had forgotten the ritual and lost the original black box, they still remembered to use stones. The pile of stones the boys had made earlier was ready; there were stones on the ground with the blowing scraps of paper that had come out of the box. Mrs. Delacroix selected a stone so large she had to pick it up with both hands and turned to Mrs. Dunbar. "Come on," she said. "Hurry up."

Mrs. Dunbar had small stones in both hands, and she said, gasping for breath, "I can't run at all. You'll have to go ahead and I'll catch up with you."

The children had stones already, and someone gave little Davy Hutchinson a few pebbles.

Tessie Hutchinson was in the center of a cleared space by now, and she held her hands out desperately as the villagers moved in on her. "It isn't fair," she said. A stone hit her on the side of the head.

Old Man Warner was saying, "Come on, come on, everyone." Steve Adams was in the front of the crowd of villagers, with Mrs. Graves beside him.

"It isn't fair, it isn't right," Mrs. Hutchinson screamed, and then they were upon her.

Discussion

At mid morning on a late June day a peaceful village crowd

gathers on the square for the annual **lottery**. The procedures have been handed down over generations with little change. While in the harmless process of drawing lots the villagers reveal their excitement. Suddenly, when the winner is selected, the innocent game turns out to be a horrifying sacrifice: the winner is stoned to death for the welfare of the community. Such is the limited picture that could be given of Shirley Jackson's *The Lottery* if symbols were overlooked.

Most critics are puzzled by the final shock, its purpose and effect; they feel they are only (left) shaken up with a sense of an unclosed end. In fact their major concern seems to be with the anthropological allusions to the rituals of the summer solstice. Seymour Lainoff claims that anthropology provides the chief symbol so that the **lottery** is to be understood as a modern representation of the primitive annual scapegoat. Brooks and Warren explain that the story reveals "the all-too-human tendency to seize upon a scapegoat" which Virgil Scott voices as "the human tendency to 'punish' innocent and often accidentally chosen victims for our sins." If these comments are to the point they nevertheless do not disclose how the remarkable reversal of expectations is anticipated. Indeed focuses on the underlying theme — the role of tradition in man's life — but fails to consider the symbolism prevailing in the main theme — man's recurrent need of a victim. Yet symbols are Jackson's major device in her tightly-knit handling of both themes.

Although ominous symbolic details prepare for the tragic outcome, the reader's attention is skilfully distracted. With her conventional title Jackson misleads the reader into thinking that the story is merely a fable or a fairy tale. The description of the pastoral-like setting implies an idyllic atmosphere. Besides, the lively, decent and friendly population lives as harmoniously as a close community can possibly do. Since the ceremony is official and causes much excitement, its true nature is not examined, the more so as it is associated with other pleasant social occasions. No reason then for tradition to be questioned or to be given up. And indeed very little has changed: the original chips of wood may well have been replaced by slips of paper, the present box may be made with some pieces of the preceding one, the former initial recital may no longer be performed but the core of the ritual has remained unchanged. In such a tradition-abiding community there seems little point for the reader to doubt the ceremony's benevolence. Mrs Hutchinson's late arrival therefore merely seems to single her out and to cast a favourable light on her: she has almost forgotten about the **lottery** because, as a perfect housewife, she would not leave her dishes in the sink. Nobody in the crowd seems to mind. As a good-humoured wife and mother she joins her husband and children while the crowd shows the friendliest feelings. The reader is thus made to sympathise not only with her but also with the rest of the population before the actual drawing of lots. After the first round, when the Hutchinsons are selected, Tessie seems to object but is gently rebuked so that little attention is paid to her apparently inexplicable objections. The second round determines the winner in the selected family: all have blank slips of paper except Tessie who has a black spot on hers. As she does not react at all when the main official urges his folks to finish the ceremony quickly the event is felt as thoroughly natural and in keeping with the general harmony. Then, suddenly, without apparent break, the reader is thrust into a symbolic realm: with no warning Tessie is stoned by all the villagers including her youngest child Davy. Taken at their face value the cold description of seemingly inoffensive and habitual circumstances, the banal structure and narration contrast with the abrupt ending. The shock is thus inevitably enhanced, the more so as the villagers' relaxed attitudes and lively speech do not prepare the reader for the gory outcome. Clearly the pastoral setting, commonplace characterisation, familiar down-to-earth vocabulary, impersonal and unimaginative style, detached point of view and plain chronological structure, all contribute to mislead the reader.

    Yet, all along tension should be felt as several allusions to the villagers' nervousness are made. The talk about giving up tradition, Mrs Hutchinson's emotional outburst, the increasing rhythm also point — even if indirectly — to the unhappy issue. Moreover the author's recurrent use of symbols stresses the duality of things and beings, which paves the way for the final horrendous revelation. Nothing — as a careful analysis of symbols reveals — is left to chance; tension lies at the heart of the story. Most numbers, colours, objects, stars, surnames in the text are ambivalent. Their ambivalence corroborates the message of the story, namely that first-hand impressions may well be deceptive; on the surface, things are smooth; deep down, reality is cruder. The usually positive value of any symbol is to be counterbalanced by its hidden or less well-known negative value so as to have a clearer picture of the text. Its richness and quality result from the mixture of opposite values. Instead of a straightforward account of small-town life, the reader gets a fuller picture of Life with its inescapable conjunction of opposites.

  Tension is already present in the description of the setting and in the atmosphere. The sun is felt throughout as an ambiguous presence. Its generative heat associated with youth, vitality and fertility heals and restores, but Midsummer and its scorching heat leads to the poisoning, burning madness of the solstice rite. The sun will provide better crops but only at the cost of the ritual murder of an innocent villager. Besides, the ambivalent character of the rite is stressed by the profusely blossoming flowers. By their very nature they symbolise beauty as well as point to the transitory stages of the vegetal cycle. They suggest not only virtue, goodness and purity but also temptation and deceit. As such they are part of pleasant occasions but also of distressing functions — as a last tribute paid at a funeral, Tessie's for example. The green grass too reveals the discrepancy between the character's appearance and deeds. Indeed, on the one hand, green denotes fertility, peace, balance, harmony, freshness, youth: these qualities, at first sight, seem to fit the description of the population. But, on the other hand, green implies ignorance, unripeness, inexperience —

the very characteristics attributed to pagan sacrifices. Significantly too, prior to the insane murder of Tessie Hutchinson, the villagers gather in the square. As the square stands for firmness and stability, organisation and construction, it is the source of order. No wonder then that traditions are perpetuated in the square, particularly those regulating the material stability of the community. And if stability is to be gained at the expense of one villager no one need to worry: the existence of the square justifies such injustice provided it serves the group. So the setting and atmosphere prefigure the ritual killing or confirm the villagers' rights and obligations to perform such a function.

If the setting and atmosphere reveal the dramatic denouement, so does the symbolic use of numbers. That they are not chosen at random is made obvious in the choice of the 27th of June as the date for the Midsummer solstice ceremony. Indeed according to Frazer fertility rites take place on Midsummer Eve (that is the 23rd of June) or on Midsummer Day (that is the 24th of June). One may wonder at this point which line of the cabalistic tradition Shirley Jackson follows. Indeed as 27 is not a primary number it has to be fused by mystic addition ($2+7=9$) or by succession (2, then 7), or else to be considered the result of multiplications (either 3^3 or 3×9). Now 9 is a multiple of 3, so the symbolic value attached to 3 is increased, namely completeness, perfection and fertility, and the end of a cycle (death) before the return to unity. So whether 27 is fused or merely the result of a multiplication it reveals the transitoriness of life. As a consequence it alludes to the imminent death that awaits any outcast who prevents the community from being a tightly-knit group. Once the outcast is dead, unity is restored and fertility secured. That symbolism fits the story is also true when 27 is interpreted as fused by succession. The number 27 would then reduce its conflict (as symbolised by the number 2) to its solution (as symbolised by the number 7). As 2 stands for the conjunction of opposites, such as life and death, man and woman, good and evil, and 7 for perfect completion of a cycle, the perfect solution is to grant death to either man or woman. Indeed a complete cycle implies decay or death so its perfect completion is closely linked with the death of a man or a woman. This is further emphasised in the twice-drawn lots. Furthermore by the use of the number 2 Shirley Jackson stresses the all-so-human conjunction of opposites. Man is not just good or evil but both. Since all human beings are dual there must be a way to determine which group in the population will provide a victim. The population is made of the elementary nucleus 3, namely children, men and women. As the elementary nucleus is self-sufficient the solution to its problem, in this case the selection of a victim for the material welfare of the community, lies within. And whenever there is a choice of three the magic solution is offered by the third choice. Therefore in *The Lottery* it is within the third group presented to the readers (the women) that a victim will be chosen. The whole ceremony must take place between 10 and 12 o'clock. By 10 o'clock on the 27th of June the community has fallen from its high position of perfection. By 12, salvation, holiness and perfection are restored so that the community shares with the number 12 in the inner unity and harmony of all matters. So by decoding the numbers used by Jackson the full implications of the fertility rite can be fathomed.

Such is certainly the case with the objects connected with the ritual. The black wooden box, the three-legged stool, the slips of paper for drawing lots combine the idea of death and rebirth, unexpected destructiveness and fertility. The outcome of the **lottery** could be anticipated from the sheer repetition of the adjective 'black' — the colour for death, mourning, punishment, penitence in western civilisation. The black box used to draw lots and the slip of paper with a black dot marking out the 'winner' are mentioned too frequently to be coincidental. Like Pandora's box and its unexpected, excessive and destructive gifts, the wooden box is associated with the vegetal cycle, with death followed by rebirth. The three-legged stool too participates in the cycle of fertility and is considered a divine object bringing all solutions. By allowing the

lottery to take place, that is by supporting the box, the stool helps marking out the martyr. The negative connotations ascribed to the preceding objects may well escape the reader but the ominous collecting of stones cannot be overlooked. Stones are indeed the universal symbol for punishment and martyrdom; they can only be part of a morbid ceremony. Consequently the marked emphasis on the objects related to the **lottery** can only but confirm that the **lottery** is a death-bringing ritual.

The villagers' fear of changing either the course of the **lottery** or the ritualistic objects discloses to what extent they are caught in the web of tradition. Even the pervading tension of their lives will not help change matters. This need surprise nobody as their surnames are symbolic of the overall duality which has governed their lives for generations. They are all friendly commonplace villagers who are capable of the most atrocious deeds. Most of their surnames reflect their gentility, their humanity. Indeed all but four names refer to past renowned men who have contributed to the welfare of humanity or to the world's cultural heritage. Their names obviously clash with their baffling potential destructiveness. Death is even announced in the very surname or characteristics of the two officials who conduct the ceremony. Mr Summers is indeed the head of the coal business in which capacity he has close contacts with the Underworld. His childlessness and marital disharmony are both outward signs of his morbid role. None but Mr Graves could best assist Mr Summers to preserve the ceremony. To crown it all the Delacroix are singled out as the most fervent participants in the ritualistic killing: Dickie is said to stack up masses of stones in advance while Mrs Delacroix is seen picking up a huge stone and hurrying on whole-heartedly to stone her friend. The latter's surname is strikingly indicative of her fate as it refers to Anne Hutchinson, a seventeenth-century American religious enthusiast who founded the Puritan colony of Rhode Island. She had new theological views which opposed her to other ministers. After a local trial banished her she was tried before the Boston Church and formally excommunicated. The parallelism between her story and Tessie's is clear: to her excommunication meant spiritual death just as to Tessie being cast out from the group implies death. The symbolic use of names thus reveals that human nature is an unaccountable mixture of the creative and the destructive: normal people can turn out to be real monsters capable of the worst atrocities.

Despite its apparently conventional start and artless narration the story, with its shift from realism to symbolism, brings about a striking shock and the sudden realisation that appearances are deceptive. The unexpected awe-inspiring contrast between man's appearance and deeds as well as the abrupt ending after a crime that allows no hope force the reader to ponder over human habits and more specifically over man's need of a scapegoat. He becomes conscious that he too may be a victim or a persecutor if he resorts unquestioningly to tradition as a line of conduct. This newly acquired awareness then prompts him to be suspicious of any systematic line of conduct, arbitrary deeds and sterile habits of mind. In this respect the victim's first and last words throw light on man's contradictory attitudes: at first Tessie's forgetfulness — possibly a premonitory sign of her imminent death — does not result from her questioning the ritual; in the end her cry words her sudden awareness of human irrationality and injustice. Her case is universal: man's awareness of absurd habits of mind always comes too late, that is when victimised and no longer in a position to change things.

(Danielle Schaub)

Questions

1. Where do you think "The Lottery" takes place? Why do you suppose the writer has made this setting appear familiar and ordinary?

2. In paragraphs 2 and 3, what details foreshadow the ending of the story?
3. Take a close look at the author's description of the black wooden box (paragraph 5) and of the black spot on the fatal slip of paper (paragraph 72). What do these objects suggest to you? Are there any other symbols in the story? What do they contribute to the theme of the story?
4. What do you make of Old Man Warner's saying, "Lottery in June, corn be heavy soon"?
5. What do you understand to be the writer's own attitude towards the lottery and the stoning? Exactly what in the story makes her attitude clear to us? What do you think Shirley Jackson is driving at? Transferring playfully a primitive fertility rite to a small town in modern times? Expressing her horror at the massacre of the Jews by people like these villagers during World War II? Satirizing our own society in which men are selected to do whatever they are not willing to do? Or simply writing a story that signifies nothing at all?

Chapter Eight

Reading Long Stories and Novels

   Novel is used in its broadest sense to designate any fictional prose narrative. In practice, its use is customarily restricted to book-length narratives in which the representation of character occurs either in a static condition or in the process of development at the result of events or actions (Holman and Harmon, *A Handbook to Literature*, 1986). The term *novel* is an English counterpart of the Italian word **novella** (from the plural of Latin *novellus*, a late variant of *novus*, meaning "new"), a short, compact, broadly realistic anecdote popular in the Medieval period, perhaps best represented by the tales in Boccaccio's *Decameron* (ca. 1348). The tales are novelties, freshly minted diversions, and they are short of moral earnestness. The term now, expressing its etymology well, still carries overtones of lightness and frivolity exemplified in *Decameron*. In European countries the word *roman* was used rather than *novel*, thus linking the novel with legendary material associated with the older *romance* (the English term carries a pejorative connotation). France, like Italy, produced *novelle* about a century later. It was at the beginning of the 17th century that the novel as a literary genre achieved its first great flowering in Spain in a mock-legendary, comic masterpiece—*Don Quixote* by Cervantes. But the English novel is essentially an eighteenth-century product. English writers of the eighteenth century had a background of the experience of continental Europe. The classical literature of Greece and Rome, the popular romance, pastoral literature, picaresque tales of adventure, miscellaneous writings on human character—all these elements and others were eventually to

Chapter Eight

crystallize into the English novel. In addition to these beginnings from Europe, the English novelists had native preparations of their own: Arthurian legends, *Eupheus* of Lyly (1579), *Arcadia* of Sir Philip Sidney (1581), picaresque elements in Nash's *The Unfortunate Traveller* (1594), an extended narrative of moral significance in John Bunyan's *Pilgrim's Progress* (1678-84), and character trait in the *Spectator* papers of Addison and Steele. Defoe, through loose narrative structure in *Robinson Crusoe* and *Moll Flanders*, and Swift, through satiric allegory in *Gulliver's Travels*, had brought verisimilitude to the chronicling of human life. These were to be two component parts of the later novel form. The works of Defoe and Swift, like any other fictional form, are not merely devices for telling tales, but means of envisaging human experience. Defoe was the first writer to be recognizably a novelist, but Swift and Bunyan were both of them profounder writers than Defoe, and contributed even more to the development of the novel-form as the most prevalent medium for the recording of modern experience in depth.

With these narrative qualities already rooted in various types of English writing, the soil was fertile when Samuel Richardson issued his *Pamela* in 1740, the first English book that critics are willing to call a fully realized novel, though it took epistolary form. After Richardson's success with *Pamela*, other significant novels came rapidly. In 1742 Henry Fielding published his *Joseph Andrews*, which was a result of criticism of *Pamela*; in 1748 Smollett brought out *Roderick Random*; and in 1749 came Fielding's greatest novel, *Tom Jones*, which shows a conscious attempt at the structure of this literary form and involves an apparently realistic interpretation of social life.

The question of how to write a novel began to occupy the minds of novelists increasingly, as they became more and more aware of the newness of the form. The most original of these experiments was Laurence Sterne's as carried out in the successive volumes of *Tristram Shandy* published from 1760 to 1767. At what point should the writer begin his narrative? In what sense is the writer digressing when he is elaborating the minor characters that surround his central character? What are the limitations to the devices that the writer may use to affect the reader? Sterne underwent an enlightened attempt at these and other problems in his work and succeeded in writing one of the most entertaining novels in English literature. *Tristram Shandy* marked the point that English novel had reached its maturity.

  The first novelist in English literature to understand what the novel should not attempt versus what it can do supremely well was Jane Austen. Her restricted subject matter has been attributed to her restricted experience of life. But the real explanation is artistic. She knew that significance did not always or necessarily arise from extraordinary conditions, that conversations about what was commonplace may reveal character even more effectively than those about grand subjects, and that the depth of the reader's impression of a story was proportionate to the extent to which the story convinced him. With the skill of irony, she exposed the internal life of her characters even as they ceaselessly conformed to the outward social circumstances. In this may she unified the inner and outer imaginative approaches of Richardson and Fielding. Hers are the first novels in English to show full and true artistic discipline without sacrificing human depth (Gillie, *Longman Companion to English Literature*, 1977).

  Attempts to classify the novel with respect to style (here in the broad sense of the general tendency of literary creation) usually come to grief, for the terms are by no means mutually exclusive. However, most novels do manifest obvious tendencies in its style, and it might be helpful to get a rough idea about the special forms of the novel classified according to subject matter.

  One of the early forms of the novel is **picaresque**: generally a chronicle, usually autobiographical, presenting of the life story of the adventures of a rascal of low degree, who makes a living more

Chapter Eight

by his wits than by his industry. The name comes from Spanish: *picaro*, "rascal" or "rogue." From the earliest times the rogue has been a favorite character presentation. In the Middle Ages, many fables adopted this approach, though they translated roguery from people to animals. But it was in the sixteenth century that this rogue literature crystallized into a definite type. A Spanish novel called *Life of Lazarillo de Tormes* was a widely read book; of french picaresque novels, Le Sage's *Gil Blas* was the most popular; and such English novels as Defoe's *Moll Flanders* can be regarded as picaresque in the etymological sense, since it presents the life record of a female picaroon. Fielding's *Jonathan Wild the Great* and *Tom Jones*, and Smollett's *Ferdinand, Count Fathom* have been called picaresque, and the *Pickwick Papers* of Dickens, whose eponym is a respectable and childishly ingenuous scholar, can be accommodated in the category.

Picaresque novels, characteristic of a loose structure, are crammed with episodes of intrigue, fights, amorous adventure, and stories within the main narrative. Perhaps such a structure indicates a roguish rejection of the settled bourgeois life, a desire for the open road, and a pursuit of an unrestrained life. In the modern period, Mark Twain's *Huckleberry Finn* owes something to the tradition: like early picaresque novels, it is told in episodic rather than in a unifying plot and is narrated in the first person by a hero, though not a rogue, at odds with the respectable society. Saul Bellow's *The Adventures of Augie March* and Jack Kerouac's *Dharma Bums* have something of the right episodic, wandering, free, questing character. Other modern novels worthy of the name are J. P. Donleavy's *The Ginger Man*, Erica Jong's *Fanny*, and Seth Morgan's *Homeboy*.

Holman and Harmon (*A Handbook to Literature*, 1986) summarize seven major traits, which are generally, not absolutely, found in the picaresque novel. (1) It chronicles the whole or a part of a rogue, and is likely to be told in the first person, but not necessarily. (2) The chief character is drawn from a low social level according to the convention of standards and he usually does some menial work. (3) The novel presents little serious structure of plot, but just a series of episodes slightly connected. (4) There is little character interest and the central figure starts as a *picaro* and ends as a *picaro*, with no or little (internal) development of character. (5) The method is realistic though the story may be romantic itself, presented with a plainness of language, a freedom in vocabulary, and a vividness of detail characteristic of realism. (6) Satire is prominent, with the *picaro* serving intimately people from various classes and from different parts of the world and imitating their foibles and frailties. The picaresque novel may in this way be made to satirize social castes, national styles, and racial peculiarities. (7) The hero of the picaresque novel, carefree and amoral, usually stops just short of being an actual criminal. The line between crime and rascality is a hazy one, but somehow the *picaro* always manages to draw it and to avoid actual crime.

  Another early form of the novel is **epistolary**: the narrative in the novel is carried forward by letters written by one or more of the characters. It has the merit of giving the author an advantage of expressing a free outpouring of the character's inner heart without apparent intervention of the author; it enables the author to present multiple points of view on the same event through the use of several correspondents; it is also a device for creating verisimilitude, with the author merely serving as "editor" for the correspondence. Its obvious disadvantage lies in the fact the enforced objectivity of the "editor" shuts the author off from comment on the actions of the characters.

  Samuel Richardson's *Pamela* is generally considered the first English epistolary novel, though the use of letters to tell stories can be traced back to over a century earlier, and his *Clarissa* is the greatest among the epistolary novels. At that time, letter writing was regarded as an art on which could be expended the literary care appropriate to fiction, and, for Richardson, the creation of epistolary novels entailed a constructive step from the actual world into that of imagination. The phenomenal success of Richardson brought about the popularity of the form all over Europe in the eighteenth century. The epistolary method has not been quite successful in the nineteenth and twentieth centuries, though the use of letters has been common in novels. Modern instances of epistolary novels are Christopher Isherwood's *Meeting by the River* which, focusing on a profoundly serious theme of religious conversation, seems to fail because of the informality and chattiness of the letters, and Alice Walker's *The Color Purple*, in which some of the letters that tell the story are addressed to God. Epistolary method in modern times has become a device for expressing alienation while sharing with the Richardsonian epistle the power of granting direct communication with the fictional character.

    Another important term concerning the early period novels (and of course not confined to novel), also related to Richardson, is **sentimental**. In its mid-eighteenth-century usage, it signified refined or elevated feeling, and it is in this sense that Laurence Sterne's *Sentimental Journey* should be understood. Richardson's *Pamela* and Rousseau's *Nouvelle Héloïse* are sentimental in that they exhibit a passionate attachment between sexes that rises above mere physical attraction. Although some writers wrote realistic novels (for example, Henry Fielding's *Tom Jones*) in protest, the sentimental novel continued to be popular for many years. Among the well-known ones are Goldsmith's *The Vicar of Wakefield*, Laurence Sterne's *Tristram Shandy*, and Henry Mackenzie's *Man of Feeling*. Sentimental novels of this period were characterized by an overindulgence in emotion, especially the conscious effort to induce emotion in order to enjoy it, and an overemphasis on the goodness of humanity. In the nineteenth century, neither Dickens nor Thackeray was immune to the temptation of sentimentality, though neither of them can be called sentimental novelists. The reported death of Tiny Tim in *A Christmas Carol* is an example of Dickens's obvious employment of sentimentality to provoke two tearful responses from a single situation — one of sorrow at a young death, the other of relief at the subsequent discovery that the death never occurred. The sentimental novel well pressed forward into the twentieth century and has proved capable of appeal even in the post-modern age; the success of the *Love Story* (1970) by Erich Segal is only one example.

We are aware of the pastoral—a poem about a shepherd's life or rural life. However, we may also classify some novels as **pastoral**: fiction that presents rural life as an idyllic condition. Such fictional work is as ancient as a pastoral poem. In as early as the second or third century AD, Longus wrote *Daphnis and Chloë* in Greek. It can be taken as the progenitor of Renaissance pastoral romances such as Boccaccio's *Ameto*, Sir Philip Sidney's *Arcadia*, and Thomas Lodge's *Rosalynde*, the source book of Shakespeare's *As You Like It*. The attempt to build a pastoral utopia in the natural world of innocence pervades such romances. In modern time, the image of a rural Eden is persistent in literary creations. For example, the elements of this image loom large in D. H. Lawrence's *Rainbow* and *Lady Chatterley's Lover*. In some novels we see a realistic and ironic picture of this pastoral life; the incompatible friction between the pastoral tradition and modern civilization under the pen of Thomas Hardy. Although it has been difficult for English novelists to take pastoral lyricism seriously, the increasing stresses of urban life makes the rural theme still available to serious novels, as in Saul Bellow's *Herzog*.

A familiar kind of fiction is the **historical novel**: a detailed reconstruction of a personage, a movement, a series of events, or the spirit of an age in the past that is based on facts. This form of literature requires a historical imagination: an awareness of the differences of outlook, customs and environment of the given period of the past. In some historical novels, the author attempts to create a faithful picture of daily life in another era; in some, history is the background for an exciting story of heroic adventure; and in others, important bearings on the society of the author's own day stream across the pages. Although writers have combined

Chapter Eight

fiction and history since time began and chronicles in the Middle Ages were not uncommon (serving as sources for historical plays such as Shakespeare's *Julius Caesar* and *Coriolanus*), it remained for Sir Walter Scott to establish the form. The eighteenth century saw the flowering of historical interest in Britain: Humes's *History of England*, Robertson's *History of Scotland*, and, especially, Gibbon's *Decline and Fall of the Roman Empire* all appeared in the eighteenth century. This spirit of the age led to a passion for historical fiction. Scott was a prominent figure who, combining the Romantic taste with an ardour for antiquities, pioneered historical fiction with his "Waverley" novels. In these, fictional characters are introduced to participate in actual historical events and move among actual personages from history. In his *Ivanhoe*, depicting a disinherited Saxon hero in a Norman world, we see an age in which two cultures came into tumultuous conflict, and thus are made aware of the impact of the historical events upon people in the process of the new replacing the old. Scott seemed to have an imaginative bond with the period of the seventeenth and eighteenth centuries that marked the establishment of Scotland. And what is true for Scott seems to be true for later historical fiction. Perhaps this accounts for the fact that only a few among the large number of historical novels written during the last 170 years are great works. Thus Thackeray's *Esmond* is distinguished, because Thackeray's emotional bond with the early eighteenth-century aristocracy and literary spirit of England gives his historical reconstruction conviction and force. Goerge Eliot's *Romola* is generally regarded as the dullest of her books because the close historical reconstruction of the fifteenth-century Florence lacks an imaginative bond with the actual life of that age.

However, historical themes have inspired some of the greatest novelists of the world, as Tolstoy's *War and Peace* and Stendhal's *Charterhouse of Parma* reveal. In the twentieth century, distinguished historical novels such as Robert Grave's *I, Claudius*, Zoé Oldenbourg's *Destiny of Fire*, and Mary

Renauld's *The King Must Die* exemplify an important function of fictional imagination—to "interpret remote events in human and particular terms, to transform documentary fact, with the assistance of imaginative conjecture, into immediate sensuous and emotional experience" (*The New Encyclopaedia Britanica*, Vol 23, 1993). The American novelist John Barth shows in *The Sot-Weed Factor* that mock historical scholarship may constitute a viable approach to the past. Virginia Woolf in *Orlandor* and *Between the Acts* attempts to squeeze vast tracts of historical time into a small space and thus make them as fictionally manageable as the events of a single day. And John Passos's *U.S.A.*, which focuses upon a phase in America's development, can be taken as an experiment in bringing great historical themes to the novel.

  The eighteenth-century's zeal for historical exploration aroused not only the burgeoning of historical fiction but also a non-historical mania for **Gothic novels.** The Goths were a barbaric Germanic tribe of ancient and early medieval times, and the term Gothic was used by the eighteenth-century Neo-Classicists as synonymous with "barbaric" to indicate any style that offended their classic tastes in fine arts (especially architecture) and literature. The eighteenth century stressed the supreme sovereignty of reason and the values that went with reason. This emphasis, however, tended to repress emotion and other mysterious forces in the personality, which were thought of as barbaric, and therefore medieval and gothic. Gothic thus became associated with all that was felt to be fantastic, grotesque, wild, savage, mysterious, and capable of strong appeal to emotion.

  Horace Walpole is generally regarded as the originator of the Gothic novel, his *Castle of Otranto* (1764) being the first. Its setting is a medieval castle with long underground passages, trap doors, dark stairways, and mysterious rooms with unexpected clanking and clashing of swords and chains—all these impart an uncanny atmosphere of terror. Anne Radcliffe's *The Mysteries of Udolpho* and Matthew Lewis's *The Monk* added to the popularity of the form. The emphasis on setting and story rather than on character is typical of Gothic novels, and the atmosphere is usually dark, tempestuous, ghostly, and full of madness, superstition, and revenge. Mary Shelley's *Frankenstein* is impregnated with weird God-defying experiments, horrible shrieks, and pestilent monsters in addition to the traditional Gothic ingredients. Sir Walter Scott endowed the Gothic novel with an entirely new kind of interest. As a Scotsman, he was the native of a country scenically more wild and socially more savage than England, so that his Scottish novels were both Gothic and realistic; and as a writer who had a strong interest in antiquities, he took the Middle Ages in both England and Scotland quite seriously and made them fascinating merely because anything pleasantly shocking or fantastic was likely to happen (Gillie, *Longman Companion to English Literature*, 1977). In America, Edgar Allan Poe developed the Gothic style brilliantly, with his measured elaboration of the plot and the nightmarish spell of a delicate and dimly or luridly lit atmosphere set in ruined abbeys or desolate castles. The term is today often applied to works, such as Daphne du Maurier's *Rebecca*, which attempt to create the same atmosphere of brooding and unnamed terror as the true Gothic novel, though they are short of typical Gothic settings. The Danish writer Isak Dinesen has used "Gothic" in the titles of his novels to indicate a fantastic spirit combining horror, crime, romance, and realism.

To label some novels as psychological is likely to arouse the objection that no novel is not psychological since no character is completely deprived of the working of mind, even if the character is an idiot. However, in literary criticism critics tend to call the novel that places special emphasis upon interior characterization a **psychological novel**. The psychological novel pays more attention to the explanation and analysis of the motives of action than a statement of what happens in a story. The psychological novel is, as one critic has said, an interpretation of "the invisible life" (Holman and Harmon, *A Handbook to Literature*, 1986). The term was first applied to a group of novelists in the middle of the nineteenth century with George Eliot, Mrs. Gaskell, and George Meredith as the representatives, though psychological stories are as old as any other literary form. It has been assumed since then that a serious novelist's prime concern must be the workings of the human mind, and hence many of the greatest novels ever produced are termed psychological. Dostoyevsky's *Crime and Punishment* deals less with the ethical significance of a murder than with the soul of the murderer; Flaubert's interest in Emma Bovary has less to do with the consequences of her mode of life than with the patterns of her mind; in *Anna Karenina*, Tolstoy presents an obsessive study of feminine psychology that is almost excruciating in its relentless probing (*The New Encyclopaedia Britanica*, Vol 23, 1993). Dickens and Thackeray were so interested in motives and mental states that they can be classified, in a loose sense, as psychological novelists. Hardy and Conrad were also interested in exploring interior motive and psychological effect. Henry James, with his intense concern for the psychological life of his characters and with his development of a novelistic technique that best suits the representation of the inner life effected by external events, pioneered the modern psychological novel. With the advance of scientific psychology in the twentieth century, the term has come into popular use. The theories of Sigmund Freud particularly gave impetus to the type and ushered in what critics call the psychoanalytical novel. However, two twentieth-century novelists of great psychological depth—Joyce and Nabokov—professed a disdain for Freud. Indeed, to write a novel with close attention to the Freudian or Jungian techniques of analysis does not necessarily produce new insights of psychological revelation, and Oedipus and Electra complexes have become commonplaces of superficial novels. Human motivation is not so simple as to be rooted merely in one or two complexes or in just a few childhood accidents.

The modern psychological novel may at one extreme record the inner experience of characters as reported by the author, as James tends to do, or at the other extreme employ **interior monologue** to express the nonverbalized and subconscious life of a character, as in some of the works of James Joyce and William Faulkner. Interior monologues convey the internal experience of the character so as to produce an effect as if the reader were overhearing an articulation of the stream of thought and feeling flowing through the character's mind. The novel of this type is generally known as the **stream-of-consciousness novel**. The stream-of-consciousness novel takes the unorganized flow of the mind as its subject matter and uses various techniques to put words to its uninterrupted, incoherent, and endlessly flowing stream of thought and feeling. In general, most psychological novels record the flow of conscious and ordered thought and feeling, as in Henry James, or the flow of memory activated by association, as in Marcel Proust; but the stream-of-consciousness novel tends to concentrate its focus chiefly on the pre-speech, nonverbalized level, where images must be employed to articulate the internal experience and where grammar belongs to another world. The techniques employed may vary under different novelists, though, the writers of the stream-of-consciousness novel seem to share certain common assumptions, as Holman and Harmon put it: (1) that the significant existence of human beings is to be found in their mental-emotional processes and not in the outside world, (2) that this mental-emotional life is illogical and disjointed, and (3) that free psychological association rather than logical relation in the working of mind manifests the ordinary sequence of thought and feeling (*A Handbook to Literature*, 1986).

Attempts to concentrate the subject matter of fiction on the inner consciousness can be traced back to Laurence Sterne's *Tristram Shandy*, in which a deliberate effort to free the sequence of thought from logical organization is discernible. The representation of the major character's consciousness remains in the speech level, however. It was a minor French novelist, Edouard Dujardin, who first used interior monologue in *Les Laurier sont coupes* (1888) in the modern sense. At the beginning of the twentieth century, James Joyce in *A Portrait of the Artist as a Young Man* (1916), Dorothy Richardson in her 13-volume *Pilgrimage* (1915-38), and Marcel Proust in his ambitious *A la recherche du temps perdu* (1913-27) all showed an interest in the technique of stream of consciousness. Henry James and Dostoyevsky also indicated, through long introspective passages, that they were aware of something like the stream-of-consciousness technique. It seems that several original minds had been working towards a new method of writing fiction independently. Of course, it is James Joyce who deliberately exploited the stream of consciousness to the uttermost point in *Ulysses*, which purports to be an account of the experiences (thoughts and feelings) of two men, Leopold Bloom and Stephen Daedalus, in just one day in Dublin. The climax of the utility of stream of consciousness is the forty-odd page interior monologue of Bloom, a passage with only one punctuation mark. Other important novelists who have used stream of consciousness as the subject matter or interior monologue as the chief technique in their fiction writing are Virginia Woolf (*Mrs Dalloway* and *To the Lighthouse*) and William Faulkner (*The Sound and Fury*).

In literary criticism, **realism** refers, in a broad sense, to literature that representats life with fidelity. In this sense realism has been a significant element in almost every school in literary history. But when we speak of realism or realists with respect to creative style, we are talking about a literary method, a philosophical attitude, and a particular scope of subject matter which prevailed especially in the nineteenth century. That the novel is realistic in nature seems an uncontroversial fact, since the rise of the novel was in a sense meant to reflect the ordinary life perceived and/or experienced by a novelist, and set against the traditional practice of poetry and play-writing that had drawn materials from mythology, legends, or history. The novel was used as a new method for the novelist to manifest vividly his/her cognition of reality, and this went without saying for most novelists in the eighteenth and nineteenth centuries. Especially the nineteenth-century important novelists in France, England, and America, such as Honoré Balzac, Stendhal, Goerge Eliot, Charles Dickens, and Mark Twain, reacted, at least partially, against romanticism by eliminating from their work those "soft" qualities—sentimentality, idealism, chivalric passion, and the like—in literary creation. They took a grim view of human life, and sought the faithful representation of reality and the truthful treatment of material in their novel writing. (The rivals of Balzac ridiculed Balzac for his special interest in contemporary life, which they thought was merely short-lived reality.) Such novelists are generally called realists and their work, **realistic novels**. In twentieth century, many writers such as John Galsworthy, Henry James, and Sinclare Lewis kept the realistic tradition, though their literary creation was not void of other significant methods.

Realists espouse what is essentially a mimetic theory of art, focusing their attention on the thing imitated and asking for a close correspondence between the representation and the subject. They keep an eye on the audience while writing their work, feeling it to be their obligation to present to them what is absolutely true. Thus they care much about the effect of their work upon the audience. George Eliot in *Adam Bede* expressed her idea that her representation of common life and experience should knit tightly the bonds of human sympathy among her readers. William Dean Howells was so concerned about the young ladies among his audience that he took on the responsibility not to do them moral injury, thus shut the doors of his works to most parts of life connected with passion and sex. Realists pay more attention to incidents of story than to a deliberate knitting of plot, since life is full of incidents and lacks symmetry. They emphasize characterization and their characterization is based on the effect of action, since they take the issue of conduct as the central one of all ethical issues in their concern. So they show an obvious tendency to explore the psychology of the actors in their stories. In Henry James, one of the greatest realists, the elaboration of this tendency to explore the inner selves of character with complex ethical choices earned for him not only the title of "father of the psychological novel" but also that of "biographer of fine consciences" (Holman and Harmon, *A Handbook to Literature*, 1986).

However, some realistic novelists in the late nineteenth and early twentieth centuries rejected romanticism so energetically that they swung to an extreme. Their works were endowed with a strong touch of pessimism and determinism. Close attention is paid to the sordid side of rural life and to human nature. If "nature" connotes a kind of divine benevolence in works by romantic poets like William Wordsworth, only the "red of tooth and claw" aspect can be seen in the novels of such realists. Thus realism is a skillful instrument in war novels, novels about human sufferings, and studies of human degradations. In Thomas Hardy, determinism is all-pervasive, and *Jude the Obscure*, his last novel, represents the limits of pessimism. However, pessimistic determinism merely reduces human character to pain, frustration, and impotency in Hardy's novel. But in Upton Sinclare's *Jungle* or Erich Maria Remarque's *All Quiet on the Western Front*, all pain, frustration, and impotency are not only inevitable but result from the human will—human will itself becomes the very force that destroys human beings. Behind this mood of pessimism and determinism is a new science, initiated by Charles Darwin and T. H. Huxley, which degrades man to the control of blind mechanistic forces. When novelists apply this view to their treatment of subject matter, the result is extreme realism—what literary critics usually called naturalism.

In its simplest sense **naturalism** is application of the principles of scientific determinism to fiction. It draws its name from the basic assumption that everything that exists is a part of nature and can be explained by natural and material causes rather than by supernatural or spiritual causes, and thus yields to objective scientific inquiry. The main influences that went into forming this view were Darwin's biological theories (including his metaphor of the competitive jungle), Comte's social and environmental determinism (including his application of scientific ideas to the study of society), and Taine's application of deterministic theories to literature. The naturalistic view takes human beings as animals in the natural world, subject to environmental forces and instinctive drives, which they can neither control nor fully understand. Man is no other than a product of natural forces, of genetic and social influences. Thus the novelist's task is to present the physical essence of man and his environment. The first naturalistic novel appeared in France, by Émila Zola. In his preface to *Thérèse Raquin* (1868), he declared that he himself was a *naturaliste* and that his method was scientifically clinical—that of the pathologist and psychologist. In his view men's lives and actions were determined by environment and heredity: "men are but phenomena and the conditions of phenomena." In his series of novels, with the best known *L'Assommoir* and *Germinal* among them, he concentrated on the seamy aspects of human existence: on the impoverished and the underprivileged, on the ugly and the diseased. Zola was experimenting his naturalistic view that a novelist's task was to select truthfully the instances subjected to laboratory conditions and to dissect life.

 Zola's influence was considerable. Strong elements of naturalism are to be seen in the work of Maupassant and J-K. Huysmans. In Germany, movement of naturalism flourished for a time in Berlin and Munich, with the dramatist Gerhart Hauptmann being the most distinguished exponent of German naturalism. In America across the Atlantic, Frank Norris wrote naturalistic novels in conscious imitation of Zola. Other notable naturalistic novelists are Stephen Crane, Jack London, and Theodore Dreiser, whose *An American Tragedy* is an archetypal American example.

 The desire to present life with frank objectivity led certain early twentieth-century novelists to question the validity of the conventions of a traditional novel. Realistic authors seek to represent what is "out there," but they will always be bound by principles of selection which makes pure objectivity impossible. So literary naturalism proposed to communicate a scientifically valid truth or natural law as revealed in the observation of objective things. With regard to narrative, if truth is to be gained, the traditional omniscient narrator should be replaced by one involved in the story and hence subject to the objective and naturalistic approach. But some French painters in the late nineteenth century, prominently Monet, Manet, Degas, and Renoir, had proclaimed a revision of the process of seeing: they distinguished between what the observer assumed he was observing and what he actually observed. Instead of painting a tree, they painted the effect of a tree: the visible world became less definite, more fluid, resolving into colour and light. For them, retaining the impressions that an object made on the observer was more important than presenting the appearance of that object by precise detail and realistic finish. (Claude Monet exhibited a painting named *Impression: Soleil Levant* in Paris in 1874.) Such painters are known as the **impressionists.**

Ford Madox Ford, Joseph Conrad, and Henry James, moving away from the realist tradition, which concentrated on closely notated detail in the exterior world, sought to create the illusion of reality by combining description of an objective, material world with its effect on the individual perceiver. For them, life does not narrate but renders impressions, and therefore, Ford says, an author "must write... as if... rendering the impressions of a person present at the scene" (Bender, *Modernism in Literature*, 1977). In Ford's *Paradise's End*, a series of novels, the reader moves freely within the time continuum, as if it were spatial, and the total picture is perceived through an accumulation of fragmentary impressions. The effect of life, the illusion of reality, then, is not produced by the report or the chronicle, but by the impression in all of its detail and seeming irrelevance. The structure of the traditional novel consequently undergoes radical change. Plot disappears, or it is no longer a tidy causal sequence of reported events. In Conrad's *Heart of Darkness*, the narrator's description of Marlow's tale as an "inconclusive" experience is a description of typical impressionist method. Conventional resolutions of narrations are defied in impressionist fiction, with the narrator subject to criticism by outside observers. Actions in the work as well as their significance may be unsolved, forcing the reader to make over and over again the possible critical structures. With respect to characterization, more attention is paid to psychological reaction to events as reflected in a record of personal impressions. Thus the narrator's description of Marlow as seated like a Buddha tells us more about his own impression about Marlow than about Marlow himself. The impressionist writer will often widen the scope of immediate impressions of a character by supplying us with a character's reveries or recollections, increasing the potential for ambiguity. Just as the impressionist painter makes the viewer conscious that he is looking at the pigment and not a real scene, the literary impressionist makes us conscious of words and how they are arranged rather than of what the words signify; he/she makes the reader aware that language is always separate from experience. The relationship between any word and the world is basically arbitrary, whether the object to be represented is a material fact or subjective experience. The dialogue in a book that Ford wrote jointly with Conrad—*The Inheritors*—manifests a particular aspect of literary impressionism. The halting utterances of real-life speech are given to clarity and conciseness. Ford and Conrad attempted to present speech as it was actually spoken.

    The interior monologue may be regarded as a development of this technique. To show pre-articulatory thought, feeling, and sensuous perception unordered into a rational sequence is an impressionistic device, which has served fiction of high importance, from Dorothy Richardson, James Joyce, and Virginia Woolf to Samuel Beckett and William Faulkner.

    Another literary style that followed and even went beyond impressionism in its emphasis on the emotional atmosphere and in opposition to the principles of realism is **expressionism**. The term, probably used after a series of paintings by Julien-Auguste Hervé exhibited in 1901 under the title *Expressionisms*, historically refers to a movement in Germany that found its congenial media in paintings and plays in the very early period of the twentieth century. (Bertolt Brecht is the important representative playwright of typical expressionist plays.) Later it is used in a broader sense to apply to artists and writers who seek to express the perceiver rather than to describe the object perceived. In literary creation, these writers appear either as creator of language conventions or as the person deliberately going beyond verbal conventions in order to represent psychic truth. They maintain that we cannot perceive or understand the world objectively and that even direct observations and sensations do not bring knowledge of the world. Instead, direct observation, as supposed by literary realism, would yield some knowledge of our own human experience. Walter Pater, one of the originators of expressionism in England, claims that if we analyze the way we perceive physical things, we shall see how subjective our experience of the world really is. He suggests in *The Renaissance* that all our ideas are derived from primary impressions of the world outside, and we understand the world only as we reconstruct it in our mind. And, since we each live in a world of our own making, it follows that artists can imitate only their own personalities in works of art (Bender, *Modernism in Literature*, 1977).

A writer who assumes that the subjective experience is real will naturally conclude that representation of a writer's highly developed imaginative processes is the most worthy subject. Therefore an appropriate novel would trace the development of the artistic mind. Joyce's *A Portrait of the Artist as a Young Man* can be regarded as such a novel. We have read a similar kind of story in the realist sense of personal development. In fact, Such a work can also be classified into the category of the **apprenticeship novel**—novel about a young man's bringing-up and education, about his discovery of the meaning of life or his knowledge of the world, with Goethe's *Wilhelm Meisters*, Charles Dickens's *Great Expectations*, and J. D. Salinger's *Catcher in the Rye* as typical examples, along with Joyce's *Portrait*. Faulkner's "Barn Burning" traces the tensions and conflicts repressed in the development of a social personality. But Joyce was interested in the representation of the unique consciousness of an individual's development rather than in that kind of social type. Joyce's novel consists of the protagonist's experience from within his own consciousness of language acquisition and use, from the fragmentary babbling of an infant on the first page through the connected but limited range or expression characteristic of a schoolboy to the sophistication of a fully articulate university student. And his unique artistic power becomes evident when he distorts the conventions of his culture to construct his own experience of the world.

The Austro-Czech Franz Kafka (1883-1924), the greatest of the expressionist novelists, sought to convey what may crudely be termed man's alienation from his world. His novels *The Trial* and *The Castle* produce a hallucinatory atmosphere similar to nightmare, which Europe was compelled to live in World War I. Of course, the significance is more subtle and universal. In *The Metamorphosis*, a young man changes into an enormous insect, and the nightmare of alienation reaches its limit.

Kafka's influence can be found in both Britain and America. The British writer Rex Warner's novels *Wild Goose* and *Aerodrome*, using fantasy, symbol, and improper action, describe such human condition as caught in a monstrously oppressive web that is both totalitarian and paternal tyranny. The American writer William Burroughs developed his own expressionistic techniques in *The Naked Lunch*, which is concerned with the social alienation of a drug addict. His *Nova Express* and *The Ticket That Exploded* use obscene fantasy to present a kind of metaphysical struggle between free spirit and enslaved flesh. Certain more recent novelists, such as Kurt Vonnegut, Jr., and Thomas Pynchon, are also included in the expressionistic tradition.

The literary creation in novel writing that goes the farthest away from traditional novel form is, perhaps, the **anti-novel**: a work of fictional imagination that abandons the conventions of plot development, characterization, dialogue, human interest, and narrative mode. It is also the French novelists who pioneered this form of the novel. French novelists like Allain Robbe-Grillet in *Jealousy*, Nathalie Sarraute in *Tropisms* and *The Planetarium*, Albert Camus in *The Stranger*, and Michel Butor in *Passing Time* and *Degrees*, attempted to remove pathetic fallacy from the fiction and thus to deter the reader from self-identification with the characters. In their writings, individual character is not important, and consciousness dissolves into sheer perception. Time is reversible, since perceptions have nothing to do with chronology, and memories can be handled backwards. Ultimately, the very appearance of the novel undergoes terrible changes: it is not obligatory to start at page 1 and work through to the end, and a reader can start reading the novel from any point at any page to which he/she just opens the book.

  British writers of the anti-novel such as Christine Brooke-Rose and Rayner Heppenstall object mainly to the falsification of the external world that is imposed upon the traditional novel by plot and character, and they insist on notating the minutiae of the surface of life rather then suggesting any meaning. Heppenstall's *Connecting the Door*, in which the narrator-hero does not even possess a name, is totally unconcerned with action but very interested in buildings, streets, and the sound of music. It is the same with their American counterparts. The only meaning of the world that the anti-novel writers such as Donald Barthelme, John Barth, and Kurt Vonnegut, Jr. intend to convey in their works is the meaninglessness of the world. So they employ the technique of "black humour"—they crack a joke upon very serious issues like religious belief, social violence, and a father's death. And they make fun of their works—they are nothing but collages of disjointed, incoherent fragments. Barthelme said that he merely believed in fragments, and Vonnegut said that he made chaos out of order while others made order out of chaos. Their remarks indicate the basic characteristic of anti-novel techniques. They care nothing about the portrayal of character, and thus characters are usually stolid, mechanical, abstract, and short of identity, since the anti-novel writers think that human beings are deprived of their personalities in this stolid and mechanized world.

However, although the writers of the anti-novel have gone so far in their opposition against realism with regard to writing techniques and treatment of subject matters, there is nothing new in the epistemology as applied to the novel. It is worth noting that as far back as 1627 Charles Sorel subtitled his novel *Le Berger extravagant* an *anti-roman*. The narrative mode of going backwards is present in Laurence Sterne's *Tristram Shandy*, and the process of anti-novel innovation can be seen in the major experiments of James Joyce (*Ulysses* and *Finnegans Wake*), Virginia Woolf (*The Waves* and *To the Lighthouse*), and in the earlier fiction of Samuel Becket (for example, *Molloy and Murphy*). Anyway, the anti-novel provides a way, perhaps a post-modernist way, of looking at the world, both objective and subjective.

Innovations in fiction are not confined to the categories already considered though many other endeavours apparently share similar characteristics with them. Even so revolutionary a work as Joyce's *Finnegans Wake* manifests an attempt to reveal the true nature of dream, which can be regarded as a kind of combination of impressionism and surrealism (which emphasizes the expression of imagination as realized in dreams and presented without conscious control). However, we prefer to treat the French novelist Michel Butor's *Mobile* as avant-garde more than an anti-novel, although it is similar to the anti-novel's collage in its presentation of material in the form of an encyclopaedia. Nabokov presents his novel *Pale Fire* in the form of a 999-line poem and provides the reader with critical comments assembled by a madman. We may classify this kind of novel as avant-garde or experimental. Whatever the label may be to a fictional work that seeks an innovation in techniques, one thing is clear, that is, it can never disclaim any interest in the world of feeling, thought, or sense, although the novelist can do anything he/she pleases with his/her art to interpret, or merely present, a world that the reader recognizes as existing, whether in actuality or in dream.

The categories briefly discussed above are among the common fictional forms. Theoretically there is no limit to the number available, since changing social patterns always provide fresh subjects, and new epistemological methods may lead to new fictional approaches and techniques. Other categories of fictional art, though not uncommon, include the **novel of manners**, whose major concern is to present the customs, conventions, manners, and habits of a definite social class at a particular time and place, as works by Jane Ausden, Edith Wharton, and Evelyn Waugh exemplify; the **regional novel** (See also Chapter Four), which concentrates on the representation of the habits, speech, manner, history, and customs of a particular area, in which respect the work of Willa Cather, Ellen Glasgow, and William Faulkner has great distinction; the **novel of character**, which places the major emphasis on characterization rather than on other elements of fiction; the **novel of incident**, in which special attention is paid to incidents or episodes in a loosely structured story, as shown in Defoe's *Robinson Crusoe* and Dumas' *Three Musketeers*; the **colonial novel**, which, exemplified by E. M. Foster's *Passage to India* and the African sequence of Joyce Cary, has suffer a lapse of no practice (but perhaps some writers will pick it up again with new connotations in the so-called post-colonialist age); the **detective story**; the **allegorical novel**; the **erotic novel** (which may or may not be pornographic); the **satirical novel**; **science fiction**; the **best-seller**; and so on. The novel is the all-embracing form of literature. New techniques will be experimented and employed in the creation of the novel, and new labels will then be attached to new types of novel, as is the label of the **structuralist novel** (following the linguistic sociologists and anthropologists). The novelist may emphasize this element (or these elements) and ignore that element (or those elements), but what is essential to the novel is always there. Thus, when reading a long novel, we may find it

Chapter Eight

helpful to look for the same elements that we have noticed in reading short stories, and, by asking ourselves those leading questions concerning short stories and at the same time keeping an eye on the deviations from conventions, we may be drawn more deeply into the novel's world and may come to a more subtle appreciation of the techniques of the novelist.

The Metamorphosis

by Franz Kafka, 1915

Translated by Willa and Edwin Muir

I

As Gregor Samsa awoke one morning from uneasy dreams he found himself transformed in his bed into a gigantic insect. He was lying on his hard, as it were armor-plated, back and when he lifted his head a little he could see his dome-like brown belly divided into stiff arched segments on top of which the bed quilt could hardly keep in position and was about to slide off completely. His numerous legs, which were pitifully thin compared to the rest of his bulk, waved helplessly before his eyes.

What has happened to me? he thought. It was no dream. His room, a regular human bedroom, only rather too small, lay quiet between the four familiar walls. Above the table on which a collection of cloth samples was unpacked and spread out—Samsa was a commercial traveler[1]—hung the picture which he had recently cut out of an illustrated magazine and put into a pretty gilt frame. It showed a lady, with a fur cap on and a fur stole, sitting upright and holding out to the spectator a huge fur muff into which the

---

[1] commercial traveler: a traveling salesman.

whole of her forearm had vanished!

　　Gregor's eyes turned next to the window, and the overcast sky—one could hear rain drops beating on the window gutter—made him quite melancholy. What about sleeping a little longer and forgetting all this nonsense, he thought, but it could not be done, for he was accustomed to sleep on his right side and in his present condition he could not turn himself over. However violently he forced himself towards his right side he always rolled on to his back again. He tried it at least a hundred times, shutting his eyes to keep from seeing his struggling legs, and only desisted when he began to feel in his side a faint dull ache he had never experienced before.

　　Oh God, he thought, what an exhausting job I've picked on! Traveling about day in, day out. It's much more irritating work than doing the actual business in the office, and on top of that there's the trouble of constant traveling, of worrying about train connections, the bed and irregular meals, casual acquaintances that are always new and never become intimate friends. The devil take it all! He felt a slight itching up on his belly; slowly pushed himself on his back nearer to the top of the bed so that he could lift his head more easily; identified the itching place which was surrounded by many small white spots the nature of which he could not understand and made to touch it with a leg, but drew the leg back immediately, for the contact made a cold shiver run through him.

5　　He slid down again into his former position. This getting up early, he thought, makes one quite stupid. A man needs his sleep. Other commercials live like harem women. For instance, when I come back to the hotel of a morning to write up the orders I've got, these others are only sitting down to breakfast. Let me just try that with my chief; I'd be sacked on the spot. Anyhow, that might be quite a good thing for me, who can tell? If I didn't have to hold my hand because of my parents I'd have given notice long ago, I'd have gone to the chief and told him exactly what I think of him. That would knock him endways from his desk! It's a queer way of doing, too, this sitting on high at a desk and talking down

Chapter Eight

to employees, especially when they have to come quite near because the chief is hard of hearing. Well, there's still hope; once I've saved enough money to pay back my parents' debts to him—that should take another five or six years—I'll do it without fail. I'll cut myself completely loose then. For the moment, though, I'd better get up, since my train goes at five.

He looked at the alarm clock ticking on the chest. Heavenly Father! he thought. It was half-past six o'clock and the hands were quietly moving on, it was even past the half-hour, it was getting on toward a quarter to seven. Had the alarm clock not gone off? From the bed one could see that it had been properly set for four o'clock; of course it must have gone off. Yes, but was it possible to sleep quietly through that ear-splitting noise? Well, he had not slept quietly, yet apparently all the more soundly for that. But what was he to do now? The next train went at seven o'clock; to catch that he would need to hurry like mad and his samples weren't even packed up, and he himself wasn't feeling particularly fresh and active. And even if he did catch the train he wouldn't avoid a row with the chief, since the firm's porter would have been waiting for the five o'clock train and would have long since reported his failure to turn up. The porter was a creature of the chiefs, spineless and stupid. Well, supposing he were to say he was sick? But that would be most unpleasant and would look suspicious, since during his five year's employment he had not been ill once. The chief himself would be sure to come with the sick-insurance doctor, would reproach his parents with their son's laziness and would cut all excuses short by referring to the insurance doctor, who of course regarded all mankind as perfectly healthy malingerers. And would he be so far wrong on this occasion? Gregor really felt quite well, apart from a drowsiness that was utterly superfluous after such a long sleep, and he was even unusually hungry.

As all this was running through his mind at top speed without his being able to decide to leave his bed—the alarm clock had just struck a quarter to seven—there came a cautious tap at the door behind the head of his bed. "Gregor," said a voice—it was his mother's—"it's a quarter to seven. Hadn't you a train to catch?" That gentle voice! Gregor had a shock as he heard his own voice answering hers, unmistakably his own voice, it was true, but with a persistent horrible twittering squeak behind it like an undertone, that left the words in their clear shape only for the first moment and then rose up reverberating round them to destroy their sense, so that one could not be sure one had heard them rightly. Gregor wanted to answer at length and explain everything, but in the circumstances he confined himself to saying: "Yes, yes, thank you, Mother, I'm getting up now." The wooden door between them must have kept the change in his voice from being noticeable outside, for his mother contented herself with this statement and shuffled away. Yet this brief exchange of words had made the other members of the family aware that Gregor was still in the house, as they had not expected, and at one of the side doors his father was already knocking, gently, yet with his fist. "Gregor, Gregor," he called, "what's the matter with you?" And after a little while he called again in a deeper voice: "Gregor! Gregor!" At the other side door his sister was saying in a low, plaintive tone: "Gregor? Aren't you well? Are you needing anything?" He answered them both at once: "I'm just ready," and did his best to make his voice sound as normal as possible by enunciating the words very clearly and leaving long pauses between them. So his father went back to his breakfast, but his sister whispered: "Gregor, open the door, do." However, he was not thinking of opening the door, and felt thankful for the prudent habit he had acquired in traveling of locking all doors during the night, even at home.

  His immediate intention was to get up quietly without being disturbed, to put on his clothes and above all eat his breakfast, and only then to consider what else was to be done, since in bed, he was well aware, his meditations would come to no sensible conclusion. He remembered that often enough in bed he had felt small aches and pains, probably caused by awkward postures,

Chapter Eight

which had proved purely imaginary once he got up, and he looked forward eagerly to seeing this morning's delusions gradually fall away. That the change in his voice was nothing but the precursor of a severe chill, a standing ailment of commercial travelers, he had not the least possible doubt.

To get rid of the quilt was quite easy; he had only to inflate himself a little and it fell off by itself. But the next move was difficult, especially because he was so uncommonly broad. He would have needed arms and hands to hoist himself up; instead he had only the numerous little legs which never stopped waving in all directions and which he could not control in the least. When he tried to bend one of them it was the first to stretch itself straight; and did he succeed at last in making it do what he wanted, all the other legs meanwhile waved the more wildly in a high degree of unpleasant agitation. "But what's the use of lying idle in bed," said Gregor to himself.

10   He throught that he might get out of bed with the lower part of his body first, but this lower part, which he had not yet seen and of which he could form no clear conception, proved too difficult to move; it shifted so slowly; and when finally, almost wild with annoyance, he gathered his forces together and thrust out recklessly, he had miscalculated the direction and bumped heavily against the lower end of the bed, and the stinging pain he felt informed him that precisely this lower part of his body was at the moment probably the most sensitive.

So he tried to get the top part of himself out first, and cautiously moved his head towards the edge of the bed. That proved easy enough, and despite its breadth and mass the bulk of his body at last slowly followed the movement of his head. Still, when he finally got his head free over the edge of the bed he felt too scared to go on advancing, for after all if he let himself fall in this way it would take a miracle to keep his head from being injured. And at all costs he must not lose consciousness now, precisely now; he would rather stay in bed.

But when after a repetition of the same efforts he lay in his former position again, sighing, and watched his little legs struggling against each other more wildly than ever, if that were possible, and saw no way of bringing any order into this arbitrary confusion, he told himself again that it was impossible to stay in bed and that the most sensible course was to risk everything for the small-est hope of getting away from it. At the same time he did not forget meanwhile to remind himself that cool reflection, the coolest possible, was much better than desperate resolves. In such moments he focused his eyes as sharply as possible on the window, but unfortunately, the prospect of the morning fog, which muffled even the other side of the narrow street, brought him little encouragement and comfort. "Seven o'clock already," he said to himself when the alarm clock chimed again, "seven o'clock already and still such a thick fog." And for a little while he lay quiet, breathing lightly, as if perhaps expecting such complete repose to restore all things to their real and normal condition.

But then he said to himself: "Before it strikes a quarter past seven I must be quite out of this bed, without fail. Anyhow, by that time someone will have come from the office to ask for me, since it opens before seven." And he set himself to rocking his whole body at once in a regular rhythm, with the idea of swinging it out of the bed. If he tipped himself out in that way he could keep his head from injury by lifting it at an acute angle when he fell. His back seemed to be hard and was not likely to suffer from a fall on the carpet. His biggest worry was the loud crash he would not be able to help making, which would probably cause anxiety, if not terror, behind all the doors. Still, he must take the risk.

When he was already half out of the bed—the new method was more a game than an effort, for he needed only to hitch himself across by rocking to and fro—it struck him how simple it would be if he could get help. Two strong people—he thought of his father and the servant girl—would be amply sufficient; they would only have to thrust their arms under his convex back, lever him out of

Chapter Eight

the bed, bend down with their burden and then be patient enough to let him turn himself right over on to the floor, where it was to be hoped his legs would then find their proper function. Well, ignoring the fact that the doors were all locked, ought he really to call for help? In spite of his misery he could not suppress a smile at the very idea of it.

15   He had got so far that he could barely keep his equilibrium when he rocked himself strongly, and he would have to nerve himself very soon for the final decision since in five minutes' time it would be a quarter past seven—when the front doorbell rang. "That's someone from the office," he said to himself, and grew almost rigid, while his little legs only jigged about all the faster. For a moment everything stayed quiet. "They're not going to open the door," said Gregor to himself, catching at some kind of irrational hope. But then of course the servant girl went as usual to the door with her heavy tread and opened it. Gregor needed only to hear the first good morning of the visitor to know immediately who it was—the chief clerk himself. What a fate, to be condemned to work for a firm where the smallest omission at once gave rise to the gravest suspicion! Were all employees in a body nothing but scoundrels, was there not among them one single loyal devoted man who, had he wasted only an hour or so of the firm's time in a morning, was so tormented by conscience as to be driven out of his mind and actually incapable of leaving his bed? Wouldn't it really have been sufficient to send an apprentice to inquire—if any inquiry were necessary at all—did the chief clerk himself have to come and thus indicate to the entire family, an innocent family, that this suspicious circumstance could be investigated by no one less versed in affairs than himself? And more through the agitation caused by these reflections than through any act of will Gregor swung himself out of bed with all his strength. There was a loud thump, but it was not really a crash. His fall was broken to some extent by the carpet, his back, too, was less stiff than he thought, and so there was merely a dull thud, not so very startling. Only he had not

lifted his head carefully enough and had hit it; he turned it and rubbed it on the carpet in pain and irritation.

"That was something falling down in there," said the chief clerk in the next room to the left. Gregor tried to suppose to himself that something like what had happened to him today might some day happen to the chief clerk; one really could not deny that it was possible. But as if in brusque reply to this supposition the chief clerk took a couple of firm steps in the next-door room and his patent leather boots creaked. From the right-hand room his sister was whispering to inform him of the situation: "Gregor, the chief clerk's here. " "I know," muttered Gregor to himself; but he didn't dare to make his voice loud enough for his sister to hear it.

"Gregor," said his father now from the left-hand room, "the chief clerk has come and wants to know why you didn't catch the early train. We don't know what to say to him. Besides, he wants to talk to you in person. So open the door, please. He will be good enough to excuse the untidiness of your room." "Good morning, Mr. Samsa," the chief clerk was calling amiably meanwhile. "He's not well," said his mother to the visitor, while his father was still speaking through the door, "he's not well, sir, believe me. What else would make him miss a train! The boy thinks about nothing but his work. It makes me almost cross the way he never goes out in the evenings; he's been here the last eight days and has stayed at home every single evening. He just sits there quietly at the table reading a newspaper or looking through railway timetables. The only amusement he gets is doing fretwork. For instance, he spent two or three evenings cutting out a little picture frame; you would be surprised to see how pretty it is; it's hanging in his room; you'll see it in a minute when Gregor opens the door. I must say I'm glad you've come, sir; we should never have got him to unlock the door by ourselves; he's so obstinate; and I'm sure he's unwell, though he wouldn't have it to be so this morning." "I'm just coming," said Gregor slowly and carefully, not moving an inch for fear of losing one word of the conversation. "I can't think of

Chapter Eight

any other explanation, madam," said the chief clerk, "I hope it's nothing serious. Although on the other hand I must say that we men of business—fortunately or unfortunately—very often simply have to ignore any slight indisposition, since business must be attended to." "Well, can the chief clerk come in now?" asked Gregor's father impatiently, again knocking on the door. "No," said Gregor. In the left-hand room a painful silence followed this refusal, in the right-hand room his sister began to sob.

Why didn't his sister join the others? She was probably newly out of bed and hadn't even begun to put on her clothes yet. Well, why was she crying? Because he wouldn't get up and let the chief clerk in, because he was in danger of losing his job, and because the chief would begin dunning his parents again for the old debts? Surely these were things one didn't need to worry about for the present. Gregor was still at home and not in the least thinking of deserting the family. At the moment, true, he was lying on the carpet and no one who knew the condition he was in could seriously expect him to admit the chief clerk. But for such a small discourtesy, which could plausibly be explained away somehow later on, Gregor could hardly be dismissed on the spot. And it seemed to Gregor that it would be much more sensible to leave him in peace for the present than to trouble him with tears and entreaties. Still, of course, their uncertainty bewildered them all and excused their behavior.

"Mr. Samsa," the chief clerk called now in a louder voice, "what's the matter with you? Here you are, barricading yourself in your room, giving only 'yes' and 'no' for answers, causing your parents a lot of unnecessary trouble and neglecting—I mention this only in passing—neglecting your business duties in an incredible fashion. I am speaking here in the name of your parents and of your chief, and I beg you quite seriously to give me an immediate and precise explanation. You amaze me, you amaze me. I thought you were a quiet, dependable person, and now all at once you seem bent on making a disgraceful exhibition of yourself. The chief did hint to me early this morning a possible explanation for your disappearance—with reference to the cash payments that were entrusted to you recently—but I almost pledged my solemn word of honor that this could not be so. But now that I see how incredibly obstinate you are, I no longer have the slightest desire to take your part at all. And your position in the firm is not so unassailable. I came with the intention of telling you all this in private, but since you are wasting my time so needlessly I don't see why your parents shouldn't hear it too. For some time past your work has been most unsatisfactory; this is not the season of the year for a business boom, of course, we admit that, but a season of the year for doing no business at all, that does not exist, Mr. Samsa, must not exist."

20   "But, sir," cried Gregor, beside himself and in his agitation forgetting everything else, "I'm just going to open the door this very minute. A slight illness, an attack of giddiness, has kept me from getting up. I'm still lying in bed. But I feel all right again. I'm getting out of bed now. Just give me a moment or two longer! I'm not quite so well as I thought. But I'm all right, really. How a thing like that can suddenly strike one down! Only last night I was quite well, my parents can tell you, or rather I did have a slight presentiment. I must have showed some sign of it. Why didn't I report it at the office! But one always thinks that an indisposition can be got over without staying in the house. Oh sir, do spare my parents! All that you're reproaching me with now has no foundation; no one has ever said a word to me about it. Perhaps you haven't looked at the last orders I sent in. Anyhow, I can still catch the eight o'clock train, I'm much the better for my few hours' rest. Don't let me detain you here, sir; I'll be attending to business very soon, and do be good enough to tell the chief so and to make my excuses to him!"

And while all this was tumbling out pell-mell and Gregor hardly knew what he was saying, he had reached the chest quite easily, perhaps because of the practice he had had in bed, and was

Chapter Eight

now trying to lever himself upright by means of it. He meant actually to open the door, actually to show himself and speak to the chief clerk; he was eager to find out what the others, after all their insistence, would say at the sight of him. If they were horrified then the responsibility was no longer his and he could stay quiet. But if they took it calmly, then he had no reason either to be upset, and could really get to the station for the eight o'clock train if he hurried. At first he slipped down a few times from the polished surface of the chest, but at length with a last heave he stood upright; he paid no more attention to the pains in the lower part of his body, however they smarted. Then he let himself fall against the back of a near-by chair, and clung with his little legs to the edges of it. That brought him into control of himself again and he stopped speaking, for now he could listen to what the chief clerk was saying.

"Did you understand a word of it ?" the chief clerk was asking; "surely he can't be trying to make fools of us?" "Oh dear," cried his mother, in tears, "perhaps he's terribly ill and we're tormenting him. Grete! Grete!" she called out then. "Yes, Mother?" called his sister from the other side. They were calling to each other across Gregor's room. "You must go this minute for the doctor. Gregor is ill. Go for the doctor, quick. Did you hear how he was speaking?" "That was no human voice," said the chief clerk in a voice noticeably low beside the shrillness of the mother's. "Anna! Anna!" his father was calling through the hall to the kitchen, clapping his hands, "get a locksmith at once!" And the two girls were already running through the hall with a swish of skirts—how could his sister have got dressed so quickly? —and were tearing the front door open. There was no sound of its closing again; they had evidently left it open, as one does in houses where some great misfortune has happened.

But Gregor was now much calmer. The words he uttered were no longer understandable, apparently, although they seemed clear enough to him, even clearer than before, perhaps because his ear had grown accustomed to the sound of them. Yet at any rate people now believed that something was wrong with him, and were ready to help him. The positive certainty with which these first measures had been taken comforted him. He felt himself drawn once more into the human circle and hoped for great and remarkable results from both the doctor and the locksmith, without really distinguishing precisely between them. To make his voice as clear as possible for the decisive conversation that was now imminent he coughed a little, as quietly as he could, of course, since this noise too might not sound like a human cough for all he was able to judge. In the next room meanwhile there was complete silence. Perhaps his parents were sitting at the table with the chief clerk, whispering, perhaps they were all leaning against the door and listening.

  Slowly Gregor pushed the chair towards the door, then let go of it, caught hold of the door for support—the soles at the end of his little legs were somewhat sticky—and rested against it for a moment after his efforts. Then he set himself to turning the key in the lock with his mouth. It seemed, unhappily, that he hadn't really any teeth—what could he grip the key with? —but on the other hand his jaws were certainly very strong; with their help he did manage to set the key in motion, heedless of the fact that he was undoubtedly damaging them somewhere, since a brown fluid issued from his mouth, flowed over the key and dripped on the floor. "Just listen to that," said the chief clerk next door; "he's turning the key." That was a great encouragement to Gregor; but they should all have shouted encouragement to him, his father and mother too: "Go on, Gregor," they should have called out, "keep going, hold on to that key!" And in the belief that they were all following his efforts intently, he clenched his jaws recklessly on the key with all the force at his command. As the turning of the key progressed he circled round the lock, holding on now only with his mouth, pushing on the key, as required, or pulling it down again with all the weight of his body. The louder click of the finally yielding lock literally quickened Gregor. With a deep breath of

Chapter Eight

relief he said to himself: "So I didn't need the locksmith," and laid his head on the handle to open the door wide.

25   Since he had to pull the door towards him, he was still invisible when it was really wide open. He had to edge himself slowly round the near half of the double door, and to do it very carefully if he was not to fall plump upon his back just on the threshold. He was still carrying out this difficult manoeuvre, with no time to observe anything else, when he heard the chief clerk utter a loud "Oh!"—it sounded like a gust of wind—and now he could see the man, standing as he was nearest to the door, clapping one hand before his open mouth and slowly backing away as if driven by some invisible steady pressure. His mother—in spite of the chief clerk's being there her hair was still undone and sticking up in all directions—first clasped her hands and looked at his father, then took two steps towards Gregor and fell on the floor among her outspread skirts, her face hidden on her breast. His father knotted his fist with a fierce expression on his face as if he meant to knock Gregor back into his room, then looked uncertainly round the living room, covered his eyes with his hands and wept till his great chest heaved.

Gregor did not go now into the living room, but leaned against the inside of the firmly shut wing of the door, so that only half his body was visible and his head above it bending sideways to look at the others. The light had meanwhile strengthened; on the other side of the street one could see clearly a section of the endlessly long, dark gray building opposite—it was a hospital—abruptly punctuated by its row of regular windows; the rain was still falling, but only in large singly discernible and literally singly splash-ing drops. The breakfast dishes were set out on the table lavishly, for breakfast was the most important meal of the day to Gregor's father, who lingered it out for hours over various newspapers. Right opposite Gregor on the wall hung a photograph of himself on military service, as a lieutenant, hand on sword, a carefree smile on his face, inviting one to respect his uniform and military bearing. The door leading to the hall was open, and one could see that the front door stood open too, showing the landing beyond and the beginning of the stairs going down.

"Well," said Gregor, knowing perfectly that he was the only one who had retained any composure, "I'll put my clothes on at once, pack up my samples and start off. Will you only let me go? You see, sir, I'm not obstinate, and I'm willing to work; traveling is a hard life, but I couldn't live without it. Where are you going, sir? To the office? Yes? Will you give a true account of all this? One can be temporarily incapacitated, but that's just the moment for remembering former services and bearing in mind that later on, when the incapacity has been got over, one will certainly work with all the more industry and concentration. I'm loyally bound to serve the chief, you know that very well. Besides, I have to provide for my parents and my sister. I'm in great difficulties, but I'll get out of them again. Don't make things any worse for me than they are. Stand up for me in the firm. Travelers are not popular there, I know. People think they earn sacks of money and just have a good time. A prejudice there's no particular reason for revising. But you, sir, have a more comprehensive view of affairs than the rest of the staff, yes, let me tell you in confidence, a more comprehensive view than the chief himself, who, being the owner, lets his judgment easily be swayed against one of his employees. And you know very well that the traveler, who is never seen in the office almost the whole year round, can so easily fall a victim to gossip and ill luck and unfounded complaints, which he mostly knows nothing about, except when he comes back exhausted from his rounds, and only then suffers in person from their evil consequences, which he can no longer trace back to the original causes. Sir, sir, don't go away without a word to me to show that you think me in the right at least to some extent!"

But at Gregor's very first words the chief clerk had already backed away and only stared at him with parted lips over one twitching shoulder. And while Gregor was speaking he did not

Chapter Eight

stand still one moment but stole away towards the door, without taking his eyes off Gregor, yet only an inch at a time, as if obeying some secret injunction to leave the room. He was already at the hall, and the suddenness with which he took his last step out of the living room would have made one believe he had burned the sole of his foot. Once in the hall he stretched his right arm before him towards the staircase, as if some supernatural power were waiting there to deliver him.

Gregor perceived that the chief clerk must on no account be allowed to go away in this frame of mind if his position in the firm were not to be endangered to the utmost. His parents did not understand this so well; they had convinced themselves in the course of years that Gregor was settled for life in this firm, and besides they were so occupied with their immediate troubles that all foresight had forsaken them. Yet Gregor had this foresight. The chief clerk must be detained, soothed, persuaded and finally won over; the whole future of Gregor and his family depended on it! If only his sister had been there! She was intelligent; she had begun to cry while Gregor was still lying quietly on his back. And no doubt the chief clerk, so partial to ladies, would have been guided by her; she would have shut the door of the flat and in the hall talked him out of his horror. But she was not there, and Gregor would have to handle the situation himself. And without remembering that he was still unaware what powers of movement he possessed, without even remembering that his words in all possibility, indeed in all likelihood, would again be unintelligible, he let go the wing of the door, pushed himself through the opening, started to walk towards the chief clerk, who was already ridiculously clinging with both hands to the railing on the landing; but immediately, as he was feeling for a support, he fell down with a little cry upon all his numerous legs. Hardly was he down when he experienced for the first time this morning a sense of physical comfort; his legs had firm ground under them; they were completely obedient, as he noted with joy; they even strove to carry him forward in whatever direction he chose; and he was inclined to believe that a final relief from all his sufferings was at hand. But in the same moment as he found himself on the floor, rocking with suppressed eagerness to move, not far from his mother, indeed just in front of her, she, who had seemed so completely crushed, sprang all at once to her feet, her arms and fingers outspread, cried: "Help, for God's sake, help!" bent her head down as if to see Gregor better, yet on the contrary kept backing senselessly away; had quite forgotten that the laden table stood behind her; sat upon it hastily, as if in absence of mind, when she bumped into it; and seemed altogether unaware that the big coffee pot beside her was upset and pouring coffee in a flood over the carpet.

30　　"Mother, Mother," said Gregor in a low voice, and looked up at her. The chief clerk, for the moment, had quite slipped from his mind; instead, he could not resist snapping his jaws together at the sight of the streaming coffee. That made his mother scream again, she fled from the table and fell into the arms of his father, who hastened to catch her. But Gregor had now no time to spare for his parents; the chief clerk was already on the stairs; with his chin on the banisters he was taking one last backward look. Gregor made a spring, to be as sure as possible of overtaking him; the chief clerk must have divined his intention, for he leaped down several steps and vanished; he was still yelling "Ugh!" and it echoed through the whole staircase.

　　Unfortunately, the flight of the chief clerk seemed completely to upset Gregor's father, who had remained relatively calm until now, for instead of running after the man himself, or at least not hindering Gregor in his pursuit, he seized in his right hand the walking stick which the chief clerk had left behind on a chair, together with a hat and greatcoat, snatched in his left hand a large newspaper from the table and began stamping his feet and flourishing the stick and the newspaper to drive Gregor back into his room. No entreaty of Gregor's availed, indeed no entreaty was

Chapter Eight

even understood, however humbly he bent his head his father only stamped on the floor the more loudly. Behind his father his mother had torn open a window, despite the cold weather, and was leaning far out of it with her face in her hands. A strong draught set in from the street to the staircase, the window curtains blew in, the newspapers on the table fluttered, stray pages whisked over the floor. Pitilessly Gregor's father drove him back, hissing and crying "Shoo!" like a savage. But Gregor was quite unpracticed in walking backwards, it really was a slow business. If he only had a chance to turn round he could get back to his room at once, but he was afraid of exasperating his father by the slowness of such a rotation and at any moment the stick in his father's hand might hit him a fatal blow on the back or on the head. In the end, however, nothing else was left for him to do since to his horror he observed that in moving backwards he could not even control the direction he took; and so, keeping an anxious eye on his father all the time over his shoulder, he began to turn round as quickly as he could, which was in reality very slowly. Perhaps his father noted his good intentions, for he did not interfere except every now and then to help him in the manoeuvre from a distance with the point of the stick. If only he would have stopped making that unbearable hissing noise! It made Gregor quite lose his head. He had turned almost completely round when the hissing noise so distracted him that he even turned a little the wrong way again. But when at last his head was fortunately right in front of the doorway, it appeared that his body was too broad simply to get through the opening. His father, of course, in his present mood was far from thinking of such a thing as opening the other half of the door, to let Gregor have enough space. He had merely the fixed idea of driving Gregor back into his room as quickly as possible. He would never have suffered Gregor to make the circumstantial preparations for standing up on end and perhaps slipping his way through the door. Maybe he was now making more noise than ever to urge Gregor forward, as if no obstacle impeded him; to Gregor, anyhow, the noise in his rear sound-ed no longer like the voice of one single father; this was really no joke, and Gregor thrust himself—come what might—into the doorway. One side of his body rose up, he was tilted at an angle in the doorway, his flank was quite bruised, horrid blotches stained the white door, soon he was stuck fast and, left to himself, could not have moved at all, his legs on one side fluttered trembling to the air, those on the other were crushed painfully to the floor—when from behind his father gave him a strong push which was literally a deliverance and he flew far into the room, bleeding freely. The door was slammed behind him with the stick, and then at last there was silence.

II

Not until it was twilight did Gregor awake out of a deep sleep, more like a swoon than a sleep. He would certainly have waked up of his own accord not much later, for he felt himself sufficiently rested and well-slept, but it seemed to him as if a fleeting step and a cautious shutting of the door leading into the hall had aroused him. The electric lights in the street cast a pale sheen here and there on the ceiling and the upper surfaces of the furniture, but down below, where he lay, it was dark. Slowly, awkwardly trying out his feelers, which he now first learned to appreciate, he pushed his way to the door to see what had been happening there. His left side felt like one single long, unpleasant tense scar, and he had actually to limp on his two rows of legs. One little leg, moreover, had been severely damaged in the course of that morning's events—it was almost a miracle that only one had been damaged— and trailed uselessly behind him.

He had reached the door before he discovered what had really drawn him to it: the smell of food. For there stood a basin filled with fresh milk in which floated little sops of white bread. He could almost have laughed with joy, since he was now still hungrier than in the morning, and he dipped his head almost over the eyes straight into the milk. But soon in disappointment he withdrew it

Chapter Eight

again; not only did he find it difficult to feed because of his tender left side —and he could only feed with the palpitating collaboration of his whole body—he did not like the milk either, although milk had been his favorite drink and that was certainly why his sister had set it there for him, indeed it was almost with repulsion that he turned away from the basin and crawled back to the middle of the room.

    He could see through the crack of the door that the gas was turned on in the living room, but while usually at this time his father made a habit of reading the afternoon newspaper in a loud voice to his mother and occasionally to his sister as well, not a sound was now to be heard. Well, perhaps his father had recently given up this habit of reading aloud, which his sister had mentioned so often in conversation and in her letters. But there was the same silence all around, although the flat was certainly not empty of occupants. "What a quiet life our family has been leading," said Gregor to himself, and as he sat there motionless staring into the darkness he felt great pride in the fact that he had been able to provide such a life for his parents and sister in such a fine flat. But what if all the quiet, the comfort, the contentment were now to end in horror? To keep himself from being lost in such thoughts Gregor took refuge in movement and crawled up and down the room.

35   Once during the long evening one of the side doors was opened a little and quickly shut again, later the other side door too; someone had apparently wanted to come in and then thought better of it. Gregor now stationed himself immediately before the living room door, determined to persuade any hesitating visitor to come in or at least to discover who it might be; but the door was not opened again and he waited in vain. In the early morning, when the doors were locked, they had all wanted to come in, now that he had opened one door and the other had apparently been opened during the day, no one came in and even the keys were on the other side of the doors.

    It was late at night before the gas went out in the living room, and Gregor could easily tell that his parents and his sister had all stayed awake until then, for he could clearly hear the three of them stealing away on tiptoe. No one was likely to visit him, not until the morning, that was certain; so he had plenty of time to meditate at his leisure on how he was to arrange his life afresh. But the lofty, empty room in which he had to lie flat on the floor filled him with an apprehension he could not account for, since it had been his very own room for the past five years—and with a half-unconscious action, not without a slight feeling of shame, he scuttled under the sofa, where he felt comfortable at once, although his back was a little cramped and he could not lift his head up, and his only regret was that his body was too broad to get the whole of it under the sofa.

He stayed there all night, spending the time partly in a light slumber, from which his hunger kept waking him up with a start, and partly in worrying and sketching vague hopes, which all led to the same conclusion, that he must lie low for the present and, by exercising patience, and the utmost consideration, help the family to bear the inconvenience he was bound to cause them in his present condition.

Very early in the morning, it was still almost night, Gregor had the chance to test the strength of his new resolutions, for his sister, nearly fully dressed, opened the door from the hall and peered in. She did not see him at once, yet when she caught sight of him under the sofa—well, he had to be somewhere, he couldn't have flown away, could he? —she was so startled that without being able to help it she slammed the door shut again. But as if regretting her behavior she opened the door again immediately and came in on tiptoe, as if she were visiting an invalid or even a stranger. Gregor had pushed his head forward to the very edge of the sofa and watched her. Would she notice that he had left the milk standing, and not for lack of hunger, and would she bring in some other kind of food more to his taste? If she did not do it of her own accord, he would rather starve than draw her attention to the fact, although he felt a wild impulse to dart out from under the

Chapter Eight

sofa, throw himself at her feet and beg her for something to eat. But his sister at once noticed, with surprise, that the basin was still full, except for a little milk that had been spilt all around it, she lifted it immediately, not with her bare hands, true, but with a cloth and carried it away. Gregor was wildly curious to know what she would bring instead, and made various speculations about it. Yet what she actually did next, in the goodness of her heart, he could never have guessed at. To find out what he liked she brought him a whole selection of food, all set out on an old newspaper. There were old, half-decayed vegetables, bones from last night's supper covered with a white sauce that had thickened; some raisins and almonds; a piece of cheese that Gregor would have called uneatable two days ago; a dry roll of bread, a buttered roll, and a roll both buttered and salted. Besides all that, she set down again the same basin, into which she had poured some water, and which was apparently to be reserved for his exclusive use. And with fine tact, knowing that Gregor would not eat in her presence, she withdrew quickly and even turned the key, to let him understand that he could take his ease as much as he liked. Gregor's legs all whizzed towards the food. His wounds must have healed completely, moreover, for he felt no disability, which amazed him and made him reflect how more than a month ago he had cut one finger a little with a knife and had still suffered pain from the wound only the day before yesterday. Am I less sensitive now? he thought, and sucked greedily at the cheese, which above all the other edibles attracted him at once and strongly. One after another and with tears of satisfaction in his eyes he quickly devoured the cheese, the vegetables and the sauce; the fresh food, on the other hand, had no charms for him, he could not even stand the smell of it and actually dragged away to some little distance the things he could eat. He had long finished his meal and was only lying lazily on the same spot when his sister turned the key slowly as a sign for him to retreat. That roused him at once, although he was nearly asleep, and he hurried under the sofa again. But it took considerable self-control for him to stay under the sofa, even for the short time his sister was in the room, since the large meal had swollen his body somewhat and he was so cramped he could hardly breathe. Slight attacks of breathlessness afflicted him and his eyes were starting a little out of his head as he watched his unsuspecting sister sweeping together with a broom not only the remains of what he had eaten but even the things he had not touched, as if these were now of no use to anyone, and hastily shoveling it all into a bucket, which she covered with a wooden lid and carried away. Hardly had she turned her back when Gregor came from under the sofa and stretched and puffed himself out.

In this manner Gregor was fed, once in the early morning while his parents and the servant girl were still asleep, and a second time after they had all had their midday dinner, for then his parents took a short nap and the servant girl could be sent out on some errand or other by his sister. Not that they would have wanted him to starve, of course, but perhaps they could not have borne to know more about his feeding than from hearsay, perhaps too his sister wanted to spare them such little anxieties wherever possible, since they had quite enough to bear as it was.

40　　Under what pretext the doctor and the locksmith had been got rid of on that first morning Gregor could not discover, for since what he had said was not understood by the others it never struck any of them, not even his sister, that he could understand what they said, and so whenever his sister came into his room he had to content himself with hearing her utter only a sigh now and then and an occasional appeal to the saints. Later on, when she had got a little used to the situation—of course she could never get completely used to it—she sometimes threw out a remark which was kindly meant or could be so interpreted. "Well, he liked his dinner today," she would say when Gregor had made a good clearance of his food; and when he had not eaten, which gradually happened more and more often, she would say almost sadly: "Everything's been left standing again."

Chapter Eight

But although Gregor could get no news directly, he overheard a lot from the neighboring rooms, and as soon as voices were audible, he would run to the door of the room concerned and press his whole body against it. In the first few days especially there was no conversation that did not refer to him somehow, even if only indirectly. For two whole days there were family consultations at every mealtime about what should be done; but also between meals the same subject was discussed, for there were always at least two members of the family at home, since no one wanted to be alone in the flat and to leave it quite empty was unthinkable. And on the very first of these days the household cook—it was not quite clear what and how much she knew of the situation—went down on her knees to his mother and begged leave to go, and when she departed, a quarter of an hour later, gave thanks for her dismissal with tears in her eyes as if for the greatest benefit that could have been conferred on her, and without any prompting swore a solemn oath that she would never say a single word to anyone about what had happened.

Now Gregor's sister had to cook too, helping her mother; true, the cooking did not amount to much, for they are scarcely anything. Gregor was always hearing one of the family vainly urging another to eat and getting no answer but: "Thanks, I've had all I want," or something similar. Perhaps they drank nothing either. Time and again his sister kept asking his father if he wouldn't like some beer and offered kindly to go and fetch it herself, and when he made no answer suggested that she could ask the concierge[1] to fetch it, so that he need feel no sense of obligation, but then a round "No" came from his father and no more was said about it.

In the course of that very first day Gregor's father explained the family's financial position and prospects to both his mother and his sister. Now and then he rose from the table to get some voucher or memorandum out of the small safe he had rescued from

---

[1] concierge: the attendant at the entrance of a building who often provides services for the residents; the doorman.

the collapse of his business five years earlier. One could hear him opening the complicated lock and rustling papers out and shutting it again. This statement made by his father was the first cheerful information Gregor had heard since his imprisonment. He had been of the opinion that nothing at all was left over from his father's business, at least his father had never said anything to the contrary, and of course he had not asked him directly. At the time Gregor's sole desire was to do his utmost to help the family to forget as soon as possible the catastrophe which had overwhelmed the business and thrown them all into a state of complete despair. And so he had set to work with unusual ardor and almost overnight had become a commercial traveler instead of a little clerk, with of course much greater chances of earning money, and his success was immediately translated into good round coin which he could lay on the table for his amazed and happy family. These had been fine times, and they had never recurred, at least not with the same sense of glory, although later on Gregor had earned so much money that he was able to meet the expenses of the whole household and did so. They had simply got used to it, both the family and Gregor; the money was gratefully accepted and gladly given, but there was no special uprush of warm feeling. With his sister alone had he remained intimate, and it was a secret plan of his that she, who loved music, unlike himself, and could play movingly on the violin, should be sent next year to study at the Conservatorium[1], despite the great expense that would entail, which must be made up in some other way. During his brief visits home the Conservatorium was often mentioned in the talks he had with his sister, but always merely as a beautiful dream which could never come true, and his parents discouraged even these innocent references to it; yet Gregor had made up his mind firmly about it and meant to announce the fact with due solemnity on Christmas Day.

  Such were the thoughts, completely futile in his present

---

[1] Conservatorium: a music school for advanced students.

Chapter Eight

condition, that went through his head as he stood clinging upright to the door and listening. Sometimes out of sheer weariness he had to give up listening and let his head fall negligently against the door, but he always had to pull himself together again at once, for even the slight sound his head made was audible next door and brought all conversation to a stop. "What can he be doing now?" his father would say after a while, obviously turning towards the door, and only then would the interrupted conversation gradually be set going again.

45   Gregor was now informed as amply as he could wish—for his father tended to repeat himself in his explanations, partly because it was a long time since he had handled such matters and partly because his mother could not always grasp things at once—that a certain amount of investments, a very small amount it was true, had survived the wreck of their fortunes and had even increased a little because the dividends had not been touched meanwhile. And besides that, the money Gregor brought home every month—he had kept only a few dollars for himself—had never been quite used up and now amounted to a small capital sum. Behind the door Gregor nodded his head eagerly, rejoiced at this evidence of unexpected thrift and foresight. True, he could really have paid off some more of his father's debts to the chief with his extra money, and so brought much nearer the day on which he could quit his job, but doubtless it was better the way his father had arranged it.

Yet this capital was by no means sufficient to let the family live on the interest of it; for one year, perhaps, or at the most two, they could live on the principal, that was all. It was simply a sum that ought not to be touched and should be kept for a rainy day; money for living expenses would have to be earned. Now his father was still hale enough but an old man, and he had done no work for the past five years and could not be expected to do much; during these five years, the first years of leisure in his laborious though unsuccessful life, he had grown rather fat and become sluggish. And Gregor's old mother, how was she to earn a living with her asthma, which troubled her even when she walked through the flat and kept her lying on a sofa every other day panting for breath beside an open window? And was his sister to earn her bread, she who was still a child of seventeen and whose life hitherto had been so pleasant, consisting as it did in dressing herself nicely, sleeping long, helping in the housekeeping, going out to a few modest entertainments and above all playing the violin? At first whenever the need for earning money was mentioned Gregor let go his hold on the door and threw himself down on the cool leather sofa beside it, he felt so hot with shame and grief.

Often he just lay there the long nights through without sleeping at all, scrabbling for hours on the leather. Or he nerved himself to the great effort of pushing an armchair to the window, then crawled up over the window sill and, braced against the chair, leaned against the windowpanes, obviously in some recollection of the sense of freedom that looking out of a window always used to give him. For in reality day by day things that were even a little way off were growing dimmer to his sight; the hospital across the street, which he used to execrate for being all too often before his eyes, was now quite beyond his range of vision, and if he had not known that he lived in Charlotte Street, a quiet street but still a city street, he might have believed that his window gave on a desert waste where gray sky and gray land blended indistinguishably into each other. His quick-witted sister only needed to observe twice that the armchair stood by the window; after that whenever she had tidied the room she always pushed the chair back to the same place at the window and even left the inner casements open.

If he could have spoken to her and thanked her for all she had to do for him, he could have borne her ministrations better; as it was, they oppressed him. She certainly tried to make as light as possible of whatever was disagreeable in her task, and as time went on she succeeded, of course, more and more, but time brought more enlightenment to Gregor too. The very way she came in distressed him. Hardly was she in the room when she rushed to the

Chapter Eight

window, without even taking time to shut the door, careful as she was usually to shield the sight of Gregor's room from the others, and as if she were almost suffocating tore the casements open with hasty fingers, standing then in the open draught for a while even in the bitterest cold and drawing deep breaths. This noisy scurry of hers upset Gregor twice a day; he would crouch trembling under the sofa all the time, knowing quite well that she would certainly have spared him such a disturbance had she found it at all possible to stay in his presence without opening a window.

On one occasion, about a month after Gregor's metamorphosis, when there was surely no reason for her to be still startled at his appearance, she came a little earlier than usual and found him gazing out of the window, quite motionless, and thus well placed to look like a bogey[1]. Gregor would not have been surprised had she not come in at all, for she could not immediately open the window while he was there, but not only did she retreat, she jumped back as if in alarm and banged the door shut; a stranger might well have thought that he had been lying in wait for her there meaning to bite her. Of course he hid himself under the sofa at once, but he had to wait until midday before she came again, and she seemed more ill at ease than usual. This made him realize how repulsive the sight of him still was to her, and that it was bound to go on being repulsive, and what an effort it must cost her not to run away even from the sight of the small portion of his body that stuck out from under the sofa. In order to spare her that, therefore, one day he carried a sheet on his back to the sofa—it cost him four hours' labor—and arranged it there in such a way as to hide him completely, so that even if she were to bend down she could not see him. Had she considered the sheet unnecessary, she would certainly have stripped it off the sofa again, for it was clear enough that this curtaining and confining of himself was not likely to conduce Gregor's comfort, but she left it where it was, and

---

[1] bogey: goblin or phantom.

Gregor even fancied that he caught a thankful glance from her eye when he lifted the sheet carefully a very little with his head to see how she was taking the new arrangement.

50　　　For the first fortnight his parents could not bring themselves to the point of entering his room, and he often heard them expressing their appreciation of his sister's activities, whereas formerly they had frequently scolded her for being as they thought a somewhat useless daughter. But now, both of them often waited outside the door, his father and his mother, while his sister tidied his room, and as soon as she came out she had to tell them exactly how things were in the room, what Gregor had eaten, how he had conducted himself this time and whether there was not perhaps some slight improvement in his condition. His mother, moreover, began relatively soon to want to visit him, but his father and sister dissuaded her at first with arguments which Gregor listened to very attentively and altogether approved. Later, however, she had to be held back by main force, and when she cried out: "Do let me in to Gregor, he is my unfortunate son! Can't you understand that I must go to him?" Gregor thought that it might be well to have her come in, not every day, of course, but perhaps once a week; she understood things, after all, much better than his sister, who was only a child despite the efforts she was making and had perhaps taken on so difficult a task merely out of childish thoughtlessness.

　　　Gregor's desire to see his mother was soon fulfilled. During the daytime he did not want to show himself at the window, out of consideration for his parents, but he could not crawl very far around the few square yards of floor space he had, nor could he bear lying quietly at rest all during the night, while he was fast losing any interest he had ever taken in food, so that for mere recreation he had formed the habit of crawling crisscross over the walls and ceiling. He especially enjoyed hanging suspended from the ceiling; it was much better than lying on the floor; one could breathe more freely; one's body swung and rocked lightly; and in the almost blissful absorption induced by this suspension it could

Chapter Eight

happen to his own surprise that he let go and fell plump on the floor. Yet he now had his body much better under control than formerly, and even such a big fall did him no harm. His sister at once remarked the new distraction Gregor had found for himself— he left traces behind him of the sticky stuff on his soles wherever he crawled—and she got the idea in her head of giving him as wide a field as possible to crawl in and of removing the pieces of furniture that hindered him, above all the chest of drawers and the writing desk. But that was more than she could manage all by herself; she did not dare ask her father to help her; and as for the servant girl, a young creature of sixteen who had had the courage to stay on after the cook's departure, she could not be asked to help, for she had begged as an especial favor that she might keep the kitchen door locked and open it only on a definite summons; so there was nothing left but to apply to her mother at an hour when her father was out. And the old lady did come, with exclamations of joyful eagerness, which, however, died away at the door of Gregor's room. Gregor's sister, of course, went in first, to see that everything was in order before letting his mother enter. In great haste Gregor pulled the sheet lower and rucked it more in folds so that it really looked as if it had been thrown accidentally over the sofa. And this time he did not peer out from under it; he renounced the pleasure of seeing his mother on this occasion and was only glad that she had come at all. "Come in, he's out of sight," said his sister, obviously leading her mother in by the hand. Gregor could now hear the two women sttuggling to shift the heavy old chest from its place, and his sister claiming the greater part of the labor for herself, without listening to the admonitions of her mother who feared she might overstrain herself. It took a long time. After at least a quarter of an hour's tugging his mother objected that the chest had better be left where it was, for in the first place it was too heavy and could never be got out before his father came home, and standing in the middle of the room like that it would only hamper Gregor's movements, while in the second place it was not at all certain that removing the furniture would be doing a service to Gregor. She was inclined to think to the contrary; the sight of the naked walls made her own heart heavy, and why shouldn't Gregor have the same feeling, considering that he had been used to his furniture for so long and might feel forlorn without it. "And doesn't it look," she concluded in a low voice—in fact she had been almost whispering all the time as if to avoid letting Gregor, whose exact where-abouts she did not know, hear even the tones of her voice, for she was convinced that he could not understand her words—"doesn't it look as if we were showing him, by taking away his furniture, that we have given up hope of his ever getting better and are just leaving him coldly to himself? I think it would be best to keep his room exactly as it has always been, so that when he comes back to us he will find everything unchanged and be able all the more easily to forget what has happened in between."

On hearing these words from his mother Gregor realized that the lack of all direct human speech for the past two months together with the monotony of family life must have confused his mind, otherwise he could not account for the fact that he had quite earnestly looked forward to having his room emptied of furnishing. Did he really want his warm room, so comfortably fitted with old family furniture, to be turned into a naked den in which he would certainly be able to crawl unhampered in all directions but at the price of shedding simultaneously all recollection of his human background? He had indeed been so near the brink of forgetfulness that only the voice of his mother, which he had not heard for so long, had drawn him back from it. Nothing should be taken out of his room; everything must stay as it was; he could not dispense with the good influence of the furniture on his state of mind; and even if the furniture did hamper him in his senseless crawling round and round, that was no drawback but a great advantage.

Unfortunately his sister was of the contrary opinion; she had grown accustomed, and not without reason, to consider herself an expert in Gregor's affairs as against her parents, and so her

Chapter Eight

mother's advice was now enough to make her determined on the removal not only of the chest and the writing desk, which had been her first intention, but of all the furniture except the indispensable sofa. This determination was not, of course, merely the outcome of childish recalcitrance and of the self-confidence she had recently developed so unexpectedly and at such cost; she had in fact perceived that Gregor needed a lot of space to crawl about in, while on the other hand he never used the furniture at all, so far as could be seen. Another factor might have been also the enthusiastic temperament of an adolescent girl, which seeks to indulge itself on every opportunity and which now tempted Grete to exaggerate the horror of her brother's circumstances in order that she might do all the more for him. In a room where Gregor lorded it all alone over empty walls no one save herself was likely ever to set foot.

And so she was not to be moved from her resolve by her mother who seemed moreover to be ill at ease in Gregor's room and therefore unsure of herself, was soon reduced to silence and helped her daughter as best she could to push the chest outside. Now, Gregor could do without the chest, if need be, but the writing desk he must retain. As soon as the two women had got the chest out of his room, groaning as they pushed it, Gregor stuck his head out from under the sofa to see how he might intervene as kindly and cautiously as possible. But as bad luck would have it, his mother was the first to return, leaving Grete clasping the chest in the room next door where she was trying to shift it all by herself, without of course moving it from the spot. His mother however was not accustomed to the sight of him, it might sicken her and so in alarm Gregor backed quickly to the other end of the sofa, yet could not prevent the sheet from swaying a little in front. That was enough to put her on the alert. She paused, stood still for a moment and then went back to Grete.

55   Although Gregor kept reassuring himself that nothing out of the way was happening, but only a few bits of furniture were being changed round, he soon had to admit that all this trotting to and

fro of the two women, their little ejaculations and the scraping of furniture along the floor affected him like a vast disturbance coming from all sides at once, and however much he tucked in his head and legs and cowered to the very floor he was bound to confess that he would not be able to stand it for long. They were clearing his room out; taking away everything he loved; the chest in which he kept his fret saw and other tools was already dragged off; they were now loosening the writing desk which had almost sunk into the floor, the desk at which he had done all his homework when he was at the commercial academy, at the grammar school before that, and, yes, even at the primary school—he had no more time to waste in weighing the good intentions of the two women, whose existence he had by now almost forgotten, for they were so exhausted that they were laboring in silence and nothing could be heard but the heavy scuffling of their feet.

And so he rushed out —the women were just leaning against the writing desk in the next room to give themselves a breather— and four times changed his direction, since he really did not know what to rescue first, then on the wall opposite, which was already otherwise cleared, he was struck by the picture of the lady muffled in so much fur and quickly crawled up to it and pressed himself to the glass, which was a good surface to hold on to and comforted his hot belly. This picture at least, which was entirely hidden beneath him, was going to be removed by nobody. He turned his head towards the door of the living room so as to observe the women when they came back.

They had not allowed themselves much of a rest and were already coming; Grete had twined her arm round her mother and was almost supporting her. "Well, what shall we take now?" said Grete, looking round. Her eyes met Gregor's from the wall. She kept her composure, presumably because of her mother, bent her head down to her mother, to keep her from looking up, and said, although in a fluttering, unpremeditated voice: "Come, hadn't we better go back to the living room for a moment?" Her intentions

Chapter Eight

were clear enough to Gregor, she wanted to bestow her mother in safety and then chase him down from the wall. Well, just let her try it! He clung to his picture and would not give it up. He would rather fly in Grete's face.

But Grete's words had succeeded in disquieting her mother, who took a step to one side, caught sight of the huge brown mass on the flowered wallpaper, and before she was really conscious that what she saw was Gregor screamed in a loud, hoarse voice: "Oh God, oh God!" fell with outspread arms over the sofa as if giving up and did not move. "Gregor!" cried his sister, shaking her fist and glaring at him. This was the first time she had directly addressed him since his metamorphosis. She ran into the next room for some aromatic essence[1] with which to rouse her mother from her fainting fit. Gregor wanted to help too—there was still time to rescue the picture—but he was stuck fast to the glass and had to tear himself loose; he then ran after his sister into the next room as if he could advise her, as he used to do; but then had to stand helplessly behind her; she meanwhile searched among various small bottles and when she turned round started in alarm at the sight of him; one bottle fell on the floor and broke; a splinter of glass cut Gregor's face and some kind of corrosive medicine splashed him; without pausing a moment longer Grete gathered up all the bottles she could carry and ran to her mother with them; she banged the door shut with her foot. Gregor was now cut off from his mother, who was perhaps nearly dying because of him; he dared not open the door for fear of frightening away his sister, who had to stay with her mother; there was nothing he could do but wait; and harassed by self-reproach and worry he began now to crawl to and fro, over everything, wall, furniture and ceiling, and finally in his despair, when the whole room seemed to be reeling round him, fell down on to the middle of the big table.

A little while elapsed, Gregor was still lying there feebly and

---

[1] aromatic essence: an aromatic medicine like smelling salts.

all around was quiet, perhaps that was a good omen. Then the doorbell rang. The servant girl was of course locked in her kitchen, and Grete would have to open the door. It was his father. "What's been happening?" were his first words; Grete's face must have told him everything. Grete answered in a muffled voice, apparently hiding her head on his breast: "Mother has been fainting, but she's better now. Gregor's broken loose." "Just what I expected," said his father, "just what I've been telling you, but you women would never listen." It was clear to Gregor that his father had taken the worst interpretation of Grete's all too brief statement and was assuming that Gregor had been guilty of some violent act. Therefore Gregor must now try to propitiate his father, since he had neither time nor means for an explanation. And so he fled to the door of his own room and crouched against it, to let his father see as soon as he came in from the hall that his son had the good intention of getting back into his room immediately and that it was not necessary to drive him there, but that if only the door were opened he would disappear at once.

60 Yet his father was not in the mood to perceive such fine distinctions. "Ah!" he cried as soon as he appeared, in a tone which sounded at once angry and exultant. Gregor drew his head back from the door and lifted it to look at his father. Truly, this was not the father he had imagined to himself; admittedly he had been too absorbed of late in his new recreation of crawling over the ceiling to take the same interest as before in what was happening elsewhere in the flat, and he ought really to be prepared for some changes. And yet, and yet, could that be his father? The man who used to lie wearily sunk in bed whenever Gregor set out on a business journey; who welcomed him back of an evening lying in a long chair in a dressing gown; who could not really rise to his feet but only lifted his arms in greeting, and on the rare occasions when he did go out with his family, on one or two Sundays a year and on high holidays, walked between Gregor and his mother, who were slow walkers anyhow, even more slowly than they did, muffled in

Chapter Eight

his old greatcoat, shuffling laboriously forward with the help of his crook-handled stick which he set down most cautiously at every step and, whenever he wanted to say anything, nearly always came to a full stop and gathered his escort around him? Now he was standing there in fine shape; dressed in a smart blue uniform with gold buttons, such as bank messengers wear; his strong double chin bulged over the stiff high collar of his jacket; from under his bushy eyebrows his black eyes darted fresh and penetrating glances; his onetime tangled white hair had been combed flat on either side of a shining and carefully exact parting. He pitched his cap, which bore a gold monogram, probably the badge of some bank, in a wide sweep across the whole room on to a sofa and with the tail-ends of his jacket thrown back, his hands in his trouser pockets, advanced with a grim visage towards Gregor. Likely enough he did not himself know what he meant to do; at any rate he lifted his feet uncommonly high, and Gregor was dumbfounded at the enormous size of his shoe soles. But Gregor could not risk standing up to him, aware as he had been from the very first day of his new life that his father believed only the severest measures suitable for dealing with him. And so he ran before his father, stopping when he stopped and scuttling forward again when his father made any kind of move. In this way they circled the room several times without anything decisive happening; indeed the whole operation did not even look like a pursuit because it was carried out so slowly. And so Gregor did not leave the floor, for he feared that his father might take as a piece of peculiar wickedness any excursion of his over the walls or the ceiling. All the same, he could not stay this course much longer, for while his father took one step he had to carry out a whole series of movements. He was already beginning to feel breathless, just as in his former life his lungs had not been very dependable. As he was staggering along, trying to concentrate his energy on running, hardly keeping his eyes open; in his dazed state never even thinking of any other escape than simply going forward; and having almost forgotten that the walls were free to him, which in this room were well provided with finely carved pieces of furniture full of knobs and crevices—suddenly something lightly flung landed close behind him and rolled before him. It was an apple; a second apple followed immediately; Gregor came to a stop in alarm; there was no point in running on, for his father was determined to bombard him. He had filled his pockets with fruit from the dish on the sideboard and was now shying apple after apple, without taking particularly good aim for the moment. The small red apples rolled about the floor as if magnetized and cannoned into each other. An apple thrown without much force grazed Gregor's back and glanced off harmlessly. But another following immediately landed right on his back and sank in; Gregor wanted to drag himself forward, as if this startling, incredible pain could be left behind him; but he felt as if nailed to the spot and flattened himself out in a complete derangement of all his senses. With his last conscious look he saw the door of his room being torn open and his mother rushing out ahead of his screaming sister, in her under-bodice, for her daughter had loosened her clothing to let her breathe more freely and recover from her swoon, he saw his mother rushing towards his father, leaving one after another behind her on the floor her loosened petticoats, stumbling over her petticoats straight to his father and embracing him, in complete union with him—but here Gregor's sight began to fail—with her hands clasped round his father's neck as she begged for her son's life.

III

The serious injury done to Gregor, which disabled him for more than a month—the apple went on sticking in his body as a visible reminder, since no one ventured to remove it—seemed to have made even his father recollect that Gregor was a member of the family, despite his present unfortunate and repulsive shape, and ought not to be treated as an enemy, that, on the contrary, family duty required the suppression of disgust and the exercise of

Chapter Eight

patience, nothing but patience.

And although his injury had impaired, probably forever, his power of movement, and for the time being it took him long, long minutes to creep across his room like an old invaild—there was no question now of crawling up the wall—yet in his own opinion he was sufficiently compensated for this worsening of his condition by the fact that towards evening the living-room door, which he used to watch intently for an hour or two beforehand, was always thrown open, so that lying in the darkness of his room, invisible to the family, he could see them all at the lamp-lit table and listen to their talk, by general consent as it were, very different from his earlier eavesdropping.

True, their intercourse lacked the lively character of former times, which he had always called to mind with a certain wistfulness in the small hotel bedrooms where he had been wont to throw himself down, tired out, on damp bedding. They were now mostly very silent. Soon after supper his father would fall asleep in his armchair; his mother and sister would admonish each other to be silent; his mother, bending low over the lamp, stitched at fine sewing for an underwear firm; his sister, who had taken a job as a salesgirl, was learning shorthand and French in the evenings on the chance of bettering herself. Sometimes his father woke up, and as if quite unaware that he had been sleeping said to his mother: "What a lot of sewing you're doing today!" and at once fell asleep again, while the two women exchanged a tired smile.

With a kind of mulishness his father persisted in keeping his uniform on even in the house; his dressing gown hung uselessly on its peg and he slept fully dressed where he sat, as if he were ready for service at any moment and even here only at the beck and call of his superior. As a result, his uniform, which was not brand-new to start with, began to look dirty, despite all the loving care of the mother and sister to keep it clean, and Gregor often spent whole evenings gazing at the many greasy spots on the garment, gleaming with gold buttons always in a high state of polish, in which the old man sat sleeping in extreme discomfort and yet quite peacefully.

65   As soon as the clock struck ten his mother tried to rouse his father with gentle words and to persuade him after that to get into bed, for sitting there he could not have a proper sleep and that was what he needed most, since he had to go to duty at six. But with the mulishness that had obsessed him since he became a bank messenger he always insisted on staying longer at the table, although he regularly fell asleep again and in the end only with the greatest trouble could be got out of his armchair and into his bed. However insistently Gregor's mother and sister kept urging him with gentle reminders, he would go on slowly shaking his head for a quarter of an hour, keeping his eyes shut, and refuse to get to his feet. The mother plucked at his sleeve, whispering endearments in his ear, the sister left her lessons to come to her mother's help, but Gregor's father was not to be caught. He would only sink down deeper in his chair. Not until the two women hoisted him up by the armpits did he open his eyes and look at them both, one after the other, usually with the remark: "This is a life. This is the peace and quiet of my old age." And leaning on the two of them he would heave himself up, with difficulty, as if he were a great burden to himself, suffer them to lead him as far as the door and then wave them off and go on alone, while the mother abandoned her needlework and the sister her pen in order to run after him and help him farther.

   Who could find time, in this overworked and tired-out family, to bother about Gregor more than was absolutely needful? The household was reduced more and more; the servant girl was turned off; a gigantic bony charwoman with white hair flying round her head came in morning and evening to do the rough work; everything else was done by Gregor's mother, as well as great piles of sewing. Even various family ornaments, which his mother and sister used to wear with pride at parties and celebrations, had to be sold, as Gregor discovered of an evening from hearing them all discuss the prices obtained. But what they lamented most was

Chapter Eight

the fact that they could not leave the flat which was much too big for their present circumstances, because they could not think of any way to shift Gregor. Yet Gregor saw well enough that consideration for him was not the main difficulty preventing the removal, for they could have easily shifted him in some suitable box with a few air holes in it; what really kept them from moving into another flat was rather their own complete hopelessness and the belief that they had been singled out for a misfortune such as had never happened to any of their relations or acquaintances. They fulfilled to the uttermost all that the world demands of poor people, the father fetched breakfast for the small clerks in the bank, the mother devoted her energy to making underwear for strangers, the sister trotted to and fro behind the counter at the behest of customers, but more than this they had not the strength to do. And the wound in Gregor's back began to nag at him afresh when his mother and sister, after getting his father into bed, came back again, left their work lying, drew close to each other and sat cheek by cheek; when his mother, pointing towards his room, said: "Shut that door now, Grete," and he was left again in darkness, while next door the women mingled their tears or perhaps sat dry-eyed staring at the table.

Gregor hardly slept at all by night or by day. He was often haunted by the idea that next time the door opened he would take the family's affairs in hand again just as he used to do; once more, after this long interval, there appeared in his thoughts the figures of the chief and the chief clerk, the commercial travelers and the apprentices, the porter who was so dull-witted, two or three friends in other firms, a chambermaid in one of the rural hotels, a sweet and fleeting memory, a cashier in a milliner's shop, whom he had wooed earnestly but too slowly— they all appeared, together with strangers or people he had quite forgotten, but instead of helping him and his family they were one and all unapproachable and he was glad when they vanished. At other times he would not be in the mood to bother about his family, he was only filled with rage at the way they were neglecting him, and although he had no clear idea of what he might care to eat he would make plans for getting into the larder to take the food that was after all his due, even if he were not hungry. His sister no longer took thought to bring him what might especially please him, but in the morning and at noon before she went to business hurriedly pushed into his room with her foot any food that was available, and in the evening cleared it out again with one sweep of the broom, heedless of whether it had been merely tasted, or—as most frequently happened—left untouched. The cleaning of his room, which she now did always in the evenings, could not have been more hastily done. Streaks of dirt stretched along the walls, here and there lay balls of dust and filth. At first Gregor used to station himself in some particularly filthy corner when his sister arrived, in order to reproach her with it, so to speak. But he could have sat there for weeks without getting her to make any improvements; she could see the dirt as well as he did, but she had simply made up her mind to leave it alone. And yet, with a touchiness that was new to her, which seemed anyhow to have infected the whole family, she jealously guarded her claim to be the sole caretaker of Gregor's room. His mother once subjected his room to a thorough cleaning, which was achieved only by means of several buckets of water—all this dampness of course upset Gregor too and he lay widespread, sulky and motionless on the sofa—but she was well punished for it. Hardly had his sister noticed the changed aspect of his room than she rushed in high dudgeon into the living room and, despite the imploringly raised hands of her mother, burst into a storm of weeping, while her parents—her father had of course been startled out of his chair—looked on at first in helpless amazement; then they too began to go into action; the father reproached the mother on his right for not having left the cleaning of Gregor's room to his sister; shrieked at the sister on his left that never again was she to be allowed to clean Gregor's room; while the mother tried to pull the father into his bedroom, since he was beyond

Chapter Eight

himself with agitation; the sister, shaken with sobs, then beat upon the table with her small fists; and Gregor hissed loudly with rage because not one of them thought of shutting the door to spare him such a spectacle and so much noise.

Still, even if the sister, exhausted by her daily work, had grown tired of looking after Gregor as she did formerly, there was no need for his mother's intervention or for Gregor's being neglected at all. The charwoman was there. This old widow, whose strong bony frame had enabled her to survive the worst a long life could offer, by no means recoiled from Gregor. Without being in the least curious she had once by chance opened the door of his room and at the sight of Gregor, who, taken by surprise, began to rush to and fro although no one was chasing him, merely stood there with her arms folded. From that time she never failed to open his door a little for a moment, morning and evening, to have a look at him. At first she even used to call him to her, with words which apparently she took to be friendly, such as: "Come along, then, you old dung beetle!" or "Look at the old dung beetle, then!" To such allocutions Gregor made no answer, but stayed motionless where he was, as if the door had never been opened. Instead of being allowed to disturb him so senselessly whenever the whim took her, she should rather have been ordered to clean out his room daily, that charwoman! Once, early in the morning—heavy rain was lashing on the windowpanes, perhaps a sign that spring was on the way—Gregor was so exasperated when she began addressing him again that he ran at her, as if to attack her, although slowly and feebly enough. But the charwoman instead of showing fright merely lifted high a chair that happened to be beside the door, and as she stood there with her mouth wide open it was clear that she meant to shut it only when she brought the chair down on Gregor's back. "So you're not coming any nearer?" she asked, as Gregor turned away again, and quietly put the chair back into the corner.

Gregor was now eating hardly anything. Only when he happened to pass the food laid out for him did he take a bit of something in his mouth as a pastime, kept it there for an hour at a time and usually spat it out again. At first he thought it was chagrin over the state of his room that prevented him from eating, yet he soon got used to the various changes in his room. It had become a habit in the family to push into his room things there was no room for elsewhere and there were plenty of these now, since one of the rooms had been let to three lodgers. These serious gentlemen—all three of them with full beards, as Gregor once observed through a crack in the door—had a passion for order, not only in their own room but, since they were now members of the household, in all its arrangements, especially in the kitchen. Superfluous, not to say dirty, objects they could not bear. Besides, they had brought with them most of the furnishings they needed. For this reason many things could be dispensed with that it was no use trying to sell but that should not be thrown away either. All of them found their way into Gregor's room. The ash can likewise and the kitchen garbage can. Anything that was not needed for the moment was simply flung into Gregor's room by the charwoman, who did everything in a hurry; fortunately Gregor usually saw only the object, whatever it was, and the hand that held it. Perhaps she intended to take the things away again as time and opportunity offered, or to collect them until she could throw them all out in a heap, but in fact they just lay wherever she happened to throw them, except when Gregor pushed his way through the junk heap and shifted it somewhat, at first out of necessity, because he had not room enough to crawl, but later with increasing enjoyment, although after such excursions, being sad and weary to death, he would lie motionless for hours. And since the lodgers often ate their supper at home in the common living room, the living room door stayed shut many an evening, yet Gregor reconciled himself quite easily to the shutting of the door, for often enough on evenings when it was opened he had disregarded it entirely and lain in the darkest corner of his room, quite unnoticed by the family. But on one occasion the charwoman left the door open a little and it stayed ajar even when the lodgers came in for supper and the lamp was lit. They set themselves at the top end of the table where formerly Gregor and his father and mother had eaten their meals, unfolded their napkins and took knife and fork in hand. At once his mother appeared in the other doorway with a dish of meat and close behind her his sister with a dish of potatoes piled high. The food steamed with a thick vapor. The lodgers bent over the food set before them as if to scrutinize it before eating, in fact the man in the middle, who seemed to pass for an authority with the other two, cut a piece of meat as it lay on the dish, obviously to discover if it were tender or should be sent back to the kitchen. He showed satisfaction, and Gregor's mother and sister, who had been watching anxiously, breathed freely and began to smile.

70   The family itself took its meals in the kitchen. Nonetheless, Gregor's father came into the living room before going in to the kitchen and with one prolonged bow, cap in hand, made a round of the table. The lodgers all stood up and murmured something in their beards. When they were alone again they ate their food in almost complete silence. It seemed remarkable to Gregor that among the various noises coming from the table he could always distinguish the sound of their masticating teeth, as if this were a sign to Gregor that one needed teeth in order to eat, and that with toothless jaws even of the finest make one could do nothing. "I'm hungry enough," said Gregor sadly to himself, "but not for that kind of food. How these lodgers are stuffing themselves, and here am I dying of starvation!"

  On that very evening—during the whole of his time there Gregor could not remember ever having heard the violin—the sound of violin-playing came from the kitchen. The lodgers had already finished their supper, the one in the middle had brought out a newspaper and given the other two a page apiece, and now they were leaning back at ease reading and smoking. When the violin began to play they pricked up their ears, got to their feet, and went on tiptoe to the hall door where they stood huddled together. Their movements must have been heard in the kitchen, for Gregor's father called out: "Is the violin-playing disturbing you, gentlemen? It can be stopped at once." "On the contrary," said the middle lodger, "could not Fräulein Samsa come and play in this room, beside us, where it is much more convenient and comfortable?" "Oh certainly," cried Gregor's father, as if he were the violin-player. The lodgers came back into the living room and waited. Presently Gregor's father arrived with the music stand, his mother carrying the music and his sister with the violin. His sister quietly made everything ready to start playing; his parents, who had never let rooms before and so had an exaggerated idea of the courtesy due to lodgers, did not venture to sit down on their own chairs; his father leaned against the door, the right hand thrust between two buttons of his livery coat, which was formally buttoned up; but his mother was offered a chair by one of the lodgers and, since she left the chair just where he had happened to put it, sat down in a corner to one side.

Gregor's sister began to play; the father and mother, from either side, intently watched the movements of her hands. Gregor, attracted by the playing, ventured to move forward a little until his head was actually inside the living room. He felt hardly any surprise at his growing lack of consideration for the others; there had been a time when he prided himself on being considerate. And yet just on this occasion he had more reason than ever to hide himself, since owing to the amount of dust which lay thick in his room and rose into the air at the slightest movement, he too was covered with dust; fluff and hair and remnants of food trailed with him, caught on his back and along his sides; his indifference to everything was much too great for him to turn on his back and scrape himself clean on the carpet, as once he had done several times a day. And in spite of his condition, no shame deterred him from advancing a little over the spotless floor of the living room.

To be sure, no one was aware of him. The family was entirely absorbed in the violin-playing; the lodgers, however, who first of

Chapter Eight

all had stationed themselves, hands in pockets, much too close behind the music stand so that they could all have read the music, which must have bothered his sister, had soon retreated to the window, half-whispering with downbent heads, and stayed there while his father turned an anxious eye on them. Indeed, they were making it more than obvious that they had been disappointed in their expectation of hearing good or enjoyable violin-playing, that they had more than enough of the performance and only out of courtesy suffered a continued disturbance of their peace. From the way they all kept blowing the smoke of their cigars high in the air through nose and mouth one could divine their irritation. And yet Gregor's sister was playing so beautifully. Her face leaned sideways, intently and sadly her eyes followed the notes of music. Gregor crawled a little farther forward and lowered his head to the ground so that it might be possible for his eyes to meet hers. Was he an animal, that music had such an effect upon him? He felt as if the way were opening before him to the unknown nourishment he craved. He was determined to push forward till he reached his sister, to pull at her skirt and so let her know that she was to come into his room with her violin, for no one here appreciated her playing as he would appreciate it. He would never let her out of his room, at least, not so long as he lived; his frightful appearance would become, for the first time, useful to him; he would watch all the doors of his room at once and spit at intruders; but his sister should need no constraint, she should stay with him of her own free will; she should sit beside him on the sofa, bend down her ear to him and hear him confide that he had had the firm intention of sending her to the Conservatorium, and that, but for his mishap, last Christmas—surely Christmas was long past? —he would have announced it to everybody without allowing a single objection. After this confession his sister would be so touched that she would burst into tears, and Gregor would then raise himself to her shoulder and kiss her on the neck, which, now that she went to business, she kept free of any ribbon or collar.

"Mr. Samsa!" cried the middle lodger, to Gregor's father, and pointed, without wasting any more words, at Gregor, now working himself slowly forwards. The violin fell silent, the middle lodger first smiled to his friends with a shake of the head and then looked at Gregor again. Instead of driving Gregor out, his father seemed to think it more needful to begin by soothing down the lodgers, although they were not at all agitated and apparently found Gregor more entertaining than the violin-playing. He hurried toward them and spreading out his arms, tried to urge them back into their own room and at the same time to block their view of Gregor. They now began to be really a little angry, one could not tell whether because of the old man's behavior or because it had just dawned on them that all unwittingly they had such a neighbor as Gregor next door. They demanded explanations of his father, they waved their arms like him, tugged uneasily at their beards, and only with reluctance backed towards their room. Meanwhile Gregor's sister, who stood there as if lost when her playing was so abruptly broken off, came to life again, pulled herself together all at once after standing for a while holding violin and bow in nervelessly hanging hands and staring at her music, pushed her violin into the lap of her mother, who was still sitting in her chair fighting asthmatically for breath, and ran into the lodgers' room to which they were now being shepherded by her father rather more quickly than before. One could see the pillows and blankets on the beds flying under her accustomed fingers and being laid in order. Before the lodgers had actually reached their room she had finished making the beds and slipped out.

The old man seemed once more to be so possessed by his mulish self-assertiveness that he was forgetting all the respect he should show to his lodgers. He kept driving them on and driving them on until in the very door of the bedroom the middle lodger stamped his foot loudly on the floor and so brought him to a halt. "I beg to announce," said the lodger, lifting one hand and looking also at Gregor's mother and sister, "that because of the disgusting conditions prevailing in this household and family"—here he spat on the floor with emphatic brevity—"I give you notice on the spot. Naturally I won't pay you a penny for the days I have lived here, on the contrary I shall consider bringing an action for damages against you, based on claims—believe me—that will be easily susceptible of proof." He ceased and stared straight in front of him, as if he expected something. In fact his two friends at once rushed into the breach with these words: "And we too give notice on the spot." On that he seized the door-handle and shut the door with a slam.

Gregor's father, groping with his hands, staggered forward and fell into his chair; it looked as if he were stretching himself there for his ordinary evening nap, but the marked jerkings of his head, which was as if uncontrollable, showed that he was far from asleep. Gregor had simply stayed quietly all the time on the spot where the lodgers had espied him. Disappointment at the failure of his plan, perhaps also the weakness arising from extreme hunger, made it impossible for him to move. He feared, with a fair degree of certainty, that at any moment the general tension would discharge itself in a combined attack upon him, and he lay waiting. He did not react even to the noise made by the violin as it fell off his mother's lap from under her trembling fingers and gave out a resonant note.

"My dear parents," said his sister, slapping her hand on the table by way of introduction, "things can't go on like this. Perhaps you don't realize that, but I do. I won't utter my brother's name in the presence of this creature, and so all I say is: we must try to get rid of it. We've tried to look after it and to put up with it as far as is humanly possible, and I don't think anyone could reproach us in the slightest."

"She is more than right," said Gregor's father to himself. His mother, who was still choking for lack of breath, began to cough hollowly into her hand with a wild look in her eyes.

His sister rushed over to her and held her forehead. His

father's thoughts seemed to have lost their vagueness at Grete's words, he sat more upright, fingering his service cap that lay among the plates still lying on the table from the lodgers' supper, and from time to time looked at the still form of Gregor.

80   "We must try to get rid of it," his sister now said explicitly to her father, since her mother was coughing too much to hear a word, "it will be the death of both of you, I can see that coming. When one has to work as hard as we do, all of us, one can't stand this continual torment at home on top of it. At least I can't stand it any longer." And she burst into such a passion of sobbing that her tears dropped on her mother's face, where she wiped them off mechanically.

"My dear," said the old man sympathetically, and with evident understanding, "but what can we do?"

Gregor's sister merely shrugged her shoulders to indicate the feeling of helplessness that had now overmastered her during her weeping fit, in contrast to her former confidence.

"If he could understand us," said her father, half questioningly; Grete, still sobbing, vehemently waved a hand to show how unthinkable that was.

"If he could understand us," repeated the old man, shutting his eyes to consider his daughter's conviction that understanding was impossible, "then perhaps we might come to some agreement with him. But as it is—"

85   "He must go," cried Gregor's sister. "That's the only solution, Father. You must just try to get rid of the idea that this is Gregor. The fact that we've believed it for so long is the root of all our trouble. But how can it be Gregor? If this were Gregor, he would have realized long ago that human beings can't live with such a creature, and he'd have gone away on his own accord. Then we wouldn't have any brother, but we'd be able to go on living and keep his memory in honor. As it is, this creature persecutes us, drives away our lodgers, obviously wants the whole apartment to himself and would have us all sleep in the gutter. Just look,

Chapter Eight

Father," she shrieked all at once, "he's at it again!" And in an access of panic that was quite incomprehensible to Gregor she even quitted her mother, literally thrusting the chair from her as if she would rather sacrifice her mother than stay so near to Gregor, and rushed behind her father, who also rose up, being simply upset by her agitation, and half-spread his arms out as if to protect her.

 Yet Gregor had not the slightest intention of frightening anyone, far less his sister. He had only begun to turn round in order to crawl back to his room, but it was certainly a startling operation to watch, since because of his disabled condition he could not execute the difficult turning movements except by lifting his head and then bracing it against the floor over and over again. He paused and looked round. His good intentions seemed to have been recognized; the alarm had only been momentary. Now they were all watching him in melancholy silence. His mother lay in her chair, her legs stiffly outstretched and pressed together, her eyes almost closing for sheer weariness; his father and his sister were sitting beside each other, his sister's arm around the old man's neck.

 Perhaps I can go on turning round now, thought Gregor, and began his labors again. He could not stop himself from panting with the effort, and had to pause now and then to take breath. Nor did anyone harass him, he was left entirely to himself. When he had completed the turn-round he began at once to crawl straight back. He was amazed at the distance separating him from his room and could not understand how in his weak state he had managed to accomplish the same journey so recently, almost without remarking it. Intent on crawling as fast as possible, he barely noticed that not a single word, not an ejaculation from his family, interfered with his progress. Only when he was already in the doorway did he turn his head round, not completely, for his neck muscles were getting stiff, but enough to see that nothing had changed behind him except that his sister had risen to her feet. His last glance fell on his mother, who was not quite overcome by sleep.

 Hardly was he well inside his room when the door was hastily pushed shut, bolted, and locked. The sudden noise in his rear startled him so much that his little legs gave beneath him. It was his sister who had shown such haste. She had been standing ready waiting and had made a light spring forward. Gregor had not even heard her coming, and she cried "At last!" to her parents as she turned the key in the lock.

"And what now?" said Gregor to himself, looking round in the darkness. Soon he made the discovery that he was now unable to stir a limb. This did not surprise him, rather it seemed unnatural that he should ever actually have been able to move on these feeble little legs. Otherwise he felt relatively comfortable. True, his whole body was aching, but it seemed that the pain was gradually growing less and would finally pass away. The rotting apple in his back and the inflamed area around it, all covered with soft dust, already hardly troubled him. He thought of his family with tenderness and love. The decision that he must disappear was one that he held to even more strongly than his sister, if that were possible. In this state of vacant and peaceful meditation he remained until the tower clock struck three in the morning. The first broadening of light in the world outside the window entered his consciousness once more. Then his head sank to the floor of its own accord and from his nostrils came the last faint flicker of his breath.

When the charwoman arrived early in the morning—what between her strength and her impatience she slammed all the doors so loudly, never mind how often she had been begged not to do so, that no one in the whole apartment could enjoy any quiet sleep after her arrival—she noticed nothing unusual as she took her customary peep into Gregor's room. She thought he was lying motionless on purpose, pretending to be in the sulks; she credited him with every kind of intelligence. Since she happened to have the long-handed broom in her hand she tried to tickle him up with it from the doorway. When that too produced no reaction she felt provoked and poked at him a little harder, and only when she had pushed him along the floor without meeting any resistance was her attention aroused. It did not take her long to establish the truth of the matter, and her eyes widened, she let out a whistle yet did not waste much time over it but tore open the door of the Samsas' bedroom and yelled into the darkness at the top of her voice: "Just look at this, it's dead; it's lying here dead and done for!"

Mr. and Mrs. Samsa started up in their double bed and before they realized the nature of the charwoman's announcement had some difficulty in overcoming the shock of it. But then they got out of bed quickly, one on either side, Mr. Samsa throwing a blanket over his shoulders, Mrs. Samsa in nothing but her nightgown; in this array they entered Gregor's room. Meanwhile the door of the living room opened, too, where Grete had been sleeping since the advent of the lodgers; she was completely dressed as if she had not been to bed, which seemed to be confirmed also by the paleness of her face. "Dead?" said Mrs. Samsa, looking questioningly at the charwoman, although she could have investigated for herself, and the fact was obvious enough without investigation. "I should say so," said the charwoman, proving her words by pushing Gregor's corpse a long way to one side with her broomstick. Mrs. Samsa made a movement as if to stop her, but checked it. "Well," said Mr. Samsa, "now thanks be to God." He crossed himself, and the three women followed his example. Grete, whose eyes never left the corpse, said: "Just see how thin he was. It's such a long time since he's eaten anything. The food came out again just as it went in." Indeed, Gregor's body was completely flat and dry, as could only now be seen when it was no longer supported by the legs and nothing prevented one from looking closely at it.

"Come in beside us, Grete, for a little while," said Mrs. Samsa with a tremulous smile, and Grete, not without looking back at the corpse, followed her parents into their bedroom. The charwoman shut the door and opened the window wide. Although it was so early in the morning a certain softness was perceptible in the fresh air. After all, it was already the end of March.

The three lodgers emerged from their room and were surprised to see no breakfast; they had been forgotten. "Where's our breakfast?" said the middle lodger peevishly to the charwoman. But she put her finger to her lips and hastily, without a word, indicated by gestures that they should go into Gregor's room. They did so and stood, their hands in the pockets of their somewhat shabby coats, around Gregor's corpse in the room where it was now fully light.

At that the door of the Samsas' bedroom opened and Mr. Samsa appeared in his uniform, his wife on one arm, his daughter on the other. They all looked a little as if they had been crying; from time to time Grete hid her face on her father's arm.

95 "Leave my house at once!" said Mr. Samsa, and pointed to the door without disengaging himself from the women. "What do you mean by that?" said the middle lodger, taken somewhat aback, with a feeble smile. The two others put their hands behind them and kept rubbing them together, as if in gleeful expectation of a fine set-to in which they were bound to come off the winners. "I mean just what I say," answered Mr. Samsa, and advanced in a straight line with his two companions towards the lodger. He stood his ground at first quietly, looking at the floor as if his thoughts were taking a new pattern in his head. "Then let us go, by all means," he said, and looked up at Mr. Samsa as if in a sudden access of humility he were expecting some renewed sanction for this decision. Mr. Samsa merely nodded briefly once or twice with meaning eyes. Upon that the lodger really did go with long strides into the hall, his two friends had been listening and had quite stopped rubbing their hands for some moments and now went scuttling after him as if afraid that Mr. Samsa might get into the hall before them and cut them off from their leader. In the hall they all three took their hats from the rack, their sticks from the umbrella stand, bowed in silence and quitted the apartment. With a suspiciousness which proved quite unfounded Mr. Samsa and the two women followed them out to the landing; leaning over the banister they watched the three figures slowly but surely going

Chapter Eight

down the long stairs, vanishing from sight at a certain turn of the staircase on every floor and coming into view again after a moment or so; the more they dwindled, the more the Samsa family's interest in them dwindled, and when a butcher's boy met them and passed them on the stairs coming up proudly with a tray on his head, Mr. Samsa and the two women soon left the landing and as if a burden had been lifted from them went back into their apartment.

 They decided to spend this day in resting and going for a stroll; they had not only deserved such a respite from work but absolutely needed it. And so they sat down at the table and wrote three notes of excuse, Mr. Samsa to his board of management, Mrs. Samsa to her employer, and Grete to the head of her firm. While they were writing, the charwoman came in to say that she was going now, since her morning's work was finished. At first they only nodded without looking up, but as she kept hovering there they eyed her irritably. "Well?" said Mr. Samsa. The charwoman stood grinning in the doorway as if she had good news to impart to the family but meant not to say a word unless properly questioned. The small ostrich feather standing upright on her hat, which had annoyed Mr. Samsa ever since she was engaged, was waving gaily in all directions. "Well, what is it then?" asked Mrs. Samsa, who obtained more respect from the charwoman than the others. "Oh," said the charwoman, giggling so amiably that she could not at once continue, "just this, you don't need to bother about how to get rid of the thing next door. It's been seen to already." Mrs. Samsa and Grete bent over their letters again, as if preoccupied; Mr. Samsa, who perceived that she was eager to begin describing it all in detail, stopped her with a decisive hand. But since she was not allowed to tell her story, she remembered the great hurry she was in, being obviously deeply huffed: "Bye, everybody," she said, whirling off violently, and departed with a frightful slamming of doors.

 "She'll be given notice tonight," said Mr. Samsa, but neither from his wife nor his daughter did he get any answer, for the charwoman seemed to have shattered again the composure they had barely achieved. They rose, went to the window and stayed there, clasping each other tight. Mr. Samsa turned in his chair to look at them and quietly observed them for a little. Then he called out: "Come along, now, do. Let bygones be bygones. And you might have some consideration for me." The two of them complied at once, hastened to him, caressed him and quickly finished their letters.

Then they all three left the apartment together, which was more than they had done for months, and went by tram into the open country outside the town. The tram, in which they were the only passengers, was filled with warm sunshine. Leaning comfortably back in their seats they canvassed their prospects for the future, and it appeared on closer inspection that these were not at all bad, for the jobs they had got, which so far they had never really discussed with each other, were all three admirable and likely to lead to better things later on. The greatest immediate improvement in their condition would of course arise from moving to another house; they wanted to take a smaller and cheaper but also better situated and more easily run apartment than the one they had, which Gregor had selected. While they were thus conversing, it struck both Mr. and Mrs. Samsa, almost at the same moment, as they became aware of their daughter's increasing vivacity, that in spite of all the sorrow of recent times, which had made her cheeks pale, she had bloomed into a pretty girl with a good figure. They grew quieter and half unconsciously exchanged glances of complete agreement, having come to the conclusion that it would soon be time to find a good husband for her. And it was like a confirmation of their new dreams and excellent intentions that at the end of their journey their daughter sprang to her feet first and stretched her young body.

Chapter Eight

 Questions

1. What was Gregor's occupation before his transformation? How did he come to his particular job? What has kept him working for his firm?
2. When Gregor wakes to find that he has become a gigantic insect, the problems that haunt him are how to get out of bed, how to get to his job, and so on. He never wonders why and how he has been changed. What does this fact suggest about Gregor?
3. When Gregor's parents first see the gigantic insect (paragraph 25), do they recognize it as their son? What do their initial reaction suggest about their attitude about their son?
4. How does each family member react to Gregor after his transformation? What is different about each reaction? What is similar?
5. What things about Gregor have been changed? What seems to have remained the same?
6. How does the setting of the story help to shape the themes?
7. How does the family decide to "get rid of" the insect? In what specific ways does the family's decision affect Gregor? How does the family react to Gregor's death?
8. Does Grete change in the course of the story? If so, how does she change?
9. In what ways is Gregor's metamorphosis symbolic?
10. In what ways is the novel expressionistic?

Chapter Nine

New Fiction

In the middle of the 20th century, with the development of modernism, a new type of fiction came into being. In contrast to traditional fiction, plot fades out and characters are decharacterized in new fiction. What the author expresses emphatically is merely a notion. Plot, character and setting become the "objective correlative" for the presentation of the notion. Words, phrases, and clauses or sentences are simply pieced together to create a literal effect of rhythm, melody, or comprehensive imagery. All these serve to help produce an **epiphany** in the reader: the point at which a reader comes to the realization of a (certain) significance in the mess of fragmentary patches.

New fiction first appeared in France in the 50s of the 20th century, and in the 60s and 70s it became rather popular in the United States. The fiction is called "new" generally because it goes against the traditional concept of fiction. It rebels traditional fiction not only in backgrounding plot and decharacterizing character, but also in destroying the elementary structure and castrating literary language of fiction: fragmentation, dislocation, vulgarity, dullness, randomness, endless repetition, incoherence and the like turned to be characteristic. The new fiction experiments with fragmentation, randomness and dislocation on the assumption that the reader will be able to reconstruct reality from the disordered and unevaluated pieces of direct experience (*A Handbook to Literature*, 1986). Donald Barthelme says that he only believes in fragments. Kurt Vonnegut says that there is no order around us and we must be subjected to the request of disorder (*Breakfast of Champions*, 1973). And Raymond Federman says that he prefers incoherence and disorder, and his whole life is a journey to disorder (*Take It or Leave It*, 1976). The refusal to allow order into the fictional world can be soundly taken as a typical feature of such fiction. Disorder in psychological and objective reality is much concerned. And writers of new fiction, taking time also as a mess of disorder, treat time in far more complex ways than they have in previous narratives, where time is generally linear as measured by the clock, and explore the complexity of human motives and actions, including the nature of shock and trauma, sexuality, violence, and cruelty (Cleanth Brooks and R. P. Warren, *Understanding Fiction*, 1971). The outward cartooning and puppetizing of the character makes a contrast with the caprice, uncertainty, and ambiguity of human nature. Rather than being concrete and vivid, plot, character and setting are all highly abstract and mechanical, or in a way completely meaningless. They seem illogical and implausible instead of being true to life. In other words, what is real and what is fictional are labyrinthically confused. This is the experience of people in the real world, and is also the experience of people in the fictional world.

  Black humour is a substantial element of new fiction. It refers to the tone of anger and bitterness as it does to the grotesque and morbid situations for darkly comic purposes. Everything, however noble or vulgar, however holy or absurd, can be the object of comic derision, satire, joke, and irony. In Barthelme's "Views of My Father Weeping", which is entirely composed of patches, "my father" dies of a traffic accident, but then sits weeping, and then plays mischievously like a naughty boy, and in the patches here and there are inserted many indecent and wicked scenes and licentious commentaries. Even to the very end of the story, the reader is not sure whether "my father" is dead or alive. If we try to find out the meaning of the story, as a meaning is often revealed in a story or novel, we seem to be at lost. Perhaps, the only meaning the story conveys is that there is no meaning in this world, and nothing can be made sure. One can never distinguish life from death, the real from the false, and reality from nightmare, and thus nothing is meaningful. John Barth's "Lost in the Funhouse" tells of a thirteen-year-old boy who gets lost in a funhouse while taking a holiday on seashore. The funhouse is a labyrinth, which is a symbol of the human world and human life. Being "lost" suggests a permanent state of human beings. Against the traditional principle of verisimilitude of fiction, the narrator frequently reminds the reader that nothing is real and everything is fictional and absurd. He tries his best to oppose the nothingness and to establish his selfness with words, but at the same time he is aware that the words, like the fictional story, is meaningless. The author himself even comes out to make a comment of the techniques employed in this story so as to make the story of patches not only of narratives, but also of commentaries, notes and sketches. Thus the story is just a hotchpotch of quite different writing styles.

The emphasis on the intrinsic possibility of a meaningless universe reminds us of existentialism. John Barth admitted publicly that there were similarities between his treatment of the theme of suicide in *The Floating Opera* and Albert Camus's discussion of suicide in *Le Mythe de Sisyphus*, and absurdity and the sense of absurdity were influential in the contemporary academic circle. John Hawkes in *Travesty* (1976) specifically mentions the necessity of the vision of absurdity around which a novel or story establishes itself, that is, a writer is concerned mostly with the continuous and persistent creativity and representation of the potentiality of our violence and absurdity. Even if some works are not obviously based upon existentialism, their handling of nothingness and emptiness suggests a similar ideology or conception. Robert Coover time and again touches the dual state of the pressure coming from the relation with empty universal horizon and the embarrassment resulting from the freedom of writing. John Barth and John Hawkes stress the attempt to fill the emptiness in light of existentialism and seek the last vision from fragmentation and disorder. The evanescence of human life and the existence of disorder produce more "facts" than facts. Human beings become the accidents in absolute emptiness in Vladimir Nabokov's *Ada* (1969) and as a result are meaningless themselves.

A sense of tragedy prevails the dominant ideology of new fiction. However, tragedy is no longer the traditional dialectic concept of human life, namely the irreducible contradictions between innocence and guilt, freedom and necessity, and meaningfulness and meaninglessness, the resolution of which is the measure of dignity of man and the meaning of life. In new fiction, as in the modern and postmodern world, serious problems cannot be solved by way of this dialectical form of tragedy since it focuses upon individual rights rather than upon a belief of universal meanings. The writers of new fiction explore the tragic under the cover of the grotesque, or blending them into black humour, in their works. The tragic sense is mainly expressed in the death of literary form, which in turn reflects the embarrassment of emotion, action, and faith of the modern man (Sontag, *Against Interpretations and Other Essays*, 1966).

The contemplation of the tragic by writers of new fiction finds expression in John Barth's comic attitude towards it. In *Giles Goat-Boy* (1966), he regards the tragic trauma of the modern world as the first-class and the meaninglessness of human life as the tragic flaw of the modern man. Barth plays with the most serious issue of the meaning of life in a derisive tone, whereas Robert Coover rejects the notion of the tragic downright: one can never make clear the meaning of life, but there is not any hue of tragedy in this; there is only absurdity and grotesqueness (*Pricksongs and Descants*, 1969). John Hawkes in *Travesty* explores the intrinsic relation between the existentialist situation of death as a tragedy and the purely fictional scene of suicide as a means of meaning with Canus's death in a traffic accident as an example. What is even more absurd is that the chauffeur who causes the accident is the witness of his own death. The reader can hardly tell whether the accident is real or purely fictional since everything in reality is confused with everything in consciousness and there is no distinction. As John Barth says, the truth is that there is no difference in anything and the problem of Hamlet (everyone) is entirely that of meaninglessness.

The Balloon
by Donald Barthelme, 1981

  The balloon, beginning at a point on Fourteenth Street, the exact location of which I cannot reveal, expanded northward all one night, while people were sleeping, until it reached the Park. There, I stopped it; at dawn the northernmost edges lay over the Plaza; the free-hanging motion was frivolous and gentle. But experiencing a faint irritation at stopping, even to protect the trees, and seeing no reason the balloon should not be allowed to expand upward, over the parts of the city it was already covering, into the "air space" to be found there, I asked the engineers to see to it. This expansion took place throughout the morning, soft imperceptible sighing of gas through the valves. The balloon then covered forty-five blocks north-south on either side of the Avenue in some places. This was the situation, then.

  But it is wrong to speak of "situations," implying sets of circumstances leading to some resolution, some escape of tension; there were no situations, simply the balloon hanging there — muted heavy grays and browns for the most part, contrasting with walnut and soft yellows. A deliberate lack of finish, enhanced by skillful installation, gave the surface a rough, forgotten quality; sliding weights on the inside, carefully adjusted, anchored the great, vari-shaped mass at a number of points. Now we have had a flood of original ideas in all media, works of singular beauty as well

Chapter Nine

as significant milestones in the history of inflation, but at that moment, there was only *this balloon*, concrete particular, hanging there.

There were reactions. Some people found the balloon "interesting." As a response, this seemed inadequate to the immensity of the balloon, the suddenness of its appearance over the city; on the other hand, in the absence of hysteria or other societally induced anxiety, it must be judged a calm, "mature" one. There was a certain amount of initial argumentation about the "meaning" of the balloon; this subsided, because we have learned not to insist on meanings, and they are rarely even looked for now, except in cases involving the simplest, safest phenomena. It was agreed that since the meaning of the balloon could never be known absolutely, extended discussion was pointless, or at least less purposeful than the activities of those who, for example, hung green and blue paper lanterns from the warm gray underside, in certain streets, or seized the occasion to write messages on the surface, announcing their availability for the performance of unnatural acts, or the availability of acquaintances.

Daring children jumped, especially at those points where the balloon hovered close to a building, so that the gap between balloon and building was a matter of a few inches, or points where the balloon actually made contact, exerting an ever-so-slight pressure against the side of a building, so that balloon and building seemed a unity. The upper surface was so structured that a "landscape" was presented, small valleys as well as slight knolls, or mounds; once atop the balloon, a stroll was possible, or even a trip, from one place to another. There was pleasure in being able to run down an incline, then up the opposing slope, both gently graded, or in making a leap from one side to the other. Bouncing was possible, because of the pneumaticity of the surface, and even falling, if that was your wish. That all these varied motions, as well as others, were within one's possibilities, in experiencing the "up" side of the balloon, was extremely exciting for children, accustomed to the city's flat, hard skin. But the purpose of the balloon was not to amuse children.

Too, the number of people, children and adults, who took advantage of the opportunities described was not so large as it might have been; a certain timidity, lack of trust in the balloon, was seen. There was, furthermore, some hostility. Because we had hidden the pumps, which fed helium to the interior, and because the surface was so vast that the authorities could not determine the point of entry — that is, the point at which the gas was injected — a degree of frustration was evidenced by those city officers into whose province such manifestations normally fell. The apparent purposelessness of the balloon was vexing (as was the fact that it was "there" at all). Had we painted, in great letters, "LABORATORY TESTS PROVE" or "18% MORE EFFECTIVE" on the sides of the balloon, this difficulty would have been circumvented. But I could not bear to do so. On the whole, these officers were remarkably tolerant, considering the dimensions of the anomaly, this tolerance being the result of, first, secret tests conducted by night that convinced them that little or nothing could be done in the way of removing or destroying the balloon, and, secondly, a public warmth that arose (not uncolored by touches of the aforementioned hostility) toward the balloon, from ordinary citizens.

As a single balloon must stand for a lifetime of thinking about balloons, so each citizen expressed, in the attitude he chose, a complex of attitudes. One man might consider that the balloon had to do with the notion *sullied*, as in the sentence, *The big balloon sullied the otherwise clear and radiant Manhattan sky.* That is, the balloon was, in this man's view, an imposture, something inferior to the sky that had formerly been there, something interposed between the people and their "sky." But in fact it was January, the sky was dark and ugly; it was not a sky you could look up into, lying on your back in the street, with pleasure, unless pleasure, for you, proceeded from having been threatened, from having been misused. And the underside of the balloon was a pleasure to look up into, we had seen to that, muted grays and browns for the most part, contrasted with walnut and soft, forgotten yellows. And so, while this man was thinking *sullied*, still there was an admixture of pleasurable cognition in his thinking, struggling with the original perception.

    Another man, on the other hand, might view the balloon as if it were part of a system of unanticipated rewards, as when one's employer walks in and says, "Here, Henry, take this package of money I have wrapped for you, because we have been doing so well in the business here, and I admire the way you bruise the tulips, without which bruising your department would not be a success, or at least not the success that it is." For this man the balloon might be a brilliantly heroic "muscle and pluck" experience, even if an experience poorly understood.

    Another man might say, "Without the example of ——, it is doubtful that —— would exist today in its present form," and find many to agree with him, or to argue with him. Ideas of "bloat" and "float" were introduced, as well as concepts of dream and responsibility. Others engaged in remarkably detailed fantasies having to do with a wish either to lose themselves in the balloon, or to engorge it. The private character of these wishes, of their origins, deeply buried and unknown, was such that they were not much spoken of; yet there is evidence that they were widespread. It was also argued that what was important was what you felt when you stood under the balloon; some people claimed that they felt sheltered, warmed, as never before, while enemies of the balloon felt, or reported feeling, constrained, a "heavy" feeling.

    Critical opinion was divided:

      "*monstrous pourings*"
      "*harp*"
  XXXXXXX "*certain contrasts with darker portions*"
      "*inner joy*"
    "*large, square corners*"
    "*conservative eclecticism that has so far governed*

modern balloon design"
⋮⋮⋮⋮⋮ "*abnormal vigor*"
"*warm, soft, lazy passages*"
"*Has unity been sacrificed for a sprawling quality?*"
"*Quelle catastrophe!*"
"*munching*"

    People began, in a curious way, to locate themselves in relation to aspects of the balloon: "I'll be at that place where it dips down into Forty-seventh Street almost to the sidewalk, near the Alamo Chile House," or, "Why don't we go stand on top, and take the air, and maybe walk about a bit, where it forms a tight, curving line with the facade of the Gallery of Modern Art —" Marginal intersections offered entrances with a given time duration, as well as "warm, soft, lazy passages" in which... But it is wrong to speak of "marginal intersections," each intersection was crucial, none could be ignored (as if, walking there, you might not find someone capable of turning your attention, in a flash, from old exercises to new exercises, risks and escalations). Each intersection was crucial, meeting of balloon and building, meeting of balloon and man, meeting of balloon and balloon.

    It was suggested that what was admired about the balloon was finally this: that it was not limited, or defined. Sometimes a bulge, blister, or sub-section would carry all the way east to the river on its own initiative, in the manner of an army's movements on a map, as seen in a headquarters remote from the fighting. Then that part would be, as it were, thrown back again, or would withdraw into new dispositions; the next morning, that part would have made another sortie, or disappeared altogether. This ability of the balloon to shift its shape, to change, was very pleasing, especially to people whose lives were rather rigidly patterned, persons to whom change, although desired, was not available. The balloon, for the twenty-two days of its existence, offered the possibility, in its randomness, of mislocation of the self, in contradistinction to the grid of precise, rectangular pathways under our feet. The amount of specialized training currently needed, and the consequent desirability of long-term commitments, has been occasioned by the steadily growing importance of complex machinery, in virtually all kinds of operations; as this tendency increases, more and more people will turn, in bewildered inadequacy, to solutions for which the balloon may stand as a prototype, or "rough draft."

I met you under the balloon, on the occasion of your return from Norway; you asked if it was mine; I said it was. The balloon, I said, is a spontaneous autobiographical disclosure, having to do with the unease I felt at your absence, and with sexual deprivation, but now that your visit to Bergen has been terminated, it is no longer necessary or appropriate. Removal of the balloon was easy; trailer trucks carried away the depleted fabric, which is now stored in West Virginia, awaiting some other time of unhappiness, sometime, perhaps, when we are angry with one another.

Discussion

In our discussions of other stories... we have repeatedly asked whether those stories that reject the conventions of realism make accessible to the reader's imagination the alternative principles that may govern their fictive worlds. We now ask this same question of the world created in "The Balloon."

In the story's first sentence the narrator asserts that he "cannot reveal" exactly where on Fourteenth Street in New York City the balloon was inflated. This assertion naturally stimulates the reader's curiosity. What considerations prevent the narrator from giving this information? The possibilities range from psychological incapacity to national security, and it is the reader's conviction that once he knows why the narrator withholds this information he will be on his way to knowing what the world of the narrator is like, what sorts of concerns will govern his presentation; in short, what the story is about.

The narrator never gives the reader a truly satisfactory answer. He offers all manner of information about the response of the city's populace to the presence of the balloon, but not until the last paragraph of the story (except teasingly and inconclusively, when observing in the middle of the story that "the purpose of the balloon was not to amuse children") does the narrator return to his own relation to the balloon, to his reasons for having it inflated, or for writing about it. The last paragraph of the story explains that the balloon is "a spontaneous autobiographical disclosure, having to do with the unease I felt at your absence, and with sexual deprivation." This is an answer, but it is not one the reader can understand. Neither is the explanation offered at a time when, even if it were comprehensible, the reader could make use of it in developing a sense of the narrator's relation to the story he tells.

Rather, as he reads, the reader gradually comes to feel that all questions about the principles of narrative governing the story, in fact all questions about the story's meaning, are best put to one side. The narrator has said as much early on: "It is wrong to speak of 'situations,' implying sets of circumstances leading to some resolution, some escape of tension; there were no situations, simply the balloon... concrete particular, hanging there." Later in the story the narrator returns to the question of meaning, remarking that "the balloon... offered the possibility, in its randomness, of mislocation of the self, in contradistinction to the grid of precise, rectangular pathways under our feet."

The argument of "The Balloon" is thus that all efforts to understand the story's predication, like all efforts to understand the balloon itself, are wrongheaded, and that the proper course for the reader is simply to "mislocate" his self for a while, to enter into the experience of the story merely for what it is, participating in the differing reactions of the citizenry, without any overarching sense of the reason for this "mislocation," that is, of why he is reading the story. It is consistent with the story's argument that the narrator's motivations in telling the story be problematic. Were these to be clear, the reader would have a sense not only of why the narrator is telling the story but inferentially of why he (the reader), at least from the narrator's point of view, should be reading it. The reader would lose his sense of the "randomness" of his involvement in the story.

In a closed system, which every fiction is, all elements are inevitably related to all other elements. The relation may be insignificant, or shifting, but it exists, and in some fashion contributes to the dynamic of the whole. In the present instance, the narrator's reasons for telling the story are unclear. What does become clear is that he has no significant relation to the story he tells. He has the balloon inflated for reasons that, when finally revealed, are seen to have nothing to do with the events he describes, and his next action is to have the balloon deflated (and subsequently trucked to West Virginia) when the "you" whose absence prompted the balloon's inflation returns from an unexplained trip to Norway. The narrator, although he is the owner of the balloon, has nothing to do with the reported action of the story, which is concerned not with the balloon's ownership but with the reactions of the citizenry to the balloon's presence. This combination of the narrator's problematic reasons for telling the story and his peripheral relation to the actions described causes the reader to shift his attention from why the story is being told to what the story is telling.

It can be argued that "The Balloon" is a chronicle of how New Yorkers respond to an inexplicable but unquestionable fact of their environment, the presence of the balloon. How they respond is to find in the balloon gratifications and meanings and relations that are arbitrary and personal. The reader responds to the story in exactly the same fashion. He moves from paragraph to paragraph, finding gratifications and meanings in and relations among the story's individual moments, all of this within the story's arbitrary given, which is the narrator's inexplicable resolve to tell the story in the first place.

This seems to bring us to an inconsistency in the story's intentions. The narrator's assertion that the balloon, which may be taken at one level to represent the story, should be seen as nothing more than a pleasant and temporary opportunity for "mislocation of the self" is contradicted by the remarks of the last paragraph and by the introductory invitation to the reader to consider the question of the narrator's motivations. His calling the story " a spontaneous autobiographical disclosure " and his subsequent remarks to the story's "you" give further legitimacy to the reader's raising objections. These might be phrased as follows: "This story gives me inadequate information about the narrator, about his personality and concerns, about the world in which he moves and the people who share it with him. Besides, between the first and last paragraphs the story has nothing to do with the narrator."

No reader with a realistic bias would find this argument persuasive. He would, rather, feel that it is the story's erosion of the reader's sense of relation between form and content that, paradoxically, gives the story unity, and that the teasingly obscure suggestions about the narrator's private reasons for telling the story unjustifiably mislead the reader, creating a false expectation about the nature of the story. But a reader without such a bias might accept the relationships, however fantastic or difficult to locate on a psychological ground. Such a reader gets satisfaction in toying with "reality" in accepting deceptions — provisionally, of course.

Nevertheless, even a reader with a realistic bias might be led to admit that this incoherence of narrative does not diminish many of the story's virtues. We can point, for example, to the story's telling perceptions about mass psychology (had the balloon been labeled " laboratory tests prove," the narrator remarks, its presence would have caused no disturbance) as well as to the accurate parody of the clichés and jargon of "critical opinion" in its list of reactions to the balloon by the city's intelligentsia. We can point, that is, to just such individual congruences within a pleasurable randomness as the story's proper formal intention lead us to expect at the same time realizing the element of satiric parody.

To state the whole matter more succinctly, we may say that the meaning of the story is that it has no meaning. It has only the shape and pretense of meaning. It is a serious joke, as it were, on our normal demand that fiction (and life) be logically and ethically fulfilled.

(Cleanth Brooks and Robert Penn Warren)

 Questions

1. With the exception of the balloon itself, the world of "The Balloon" seems very much like the everyday world. Why is this necessary for the purposes of the story?
2. Among the quotations of "critical opinion" of the balloon, the narrator lists "munching." Is this listing credible? Can it be seen as a sort of slapstick treatment of reactions that to this point the narrator has satirized more subtly? If so, what function is served by this change in technique? Keep in mind where in the list of opinions the word appears.
3. When people use the balloon as a reference point in making plans to meet, their speech sounds rather "arty." What makes this dialogue credible?
4. Can it be argued that there is no end to the number and case, of such stories as this — stories that proclaim meaninglessness through an ingenuity of seeming to proclaim meaningfulness? If so, how many such stories do you yearn to read?

Chapter Ten

Writing about a Story

Like any coherent, forceful essay, a good discussion of fiction does not just toss forth a random lot of impressions and quotations. We begin by determining our purpose in writing and our intended reader. And our essay, like any informal everyday writing, must be designed to communicate our ideas directly and clearly to our reader. One of the obvious purposes for writing an essay on a story is to give us an opportunity to sort out our thinking and formalize it. The fiction writer and essayist E. M. Foster once said, "How do I know what I think until I see what I say?" Essay writing on literary works gives us an opportunity to see what we think or say about a topic. Unlike conversation, in which thoughts and remarks whiz by rather randomly, the physical presence of our writing summons us to look and think again. As we look back through our writing, we may find that we have not carefully enough explained a concept or that we have not grouped our ideas in their most effective manner. Thus we rewrite and clarify our own thinking. Such formal essay-writing generally assumes three phases in most of us students, though writing in its strict sense is an intensely personal activity and the methods we take in writing may vary radically. The three phases are: searching for ideas and prewriting, drafting and revising, and documenting and proofreading.

Searching for Ideas and Prewriting

In order to write a meaningful essay, then, we need something we *want* to say—a meaningful topic. Instead of choosing what we think will impress our instructor, we should choose what appeals to us when we write about a story. And how to find out what appeals? Whether we plan to write a short paper that requires no research beyond the piece of fiction or a long essay that will take us to a library, the first stage of our project is reading—reading the story closely and attentively for details, and asking ourselves the following questions (suggested by Kennedy and Gioia, *Literature*, 1995) while reading:

1. What is the point of view? In what way(s) is it appropriate (or inappropriate) and effective (or ineffective) in this story? Imagine the story told from a different point of view; would such a change be for the worse or for the better?
2. What is the tone of the story? By what means and how effectively is it communicated?
3. Does the story show us unique and individual scenes, events, and characters, or weary stereotypes?
4. What is typical of the style of the story? What is different in this story from other writings of the same author, and from the writings of other writers?
5. Are any symbols evident and foregrounded? If so, do they direct to the story's central theme? Or do they distract us from it?
6. How appropriate to the theme of the story, and to its subject matter, are its title, tone, and style? Is it difficult or impossible to sympathize with the attitudes of the author (insofar as we can tell what they are)?
7. Does our interest in the story mainly depend on following its plot, on finding out what will happen next? Or does the author go beyond the events to show us what they mean? Are the events (however fantastic) credible, or are they incredibly melodramatic? Does the plot greatly depend on farfetched coincidence or natural conflict? How is the development of the plot related to characterization, revealing of the author's

attitudes, and unfolding of the theme?
8. Has the author caused characters, events, and settings to come alive? Are they full of breath and motion, or simply told about in the abstract ("She was a lovely girl and had a highly exciting life")? What are the details in the portrayal of character that make us believe in it?

Of course, that we ask ourselves such questions while reading a story does not mean that we must stuff our paper with information concerning so many aspects. These are merely to help us choose whatever appeals us most so that we can concentrate on a **topic**—the subject we are going to write about—for our paper. The instructor will generally advise us to define our topic narrowly. Our paper will be stronger if we go deeper into our subject than if we choose some very comprehensive subject and then find ourselves merely able to touch on it superficially. We can, of course, narrow and focus a large topic while we work our way into it. A general interest in "Hemingway's Style" might lead us to the narrower topic "Cohesive Devices under Hemingway."

　　It is advisable to take notes with a pencil while we are reading a piece of fiction: mark (if the book is ours) passages and sentences or phrases that stand out in importance and jot brief notes in the margin. In a long story, we may mark passages that are subject to comparisons; for instance, all the places in which we find the same theme or symbol or all the places that carry an ironic tone. Later, at a glance, we can review the highlights of a work and quickly refer to evidence when writing a paper about it. We may also take notes on loose-leaf notebook paper, keeping one sheet beside the page in the book. In this we have the advantage of affording a lot of room for note taking.

　　However, the most popular method of note taking is perhaps to write on index cards. The advantage of taking notes on cards is that cards are easy to shuffle in organizing our materials with respect to different categories. This is especially helpful when we

Chapter Ten

read relevant critical works in a library. To save work, we can just keep a numbered list of books we are using, instead of bothering ourselves to write down the author and the title of the book on every card. When taking notes, we only need write the book's identifying number and the page number on the card in order to identify our source and translate the number into author, title, and other necessary information in the paper.

Ideas in our writing will never proceed in a straight line. They often come in fits and starts. All the while we take notes, we come up with ideas and material to write about; all the while we think about the topic in our mind, we plan. While we continue to plan, while we write a draft, and while we revise, we shall discover new thoughts, and perhaps the best thoughts of all. If we do, be sure to let them in. Remember that Rome was not built in one day and we cannot accomplish our writing in one move. Generally we shall take a few steps before we finish our paper.

Whenever we begin our paper, it is helpful to analyze the writing situation first. **A writing situation** can be analyzed in six parts, as indicated in Prentice Hall's *Literature* (1989): topic, purpose, reader, voice, content, and form. As we begin to think about a writing project, ask ourselves the following questions:

1. *Topic* (the subject we are going to write about): What, exactly, is the subject? Is our subject broad or narrow? Can we state it in a sentence?
2. *Purpose* (what we want our writing to accomplish): Is our purpose to explain? To describe? To persuade? Or to analyze? What do we want the reader to take away from the writing?
3. *Reader* (the people who will be reading our writing): What are the backgrounds of these people? Do they already know a great deal about our subject, or shall we have to provide basic information?
4. *Voice* (the way our writing will sound to the reader): What impressions do we want to make on our readers? What tone

should the writing have? Should it be formal or informal? Should it be cool and reasoned or charged with emotion?

5. *Content* (the subject and all the information provided about the subject): How much do we already know about the subject? What shall we have to find out and replenish? Shall we have to do some research in a library? What people, books, magazines, websites, or other sources should we consult?

6. *Form* (the shape that the writing will take, including its organization and length): What will the final piece of writing look like? Will it be a single paragraph or several paragraphs? In what order will the content be presented?

The answers to some of these questions will be obvious from the start. For example, our instructor may have assigned us a particular topic and may have specified a certain length for our paper. However, answers to many of these questions will be helpful in our making decisions, setting goals, and making a plan for achieving these goals, which writing always involves.

The next thing we should do is to determine what our writing plan will be. For example, if we find that we are still undecided about our topic, our plan will include clarifying what our topic will be. Our plan will also include research to find out more about the topic, in addition to gathering information from the story we are writing about, organizing our notes, prewriting or making an outline, drafting and revising.

Once we have decided the topic (which may be changed drastically as we continue) and made our writing plan, we begin to sort out our miscellaneous notes and ideas and try to get them organized. It is quite natural that we do not have a smooth train of thoughts at first, and perhaps we even do not have a clear idea how to organize our materials. In this case, we may try the following methods, also suggested in Prentice Hall, for gathering ideas and information for our paper:

| Chapter Ten |

1. *Free-writing*: Think about the topic and write rapidly and uncritically, letting our thoughts tumble onto paper as fast as our pen can capture them. Do not pause to think about spelling, grammar, or punctuation. Just write, nonstop, for ten to fifteen minutes. Then read the free-writing to find ideas that we can use in our paper. Sometimes unexpectedly good ideas will appear on the paper.
2. *Clustering*: Write the topic in the middle of a piece of paper and circle it. Then, in the space round the topic, write down ideas that are related to it and circle these ideas. Draw lines to show how the ideas are connected to one another and to the main topic. This method is particularly useful for broadening or narrowing a topic. If our topic is too broad, we might select one of the related ideas as a new topic; if our topic is too narrow, we might make a change in the topic to include some of the related ideas.
3. *Analyzing*: Divide our topic into parts and then think about each part separately and write down our thoughts about it in the notes. Also think about how the parts relate to one another and how they relate to the topic as a whole.
4. *Questing*: Make a list of questions about the topic in the notes and begin the questions with words *who*, *what*, *when*, *where*, *why*, and *how*. Then do some research to find answers to the questions.
5. *Using outside sources*: Consult books, magazines, websites, reference works such as encyclopaedias and atlases. Talk with people who are knowledgeable about our topic. Write down in our notes any relevant information that we gather from these sources.
6. *Making charts or lists*: Create charts or lists of information related to our topic, for example, a list of characteristics of the topic or a chart of pros-and-cons for the topic.

After we have tried some of the methods, we need to put our ideas and notes into some kind of logical order to make sense of the information we have gathered. The following are suggestions on the ways to organize our notes:

1. *Chronological order*: the order in which events occur
2. *Spatial order*: the order in which things appear in space, as from left to right, top to bottom, or near to far
3. *Degree order*: in increasing or decreasing order, as of size, importance, familiarity, or others
4. *Clarification order*: dividing and labeling the various parts of a subject into logical groups or classes
5. *Process order*: the order of steps according to which something is done

By the way, the above mentioned suggestions are not only useful methods in our arrangement of our notes for the facility of our drafting but also basic organizational patterns common to essay writings. For example, chronological order can be used to describe the time stages required for giving an account of a historical event or explaining the development of a theory; degree order is used when we have several points of discussion and want to put special emphasis on the first or the last point; clarification order is common when we want to explain or define a concept or term and when we have several aspects concerning a subject; and process order is most appropriate for narrative or descriptive writing. Besides, another commonly used method in writing the body of essay on literary works is *comparison order*: showing the similarities and differences between two or more parts of a subject. If only the differences are pointed out, the essay contrasts rather than compares. Generally speaking, a short essay may be structured around just one of these patterns; longer essays usually use a combination of patterns but with an emphasis upon one.

Having organized our notes, we shall usually have a comparatively clear idea about what we are going to write. Perhaps, some of us shall make a rough outline for our paper, which will probably help unless our topic already suggests some obvious way to organize the paper. All of us know how to construct a beautiful outline laid out with Roman numerals, capital letters, Arabic numerals, and lower-case letters. Not every outline needs to be detailed and elaborate. Generally, of course, we do find it helpful to outline in detail, particularly when we are planning a long term paper involving a long novel or several works, comparing and contrasting several aspects of them.

  An outline, if we use one, is not meant to stand as an achievement in itself. It should consume itself and disappear. Kennedy and Gioia (*Literature*, 1995) record a once-valuable outline, a very informal one that enabled the student to organize the paper that appears later in this chapter, "The Hearer of the Tell-Tale Heart." Before he wrote, the student jotted down the ideas that had occurred to him. Looking them over, he saw that certain ones predominated. Since the paper was to analyze the point of view in Poe's story, he began with some notes about the narrator of the story. His other leading ideas emerged as questions: Is the story supposed to be a ghost story or an account of a delusion? Can we read the whole thing as a nightmare, having no reality outside the narrator's mind? Going down his list and seeing that his thoughts were not totally disconnected, he numbered with the same numbers those ideas that belonged together.

{Point of view}
  1 Killer is mad—can listen in on hell.
  2 He is obsessed with the Evil eye.
  1 He thinks he is sane, we know he's mad.
   Old man rich—a miser?
  4 ⎰Is this a ghost story? No! Natural explorations for the heartbeat:
    His mind is playing tricks.
    Hears his <u>own</u> heart (Hoffman's idea).
 3 Maybe the whole story is only his dream?
  Poe must have been crazy too.

The number showed him the order in which he planned to discuss each of his four ideas. Labeling his remarks about the narrator with the number 1, he decided to begin his paper with them and state that they indicated the story's point of view. As we can see from his finished paper, he removed two notions that did not seem relevant to his purpose: the notion about the old man's wealth and the thought that Poe himself was mad. Having completed this rough outline, he returned to Poe's story and on rereading it noticed a few additional points, which we shall find in his paper. His outline did not tell him exactly what to write at every step, but it was clear and easy to follow.

Drafting and Revising

After we have gathered our information and made a rough outline, the next step is to put our ideas down on paper. Thus we begin to draft our essay. When first we **draft** our essay—that is, when we write it out in the rough—we shall probably write rapidly or write slowly and carefully. At this early stage, anyway, we do not need to be fussy about proper spelling, grammar, and punctuation, which are left to be concerned about later when we do a **proofreading** (going over the finished essay word by word, checking it for typographical and other mistakes). Right now, the most important thing is to get our thoughts down on paper in a steady flow. Perhaps, sometimes we need to refer to our prewriting notes and to our outline as we write, or we do not even want to look at those notes on our reading that we have collected industriously. However, when we come to a place where a note will fit, we might just insert a reminder to ourselves, such as SEE CARD 16, or SEE FORSTER ON CHARACTER. It is quite natural that we shall come up with new ideas while drafting. In this case, we may stop in the middle of our draft and do some more prewriting to develop our new ideas. A writer of effective essays will never be afraid of discarding old ideas when new ones come to mind, since a good essay always depends upon new and original ideas. Frequently, we have to make several attempts at drafting before we come up with a satisfactory draft. If we write a draft that does not seem to have a well-defined purpose or does not contain enough information to support our main idea, we might as well go back to prewriting stage: define our purpose more clearly, review our notes to discard irrelevant ideas, and gather any additional ideas and facts that we need for a new draft. "Writing and rewriting," says John Updike, "are a constant search for what one is saying."

We all know that writing about literature has a great deal to do with literary and critical terms. As a beginning critic, we are supposed to be careful when we use such terms. Nothing can be more misleading than a technical term indiscriminately, or even arrogantly, misapplied. It is far better to choose plain words with which we are already at ease. When it is necessary to use technical terms, we are supposed to be clear about their connotations and denotations and the context they are used. And sometimes we have to be informed about the theory from which they are derived. Selectively and appropriately employed, critical terms can help to sharpen a thought.

Another thing we should remember when draft our writing is to leave plenty of space between lines and enormous margins so that we can easily squeeze later thoughts in when they come to us.

To achieve effective writing, we have to have the courage to be ruthless. No reader is prepared to read our drafts. So we can treat them mercilessly—scissor them apart, rearrange their pieces, and reassemble them into a stronger order, using tape or glue. Once we have a draft that pleases us, we begin to refine and polish it. This process of reworking a draft is known as **revising**. For most of us, good writing is largely a matter of revising—of going back over our first thoughts word by word. In the process of reconsidering our words, we often discover fresher and sharper ideas. Kennedy and Gioia (*Literature*, 1995) put forth a few suggestions which may be helpful when we revise our drafts:

1. So far as the deadline allows, be ready to revise as many times as need be.
2. We must not think of revising simply as checking spelling mistakes. That is the thing we shall do in proofreading, which comes last. When revising, we should be willing to cut and slash, to discover new insights, to move blocks of words here and there so that they follow in a stronger order.
3. It is beneficial to enlist outside advice—from our instructor, from our roommates, from any friend who will read our rough draft and give us reaction—and ask them: "What isn't clear?"
4. If we (or our willing reader) find any places that are not readily understandable, we should single them out for rewriting.
5. Short paragraphs of one or two sentences may indicate places that call for more thought or more material. Can we supply them with more evidence, more explanation and interpretation, more examples and illustration?
6. A time-tested method of revising is to lay aside our manuscript for a while, forget it, and then after a long interval, go back to it for a fresh look.
7. When our paper is in the last draft, that is the time to edit it. Once we have our ideas in firm shape, we can check those uncertain spelling, see to the agreement of verbs, pronouns, and numbers, cut needless words, and replace a weak word with a stronger one. When we feel satisfied that we have made ourselves clear, we can be as fussy as we like about our writing.

Prentice Hall (*Literature*, 1989) also suggests a list of questions that we ask while we revise our draft, which are helpful to make our paper an effective one:

CHECKLIST FOR REVISION

Topic and Purpose
- [ ] Is my topic clear?
- [ ] Does my writing have a specific purpose?
- [ ] Does my writing achieve its purpose?

Audience
- [ ] Will everything that I have written be clear to my audience?
- [ ] Will my audience find the writing interesting?
- [ ] Will my audience respond in the way that I would like?

Voice and Word Choice
- [ ] Is the impression that my writing conveys the one I intended it to convey?
- [ ] Is my language appropriately formal or informal?
- [ ] Have I avoided vague, undefined terms?
- [ ] Have I avoided jargon that my audience will not understand?
- [ ] Have I avoided clichés?
- [ ] Have I avoided slang, odd connotations, euphemisms, and gobbledygook except for novelty or humor?

Content/Development
- [ ] Have I avoided including unnecessary or unrelated ideas?
- [ ] Have I developed my topic completely?
- [ ] Have I supplied examples or details that support the statements I have made?
- [ ] Are my sources of information unbiased, up-to-date, and authoritative?

Form
- [ ] Have I followed a logical method of organization?
- [ ] Have I used transitions, or connecting words, to make the organization clear?
- [ ] Does the writing have a clear introduction, body, and conclusion?

If our answer to any of the questions is no, we might as well revise the draft until we can answer yes.

The following is the editorial symbols commonly used in revising and editing a draft:

SYMBOL	MEANING	EXAMPLE
◯↑	move text	She, however, was not at home.
ℓ	delete	I also went, too.
∧	insert	of our car
⌒	close up; no space	every where
⊙	insert period	ran⊙ I
∧	insert comma	mice, bats, and rats
∨	add apostrophe	they're here
∨ ∨	add quotation marks	"The Tell-Tale Heart"
⌒⌐⌐⌒	transpose	to see clearly
¶	begin paragraph	crash. ¶ The man
/	make lower case	the ʙasketball player
≡	capitalize	president Truman

— 396 —

Chapter Ten

Documenting and Proofreading

It is natural and necessary for us to make references to other books and essays in our research paper about a story, especially when we are writing a rather long paper. So we shall want to give credit to those critics who have helped us. Whether we quote from other writers, translate them into our language, summarize their thoughts, or paraphrase their ideas, we must make sure that we give them their due: we should document what we take from other sources and identify the author, book (or essay), page, publisher, the place and year of publication and other necessary sources. In so doing, the duty to document makes us careful about our sources and helps us keep our writing accurate and responsible. It is not right that we just provide the authors and the books. (In this textbook, a selection and compiling of materials from various writers and critics is provided that the compiler thinks will best benefit students in learning how to approach fiction. This differs from research work in its strict sense.) in our research paper even if we list the sources in the bibliography at the end of the paper. We must always remember to provide the source as fully as necessary so that the reader can easily go to the original source to check up on us (though most readers will not bother) or to find more information about a special idea.

However, this does not mean that every word that has appeared in other sources has to be documented in our paper. The general rule for knowing when to document is that every direct quotation and any idea that is not common knowledge must be identified either in **footnote** (a note placed at the bottom of a page), **endnote** (a note placed at the end of the paper), or in parentheses at the end of the sentence with the author's last name and page citation. So the difficulty about this rule lies in determining what material is considered to be common knowledge. Common knowledge here does not mean what everyone in the street knows.

Instead, it refers to what most scholars and writers on the subject we are studying consider to be general information in the field. For example, we need not document "To be, or not to be," even if we put the phrase in quotation marks. The most reliable way of testing whether a bit of information is common knowledge is to survey what we have read on the subject. If seven out of ten writers mention the same bit of information, we can assume that it is common knowledge.

Another difficult thing for us Chinese students is when to quote. **Quoting** is copying word for word a complete passage or a single significant word or phrase from someone else's writing. Quoting must always be indicated by quotation marks around both ends of the copied material. But quotation marks are just one thing we need. In the final paper we should place a note number at the end of the material quoted so as to identify the source in our footnotes or endnotes, or provide the author with a page citation in parentheses. Generally speaking, quoting should be used as sparing as possible. Excessive quoting will make a research paper poor because our original ideas will be submerged in quoting and the style of writing will appear inconsistent. So if we borrow ideas from other sources, it is advisable to summarize or to paraphrase. Summarizing and paraphrasing not only test our understanding of other critics' ideas but also force us to consider the essence of what we read so that we can compare our ideas with those of others. We may wish to quote a few words that sum up especially important ideas but, whenever possible, quotations should be integrated into our own sentences and our final sentences should be smooth and grammatical. But when quoting is used appropriately and effectively, it will pungently strengthen our paper. There are three instances when quotations should be used (Robins, *The Writer's Practical Rhetoric*, 1980):

1. When citing a well-known quotation. We would not want to reword "To be, or not to be."

2. When presenting evidence for a particular style or choice of words. For instance, if we are doing a study of Faulkner's narrative style, we would quote his writing as evidence to illustrate our opinion, not paraphrase it.
3. When an idea presented concisely and effectively requires the use of someone else's words. Sometimes we would like to quote ideas that are so radical or controversial that our reader needs to see the exact words. The direct quotation assures our reader that we have not misinterpreted the statement or removed it from the correct context.

At times we shall need to quote a longer passage in our paper. Just as with short quotations, we should integrate a long quotation into our own discussion naturally and smoothly. In addition, we should use a special form if the quotation is four or more lines. The following rules are commonly followed when long quotations are used in research papers:

1. Block off the quotation, double-spacing the quotation from the rest of the paper and single-spacing the quotation itself.
2. Indent five spaces from the left margin of the paper.
3. Omit quotation marks at the beginning and end of the quoted material, since block quotations are only for word for word copying.

However, as a writer of a research paper, we should use our own words as much as possible and fit the key words from our sources into our own sentences.

The most commonly and efficiently used way for English writers to document their sources is that recommended in the *MLA Handbook for Writers of Research Papers*, 5th ed. (New York: Modern Language Association of America, 1999). In MLA documentation style, the writer acknowledges the sources by providing brief **parenthetical citations** in the text with an alphabetical list of works that appears at the end of the paper (once called a **bibliography**, now entitled "Works Cited." See Appendix III for samples of various sources in MLA style.). The parenthetical citation that appears at the end of the following sentence is typical of MLA style:

> The word "symbol" can mean any unit of literary structure with some kind of special reference that can be isolated for critical analysis (Frye 71).

The citation "(Frye 71)" tells readers that the information in the sentence was derived from page 71 of a work by an author named Frye. If readers want more information about the source, they can turn to the works-cited list, where under the name of Frye, they will find the following information:

> Frye, Northrop. *Anatomy of Criticism: Four Essays*. Princeton: Princeton UP, 1957.

This entry indicates that the work's author is Northrop Frye and its title, *Anatomy of Criticism: Four Essays*. (By the way, the punctuation marks for the titles of books, newspapers, journals etc in English are italics or underlining and for articles, poems, short stories, and chapters of a book are quotation marks.) The remaining information tells that the work was published in Princeton by Princeton University Press in 1957. If the author's name is mentioned and readers will be clear that the source is his/hers, only the page number appears in the citation:

> Northrop Frye in his monumental work talks about "symbol" in a broad sense to mean any unit of literary structure that can be isolated for critical analysis. Thus a word with some kind of special reference is taken as a symbol (71).

If more than one work by the same author is in the list of works cited, a comma after the author's last name and a shortened version of the title is given: "(Frye, *Anatomy* 71)."

If the book or essay is co-authored, the family names of both the authors are given: "(Gilbert & Gubar 231)." Here the reference is to "Gilbert, Sandra M., and Susan Gubar. The Madwoman in the Attic: The Woman Writer and the Nineteenth-Century Literay Imagination. New Haven: Yale UP, 1979." in the list of works cited.

If the citation is from more than one work, both or all the works should be referred and put a semicolon between the works:

> One widely accepted explanation of this phenomenon is that the ordering of the discourse is determined by the sender's hypotheses about what the receiver does and does not know. (Halliday 174-5; Quirk et al 1360)

The parenthetical note indicates that two works authored respectively by Halliday and Quirk and others are referred here. In the list of works cited, we shall have

> Halliday, M. A. K. System and Function in Language. Oxford: Oxford UP, 1976.

and

> Quirk, R. ,S. Greenbaum,G. N. Leech, and J. Svartvik. A Comprehensive Grammar of the English Language. London: Longman, 1985.

However, when we quote the Bible, we put the name of the book, the section number, and the sentence in the parenthesis: "Lift up your heads, O you gates; be lifted up, you ancient doors, that the King of glory may come in" (Psalms 24: 7). The entry of the Bible should be the same with the other works in a complete form: The Holy Bible. New International Version. New York: Zondervan, 1982.

Of course, MLA style is not the only way to document sources, though MLA style is widely used in the humanities. The author-date system and number system are similarly common methods of documentation. And many disciplines have their own documentation systems. For example, in the style recommended by the American Psychological Association (APA), a citation includes the date of publication and the abbreviation *p.* before the page number. Compare APA and MLA parenthetical citations for the same source:

APA: (Frye, 1957, p. 71)

MLA: (Frye 71)

In an entry in the works-cited list of APA style, the date in parenthesis immediately follows the author, whose first name is generally written as an initial, just the first word of the title is capitalized, and the publisher's full name is provided. The first line of the entry is indented, the second and subsequent lines are flush with the margin if the entry extends to two or more lines. By contrast, in an MLA entry, the author's name appears in full, every important word of the title is capitalized, the publisher's name is generally shortened, and the date of publication comes last. The first line of the entry is flush with the margin while the second and subsequent lines are indented. Compare APA and MLA for the same entry in the works-cited list:

APA:
Chamberlain, D. Frank. (1990). *Narrative perspective in fiction: a phenomenological meditation of reader, text, and world*. Toronto: University of Toronto Press.

MLA:
Chamberlain, Daniel Frank. *Narrative Perspective in Fiction: A Phenomenological Meditation of Reader, Text, and World*. Toronto: U of Toronto P, 1990.

However, still many writers use **footnotes** or **endnotes** in their research writings. The forms of footnotes and endnotes are similar except that, as the words indicate, they appear at the bottom of the page and at the end of the paper respectively. The rules for such notes are (1) they are numbered consecutively throughout the paper; (2) note numbers in the text come immediately after the information being cited and, if they should appear at the end of the sentence, after the punctuation; (3) note numbers should be raised about half a space above the line of words; and (4) no parentheses or other punctuation is placed around note numbers. In research papers, we suggest that endnotes be used. Endnotes have the advantage of providing enough space for a writer to insert any interesting information or noteworthy background that he/she thinks necessary but incongruous with the mainstream argument of the text, in addition to source reference. A judicious writer may even have a brief discussion on different ideas from various critics about a special point in an endnote. We call this kind of notes annotated notes or information notes.

Endnotes generally start on a new page numbered in sequence with the preceding page. Centre the title *Notes* one inch from the top, double-space, indent one-half inch (or five spaces) from the left margin, and add the note number (generally without punctuation) slightly above the line. Type a space and then the reference. If the note extends to two or more lines, begin the subsequent lines at the left margin. Here are a few examples (For samples of endnotes or footnotes for various sources, see Appendix III for reference):

[1] Northrop Frye, Anatomy of Criticism: Four Essays (Princeton: Princeton U P, 1957) 71.
[2] Cleanth Brooks, John T. Purser and Robert Penn Warren, eds., An Approach to Literature, 4th ed. (New York: Meredith, 1964) 348-50.
[3] Ibid, 198.

⁴ Wolfgang Iser, "Narrative Strategies as a Means of Communication," in Mario J. Valdés and Owen J. Miller (eds.), Interpretation of Narrative (Toronto: U of Toronto P, 1987) 38.

⁵ Thomas Hardy, Far from the Madding Crowd, ed. Ronald Blythe (Harmondsworth: Penguin, 1978), online, Oxford Text Archive, Internet, 24 Jan. 1994.

⁶ Louise Horton, "Who Reads Small Literary Magazines and What Good Do They Do?" Texas Review Spring/Summer 1984: 108.

⁷ Diane Elam, "Disciplining Woman: Feminism or Woman's Studies," in Surfaces 5. 101 (1995). 25 June 2008 ⟨http://tornade. ere. umontreal. ca: 80/∼ guedon/Surfaces/vol5/elam. html⟩.

⁸ Britannica Online, vers. 98. 2, Apr. 1998, Encyclopaedia Britannica, 8 May 1998 ⟨http//www. eb. com/⟩.

⁹ Joanne Merrian, "Spinoff: Monsterpiece Theatre," online posting, 30 Apr. 2006 ⟨http//www. arts. ubc. ca/english/iemls/shak-L. html⟩.

The final copy of a research paper should be clean, clear, conforming to norms, and without error. Although current software in our computers would check and even correct our errors in spelling and grammar while we are writing on a keyboard, it is worth our effort to check the paper for errors in grammar, usage, punctuation, capitalization, spelling, and manuscript form before we submit the final finished paper. This process of final checking belongs to the stage of proofreading. Here is a checklist containing the questions (suggested in Prentice Hall's *Literature*, 1989) for us to refer to while doing our proofreading. If our answer to any of the questions is no, we should make necessary correction on the revised draft:

CHECKLIST FOR PROOFREADING

Grammar and Usage

☐ Are all of my sentences complete? That is, have I avoided

sentence fragments?
- [ ] Does each of my sentences express only one complete thought? That is, have I avoided run-on sentences?
- [ ] Do the verbs I have used agree with their subjects?
- [ ] Have all the words in my paper been used correctly? Am I sure about the meanings of all of these words?
- [ ] Is the person or thing being referred to by each pronoun clear?
- [ ] Have I used adjectives and adverbs correctly?

Spelling
- [ ] Am I absolutely sure that each word has been spelled correctly?

Punctuation
- [ ] Does every sentence end with a punctuation mark?
- [ ] Have I correctly used commas, semicolons, colons, hyphens, dashes, parentheses, quotation marks, and apostrophes?

Capitalization
- [ ] Have I capitalized any words that should not be capitalized?
- [ ] Should I capitalize any words that I have not capitalized?

Manuscript Form
- [ ] Have I indented the first line(s) of my paragraph(s)?
- [ ] Have I written my name and the page number in the top right-hand corner of each page?
- [ ] Have I double-spaced the manuscript?
- [ ] Is my draft neat and legible?

In writing about a short story, we generally resort to a careful explication of it sentence by sentence or, even, word by word. **Explication** is a method involving patient unfolding of the relationships, ambiguities, and meanings of the words, images, symbols, and other literary elements in a work. It is one of the methods employed by the New Critics. A good explication dwells on details to reveal the larger meanings of the story, bringing readers' attention to what might have missed in their reading and to what is between the lines. Frequently, the method of explication is best suited to a paper that deals only with a short passage or a section of a story in relation with the story as a whole: an opening or a closing paragraph, a scene, a conversation, etc. Here is an explication, by a student, of a short passage in Edgar Allan Poe's "The Tell-Tale Heart" (recorded by Kennedy and Gioia, *Literature*, 1995). The passage occurs in the third paragraph of the story. To help us follow the explication, the student quotes it in full at the beginning of the paper.

By Lantern Light: An Explication of a Passage in "The Tell-Tale Heart"

And every night, about midnight, I turned the latch of his door and opened it—oh, so gently! And then, when I had made an opening sufficient for my head, I put in a dark lantern, all closed, closed, so that no light shone out, and then I thrust in my head. Oh, you would have laughed to see how cunningly I thrust it in! I moved it slowly—very, very slowly, so that I might not disturb the old man's sleep. It took me an hour to place my whole head within the opening so far that I could see him as he lay upon his bed. Ha! —would a madman have been so wise as this? And then, when my head was well in the room, I undid the lantern cautiously—oh, so cautiously—cautiously (for the hinges creaked)—I undid it just so much that a single thin ray fell upon the vulture eye. And this I did for seven long nights—every night just at midnight—but I found the eye always closed; and so it was impossible to do the work; for it was not the old man who vexed me, but his Evil Eye.

Chapter Ten

Although Poe has suggested in the first lines of his story that the person who addresses us is insane, it is only when we come to the speaker's account of his preparations for murdering the old man that we find his madness fully revealed. Even more convincingly than his earlier words (for we might possibly think that someone who claims to hear things in heaven and hell is a religious mystic), these preparations reveal him to be mad. What strikes us is that they are so elaborate and meticulous. A significant detail is the exactness of his schedule for spying: "every night just at midnight." The words with which he describes his motions also convey the most extreme care (and I will indicate them with italics): "how wisely I proceeded—with *what caution*," "I turned the latch of his door and opened it —oh, *so gently*!" "how *cunningly* I thrust [my head] in! I moved it *slowly, very slowly*." " I undid the lantern *cautiously*—oh, *so cautiously—cautiously*." Taking a whole hour to intrude his head into the room, he asks, "Ha! —would a madman be as wise as this?" But of course the word *wise* is unconsciously ironic, for clearly it is not wisdom the speaker displays, but an absurd degree of care, an almost fiendish ingenuity. Such behavior, I understand, is typical of certain mental illnesses. All his careful preparations that he thinks prove him sane only convince us instead that he is mad.

Obviously his behavior is self-defeating. He wants to catch the "vulture eye" open, and yet he takes all these pains not to disturb the old man's sleep. If he behaved logically, he might go barging into the bedroom with his lantern ablaze, shouting at the top of his voice. And yet, if we can see things his way, there *is* a strange logic to his reasoning. He regards the eye as a creature in itself, quite apart from its possessor. "It was not," he says, "the old man who vexed me, but his Evil Eye." Apparently, to be inspired to do his deed, the madman needs to behold the eye—at least, this is my understanding of his remark, "I found the eye always closed; and so it was impossible to do the work." Poe's choice of the word *work*, by the way, is also revealing. Murder is made to seem a duty or a job; and anyone who so regards murder is either extremely cold-blooded, like a hired killer for a gangland assassination, or else deranged. Besides, the word suggests again the curious sense of detachment that the speaker feels toward the owner of the eye.

In still another of his assumptions, the speaker shows that he is madly logical, or operating on the logic of a dream. There seems a dream-like relationship between his dark lantern "all closed, closed, so that no light shone out," and the sleeping victim. When the madman opens his lantern so that it emits a single ray, he is hoping that the eye in the old man's head will be open too, letting out its corresponding gleam. The latch that he turns so gently, too, seems like the eye, whose lid needs to be opened in order for the murderer to go ahead. It is as though the speaker is *trying* to get the eyelid to lift. By taking such great pains and by going through all this nightly ritual, he is practicing some kind of magic, whose rules are laid down not by our logic, but by the logic of dreams.

In this paper, rather than attempting to say something about everything in the selected passage from the story, the student only focuses her attention upon the details that strike her as most meaningful. In writing the paper, the student went by the following simple outline—a list of the points she wanted to explicate:

1. Speaker's extreme care and exactness—typical of some mental illnesses.
2. Speaker doesn't act by usual logic but by a crazy logic.
3. Dreamlike connection between latch & lantern and old man's eye.

The student follows the list in her writing, setting forth her ideas one at a time, one idea to a paragraph. She does not go through the passage sentence by sentence but freely takes up its details in whatever order she likes to suit her argument.

In writing a long research paper, we perhaps do not adhere to just one method all the way through. We may employ explication from time to time, especially when we want to unravel a knotty passage.

Sometimes we may write an essay of **comparison**, in which one thing is placed against another so that the points of likeliness and/or differences are brought to light for examination and/or evaluation. The methods of comparing and contrasting are fundamental to academic thinking. They not only serve as ways to present class material and information but also to elicit them—by comparing and contrasting we are forced to reconstruct and reevaluate what we have gathered from our reading of a story. We may be asked to write a paper of comparison with a title, say, "the Experience of Coming of Age in James Joyce's 'Araby' and William Faulkner's 'Barn Burning'" or "Compare the Mother Image in Katherine Anne Porter's 'The Jilting of Granny Weatherall' and Alice Walker's 'Everyday Use.'" Topics like these usually contain some germ of comparison. Once we have discovered that initial basis of comparison, we have taken the first strong step to write an effective essay. Even if we are asked to choose an essay topic on our own, thinking of comparison as one of the options open to us might plausibly kick off our train of thoughts in interesting and helpful ways, though the eventual essay may turn out not to be structured as a comparison. For example, a sense of comparison may spur us to ask ourselves to what extent something particular corresponds to something general: Does the story by Hemingway we have been assigned to write about go along with critics' general view about Hemingway's rigid ideal of masculinity?

Comparing is perhaps most intimately connected with classifying. In fact we can say that comparison depends on classification. At times we are comparing without a clear intent to do so, since someone else has done the classifying in advance. At times we only do the classifying in our mind instead of in our paper. Usually comparing helps us understand a story more clearly and look at it more freshly, since most things in fiction do have some similarities and thus they can be brought into some alignment for comparison. Comparing is useful as it is, however, a still more useful and common method of writing academic papers is analyzing (by the way, comparison may play an important role in analysis).

Analysis occurs whenever we look at something closely and selectively, interpreting what we see. Actually we have already written analytically if we have written anything about literature: if we have defined a word by examining some of the ways in which it is used; if we tried to interpret a short poem by moving through it seriously; if we have tried to say something about a group of images by sorting them into meaningful categories; and if we have attempted to summarize a story in our own words. However, in most academic situations, analysis is seldom a matter of mere looking and selecting, but rather how we look and what we select.

Supposing we are assigned to write an essay on a short story. We have read the story and have got some impression of it. We may have some idea about what to say. But we cannot hope to ground our analytical thinking on the sorts of impression or experience we have got. Without understanding of the assumptions, methods, and terminologies of literary criticism, we can hardly get very far in our analysis. If we are equipped with some learning in critical theories, we shall be on a surer ground. Of course, if we know something about the theories of other disciplines relevant to criticism of literature, we shall have fuller frameworks. After a speculation on the information we have gathered about the story, we may assume a hypothesis, or a point of view, to guide our analysis. For example, we might attempt to approach the social milieu of the story from a sociological perspective or a political perspective, or approach a character from a psychological perspective or an anthropological perspective.

Obviously, no one method can solve all the problems arising from our reading of a story; no one essay can include everything of a story; and no one element of a story presents itself in complete isolation from the story's other elements. Therefore, in our essay, even a long one, we should focus our analysis upon one or two points that most interest us and at the same time approach these points with a look at other aspects that are related to them. And we can use one method to analyze this point and another to analyze that point. For example, In "The Tell-Tale Heart," the insanity of the character apparently makes it necessary to tell the story from a special point of view and becomes the important factor that results in the author's choice of theme, setting, tone, style, and ironies (Kennedy and Gioia, *Literature*, 1995). But it would be messy and confusing to lay a finger on all those aspects in a paper. Thus, when we write an analysis, we generally study just one aspect and suggest its relation to the whole story. The following is an analysis of "The Tell-Tale Heart" by a student, dealing with just one aspect—the story's point of view, which, though contain-ing no insight so fresh as the suggestion that the madman's lantern is like the old man's head (made in the previous paper), convinces us that he understands not only the story's point of view, but also the story as a whole.

The Hearer of the Tell-Tale Heart

Although there are many things we do not know about the narrator of Edgar Allan Poe's story "The Tell-Tale

Heart" —is he a son? a servant? a companion? —there is one thing we are sure of from the start. He is mad. In the opening paragraph, Poe makes the narrator's condition unmistakable, not only from his excited and worked-up speech (full of dashes and exclamation points), but also from his wild claims. He says it is merely some disease which has sharpened his senses that has made people call him crazy. Who but a madman, however, would say, "I heard all things in the heaven and in the earth," and brag how his ear is a kind of CB radio, listening in on Hell? Such a statement leaves no doubt that the point of view in the story is an ironic one.

Because the participating narrator is telling his story in the first person, some details in the story stand out more than others. When the narrator goes on to tell how he watches the old man sleeping, he rivets his attention on the old man's "vulture eye." When a ray from his lantern finds the Evil Eye open, he says, "I could see nothing else of the old man's face or person." Actually, the reader can see almost nothing else about the old man anywhere in the rest of the story. All we are told is that the old man treated the younger man well, and we gather that the old man was rich, because his house is full of treasures. We do not have a clear idea of what the old man looks like, though, nor do we know how he talks, for we are not given any of his words. Our knowledge of him is mainly confined to his eye and its effect on the narrator. This confinement gives that symbolic eye a lot of importance in the story. The narrator tells us all we know and directs our attention to parts of it.

This point of view raises an interesting question. Since we are dependent on the narrator for all our information, how do we know the whole story isn't just a nightmare in his demented mind? We have really no way to be sure it isn't, as far as I can see. I assume, however, that there really is a dark shuttered house and an old man and real policemen who start snooping around when screams are heard in the neighborhood, because it is a more memorable story if it is a crazy man's view of reality than if it is all just a terrible dream. But we can't take stock in the madman's interpretation of what happens. Poe keeps putting distances between what the narrator says and what we are supposed to think, apparently. For instance: the narrator has boasted that he is calm and clear in the head, but as soon as he starts (in the second paragraph) trying to explain why he killed the old man, we gather that he is confused, to say the least. "I think it was his eye!" the narrator exclaims, as if not quite sure. As he goes on to explain how he conducted the murder, we realize that he is a man with a fixed idea working with a patience that is certainly mad, almost diabolical.

Some readers might wonder if "The Tell-Tale Heart" is a story of the supernatural. Is the heartbeat that the narrator hears a ghost come back to haunt him? Here, I think, the point of view is our best guide to what to believe. The simple explanation for the heartbeat is this: it is all in the madman's mind. Perhaps he feels such guilt that he starts hearing things. Another explanation is possible, one suggested by Daniel Hoffman, a critic who has discussed the story: the killer hears the sound of his own heart.* Hoffman's explanation (which I don't like as well as mine) also is a natural one, and it fits the story as a whole. Back when the narrator first entered the old man's bedroom to kill him, the heartbeat sounded so loud to him that he was afraid the neighbors would hear it too. Evidently they didn't, and so Hoffman may be right in thinking that the sound was only that of his own heart pounding in his ears. Whichever explanation you take, it is a more down-to-earth and reasonable explanation than that (as the narrator believes) the heart is still alive, even though its owner has been cut to pieces. Then, too, the police keep chatting. If they heard the heartbeat too, wouldn't they leap to their feet, draw their guns, and look all around the room? As the author has kept showing us in the rest of the story, the narrator's view of things is untrustworthy. You don't kill someone just because you dislike the look in his eye. You don't think that such a murder is funny. For all its Gothic atmosphere of the old dark house with a secret hidden inside, "The Tell-Tale Heart" is not a ghost story. We have only to see its point of view to know it is a study in abnormal psychology.

* Poe Poe Poe Poe Poe Poe Poe (New York: Anchor, 1973), 227.

Appendix I

Why Do We Read Fiction?

by Robert Penn Warren, 1964

  Why do we read fiction? The answer is simple. We read it because we like it. And we like it because fiction, as an image of life, stimulates and gratifies our interest in life. But whatever interests may be appealed to by fiction, the special and immediate interest that takes us to fiction is always our interest in a story.

  A story is not merely an image of life, but of life in motion—specifically, the presentation of individual characters moving through their particular experiences to some end that we may accept as meaningful. And the experience that is characteristically presented in a story is that of facing a problem, a conflict. To put it bluntly: No conflict, no story.

  It is no wonder that conflict should be at the center of fiction, for conflict is at the center of life. But why should we, who have the constant and often painful experience of conflict in life and who yearn for inner peace and harmonious relation with the outer world, turn to fiction, which is the image of conflict? The fact is that our attitude toward conflict is ambivalent. If we do find a totally satisfactory adjustment in life, we tend to sink into the drowse of the accustomed. Only when our surroundings—or we ourselves—become problematic again do we wake up and feel that surge of energy which is life. And life more abundantly lived is what we seek.

So we, at the same time that we yearn for peace, yearn for the problematic. The adventurer, the sportsman, the gambler, the child playing hide-and-seek, the teen-age boys choosing up sides for a game of sandlot baseball, the old grad cheering in the stadium—we all, in fact, seek out or create problematic situations of greater or lesser intensity. Such situations give us a sense of heightened energy, of life. And fiction, too, gives us that heightened awareness of life, with all the fresh, uninhibited opportunity to vent the rich emotional charge—tears, laughter, tenderness, sympathy, hate, love, and irony—that is stored up in us and short-circuited in the drowse of the accustomed. Furthermore, this heightened awareness can be more fully relished now, because what in actuality would be the threat of the problematic is here tamed to mere imagination, and because some kind of resolution of the problem is, owing to the very nature of fiction, promised.

The story promises us a resolution, and we wait in suspense to learn how things will come out. We are in suspense, not only about what will happen, but even more about what the event will mean. We are in suspense about the story in fiction because we are in suspense about another story far closer and more important to us—the story of our own life as we live it. We do not know how that story of our own life is going to come out. We do not know what it will mean. So, in that deepest suspense of life, which will be shadowed in the suspense we feel about the story in fiction, we turn to fiction for some slight hint about the story in the life we live. The relation of our life to the fictional life is what, in a fundamental sense, takes us to fiction.

Even when we read, as we say, to "escape," we seek to escape not from life but to life, to a life more satisfying than our own drab version. Fiction gives us an image of life—sometimes of a life we actually have and like to dwell on, but often and poignantly of one we have had but do not have now, or one we have never had and can never have. The ardent fisherman, when his rheumatism keeps him housebound, reads stories from *Field and Stream*. The

Appendix I

baseball fan reads *You Know Me, Al*, by Ring Lardner. The little coed, worrying about her snub nose and her low mark in Sociology 2, dreams of being a debutante out of F. Scott Fitzgerald; and the thin-chested freshman, still troubled by acne, dreams of being a granite-jawed Neanderthal out of Mickey Spillane. When the Parthians in 53 B. C. beat Crassus, they found in the baggage of Roman officers some very juicy items called *Milesian Tales*, by a certain Aristides of Miletus; and I have a friend who in A. D. 1944, supplemented his income as a GI by reading aloud *Forever Amber*, by a certain Kathleen Winsor, to buddies who found that the struggle over three-syllable words somewhat impaired their dedication to that improbable daydream.

And that is what, for all of us, fiction, in one sense, is—a daydream. It is, in other words, an imaginative enactment. In it we find, in imagination, not only the pleasure of recognizing the world we know and of reliving our past, but also the pleasure of entering worlds we do not know and of experimenting with experiences which we deeply crave but which the limitations of life, the fear of consequences, or the severity of our principles forbid to us. Fiction can give us this pleasure without any painful consequences, for there is no price tag on the magic world of imaginative enactment. But fiction does not give us only what we want; more importantly, it may give us things we hadn't even known we wanted.

In this sense then, fiction painlessly makes up for the defects of reality. Long ago Francis Bacon said that poetry—which, in his meaning, would include our fiction—is "agreeable to the spirit of man" because it affords "a greater grandeur of things, a more perfect order, and a more beautiful variety" than can "anywhere be found in nature. ..." More recently we find Freud putting it that the "meagre satisfactions" that man "can extract from reality leave him starving," and John Dewey saying that art "was born of need, lack, deprivation, incompleteness." But philosophers aside, we all know entirely too well how much we resemble poor Walter Mitty[1].

If fiction is—as it clearly is for some readers—merely a fantasy to redeem the liabilities of our private fate, it is flight from reality and therefore the enemy of growth, of the life process. But is it necessarily this? Let us look at the matter in another way.

The daydream which is fiction differs from the ordinary daydream in being publicly available. This fact leads to consequences. In the private daydream you remain yourself—though nobler, stronger, more fortunate, more beautiful than in life. But when the little freshman settles cozily with his thriller by Mickey Spillane, he finds that the granite-jawed hero is not named Slim Willett, after all—as poor Slim, with his thin chest, longs for it to be. And Slim's college instructor, settling down to *For Whom the Bell Tolls*, finds sadly that this other college instructor who is the hero of the famous tale of sleeping bags, bridge demolition, tragic love and lonely valor, is named Robert Jordan.

In other words, to enter into that publicly available daydream which fiction is, you have to accept the fact that the name of the hero will never be your own; you will have to surrender something of your own identity to him, have to let it be absorbed in him. But since that kind of daydream is not exquisitely custom-cut to the exact measure of your secret longings, the identification can never be complete. In fact, only a very naïve reader tries to make it thrillingly complete. The more sophisticated reader plays a deep double game with himself; one part of him is identified with a character—or with several in turn—while another part holds aloof to respond, interpret and judge. How often have we heard some sentimental old lady say of a book: "I just loved the heroine—I mean I just went through everything with her and I knew exactly how she felt. Then when she died I just cried." The sweet old lady, even if she isn't very sophisticated, is instinctively playing

[1] Walter Mitty: the main character in J. Thurber's *The Secret Life of Walter Mitty*.

the double game too: She identifies herself with the heroine, but she survives the heroine's death to shed the delicious tears. So even the old lady knows how to make the most of what we shall call her role-taking. She knows that doubleness, in the very act of identification, is of the essence of role-taking: There is the taker of the role and there is the role taken. And fiction is, in imaginative enactment, a role-taking.

For some people—those who fancy themselves hardheaded and realistic—the business of role-taking is as reprehensible as indulgence in a daydream. But in trying to understand our appetite for fiction, we can see that the process of role-taking not only stems from but also affirms the life process. It is an essential part of growth.

Role-taking is, for instance, at the very center of children's play. This is the beginning of the child's long process of adaptation to others, for only by feeling himself into another person's skin can the child predict behavior; and the stakes in the game are high, for only thus does he learn whether to expect the kiss or the cuff. In this process of role-taking we find, too, the roots of many of the massive intellectual structures we later rear—most obviously psychology and ethics, for it is only by role-taking that the child comes to know, to know "inwardly" in the only way that finally counts, that other people really exist and are, in fact, persons with needs, hopes, fears and even rights. So the role-taking of fiction, at the same time that it gratifies our deep need to extend and enrich our own experience, continues this long discipline in human sympathy. And this discipline in sympathy, through the imaginative enactment of role-taking, gratifies another need deep in us: our yearning to enter and feel at ease in the human community.

Play when we are children, and fiction when we are grown up, lead us, through role-taking, to an awareness of others. But all along the way role-taking leads us, by the same token, to an awareness of ourselves; it leads us, in fact, to the creation of the self. For the individual is not born with a self. He is born as a mysterious bundle of possibilities which, bit by bit, in a long process of trial and error, he sorts out until he gets some sort of unifying self, the ringmaster self, the official self.

The official self emerges, but the soul, as Plato long ago put it, remains full of "ten thousand opposites occurring at the same time," and modern psychology has said nothing to contradict him. All our submerged selves, the old desires and possibilities, are lurking deep in us, sleepless and eager to have another go. There is knife-fighting in the inner dark. The fact that most of the time we are not aware of trouble does not mean that trouble is any the less present and significant; and fiction, most often in subtly disguised forms, liberatingly reenacts for us such inner conflict. We feel the pleasure of liberation even when we cannot specify the source of the pleasure.

Fiction brings up from their dark oubliettes our shadowy, deprived selves and gives them an airing in, as it were, the prison yard. They get a chance to participate, each according to his nature, in the life which fiction presents. When in Thackeray's *Vanity Fair* the girl Becky Sharp, leaving school for good, tosses her copy of Doctor Johnson's *Dictionary* out of the carriage, something in our own heart leaps gaily up, just as something rejoices at her later sexual and pecuniary adventures in Victorian society, and suffers, against all our sense of moral justice, when she comes a cropper. When Holden Caulfield, of Salinger's *Catcher in the Rye*, undertakes his gallant and absurd little crusade against the "phony" in our world, our own nigh-doused idealism flares up again, for the moment without embarrassment. When in Faulkner's *Light in August* Percy Grimm pulls the trigger of the black, blunt-nosed automatic and puts that tight, pretty little pattern of slugs in the top of the overturned table behind which Joe Christmas cowers, our trigger finger tenses, even while, at the same time, with a strange joy of release and justice satisfied, we feel those same slugs in our heart. When we read Dostoevski's

Appendix I

Crime and Punishment, something in our nature participates in the bloody deed, and later, something else in us experiences, with the murderer Raskolnikov, the bliss of repentance and reconciliation.

For among our deprived selves we must confront the redeemed as well as the damned, the saintly as well as the wicked; and strangely enough, either confrontation may be both humbling and strengthening. In having some awareness of the complexity of self we are better-prepared to deal with that self. As a matter of fact, our entering into the fictional process helps to redefine this dominant self—even, as it were, to recreate, on a sounder basis— sounder because better understood—that dominant self, the official "I." As Henri Bergson says, fiction "brings us back into our own presence"—the presence in which we must make our final terms with life and death.

The knowledge in such confrontations does not come to us with intellectual labels. We don't say, "Gosh, I've got 15 percent of sadism in me"—or 13 percent of unsuspected human charity. No, the knowledge comes as enactment; and as imaginative enactment, to use our old phrase, it comes as knowledge. It comes, rather, as a heightened sense of being, as the conflict in the story evokes the conflict in ourselves, evokes it with some hopeful sense of meaningful resolution, and with, therefore, an exhilarating sense of freedom.

Part of this sense of freedom derives, to repeat ourselves, from the mere fact that in imagination we are getting off scot-free with something which we, or society, would never permit in real life; from the fact that our paradoxical relation to experience presented in fiction—our involvement and noninvolvement at the same time—gives a glorious feeling of mastery over the game of life. But there is something more important that contributes to this sense of freedom, the expansion and release that knowledge always brings; and in fiction we are permitted to know in the deepest way, by imaginative participation, things we would otherwise never know—including ourselves. We are free from the Garden curse: We may eat of the Tree of Knowledge, and no angel with flaming sword will appear.

But in the process of imaginative enactment we have, in another way, that sense of freedom that comes from knowledge. The image that fiction presents is purged of the distractions, confusions and accidents of ordinary life. We can now gaze at the inner logic of things—of a personality, of the consequences of an act or a thought, of a social or historical situation, of a lived life. One of our deepest cravings is to find logic in experience, but in real life how little of our experience comes to us in such a manageable form!

We have all observed how a person who has had a profound shock needs to tell the story of the event over and over again, every detail. By telling it he objectifies it, disentangling himself, as it were, from the more intolerable effects. This objectifying depends, partly at least, on the fact that the telling is a way of groping for the logic of the event, and attempt to make the experience intellectually manageable. If a child—or a man—who is in a state of blind outrage at his fate can come to understand that the fate which had seemed random and gratuitous is really the result of his own previous behavior or is part of the general pattern of life, his emotional response is modified by that intellectual comprehension. What is intellectually manageable is, then, more likely to be emotionally manageable.

This fiction is a "telling" in which we as readers participate and is, therefore, an image of the process by which experience is made manageable. In this process experience is foreshortened, is taken out of the ruck of time, is put into an ideal time where we can scrutinize it, is given an interpretation. In other words, fiction shows, as we have said, a logical structure which implies a meaning. By showing a logical structure, it relieves us, for the moment at least, of what we sometimes feel as the greatest and most mysterious threat of life—the threat of the imminent but "unknowable," of the urgent but "unsayable." Insofar as a piece of fiction is original and not merely a conventional repetition of the known and predictable, it is a movement through the "unknowable" toward the "knowable"—the imaginatively knowable. It says the "unsayable."

This leads us, as a sort of aside, to the notion that fiction sometimes seems to be, for the individual or for society, prophetic. Now looking back we can clearly see how Melville, Dostoevski, James, Proust, Conrad and Kafka tried to deal with some of the tensions and problems which have become characteristic of our time. In this sense they foretold our world—and even more importantly, forefelt it. They even forefelt us.

Or let us remember that F. Scott Fitzgerald and Hemingway did not merely report a period, they predicted it in that they sensed a new mode of behavior and feeling. Fiction, by seizing on certain elements in its time and imaginatively pursuing them with the unswerving logic of projected enactment, may prophesy the next age. We know this from looking back on fiction of the past. More urgently we turn to fiction of our own time to help us envisage the time to come and our relation to it.

But let us turn to more specific instances of that inner logic which fiction may reveal. In *An American Tragedy* Dreiser shows us in what subtle and pitiful ways the materialism of America and the worship of what William James called the "bitch-goddess Success" can corrupt an ordinary young man and bring him to the death cell. In *Madame Bovary* Flaubert shows us the logic by which Emma's yearning for color and meaning in life leads to the moment when she gulps the poison. In both novels we sense this logic most deeply because we, as we have seen, are involved, are accomplices. We, too, worship the bitch-goddess—as did Dreiser. We, too, have yearnings like Emma's, and we remember that Flaubert said that he himself was Emma Bovary.

We see the logic of the enacted process, and we also see the logic of the end. Not only do we have now, as readers, the freedom that leads to a knowledge of the springs of action; we have also the more difficult freedom that permits us to contemplate the consequences of action and the judgment that may be passed on it. For judgment, even punishment, is the end of the logic we perceive. In our own personal lives, as we well know from our endless secret monologues of extenuation and alibi, we long to escape from judgment; but here, where the price tag is only that of imaginative involvement, we can accept judgment. We are reconciled to the terrible necessity of judgment—upon our surrogate self in the story, our whipping boy and scapegoat. We find a moral freedom in this fact that we recognize a principle of justice, with also perhaps some gratification of the paradoxical desire to suffer.

It may be objected here that we speak as though all stories were stories of crime and punishment. No, but all stories, from the gayest farce to the grimmest tragedy, are stories of action and consequence—which amounts to the same thing. All stories, as we have said, are based on conflict; and the resolution of the fictional conflict is, in its implications, a judgment too, a judgment of values. In the end some shift of values has taken place. Some new awareness has dawned, some new possibility of attitude has been envisaged.

Not that the new value is necessarily "new" in a literal sense. The point, to come back to an old point, is that the reader has, by imaginative enactment, lived through the process by which the values become valuable. What might have been merely an abstraction has become vital, has been lived, and is, therefore, "new"—new because newly experienced. We can now rest in the value as experienced; we are reconciled in it, and that is what counts.

It is what counts, for in the successful piece of fiction, a comic novel by Peter de Vries or a gut-tearing work like Tolstoy's *War and Peace*, we feel, in the end, some sense of reconciliation with the world and with ourselves. And this process of moving through conflict to reconciliation is an echo of our own life process. The life process, as we know it from babyhood on, from our early relations with our parents on to our adult relation with the world, is a long process of conflict and reconciliation. This process of enriching and deepening experience is a pattern of oscillation—a pattern resembling that of the lovers' quarrel: When lovers quarrel, each asserts his special ego against that of the beloved and then in the moment of making up finds more keenly than before the joy of losing the self in the love of another. So in fiction we enter imaginatively a situation of difficulty and estrangement—a problematic situation that, as we said earlier, sharpens our awareness of life—and move through it to a reconciliation which seems fresh and sweet.

Reconciliation—that is what we all, in some depth of being, want. All religion, all philosophy, all psychiatry, all ethics involve this human fact. And so does fiction. If fiction begins in daydream, if it springs from the cramp of the world, if it relieves us from the burden of being ourselves, it ends, if it is good fiction and we are good readers, by returning us to the world and to ourselves. It reconciles us with reality.

Let us pause to take stock. Thus far what we have said sounds as though fiction were a combination of opium addiction, religious conversion without tears, a home course in philosophy and the poor man's psychoanalysis. But it is not; it is fiction.

It is only itself, and that *itself* is not, in the end, a mere substitute for anything else. It is an art—an image of experience formed in accordance with its own laws of imaginative enactment, laws which, as we have seen, conform to our deep needs. It is an "illusion of life" projected through language, and the language is that of some individual man projecting his own feeling of life.

The story, in the fictional sense, is not something that exists of and by itself, out in the world like a stone or a tree. The materials of stories—certain events or characters, for example—may exist out in the world, but they are not fictionally meaningful to us until a human mind has shaped them. We are, in other words, like the princess in one of Hans Christian Andersen's tales; she refuses her suitor when she discovers that the bird with a ravishing song which he has offered as a token of love is only a real bird after all. We, like the princess, want an artificial bird—an artificial bird with a real song. So we go to fiction because it is a *created* thing.

Because it is created by a man, it draws us, as human beings, by its human significance. To begin with, it is an utterance, in words. No words, no story. This seems a fact so obvious, and so trivial, as not to be worth the saying, but it is of fundamental importance in the appeal fiction has for us. We are creatures of words, and if we did not have words we would have no inner life. Only because we have words can we envisage and think about experience. We find our human nature through words. So in one sense we may say that insofar as the language of the story enters into the expressive whole of the story we find the deep satisfaction, conscious or unconscious, of a fulfillment of our very nature.

As an example of the relation of words, of style, to the expressive whole which is fiction, let us take Hemingway. We readily see how the stripped, laconic, monosyllabic style relates to the tight-lipped, stoical ethic, the cult of self-discipline, the physicality and the anti-intellectualism and the other such elements that enter into his characteristic view of the world. Imagine Henry James writing Hemingway's story *The Killers*. The complicated sentence structure of James, the deliberate and subtle rhythms, the careful parentheses—all these things express the delicate intellectual, social and aesthetic discriminations with which James concerned himself. But what in the Lord's name would they have to do with the shocking blankness of the moment when the gangsters enter the lunchroom, in their tight-buttoned identical blue overcoats, with gloves on their hands so as to leave no fingerprints when they kill the Swede?

The style of a writer represents his stance toward experience, toward the subject of his story; and it is also the very flesh of our experience of the story, for it is the flesh of our experience as we read. Only through his use of words does the story come to us.

And with language, so with the other aspects of a work of fiction. Everything there—the proportioning of plot, the relations among the characters, the logic of motivation, the speed or retardation of the movement—is formed by a human mind into what it is, into what, if the fiction is successful, is an expressive whole, a speaking pattern, a form. And in recognizing and participating in this form, we find a gratification, though often an unconscious one, as fundamental as any we have mentioned.

We get a hint of the fundamental nature of this gratification in the fact that among primitive peoples decorative patterns are developed long before the first attempts to portray the objects of nature, even those things on which the life of the tribe depended. The pattern images a rhythm of life and intensifies the tribesman's sense of life.

Or we find a similar piece of evidence in psychological studies made of the response of children to comic books. "It is not the details of development," the researchers tell us, "but rather the general aura which the child finds fascinating." What the child wants is the formula of the accelerating buildup of tension followed by the glorious release when the righteous Superman appears just in the nick of time. What the child wants, then, is a certain "shape" of experience. Is his want, at base, different from our own?

At base, no. But if the child is satisfied by a nearly abstract pattern for the feelings of tension and release, we demand much more. We, too, in the build and shape of experience, catch the echo of the basic rhythm of our life. But we know that the world is infinitely more complicated than the child thinks. We, unlike the child, must scrutinize the details of development, the contents of life and of fiction. So the shaping of experience to satisfy us must add to the simplicity that satisfies the child something of the variety, roughness, difficulty, subtlety and delight which belongs to the actual business of life and our response to it. We want the factual richness of life absorbed into the pattern so that content and form are indistinguishable in one expressive flowering in the process that John Dewey says takes "life and experience in all its uncertainties, mystery, doubt and half-knowledge and turns that experience upon itself to deepen and intensify its own qualities." Only then will it satisfy our deepest need—the need of feeling our life to be, in itself, significant.

Appendix II

How I Write

by Eudora Welty

"HOW do I write my stories?" is a blessedly open question. For the writer it is forever in the course of being studied through doing and new doing, and wouldn't last very long as a matter of selfobservation, which could very well turn him to stone. Apart from what he's learned about his separate stories, out of passion, the renewable passion, of doing each in the smallest part better (at least nearer the way he wants it), he may or may not be a good judge of his work in the altogether. To him if a story is good enough to be called finished, as far as he can see, it is detached on the dot from the hand that wrote it, and the luster goes with it; what *is* attached is the new story. "How I wrote," past tense, may be seen into from this detachment, but not with the same insight — that too is gone, displaced. Looking backward can't compete with looking forward with the story in progress — that invites and absorbs and uses every grain of his insight, and his love and wits and curiosity and strength of purpose. "How do I write *this* story?" is really the question, the vital question; but its findings can be set down only in terms of the story's own — terms of fiction. (At least, ordinarily. Story writing and an independently operating power of critical analysis are separate gifts, like spelling and playing the flute, and one person proficient in both has been doubly endowed. But even he can't rise and do both at the same time.)

I feel myself that any *generalization* about writing is remote from anything I have managed to learn about it. I believe I can make one wide one, and others must have often nailed it down, but I shall have to hold my blow till I get there. The only things I feel I really know well are stuck to the stories, part of the animal. The main lesson I've learned from work so far is the simple one that each story is going to open up a different prospect and pose a new problem; no story bears on another or helps another, even if the writing mind had room for help and the wish that it would come. Help would be a blight. I could add that it's hard for me to think that a writer's stories are a unified whole in any respect except perhaps their lyric quality. I don't believe they are written in any typical, predictable, logically developing, or even chronological way (for all that a good writer's stories are, to the reader, so immediately identifiable as his) — or in any way that after enough solid tries guarantees him a certain measure of excellence, safety (spare the word!), or delight.

I do have the feeling that all stories by one writer tend to spring from the same source within him. However they differ in subject or approach, however they vary in excellence or fluctuate in their power to alter the mind or mood or move the heart, all of one writer's stories must take on their quality, carry their signature, because of one characteristic, lyrical impulse of his mind — the impulse to praise, to love, to call up, to prophesy. But then what countless stories share a common source! All writers write out of the same few, few and eternal — love, pity, terror do not change.

Sources of stories could be examined with less confusion, perhaps, not in the subjective terms of emotion, but through finding what in the outside world leads back to those emotions most directly and tautly and specifically. The surest clue is the pull on the line, the "inspiration," the outside signal that has startled or moved the creative mind to complicity and brought the story to active being: the irresistible, the magnetic, the alarming (pleasurable or disturbing), the overwhelming person, place, or

Appendix II

thing.

Surely, for the writer this is the world where stories come from, and where their origins are living reference plain to his eyes. The dark changes of the mind and heart, where all in the world is constantly *becoming* something — the poetic, the moral, the passionate, hence the *shaping* idea — are not mapped and plotted yet, except as psychiatry has applied the healing or tidying hand, and their being so would make no change in their processes, or their climates, or their way of life and death (any more than a map hung on the wall changes the world); or schedule or pigeonhole or allot or substitute or predict the mysteries rushing unsubmissively through them by the minute; or explain a single work of art that came out the other side. The artist at work functions, while whoever likes to may explain how he does it (or failing that, why) — without, however, the least power of prevention or prophecy or even cure — for some alarmists say that literature has come out of a disease of society, as if stamping out the housefly would stop it, and I've heard there's another critic who says writing is nothing but the death wish. (Exactly where in all this *standards* come in I don't know.)

It is of course the *way* of writing that gives a story, however humble, its whole distinction and glory — something learned, and learned each writer for himself, by dint of each story's unique challenge and his work that rises to meet it — work scrupulous, questioning, unprecedented, ungeneralized, uncharted, and his own. It is the changeable outside world and the learnable way of writing that are the different quotients. Always different, always differing, from writer to writer and story to story, they are — or so I believe — most intimately connected with each other.

Like a good many other writers, I am myself touched off by place. The place where I am and the place I know, and other places that familiarity with and love for my own make strange and lovely and enlightening to look into, are what set me to writing my stories. To such writers I suppose place opens a door in the mind;

either spontaneously or through beating it down, attrition. The impression of place as revealing something is an indelible one — which of course is not to say it isn't highly personal and very likely distorted. The imagination further and further informs and populates the impression according to present mood, intensification of feeling, beat of memory, accretion of idea, and by the blessing of being located — contained — a story so changed is now capable of being written.

The connection of this to what's called regional writing is clear but not much more informing; it does mean a lot of writers behave the same way. Regional writing itself has old deep roots; it is not the big root itself. Place is surely one of the most simple and obvious and direct sources of the short story, and one of the most ancient — as it is of lyric poetry — and, if I may presume to speak freely here for other regional writers too, the connection of story to place can go for ever so long not even conscious in the mind, because taken for granted. The regional writer's vision is as surely made of the local clay as any mud pie of his childhood was, and it's still the act of the imagination that makes the feast; only in the case of any art the feast is real, for the act of the imagination gives vision the substance and makes it last.

After we see the connection between our place and our writing, has anything changed for us? We aren't admonished in any way we weren't admonished already by pride of work, surely? Yes, something *has* changed for us; we learn that. I am the proud partisan I am of regional writing because this connection between place and story *is* deep, *does* take time, and its claims on us are deep; they, like our own mind's responsibilities, are for us to find out. To be a regional writer is not like belonging to a club or a political party; it is nothing you can take credit for — it's an endowment, but more than that. It's touchstone when you write, and shows up, before anything else does, truth and mistakes. In a way place is your honor as it is your wisdom, and would make you responsible to it for what you put down for the truth.

Appendix II

Whatever the story a reader takes up, the road from origin on isn't any the plainer for the simplicity of the start. Sometimes a reader thinks he is "supposed" to see in a story (I judge from letters from readers when they can't find it in mine) a sort of plant-from-seed development, rising in the end to a perfect Christmas tree of symmetry, branch, and ornament, with a star at the top for neatness. The reader of more willing imagination, who has specified for something else, may find the branchings not what he's expecting either, and the fulfillment not a perfect match, not at all to the letter of the promise — rather to a degree — (and to a degree of pleasure) mysterious. This is one of the short story's finest attributes. The analyst, should the story come under his eye, may miss this gentle shock and this pleasure too, for he's picked up the story at once by its heels (as if it had swallowed a button) and is examining the writing as his own process in reverse, as though a story (or any system of feeling) could be the more accessible to understanding for being hung upside down. "Sweet Analytics, 'tis thou hast ravish'd me!"

Analysis, to speak generally, has to travel backwards; the path it goes, while paved with good intentions, is an ever-narrowing one, whose goal is the vanishing point, beyond which only "influences" lie. But writing, bound in the opposite direction, works further and further always into the open. The choices get freer and wider, apparently, as with everything else that has a life and moves. "This story promises me fear and joy and so I write it" has been the writer's honest beginning. Dr. Faustus, the critic, coming to the end of his trail, may call out the starting point he's found, but the writer long ago knew the starting point for what it was to him — the jumping off place. If they coincide, it's a coincidence. I think the writer's out-bound choices seem obstructive sometimes to analysts simply because they wouldn't be there if they weren't plain evidence that they were to the writer inevitable choices, not arguable; impelled, not manipulated; that they came with an arrow inside them. Indeed they have been *fiction's* choices: one-way and fateful; strict as art, obliged as feeling, powerful in their authenticity though for slightest illusion's sake; and reasonable (in the out-of-fiction sense) only last, and by the grace of, again, coincidence — always to be welcomed and shown consideration, but never to be courted or flattered.

Certainly a story and its analysis are not the mirror opposites of each other, for all their running off in opposite directions. Criticism can be an art too and may go deeper than its object, and more times around; it may pick up a story and waltz with it, so that it's never the same. In any case it's not a reflection. But I think that's exactly why it cannot be *used* as one, whoever holds it up, even the curious author; why it's a mistake to think you can stalk back a story by analysis's footprints and even dream that's the original coming through the woods. Besides the difference in the direction of the two, there's the difference in speeds, when one has fury; but the main difference is in world-surround. One surround is a vision and the other is a pattern for good visions (which — who knows! — fashion may have tweaked a little) or the nicest, carefullest black-and-white tracing that a breath of life would do for. Each, either, or neither may be a masterpiece of construction; but the products are not to be confused.

The story is a vision; while it's being written, all choices must be its choices, and as these multiply upon one another, their field is growing too. The choices remain inevitable, in fact, through moving in a growing maze of possibilities that the writer, far from being dismayed at his presence on unknown ground (which might frighten him as a critic) has learned to be grateful for, and excited by. The fiction writer has learned (and here is my generalization) that it is the very existence, the very multitude and clamor and threat and lure of *possibility* — all possibilities his work calls up for itself as it goes — that guide his story most delicately. In the act of writing he finds, if no explanation outside fiction for what he is doing, or the need of it, no mystery about it either. What he does know is the word comes surest out of too much, not too little — just as the most exacting and sometimes the simplest-appearing work is brought off (when it does not fail) on the sharp edge of experiment, not in dim, reneging safety. He is not at the end yet, but it was for this he left all he knew behind, at the jumping off place, when he started this new story.

II

I made the remark above that I believed the changeable outside world and the learnable way of writing are connected with each other. I think it is this connection that can be specifically looked at in any story, but maybe a regional story could give us the easiest time. I offer here the clearest example I could find among my own stories of the working point I am hoping to make, since place not only suggested how to write the story but repudiated a way I had already tried it.

What happened was that I was invited to drive with a friend down south of New Orleans one summer day, to see that country for the first (and only) time, and when I got back home I realized that without being aware of it at the time I had treated a story, which I was working on then, to my ride, and it had come into my head in an altogether new form. I set to work and wrote the new version from scratch, which resulted in my throwing away the first and using the second. I learned all the specific detail of this story from the ride, though I should add that the story in neither version had any personal connection with myself and there was no conscious "gathering of material" on a pleasant holiday.

As first written, the story told, from the inside, of a girl in a claustrophobic predicament: she was caught fast in the over-familiar, monotonous life of her small town, and immobilized further by a hopeless and inarticulate love, which she had to pretend was something else. This happens all the time. As a result of my ride I extracted her. But she had been well sealed inside her world, by nature and circumstance both, and even more closely by my knowing her too well (the story had gone on too long) and too confidently. Before I could prize her loose, I had to take a primary step of getting outside her mind. I made her a girl from the Middle West — she'd been what I knew best, a Southerner, before. I kept outside her by taking glimpses of her through the curious eyes of a stranger; instead of the half-dozen characters (I knew them too well too) from the first version, I put in one single new one — a man whom I brought into the story *to be* a stranger. I had double-locked the doors behind me — you never dream the essentials can be simple again, within one story.

But the vital thing that happened to the story came from writing, as I began the work. My first realization of what it was came when I looked back and recognized that country (the once-submerged, strange land of "south from South" that had so stamped itself upon my imagination) as the image to me of the story's predicament come to life. This pointed out to me, as I wrote into the story, where the real point of view belonged. Once I was outside, I saw *it* was outside — suspended, hung in the air between the two people, fished alive from the surrounding scene, where as it carried the story along it revealed itself (I hoped) as more real, more essential, than the characters were or had any cause to be. In effect there'd come to be a sort of third character present — an identity, rather: the relationship between the two and between the two and the world. It was what grew up between them meeting as strangers, went on the trip with them, nodded back and forth from one to the other — listening, watching, persuading or denying them, enlarging or diminishing them, forgetful sometimes of who they were or what they were doing here, helping or betraying them along. Its role was that of hypnosis — it was what a relationship *does*, be it however brief, tentative, potential, happy or sinister, ordinary or extraordinary. I wanted to suggest that its being took shape as the strange, compulsive journey itself, was palpable as its climate and mood, the heat of the day — but was its spirit too, a spirit that held territory — what's seen fleeting past by two vulnerable people who might seize hands on the run. There are times in the story when I say neither "she felt" nor "he felt" but "they felt." All this is something that *doesn't* happen all the time. It merely could, or almost could, as here.

This is to grant that I rode out of the old story on the back of the girl and then threw away the girl; but I saved the story, for entirely different as the second version was, it was what I wanted to say. My subject was out in the open, provided at the same time with a place to happen and a way to say it was happening. All I had had to do was recognize it, which I did a little late.

Anyone who has visited the actual scene of this story has a chance of recognizing it when he meets it here, for the story is visual and the place is out of the ordinary. The connection between a story and its setting may not always be so plain. A reader may not see the slightest excuse for a given story after a personal inspection of the scene that called it up; the chances are good that he may not recognize it at all, and about 100 per cent that he will feel he would certainly have written something of a different sort himself. The point is, of course, that no matter whether the "likeness" is there for all to see or not, the place, once entered into the writer's mind in a story, is, in the course of writing the story, *functional*.

I wanted to make it seen and believed what was to me, in my story's grip, literally apparent — that secret and shadow are taken away in this country by the merciless light that prevails there, by the river that is like an exposed vein of ore, the road that descends as one with the heat — its nerve (these are all terms in the story), and that the heat is also a visual illusion, shimmering and dancing over the waste that stretches ahead. I was writing of a real place; but doing so in order to write about my subject. I was writing of exposure, and the shock of the world; in the end I tried to make the story's inside outside and then throw away the shell.

The vain courting of imperviousness in the face of exposure is this little story's plot. Deliver us all from the naked in heart, the girl thinks (this is what I kept of her). "So strangeness gently steels us," I read today in a poem of Richard Wilbur's. Riding down together into strange country is danger, a play at danger, secretly poetic, and the characters, in attempting it as a mutual feat, admit nothing to each other except the wicked heat and its comical inconvenience; the only time they will yield or touch is while they are dancing in the crowd that to them is comically unlikely (hence insulating, non-conducting) or taking a kiss outside time. Nevertheless it happens that they go along aware, from moment to moment, as one: as my third character, the straining, hallucinatory eyes and ears, the roused up sentiment being of that place. Exposure begins in intuition and has its end in showing the heart that has expected, while it dreads, that exposure. Writing it as I'd done before as a story of concealment, in terms of the hermetic and the familiar, had somehow resulted in my effective concealment of what I meant to say.

(I might say, for what interest it has here, that the original image of the story's first version came from an object — a grandiose, dusty, empty punch bowl of cut glass surrounded by its ring of cups, standing typically in the poor, small-town hardware store window where such things go unsold for ever, surrounded by the axes and halters, and tin mailboxes and shotguns of the country trade. Even as I write it's still provocative to me — as it is probably, also, still there in the window, still $ 13.75.)

In my second effort to show the story happen, the place had suggested to me that something demoniac was called for — the speed of the ride pitted against the danger of an easy or ignorant or tempting sympathy, too pressing, too acute, in the face of an inimical world, the heat that in itself drives on the driver. Something wilder than ordinary communication between well-disposed strangers, and more ruthless and more tender than their automatic, saving ironies and graces, I felt, and do so often feel, has to come up against a world like that.

I did my best to merge, rather to identify, the abstract with

Appendix II

the concrete, it being so happily possible in this story — however the possibilities may have been realized — where setting, characters, mood, and method of writing all appeared parts of the same thing and subject to related laws and conditionings. I cut out some odd sentences that occurred, not because they were odd — for the story is that — but because they would tantalize some cooling explanations out of the mind if they stayed in. The story had to be self-evident and hold its speed — which I think of as racing, though it may not seem so to the reader. Above all I had no wish to sound mystical, but I did expect to sound mysterious now and then, if I could: this was a circumstantial, realistic story in which the reality *was* mystery. The cry that rose up at the story's end was, I hope unmistakably, the cry of the fading relationship — personal, individual, psychic — admitted in order to be denied, a cry that the characters were first able (and prone) to listen to, and then able in part to ignore. The cry was authentic to my story and so I didn't care if it did seem a little odd: the end of a journey *can* set up a cry, the shallowest provocation to sympathy and loves does hate to give up the ghost. A relationship of the most fleeting kind has the power inherent to loom like a genie — to become vocative at the last, as it has already become present and taken up room; as it has spread out as a destination however makeshift; as it has, more faintly, more sparsely, glimmered and rushed by in the dark and dust outside. Relationship *is* pervading and changing mystery; it is not words that make it so in life, but words have to make it so in a story. Brutal or lovely, the mystery waits for people wherever they go, whatever extreme they run to. I had got back at the end of the new story to suggesting what I had started with at the beginning of the old, but there was no question in my mind which story was nearer the mark.

  This may not reflect very well on the brightness of the author; it may only serve to prove that for some writers a story has to rescue itself. This may be so, but I think it might show too what alone in the actual writing process may have interest for others besides the writer: that subject, method, form, style, all wait upon — indeed hang upon — a sort of double thunderclap at the author's ears: the break of the living world upon what is stirring inside the mind, and the answering impulse that in a moment of high consciousness fuses impact and image and fires them off together. There really never was a sound, but the impact is always recognizable, granting the author's sensitivity and sense, and if the impulse so projected is to some degree fulfilled it may give some pleasure out of reason to writer and reader. The living world remains just the same as it always was, and luckily enough for the story, among other things, for it can test and talk back to the story any day in the week.

Appendix III

Samples of MLA Style "Works Cited" in Research Papers

Here included are common entry samples of the list of "works cited" in MLA style in academic papers. The "Works Cited" attached to a research paper should arranged according to the last names of the (first) authors and the titles of the works (if the author's name is unavailable) in the alphabetical order. Note: Increasingly, it is preferred that students use italics, rather than underlining, for titles.

A Book by a Single Author:
Banfield, Ann. Unspeakable Sentences: Narration and Representation in the Language of Fiction. London: Routledge, 1982.

An Anthology or a Compilation:
Nichols, Fred J., ed. and trans. An Anthology of Neo-Latin Poetry. New Haven: Yale UP, 1979.

Two or More Books by the Same Author:
Frye, Northrop. Anatomy of Criticism: Four Essays. Princeton: Princeton UP, 1957.
---, ed. Sound and Poetry. New York: Columbia UP, 1957.

A Book by Two or More Authors:

Leech, Geoffrey N. and Micheal H. Short. <u>Style in Fiction: A Linguistic Introduction to English Fictional Prose</u>. London and New York: Longman, 1981.

Quirk, Randolph, et al. <u>A Comprehensive Grammar of the English Language</u>. London: Longman, 1985.

A Work (or an Article) in an Anthology:
Girling, Harry. "The Jew in James Joyce's *Ulysses*." <u>Jewish Presences in English Literature</u>. Ed. Derek Cohen and Deborah Heller. Montreal & Kingston: McGill-Queen's UP, 1990. 96-112.

Frye, Northrop. "Literary and Linguistic Scholarship in a Postliterate Age." <u>PMLA</u> 99 (1984): 990-95. Rpt. in <u>Myth and Metaphor: Selected Essays, 1974-88</u>. Ed. Robert D. Denham. Charlottesville: UP of Virginia, 1990. 18-27.

An Anonymous Book:
<u>Encyclopedia of Virginia</u>. New York: Somerset, 1993.

A Translation:
Dostoevsky, Feodor. <u>Crime and Punishment</u>. Trans. Jessie Coulson. Ed. Geoge Gibian. New York: Norton, 1964.
or
Coulson, Jessie, trans. <u>Crime and Punishment</u>. By Dostoevsky, Feodor. Ed. Geoge Gibian. New York: Norton, 1964.

A Book Published in a Second or Subsequent Edition:
Chaucer, Geoffrey. <u>The Works of Geoffrey Chaucer</u>. Ed. F. W. Robinson. 2nd ed. Boston: Houghton, 1957.

A Multivolume Work:
Wellek, René. <u>A History of Modern Criticism, 1750-1950</u>. 8 vols.

New Haven: Yale UP, 1955-92.

Churchill, Winston S. The Age of Revolution. New York: Dodd, 1957. Vol. 3 of A History of the English-Speaking Peoples. 4 vols. 1956-58.

A Republished Book:
Atwood, Margaret. Surfacing. 1972. New York: Fawcett, 1987.

A Presentation in the Proceedings of a Conference:
Mann, Jill. "Chaucer and the 'Woman Question.'" This Noble Craft: Proceedings of the Tenth Research Symposium of the Dutch and Belgian University Teachers of Old and Middle English and Historical Linguistics, Utrecht, 19-20 January 1989. Ed. Erik Kooper. Amsterdam: Rodopi, 1991. 173-88.

A Book in a Language Other Then English:
Bessière, Jean, ed. Mythologies de l'écriture: Champs critiques. Paris: Paris UP, 1990.

An Unpublished Dissertation:
Wu, Qiren. "A Phenomenological Study of Hemingway." Diss. Peking U, 1997.

An Article in a Scholarly Journal:
Scotto, Peter. "Censorship, Reading, and Interpretation: A Case Study from the Soviet Union." PMLA 109 (1994): 61-70.

An Article in a Newspaper:
Tagliabue, John. "Cleaned Last Judgment Unveiled." *New York Times* 9 Apr. 1994, late ed.: 13.

An Article in a Magazine:
Murphy, Cullen. "Women and the Bible." Atlantic Monthly Aug.

1993: 39-64.

A Publication on CD-ROM:
The Oxford English Dictionary. 2nd ed. CD-ROM. Oxford:
   Oxford UP, 1992.

"Brontë, Emily." Discovering Authors. Vers. 1. 0. CD-ROM.
   Detroit:Gale,1992.

A Publication on Diskette:
Joyce, Michael. Afternoon: A Story. Diskette. Watertown:
   Eastgate, 1987.

"Ellison, Ralph." Disclit: American Authors. Diskette. Boston:
   Hall, 1991.

Coleridge, Samuel Taylor. "Dejection: An Ode." The Complete
   Poetical Works of Samuel Taylor Coleridge. Ed. Ernest Hartley
   Coleridge. Vol. 1. Oxford: Clarendon, 1912. 362-68. The
   Poetical Works of Samuel Taylor Coleridge. Diskette. Oxford:
   Oxford UP, 1993.

Material Accessed through a Computer Service:
"Middle Ages." Academic American Encyclopedia. Online.
   Prodigy. 30 Mar. 1992.

Material from an Electronic Journal:
Readings, Bill. "Translatio and Comparative Literature: The
   Terror of European Humanism." Surfaces 1. 11 (Dec. 1991): 19
   pp. Online. Internet. 2 Feb. 1992.

Material from an Electronic Text:
Hardy, Thomas. Far from the Madding Crowd. Ed. Ronald
   Blythe. Harmondsworth: Penguin, 1978. Online. Oxford Text

Appendix III

Archive. Internet. 24 Jan. 1994.

Material from a Lecture:
Atwood, Margaret. "Silencing the Scream." Boundaries of the Imagination Forum. MLA Convention. Royal York Hotel, Toronto. 29 Dec. 1993.

Bibliography

Abrams, M. H. *A Glossary of Literary Terms*. New York: Holt, Rinehart and Winston, 1957.

Aitieri, Charles. *Act and Quality: A Theory of Literary Meaning and Humanistic Understanding*. Amherst: University of Massachusetts Press, 1981.

Allen, Walter. *The English Novel: A Short Critical History*. New York: Dutton, 1955.

Alter, Robert. *Rogue's Progress: Studies in the Picaresque Novel*. Cambridge: Harvard University Press, 1964.

Auerbach. Erich. *Mimesis: The Representation of Reality in Western Literature*. New York: Doubleday, 1957.

Austin, J. L. *How to Do Things with Words*. Cambridge: Harvard University Press, 1962.

Bakhtin, M. M. *The Dialogic Imagination: Four Essays*. Trans. Caryl Emerson and Micheal Holquist. Austin: University of Texas Press, 1981.

Bal, Mieke. *Narratology: Introduction to the Theory of Narrative*. Trans. Christine van Boheemen. Toronto: University of Toronto Press, 1985.

Bann, S. and J. E. Bowlt, eds. *Russian Formalism*. New York: Barnes and Noble, 1973.

Banfield, Ann. *Unspeakable Sentences: Narration and Representation in the Language of Fiction*. London: Routledge, 1982.

Barthes, Roland. *S/Z*. New York: Hill & Wang, 1974.

Bayer-Berenbaum, Linda. *The Gothic Imagination: Expansion in Gothic Literature and Art*. Rutherfold, New Jersey: Fairleigh Dickinson University Press, 1981.

Bender, Todd K. et al. *Modernism in Literature*. New York:

Holt, Rinehart & Winston, 1977.

Bonheim, Helmut. *The Narrative Modes: Techniques of the Short Story*. New York: D. S. Brewer, 1992.

Booth, Wayne C. *The Rhetoric of Fiction*. Chicago: University of Chicago Press, 1961.

---. *Critical Understanding: The Powers and Limits of Pluralism*. Chicago: University of Chicago Press, 1979.

Bronzwaer, W. J. M. *Tense in the Novel*. Groningen: Wolters-Noordhoff, 1971.

Brooks, Cleanth and Robert Penn Warren, eds. *Understanding Fiction*. Upper Saddle River, NJ: Prentice-Hall, Inc., 1971.

Brooks, Cleanth, John Thibaut Purser and Robert Penn Warren, eds. *An Approach to Literature*. 4th ed. New York: Meredith, 1964.

Brooks, Peter. *Reading for the Plot: Design and Intention in Narrative*. New York: Knopf, 1984.

Burke, Kenneth. *The Philosophy of Literary Forms: Studies in Symbolic Action*. 2nd ed. Baton Rouge: Louisiana State University Press, 1967.

Cebic, L. B. *Fictional Narrative and Truth: An Epistemic Analysis*. Lanham, Md.: University Press of America, 1984.

Chamberlain, Daniel Frank. *Narrative Perspective in Fiction: A Phenomenological Meditation of Reader, Text, and World*. Toronto: University of Toronto Press, 1990.

Chambers, Ross. *Story and Situation: Narrative Seduction and the Power of Fiction*. Minneapolis: University of Minnesota Press, 1984.

Chatman, Seymoure. *Story and Discourse: Narrative Structure in Fiction and Film*. Ithaca: Cornell University Press, 1978.

Cobley, Paul. *Narrative*. London and New York: Routledge, 2001.

Cohan, Steven and Linda M. Shires. *Telling Stories: A Theoretical Analysis of Narrative Fiction*. London and New York: Routledge, 1993.

Cohn, Dorrit. *Transparent Minds: Narrative Modes for Presenting Consciousness in Fiction*. Princeton: Princeton University Press, 1978.

Crane, Ronald S. *Critics and Criticism*. Chicago: University of Chicago Press, 1952.

Docherty, Thomas. *Reading (Absent) Character: Towards a Theory of Characterization in Fiction*. Oxford: Clarendon, 1983.

De Man, Paul. *Allegories of Reading*. New Haven: Yale University Press, 1979.

Epstein, E. L. *Language and Style*. London: Methuen, 1978.

Foster, E. M. *Aspects of the Novel*. New York: Harcourt, Brace and World, 1927.

Fowler, R., ed. *Essays on Style and Language*. London: Routledge & Kegan Parl, 1966.

———. *Style and Structure in Literature: Essays in the New Stylistics*. Oxford: Blackwell, 1975.

Freeman, D. C. *Linguistics and Literary Style*. New York: Holt, Rinehart & Winston, 1970.

Friedman, Melvin. *Stream of Consciousness: A Study in Literary Method*. New Haven: Yale University Press, 1955.

Frye, Northrop. *Anatomy of Criticism: Four Essays*. Princeton: Princeton University Press, 1957.

Gass, William. *Fiction and Figures of Life*. New York: Knopf, 1970.

Genette, Gerard. *Narrative Discourse: An Essay in Method*. Trans. James E. Lewin. Ithaca: Cornell University Press, 1980.

Gibaldi, Joseph. *MLA Handbook for Writers of Research Papers*. 4th ed. New York: The Modern Language Association of America, 1995.

Gillie, Christopher, *Longman Companion to English Literature*. London: Longman, 1977.

Halperin, John, ed. *The Theory of the Novel: New Essays*. New

York: Oxford University Press, 1974.
Harvey, W. J. *Character and the Novel*. New York: Ithaca, 1965.
Hennessy, Brenden. *The Gothic Novel*. New York: Longman, 1978.
Holloway, John. *Narrative and Structure*. Cambridge: Cambridge University Press, 1979.
Holman, C. Hugh and William Harmon. *A Handbook to Literature*. New York: Macmillan, 1986.
Hutcheon, Linda. *Narcissistic Narrative: The Metafictional Paradox*. Waterloo, Ont. : Wilfrid Laurier University Press, 1980.
Iser, Wolfgang. *The Act of Reading: A Theory of Aesthetic Response*. Baltimore: Johns Hopkins University Press, 1978.
James D. Hart, ed. *The Oxford Companion to American Literature*. 4th ed. New York: Oxford University Press, 1966.
James, Henry. *The Art of the Novel*. New York: Charles Scribner's Sons, 1934.
Kennedy, X. J. and Dana Gioia, eds. *Literature: An Introduction to Fiction, Poetry, and Drama*. New York: HarperCollins, 1995.
Kermode, Frank. *The Sense of an Ending : Studies in the Theory of Fiction*. New York: Oxford University Press, 1967.
---. *The Art of Telling : Essays on Fiction*. Cambridge: Harvard University Press, 1983.
Kiniry, Malcolm and Mike Rose. *Critical Strategies for Academic Writing*. Boston: Bedford Books of St. Martin's Press, 1990.
Knickerboker, K. L. and H. Willard Reninger, eds. *Interpreting Literature*. 5th ed. New York: Holt, Rinehart and Winston, 1974.
Kronegger, Maria Elisabeth. *Literary Impressionism*. New Haven, Connecticut: College and University Press, 1983.
Leavis, F. R. *The Great Tradition*. London: Stewart, 1948.
Leech, Geoffrey N. and Micheal H. Short. *Style in Fiction : A*

Linguistic Introduction to English Fictional Prose. London and New York: Longman, 1981.

Lodge, David. *Language of Fiction*. London: Routledge & Kegan Parl, 1966.

---. *The Modes of Modern Writing: Metaphor, Metonymy and the Typology of Modern Literature*. 1977. London: Arnold, 1996.

Lotman, Jurij. *The Structure of the Artistic Text*. Ann Arbor: University of Michigan Press, 1977.

Lubbock, Percy. *The Craft of Fiction*. New York: Viking Press, 1957.

Lukacs, G. *The Historical Novel*. London: Hannah and Stanley Mitchell, 1965.

Martin, Wallace. *Recent Theories of Narrative*. Ithaca: Cornell University Press, 1986.

O'Faolain, Sean. *The Vanishing Hero*. Boston: Little, Brown & Co., 1957.

Ohmann, Richard. "Generative Grammars and the Concept of Literary Style." 1964. Rept. in Freedman, D. C., 1970.

Pizer, Donald. *Twentieth-Century Literary Naturalism*. Carbondale: Southern Illinois University Press, 1982.

Pratt, Mary Louise. *Toward a Speech of Act Theory of Literary Discourse*. Bloomington: Indiana University Press, 1977.

Prentice Hall, ed. *Literature*. New Jersey: Simon & Schuster, 1989.

Price, Martin. *Forms of Life: Character and Moral Imagination in the Novel*. New Haven: Yale University Press, 1983.

Ricoeur, Paul. *Time and Narrative*. 3 vols. Trans. Kathleen McLaughlin and David Pellauer. Chicago: University of Chicago Press, 1984-88.

Rimmon-Kenan, Shlomith. *Narrative Fiction: Contemporary Poetics*. 1983. London and New York: Routledge, 1994.

Robins, Adrienne. *The Writer's Practical Rhetoric*. New York: John Wiley & Sons, 1980.

Rose, Margaret. *Parody/Meta-fiction : An Analysis of Parody as a Critical Mirror to the Writing and Reception of Fiction.* London: Croom Helm, 1979.
Rubinstein, Annette T. *The Great Tradition in English Literature from Shakespeare to Shaw.* 2 vols. New York and London: Modern Reader, 1953.
Scholes, Robert E. and Robert Kellogg. *The Nature of Narrative.* New York: Oxford University Press, 1966.
Sebeok, Thomas, ed. *Style in Language.* Cambridge: M. I. T. Press, 1960.
Spence, Donald. *Narrative Truth and Historical Truth : Meaning and Interpretation in Psychoanalysis.* New York: Norton, 1982.
Stanzel, Franz. *A Theory of Narrative.* Cambridge: Cambridge University Press, 1984.
Sternberg, Meir. *Expositional Modes and Temporal Ordering in Fiction.* Baltimore: Johns Hopkins University Press, 1978.
Stevick, Philip, ed. *The Theory of the Novel.* New York: Macmillan, 1967.
Strelka, Joseph P., ed. *Patterns of Literary Style.* University Park: Penn State University Press, 1971.
Todorov, Tzvetan. *The Poetics of Prose.* Ithaca: Cornell University Press, 1977.
Tomashevsky, Boris. "Thematics." In *Russian Formalist Criticism : Four Essays.* Ed. Lee Lemon and Marion Reis. Lincoln: University of Nebraska Press, 1925.
Toolan, Michael, ed. *Language, Text and Context : Essays in Stylistics.* London: Routledge, 1992.
Trilling, Lionel. *The Liberal Imagination.* New York: Viking Press, 1950.
Valdés, Mario J. and Owen J. Miller, eds. *Interpretation of Narrative.* Toronto: University of Toronto Press, 1978.
Watt, Ian. *The Rise of the Novel : Studies in Defoe, Richardson and Fielding.* 1957. Harmondsworth: Penguin, 1970.

Waugh, Patricia. *Metafiction: The Theory and Practice of Self-Conscious Fiction*. London: Methuen, 1984.
Whorf, B. L. *Language, Thought and Reality*. New York: M. I. T. Press, 1956.
Widdowson, H. G. *Stylistics and the Teaching of Literature*. London and New York: Longman, 1975.
Woolf, Virginia. *Collected Essays*. New York: Harcourt, Brace and World, 1967.